BERING'S VOYAGES:
THE REPORTS
FROM RUSSIA

T0164066

The Rasmuson Library
Historical Translation Series
Volume III
Marvin W. Falk, Editor

Additional titles published by the Elmer E. Rasmuson Translation Program:

TLINGIT INDIANS OF ALASKA by Archimandite Anatolii Kamenskii. Translated, with an Introduction and Supplementary Material by Sergei Kan. The Rasmuson Library Historical Translation Series, Volume II. Published by the University of Alaska Press: Fairbanks, Alaska, 1985.

HOLMBERG'S ETHNOGRAPHIC SKETCHES by Heinrich Johan Holmberg. Edited by Marvin W. Falk. Translated from the original German of 1855-1863 by Fritz Jaensch. The Rasmuson Library Historical Translations Series, Volume I. Published by the University of Alaska Press: Fairbanks, Alaska, 1985.

NOTES ON THE ISLANDS OF THE UNALASHKA DISTRICT by Ivan Veniaminov. Translated from the original Russian edition of 1840 by Lydia T. Black and R.H. Geoghegan. Edited with an introduction by Richard A. Pierce. Published jointly by the Elmer E. Rasmuson Library Translation Program and The Limestone Press, 1984. Available from the Limestone Press, P.O. Box 1604, Kingston, Ontario, Canada K7L 5C8.

BERING'S VOYAGES: THE REPORTS FROM RUSSIA

by
Gerhard Friedrich Müller

Translated, with commentary
by
Carol Urness

The University of Alaska Press
Fairbanks

Translation of *Nachrichten von Seareisen,* St Petersburg, 1758.

International Standard Series Number: 0890-7935
International Standard Book Number: 0-912006-22-6
Library of Congress Catalog Card Number: 86-051585
English Translation © 1986 by the University of Alaska Press.
All rights reserved. Published 1986.
First printing 1986, 1000 copies.
Second printing 1995, 500 copies.
Printed in the United States of America.

This publication was printed on acid-free paper which meets the minimum
requirements of American National Standard for Information Sciences—
Permanence for Paper for Printed Library Materials.
ANSI Z39.48-1984.

Typesetting, design and production by
University of Alaska Fairbanks Printing and Duplicating Services.

Supported in part by a publication grant from
the National Endowment for the Humanities and the
Alaska Humanities Forum, Anchorage

CONTENTS

Page

Illustrations and Maps vi

Acknowledgements viii

Preface 1

BERING'S VOYAGES

THE SETTING

    I.   Background 3

    II.   The Rebuttals 30

    III.   The Translation 65

MÜLLER TRANSLATED

    I.   The First Kamchatka Expedition 69

    II.   Events between the Two Bering Expeditions 74

    III.   Beginning of the Second Kamchatka Expedition 78

    IV.   Exploration of the Icy Sea 81

    V.   The Voyages to Japan 88

    VI.   To Kamchatka 96

    VII.   The Selection of the Route 99

    VIII. Chirikov's Voyage 101

    IX.   Bering 103

    X.   Khitrov 105

    XI.   Waxell and Steller 107

    XII.   Return 110

    XIII. Bering Island 114

    XIV. Chirikov 116

    XV.   The Wintering 117

    XVI. Return to Kamchatka 124

    XVII. Commentary on Publications 128

Glossary 141

Footnotes 145

Bibliography 199

Index 213

MAPS AND ILLUSTRATIONS

Maps   Page

I.   Sixteen century map of the northern polar regions
        by Gerhardus Mercator 5
II.   Map to accompany an account of Maerten Gerritsen Vries . . .7
III.   Guillaume Delisle's map of Russia, 1707 9
IV.   Northeastern Siberia from *Histoire genealogique
        des Tatars,* 1706 14
V.   Joseph Nicolas Delisle's sketch map 21
VI.   Homann's first map of Kamchatka 23
VII.   Cartouche and northeastern portion of Homann's
        map of Russia 24
VIII.   Cartouche and northeastern portion of Homann's
        map of Russia 26
IX.   Comparison of Homann's map with a modern map 28
X.   Comparison of Bering's map with a modern map 29
XI.   Engelbert Kaempfer's map. 33
XII.   Joseph Nicolas Delisle's manuscript "Carte dressee en 1731 . . ."35
XIII.   A portion of the Georges-Louis la Rouge map 46
XIV.   A portion of the Hasius map 47
XV.   The Joseph Nicolas Delisle map of 1750 48
XVI.   The Joseph Nicolas Delisle map of 1752 49
XVII.   Manuscript map of Bering's First Kamchatka Expedition 57
XVIII. Müller's map of 1754 58
XIX.   Portion of Müller's map relating to the Bering
        voyages of 1728-29 59
XX.   Sketch map of Gvozdev's voyage 60
XXI.   Arctic Coast, from Müller. 61
XXII.   Kamchatka to Japan, from Müller 62
XXIII. Routes of Bering and Chirikov, from Müller 63

Illustrations

I.   Report of Bering's expedition in the
        St. Petersburgische Zeitung, 1730 18
II.   Title page from the first translation of
        Müller's *Voyages,* 1761 64

ACKNOWLEDGEMENTS

I am grateful to the Elmer E. Rasmuson Library of the University of Alaska, Fairbanks, for making this publication possible. The personal interest and assistance of Dr. Marvin W. Falk, the Curator of Rare Books of that Libary, are deeply appreciated.

During the initial stages of this work, I was fortunate to discover that J.L. (Larry) Black, Carleton University, Ottawa, had written a biography of Müller as a historian. Professor Black shared his typescript with me in the fall of 1983, saving many hours of research on my part. His biography will be published by McGill-Queen's University Press. We have been conducting a friendly race into print. At this writing neither of us has won, but the reader should be reminded that the citations to his biography are to the typescript pages. I hope that this will not cause too much inconvenience. Professor Black also read the introductory chapters to this book and offered useful suggestions, for which I am most appreciative.

In preparing the translation I received help, in the initial stages, from Jean R. McGreehan. When the translation was completed, Paul Brashear provided invaluable assistance in his reading and rewriting of many troublesome passages. The readability of the translation was thus vastly improved. My own experience as a translator is limited—this translation is my first attempt. I was often reminded of Müller's statement: "But it comes to the wording. Indeed that is the whole difficulty." The wording is often much better thanks to the skill of Mr. Brashear.

In footnoting the translation, I relied on the work of earlier translators, in particular Frank A. Golder's collection of journals and texts relating to the Bering expeditions. The translation by E.A.P. Crownhart-Vaughan of Stepan Krasheninnikov's account of Kamchatka, published in 1972, has also been most helpful. In his writing Müller used the work of Sven Waxell extensively, and I have followed suit in citing Waxell's work as translated into English by Maurice A. Michael and published in 1952 as *The American Expedition*. Because of its importance to the text presented here, I wrote to the publisher to learn more about the book. In response I received a letter from the translator who lives in Lostwithiel, Cornwall. Mr. Michael is a professional publisher and translator who has translated some 130 books from six languages. Waxell's account of the expedition is fascinating. I highly recommend it to anyone interested in the Bering expeditions.

My best friends in the world of scholarship, Professor Raymond H. Fisher of the University of California, Los Angeles, and Professor John Parker, Curator of the James Ford Bell Library, have read parts of the book for me, as have two young friends, Paul Brashear and Bradley Oftelie. I have benefited from their interest and encouragement.

Superb typing assistance was provided by Bradley Oftelie and Jessie Richardson. The text was put on a word processor at the University of Alaska by Jeff Pederson, who managed to absorb the many corrections and changes of spelling (and of mind) without complaining—at least not to me. In the proofing stage, I was blessed with a bevy of willing readers: Lynn Balfour, Dorothy Bohn, Arnold Fredrickson (whose French, German, and Russian accents were unforgettable), Brad Oftelie, Jessie Richardson, Kirsten Schwappach, and Karen Sheldon. John Jenson, my colleague in the Special Collections Department of the University of Minnesota Libraries, prepared the index to the book. For all of this help, I am thankful indeed.

My home research institution is the James Ford Bell Library at the University of Minnesota, where I am Assistant Curator. The resources of this Library, together with those of the Elmer E. Rasmuson Library, made my research possible. In addition I have enjoyed the use of an excellent Interlibrary Loan service and have had special assistance from the following: Archives Nationale, Paris; Bibliothéque Nationale, Paris; Geography and Map Division, Library of Congress (John Wolter); The Hermon Dunlap Smith Center for the History of Cartography, The Newberry Library (David Buisseret); Joseph Regenstein Library, University of Chicago; Kenneth Spencer Research Library, University of Kansas (Alexandra Mason); the Library of the Academy of Sciences of the USSR, Leningrad; Lilly Library, Indiana University; Map Library, British Library (Helen Wallis); Nordenskiold Collection, Helsinki University; Rare Books Collection, Princeton University (Stephen Ferguson); Public Archives of Canada (Nadia Kazymyra-Dzioba); Yale University Library (Barbara McCorkle).

I am grateful to the University of Minnesota Libraries for a single quarter leave and to my colleagues in the libraries and in the Department of Russian and East European Studies for their interest in this work. My family and friends have been supportive beyond belief and I am grateful to them.

PREFACE

My interest in preparing a new translation of Gerhard Friedrich Müller's writings on the two Bering expeditions evolved from research for my Ph.D. dissertation, "Bering's First Kamchatka Expedition: A re-evaluation based on eighteenth century books, maps, and manuscripts," which was completed in 1982. In the course of this research I became convinced that the prevailing ideas about the purpose of Bering's First Kamchatka Expedition were not supported in the eighteenth century sources. Rather, the writings of Müller gave rise to these ideas, and I determined to undertake a study of Müller's publications to discover his part in the interpretations of the first Bering expedition. This effort led me to an examination of his writings on both expeditions, particularly the German-language account Müller published in Saint Petersburg in 1758.

Müller's publication was the only "official" account of Bering's expeditions published in the eighteenth century and it is still, indeed, a standard source. The two previous English translations of the work, published in 1761 and 1764, are incomplete and are difficult for the modern reader to follow. The discovery that the Elmer E. Rasmuson Library holds not only the 1761 edition but the 1764 as well was invaluable to me in comparing the two translations. This comparison revealed that the 1764 edition is not, as commonly assumed, a reprint of the 1761 edition. Working with the text, I found that the sources Müller used and the ways he utilized them were highly instructive, for Müller was accused by his contemporaries of concealing information about the expeditions. The emphasis in my footnoting to the translation, then, has been placed on identifying the sources Müller consulted in his writing, and I have quoted them often for comparison.

The footnoting to the translation has been restricted to English-language sources where possible. Since the primary readers of this text presumably will not be specialists, diacritical marks have been omitted (e.g., "Tobolsk" rather than "Tobol'sk") throughout. In most cases, spelling, punctuation, and, occasionally, phrasing have been updated to modern English usage.

Müller stated his own standard for a historian when he wrote:

> *Everything is in these words; be faithful to the truth, unprejudiced, and modest. The duty of a historian is hard to fulfill; you know that he must appear without country, without religion, without emperor. I do not re-*

quire that a historian should narrate all he knows, nor even all that is true, because there are things that one should not narrate and which may be of doubtful interest, so that they should be hidden from the public; but everything the historian says must be strictly true, and he must never give occasion for the suspicion of flattery to be raised against him.
(Pekarskii, I:381, translated by Cross, 1916, p. 204).

The introductory chapters of this book attempt to place Müller's writings on the Bering expeditions in the context of his life and experiences. This, plus the footnoting to his sources, gives the reader an opportunity to evaluate Müller's text against his own statement about the duty of a historian.

THE SETTING

I. BACKGROUND

In the eighteenth century, Russian expeditions explored and mapped regions of the earth that had been the subject of rumor and uncertainty in Europe for centuries. The most famous of these expeditions were the First Kamchatka Expedition (1725-30) and the Second Kamchatka Expedition (1733-43 and, unofficially, even beyond 1743), led by Vitus Bering. During the First Kamchatka Expedition Bering sailed from Okhotsk, on the eastern coast of Siberia, across the Sea of Okhotsk to the west coast of Kamchatka. He crossed the Kamchatka Peninsula by land to its east coast, built a ship there, sailed northward following the Kamchatka coast, and then continued along the Chukchi Peninsula through the strait that separates Asia from America.

After his return from this expedition a much more grandiose effort, the Second Kamchatka Expedition, was mounted. The expedition had several purposes: the arctic coasts of Russia and Siberia, from Arkhangelsk to Kamchatka, were to be explored and mapped; a voyage was to be made from Okhotsk in search of a sea route to Japan; and Bering himself was to command ships sent from Kamchatka eastward in search of America. In addition, members of the Second Kamchatka Expedition were assigned to study and record "the natural history" (roughly, everything of interest) of the areas explored.

Both expeditions made substantial contributions to the history of geographical discoveries. The records collected by participants provided a rich store of information about the areas explored. The expeditions firmly established official Russian presence in the far reaches of Siberia and, additionally, heralded Russian expansion to America. The two expeditions, incidentally, have offered historians and writers a prime opportunity for comment and debate.[1]

This is the story of how the Bering expeditions were written about in Russia during the eighteenth century by Gerhard Friedrich Müller (1705-83).[2] It is a story of books and maps, of geographical ideas, of explorations, and of how these expeditions were recorded in their own time. In 1725, as a young man, Müller, a German, took service in Russia. Like many others, Müller went to Russia because of the activities of Peter the Great (1672-1725), for Müller became one of the first members of the Russian Imperial Academy of Sciences, an institution founded by Peter. In his early association with the academy, Müller taught geography and history; he also worked in the academy's library, which was especially rich in geographical works. The printed books and maps available to Müller during his days as a student at Leipzig and later in Russia reflect the long fascination western Europe had for Russia and the lands to the east.[3] The geography of Russia and Siberia was little known; much of western European curiosity about northern Asia revolved about an interest in discovering a northeast passage to the East.

The dream of finding a sea route to "the Indies"—to Japan, China, the East Indies—has a long history. Beginning in the mid-fifteenth century, reports of rich kingdoms, eastern Christians, and fabulous trade opportunities stirred Europeans to search for a sea route to the eastern lands. Christopher Columbus led the way west in search of a direct route; many other explorers followed him in the same search. Portuguese and Spanish mariners soon dominated the long southern routes; therefore other Europeans began to search for a northern route. In 1497 and 1498 John Cabot made two voyages for the English in search of a westward sea route from Bristol to the East. Later expeditions of Danes, Dutch, French, and Italians were sent to North America for the same purpose.[4]

But attempts to find a northern sea passage were not limited to the west; voyages were also made to the northeast, around Scandinavia. In his *Commentarii rerum Moscoviticarum*, first published in 1549, Baron Sigismund von Herberstein, who had been an ambassador from the Austrian Habsburgs to Muscovy in 1517-18 and again in 1526-27, included reports of voyages around North Cape which raised hopes of a northeast passage, either by sea or by sea and river.[5] The English were not slow to seize the initiative. In the spring of 1553 three ships, under the command of Sir Hugh Willoughby, set out in search of the northeast passage to "Cathay." The ships, after rounding North Cape, were separated in a storm. Two of them anchored at the Kola Peninsula in Lapland. During the winter their crews froze to death. The third ship, under Richard Chancellor, reached the White Sea. When he learned of the English arrival, Ivan IV had them brought to Moscow. He welcomed the English with enthusiasm and offered them attractive commercial privileges, for his western neighbors had effectively cut Muscovy off from western European military weapons and personnel. Following this voyage the Muscovy Company was formed in England to develop the trade with Russia. Englishmen and Scots entered service in Russia, and English interest in Russia grew.[6] The search for a northeast passage continued. In 1556 Stephen Burough sailed between Novaia Zemlia and Vaigach Island and into the Kara Sea, before being forced to turn back. In 1580 Arthur Pet and Charles Jackman tried to cross the Kara Sea but failed because of ice.[7]

The English made loud claims about the "discovery" they had made of Russia, hoping thereby to keep the trade route their own monopoly. But the Dutch followed in the steps of the English, both in trade and in exploration. One of their merchants, Olivier Brunel, sailed from Arkhangelsk (the port established at the White Sea for the trade) in 1584, seeking the northeast passage. He died in the attempt. In 1594 three Dutch ships were sent out to find the passage, one sailing north of Novaia Zemlia and the other two following the route along the

Siberian coast. Though none of these succeeded, the next year seven Dutch ships tried the Kara Sea route. In 1596 Willem Barents, a participant in the earlier expeditions, rounded the far northern tip of Novaia Zemlia, where he wintered. Barents died on the return voyage the next summer, but some of his men returned home.[8]

Russians took this possible threat to their fur trade seriously. By 1619 foreigners were forbidden by Russia to sail east of the Iamal Peninsula.[9] For more than 50 years the Dutch and English made no further attempts to discover a northeast passage. The hope of finding one, however, did not die.

Mapmakers customarily placed a strait separating Asia from America in the far north. This strait was shown on a printed map for the first time on an Italian map dated 1566.[10] Called the "Strait of Anian" because Marco Polo (1254-1323?) mentioned a country to the north named Anian in his account of travels to China, this strait was crucial to any northern passage by the northeast or over the pole, and indeed, if land blocked the passage further south in America, to a northwest passage as well. The ideas about northern passages were summarized on a map by Gerardus Mercator (1512-94), the famous Dutch mapmaker[11] (Map I).

MAP I. Sixteenth century map of the northern polar regions by Gerhardus Mercator. (Courtesy of the James Ford Bell Library)

Russians, in the sixteenth and seventeenth centuries, were expanding their influence eastward because of the fur trade. By 1639 the cossack Ivan Moskvitin reached the Sea of Okhotsk. The Siberian river system, which the Russians were able to control by building *ostrogs* (forts) at strategic points, made possible this swift expansion to the east. In eastern Siberia the advance was spearheaded by cossacks and *promyshlenniki* (fur traders), with the government following after. The market for furs was in Europe, and the extension of control to reach the most accessible fur trading areas, along the rivers, was profitable to the government and to the fur traders.[12] Early in the seventeenth century both the Dutch and the English had broken the Iberian monopoly on trade to the East Indies and had established East India companies. Even though the route used in this trade was long and mortality on the ships was high, the trade was profitable. In western Europe, reports of Russian eastward expansion led to renewed speculation about a possible northeast passage. But very little firsthand information was available.

Nicolaas Witsen (1641-1717), a Dutchman who had been in Russia for several months in 1664-65, gathered all the information he could find about northeastern Asia. By the 1670s Witsen believed in the possibility of a northeast passage, stating in a letter: "The Samoyeds as well as the Tartars do unanimously affirm, that passing on the back of Nova Zembla, at a considerable distance from the shore, Navigators may well pass as far as Japan."[13] This letter was published in the *Philosophical Transactions* of the Royal Society; later in the same year, 1674, an article appeared describing a voyage made by a Dutch East India Company ship in search of the "famous Land of Jesso near Japan." This land was purported to be rich in silver and gold; the voyage made in 1643 to search for it was led by Maerten Gerritsen Vries.[14] Because of fogs, Vries did not see the strait between Hokkaido and Sakhalin; therefore he depicted these islands as one huge land mass on his map. The map published with this account of his voyage reflects the confusion about the area: mapmakers put the land of Jeso (Jedso, Yedso, Esso) on their maps for years to come[15] (Map II).

The next year Witsen published another article about the northeast passage, based on reports in Amsterdam that a sea had been discovered to the north of Novaia Zemlia, "free from all Ice, and very convenient for Navigation."[16] Witsen had great hopes for the northeast passage, by which, according to his estimation, ships could sail from Europe to Japan in five weeks, or six at the most.[17] At that time, voyages from Europe to the East Indies by the route around Africa required eight to nine months.

Captain John Wood led an English expedition of 1676 on a search for a northeast passage. Wood had two ships, the *Speedwell* (belonging to the king) and the *Prosperous* (supplied by a group of merchants). They sailed northeast from North Cape in hopes of finding the open northern sea. Instead, they met ice on 22 June and coasted along it hoping to find a passage. They were unable

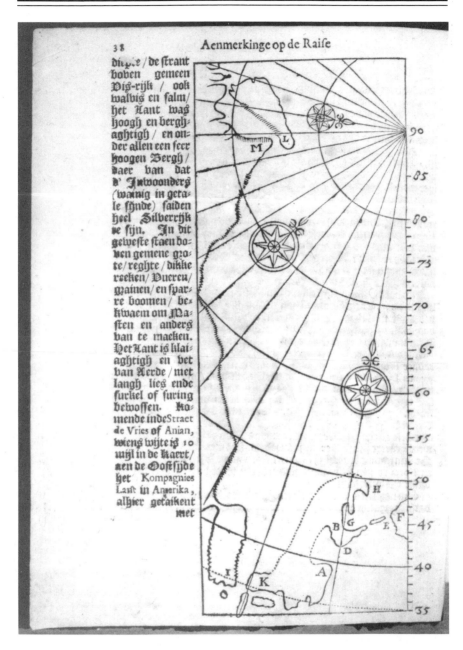

MAP II. Map to accompany an account of the voyage of Maerten Gerritsen Vries, published in 1669. Straits are shown between L and M (northern Russia and Novaia Zemlia) and I and K (Korea and Japan). A is Japan, B is the capital of Jeso. D is the southeast corner of Jeso and G is the bay reached by Vries; H is the northernmost point of the voyage. E is "Vries Strait" and F in America. (Courtesy of the James Ford Bell Library)

7

to get north of 76° and Wood concluded: "The Sea is all frozen and always will be so."[18] The ships were separated and the *Speedwell* struck ice near the northern coast of Novaia Zemlia. The ship sank, but 68 of the 70 men on board reached shore safely, only to begin arguing about which of them would take the ship's boat away from the island, and who would have to remain at Novaia Zemlia until help could come. Before their brandy gave out, the men were rescued by the arrival of the *Prosperous*. After this voyage, the exploration of the northern Siberian coasts was left to the Russians; western Europeans could only speculate about Russian success in discovering a northeast passage.

In 1687 Witsen made a large, detailed map of northeastern Siberia. Though Witsen's map was produced in only a few copies it inaugurated a series of European maps of the region.[19] The map was based on Russian sources and was dedicated to Peter the Great. In the northeast, it included an "Ice Cape" which is left unenclosed. The text with the map stated that the end of this cape was unknown. In 1692 Witsen published a massive book, *Noord en Oost Tartarye*, in which he described the geography, economy, natural history, peoples and languages of "North and East Tartary" in more than 600 folio pages. He commented on the large promontory shown in the northeastern part of his map: "Some believe that this section is attached to land and connected to North America; but this is uncertain, as neither water nor land have been tested there and the end of the same section is unknown."[20] In two other places in the same book, however, he refers to reports of mariners sailing around the northeast corner of Asia.[21]

Peter the Great visited Witsen in Amsterdam in 1697. At the time, Witsen was told by the Russians that "Ice Cape" did not join to America.[22] In 1704 Witsen published a book written by Evert Izbrandszoon Ides, who traveled to China as part of a diplomatic embassy from Russia in 1692-94. This book contains a map which shows no promontory extending from northeastern Asia. Witsen said he wrote the text for the book because Ides had died before it could be printed.[23] An eighteenth century English translation of the text includes the statement: "From Weygats to the Icy or Holy Cape, the Sea is utterly unnavigable with Ships, and should a second Christopher Columbus appear, and point out the course of the Heavens, he could not yet drive away these Mountains of Ice: For God and Nature have so invincibly fenced the Sea side of Siberia with Ice, that no Ship can come to the River Jenisea, much less can they come farther Northwards into the Sea."[24] The obstacle was not a land promontory that might be connected with America, but rather the *ice*.

In maps, however, the question of a possible land connection between northeastern Asia and America dominated. One mapmaker who followed Witsen's map was Guillaume Delisle (1675-1726), the geographer to the King of France.[25] In 1706 Delisle published "Carte de Tartarie" (Map III) which was based, largely, on Witsen's map. In northern Asia a mountainous, open-ended peninsula is

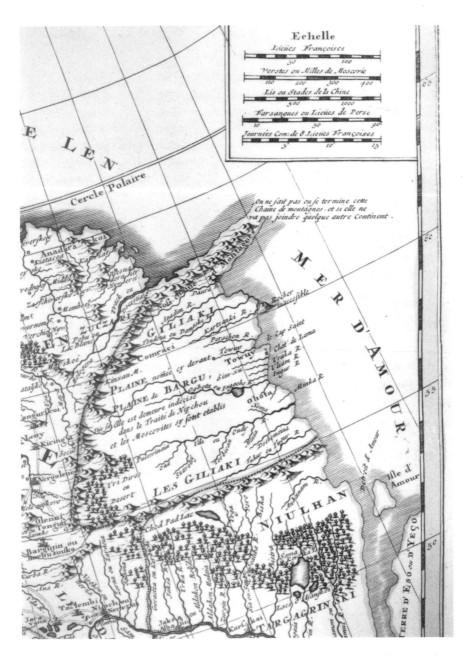

MAP III. Northeastern portion of Guillaume Delisle's map of Russia dated 1706. (Courtesy of the James Ford Bell Library)

shown with the notation "One does not know where this chain of mountains ends, and if it is not joined with some other continent." Peter the Great visited Delisle in 1717 and discussed maps with him, showing Delisle some maps which greatly interested him. Delisle made a later map based on information from Russia showing the unclosed promontory transformed into a cape, with five islands beyond it. In a similar map, bearing the date 1720, Delisle shows this same area with an even less prominent cape and many islands.[26] Russian explorations and reports of the fur traders in northern Siberia had provided a much different picture of the geography of northeastern Asia. However, the first map of Witsen and the early map of Delisle—and maps imitating them—were the ones that were widely known and copied in western Europe.

In the eighteenth century, hopes of finding a northern sea route to the East were again raised. Western Europeans had no information about the American coast north of Cape Mendocino (California); they had little information about Japan and confusing reports about the lands near it. In the absence of fact, mapmakers used their imaginations. The results of Russian explorations were scarcely known in Europe, where questions about a possible sea route to the East focused on the issue of a land junction between Asia and America.[27] Rumors about Russian explorations were viewed in the context of western European obsession with trade in the East: a Russian discovery of a northeast passage would threaten that trade.

This, briefly, was the state of geographical knowledge in western Europe about Siberia and the lands and seas to the east of it when Gerhard Friedrich Müller arrived in Russia.

*   *   *

Gerhard Friedrich Müller was born in Herford, Westphalia, on 18 October 1705. As a student at Leipzig University he worked at the library under its director, Johann Peter Kohl. Kohl was invited to become a member of the Russian Imperial Academy of Sciences as a professor of rhetoric and church history and as director of the academy's new gymnasium (secondary school). Kohl recommended Müller to the academy as a teacher at the gymnasium and as a student at the academy's university. Kohl left for St. Petersburg on 7 February 1725; from there he wrote to Müller encouraging him to accept the position with the academy, indicating that living conditions in St. Petersburg were as good as in Germany and the library was excellent.[28] After some vacillation, Müller accepted a one-year contract, planning to return to Germany at the end of the year to continue his education. He reached St. Petersburg on 5 November 1725, in time to attend the first formal meeting of the Academy of Sciences.[29]

Müller's concerns about leaving his homeland for Russia are understandable. Apart from personal feelings about leaving his family and friends, reports from western Europeans who had served in Russia were not always favorable.[30] Russia had a much different culture—or, in the eyes of some Europeans, very little culture at all. Russia was Orthodox; Russia seemed remote, oriental. On the other hand, during the reign of Peter the Great western Europe's image of Russia had changed significantly. Russia had become a European military power by defeating Sweden in the Northern War of 1700-21. Her new capital was established on the Baltic; Russian ships sailed to western ports and Russians traveled to western Europe. Peter the Great himself had traveled outside of Russia—something no Russian ruler before him had done. In 1697-98 Peter visited Germany, Holland, and England. His journey turned attention to the tsar and to his country. Wherever he went, Peter collected information, especially the technical information he wanted to introduce into Russia. Following his first visit to western Europe, Peter hired about a thousand western Europeans for Russian service, mostly for their technical skills. From this time on, Peter encouraged Russians to go to western educational institutions to study, particularly to obtain the technical and scientific education not available in Russia.[31] Toward the end of his reign, Peter the Great took steps to found the Russian Academy of Sciences, an institution for bringing western European education—not only in the sciences but in the humanities as well—to Russia.

Peter the Great's interest in founding an academy was a persistent one. He visited the Royal Society of London in 1698 and became familiar with its purposes.[32] Through correspondence with Gottfried Leibniz he was informed about the Berlin academy, the pride of Prussia's Frederick the Great, which was founded in 1700. In 1716, the year of his death, Leibniz wrote to Peter with a plan for creating an educational system in Russia.[33] In 1717 Peter attended a meeting of the Académie des Sciences in Paris.[34] Two years later he wrote to Christian Wolff, a disciple of Leibniz and a professor at Leipzig University, about a plan for an academy which would have a university and a gymnasium associated with it. This letter was delivered by Laurentii Blumentrost, Peter's personal physician, who invited Wolff to St. Petersburg. Wolff declined, though he did offer his advice and later recommended scholars for the Russian academy.[35]

Laurentii Blumentrost and Johann D. Schumacher presented a plan for the Academy of Sciences to Peter early in 1724. Peter approved the plan immediately and sent it to the Senate in January of 1724. Though it was similar to western institutions, the Russian plan for the academy was adapted to the realities of the situation in Russia. The Academy of Sciences would be supported by the Russian government. Academicians were to do their own research but were also charged with responsibilities for teaching.[36] Brought from western Europe, specialists were to do research and to teach in subjects under three broad headings: (1) mathematics (including astronomy, geography and navigation), (2) physics (anatomy, botany, and chemistry, in addition to theoretical and experimental physics), (3) humanities (including ancient and modern history, economics, law, and politics).[37] Peter's plan for the academy was an ambitious one. To a protest from one of his associates that establishing an Academy of Sciences without the other educational institutions to support it was a great waste of money, Peter replied that the Russian Academy would resemble a windmill without water, but that this "beginning would compel his successors to complete the work by digging a canal that would bring in the water. The existing ciphering and parochial schools were, he thought, at least the start of the canal."[38]

The "ciphering," or elementary, schools had been established at Peter's order in 1714. An elementary school for teaching reading, writing, arithmetic, and geometry was opened at each of the 42 provincial capitals of Russia. Peter also promoted the founding of other secular educational institutions. Through his efforts the Moscow School of Mathematics and Navigation—the first secular educational institution in Russia—opened in 1701. Peter also established schools for the study of artillery, engineering, and medicine.[39]

Peter, not surprisingly, extended his concern for education in Russia to the religious schools as well. Among churchmen he found an ally in Feofan Prokopovich (1681-1736), a churchman from Kiev Academy who came to St. Petersburg in 1716 at Peter's invitation.[40] Prokopovich is remembered in history for his association with the *Ecclesiastical Regulation* of 1721, a document which served as a justification for Peter's decision to abolish the Russian patriarchate and to place the control of the Church under a committee. The document stresses the importance of education and gives a detailed commentary on church schools. Prokopovich advocated incorporating the sciences into religious education. In his eulogy delivered after Peter the Great's death, Prokopovich asserted that, because of Peter, "...our children are now passionate students of arithmetic, geometry, and other mathematical arts."[41] Such was "the start of the canal" provided by Peter the Great.

The formal decree establishing the Academy of Sciences was issued under the hand of his widow and successor Catherine I (reigned 1725-27). Sixteen scholars were in St. Petersburg as members of it: Frenchmen, Germans, and Swiss. There were no Russian members, and no Russian students at the university. The university had eight students: six Austrians (all from Vienna) and two Germans (including Müller). In its first year the gymnasium of the academy had over a hundred students. Müller taught geography, history, and Latin at the gymnasium and tutored two students. He attended lectures at the university. But as his biographer, J.L. Black, notes, Müller had "little to do" during his first year with the academy.[42] He worked at the academy's library, as assistant to Johann D. Schumacher. Peter the Great's library of about 1600 books was given to the academy in 1725. As he was teaching geography and history, Müller undoubtedly found much of interest in the part of the collection—about 150 titles—concerning these subjects. At the time the academy's library contained about

12,000 titles.[43] In 1727 Müller was named adjunct (the rank below professor) of the academy.

The excitement and high expectations characterizing the opening of the academy were, by 1728, replaced by complaints and discord among its members. After the death of Catherine I, Peter II (reigned 1727-30) moved the court to Moscow. Laurentii Blumentrost, the academy's president, went to Moscow in January, 1728, to be with the court; he entrusted the management of the academy to Schumacher. Professors complained about their salaries; some of them returned to their homelands. Others of the initial membership died and there were squabbles over their replacements. In response to conflicts within the academy, a Chancellery (committee) of academicians was formed to serve as a governing body. In fact, however, Schumacher retained control of the academy, with only one brief interruption, until his death in 1747.[44]

In the late 1720s Müller was closely associated with Schumacher. He continued to work in the library, Schumacher's special interest. Müller acted as secretary at the academy's sessions and answered Schumacher's foreign correspondence. Müller was, inevitably, a target of the malice the academicians felt toward Schumacher. To make matters worse, when Schumacher left St. Petersburg in January, 1730, to join the court in Moscow, Müller—at age 25—was placed in control of the academy, except for "important matters." In spite of lack of endorsement by the academicians, Müller was promoted to the rank of professor in the summer of 1730.[45]

Müller served other functions within the academy in addition to those relating to administration. In January of 1728 he was transferred from the gymnasium to the academy's archives, where he handled current German-language materials.[46] In 1728, when the academy began publishing a newspaper, Müller became editor of the *Sanktpeterburgskiia Vedomosti*, which was also published in a German-language counterpart, the *St. Petersburgische Zeitung*. The newspaper was accompanied by supplements containing longer articles.[47] In one of these supplements, in 1728, Müller published the portion of Nicolaas Witsen's *Noord en Oost Tartarye* relating to the land of Jeso. He did so, he said, because "the notes to Albugazi and an accompanying map had made common the opinion, that Kamchatka and Jeso were one and the same land."[48]

The book to which he was referring was the *Histoire généalogique des Tatars*, printed in Leiden in 1726. Volume one of this work is a translation of a manuscript history of the Tatars, written by Ebulgazi Bahadir Han, Khan of Korezm, who died in 1633. Volume two is a compilation of information describing northern Asia. The compiler of it was Philip Johann Tabbert von Strahlenberg, a Swede who was taken prisoner at the battle of Poltava in 1709 and was in Siberia from 1711 to 1721. While he was at Tobolsk, Strahlenberg obtained a copy of the history of the Tatars and had it translated into German. He shared this work, and his compilation of material, with a friend, who translated it into

French and published it without Strahlenberg's permission.[49] The map accompanying the work was also made by Strahlenberg. On this map the peninsula of Kamchatka extended southward to a latitude of 40° north, almost to Japan, making Jeso appear to be part of Kamchatka (Map IV). Müller noted, "Everyone spoke about Kamchatka, as about an unknown world. The most detailed reports, which Witsen communicated about the land of Jeso, should, according to

MAP IV. Northeastern Siberia from *Histoire genealogique des Tatars*, published in 1726. (Courtesy of the Library of the Academy of Science, Leningrad)

my thought, give temporary knowledge of Kamchatka until the return of Bering."[50]

The "Abulgazi" book was interesting for another reason: one portion of it could hardly fail to excite believers in a possible northeast passage. About the far northeastern part of Siberia—the area on maps where a possible land connection between Asia and America had been placed—the text, in an eighteenth-century English translation, reads as follows:

> *It has been believed till the present that Asia was joined on the N.E. to North America, and that for this Reason it was impossible to sail from the Icy Sea into the eastern Ocean; but since the Discovery of the country of Kamtzchatka, 'tis known for certain that America is not contiguous to Asia, for the Russian Ships coasting the firm Land, pass at present Cape Suetoi Nos, or Holy Cape, and go traffick with the Kamtzchadals upon the coast of the eastern Sea, about the 50th degree of latitude but they must for this purpose pass between the Continent and a Great Island which lies to the N.E. of Cape Suetoi Nos. It is so lately discovered, and it is so remote from the other dominions of Russia, that we have not yet come to an exact Knowledge of it; what has been already related is all that I have been able to learn for certain of it, after a diligent Enquiry.*[51]

One of Müller's colleagues in the academy, Joseph Nicolas Delisle (1688-1768), also knew about this map and book. A younger brother of Guillaume Delisle, Joseph Nicolas went to St. Petersburg in 1726 to begin a four-year contract with the Academy of Sciences. He was assigned to work with Ivan Kirilovich Kirilov, director of cartographic studies for the Administrative Senate, in preparing accurate maps of Russia. Joseph Nicolas Delisle had a stormy career in Russia, largely because of his practice of sending Russian maps and information "home" to France.[52] In a letter of 25 May 1729 to Jean Frédéric Maurepas, the leading proponent of French overseas exploration, Delisle wrote that he had no better information available to him about northeastern Siberia than that found in the "*Histoire générale* [sic] *des Tatars*. The map accompanying the work, Delisle noted, was a reduction of a map printed in Amsterdam in 1725. In the same letter Delisle wrote that Peter the Great had sent Bering on an expedition "to discover the route along the north of Asia as far as the Eastern Sea."[53] When Bering returned to St. Petersburg on 1 March 1730 after an absence of five years, there were, obviously, two members of the Academy of Sciences who were anxious to learn more about the expedition to Kamchatka.

*   *   *

Vitus Jonassen Bering (1681-1741) was born in Horsens, a town on Denmark's Jutland Peninsula. As an adolescent he went to sea; as a young man he sailed on a Dutch East India Company ship on a voyage to the East Indies. The ship returned to Amsterdam in 1703. There Bering met Cornelis Cruys, a Norwegian-Dane (the two countries were united at the time) who was serving in the Russian Navy. Cruys was a close friend of Peter the Great. On the strength of recommendations of Cruys and Peter Sievers (a Dane by birth), Bering was invited to join the Russian Navy.[54]

Bering's career in the navy began in 1704, when he became a midshipman, or sublieutenant. He was promoted to lieutenant in 1707, lieutenant-captain in 1710, captain fourth rank in 1715, third in 1717, and second in 1720. Bering served with the navy in campaigns in the Sea of Azov early in his service in Russia, and later in the Baltic Sea, during the Northern War against Sweden. In the many biographical works about Bering little is written about his activities in the navy from 1716 to 1723.[55]

One of Bering's contemporaries wrote that Bering had been employed in explorations of Siberia during some of this period, including "learning the languages there," becoming governor of a province, and establishing a harbor on the east coast of Asia.[56]

Another eighteenth-century writer said that he had, in 1724, undertaken a voyage northeast from Arkhangelsk in search of a northeast passage.[57] Presumably Bering continued serving in the Baltic, but the record is incomplete.

At the end of the Northern War, a number of navy officers were promoted in recognition of their services. Bering's friends Cruys and Sievers had risen to high ranks in the Admiralty College, the navy's administrative body. Whatever Bering had been doing, it was clear he felt he was not rewarded adequately. In the spring of 1724, he asked to be relieved from service. Bering may have been a victim of factionalism that had developed within the Admiralty College. Thomas Gordon, a Scot, had won Peter the Great's favor in 1722 and had used this advantage against "the Danes" according to one authority.[58] On the other hand, it is not certain Bering had enemies in the Admiralty College; his nineteenth-century biographer, Peter Lauridsen, asserted that this idea was "entirely without foundation." According to Lauridsen, "Bering demanded and got his discharge in 1724 because he was dissatisfied with the regulations governing promotions."[59] Admiral Matseevich Apraksin, head of the Admiralty College, was reluctant to give Bering the discharge but signed the necessary papers on 3 June 1724.

Peter the Great learned about Bering's resignation from Apraksin. Two months later, at Peter's order, Bering rejoined the navy as captain of the first rank and returned to St. Petersburg in August, 1724. This dating is significant, because it was in connection with the First Kamchatka Expedition that Bering was promoted to this rank. Much of the secondary literature about the expedition stresses the presumed haste surrounding the expedition, since Peter's official instructions for it were written in January, 1725, shortly before his death. This emphasis on the last-minute preparations has been cited as a factor causing

Bering to misunderstand Peter's goals for the expedition. However, since Bering was in St. Petersburg by August, 1724, months before Peter's death on 28 January, ample time was available for discussions and planning of the expedition.[60] The official instructions for the expedition were given to Bering by Catherine I on 5 February 1725. Bering also received orders from Admiral Apraksin, together with a map for use in the expedition. The instructions, in an eighteenth-century English translation, are as follows:

> I. *You shall cause one or two convenient Vessels to be built at Kamtschatka, or elsewhere.*
>
> II. *You shall endeavour to discover, by Coasting with these Vessels, whether the Country towards the North, of which at present we have no distinct Knowledge, is a Part of America, or not.*
>
> III. *If it joins to the Continent of America, you shall endeavour, if possible, to reach some Colony belonging to some European Power; or in case you meet with any European Ship, you shall diligently enquire the Name of the Coasts, and such other Circumstances as it is in your Power to learn; and these you shall commit to Writing, so that we may have some certain Memoirs by which a Chart may be constructed.*[61]

Bering left St. Petersburg the same day he received his official instructions. A detachment of the expedition consisting of 27 men and 26 wagonloads of materials to be used for the ships had already left St. Petersburg on 24 January. The long journey across Siberia was made partly by river and partly overland; Bering reached Okhotsk in the fall of 1726. Other detachments of the expedition, with supplies, reached Okhotsk in the spring and summer of 1727. By that fall the expedition was on the west coast of Kamchatka, at Bolsheretsk; during the winter the men made the difficult overland journey to the Kamchatka River on the east coast, traveling in dogsleds provided by the Kamchadals. Some of Bering's men were already at Nizhne-Kamchatsk, on the Kamchatka River, where trees had been cut in preparation for building a ship. The ship was launched on 10 July and christened the *St. Gabriel*. The provisions were loaded and the *St. Gabriel*, with a crew of 44 men, sailed on 14 July.[62]

The route was to the north and east along the coasts of Kamchatka. Much of the time the coasts were in sight. On 8 August they met eight Chukchi and asked them, through interpreters, about the geography of the area. By 15 August Bering had reached 67° 18' north. He had sailed through the strait separating Asia from America. At that point he turned back, he said, "because the coast did not extend farther north and no land was near the Chukchi or East Cape and therefore it seemed to me that the instructions of His Imperial Majesty of illustrious and immortal memory had been carried out."[63] The expedition wintered again at Nizhne-Kamchatsk. The following summer they sailed eastward in a futile search for land that was believed to be there; then they sailed around the southern point of Kamchatka and stopped briefly at Bolsheretsk. They sailed for Okhotsk and arrived there 23 July. From there Bering headed home, arriving in St. Petersburg in March 1730 to make his report to the Admiralty College.

) 87 (

genennet wird, und bestehet derselbe aus nachfolgenden 21. Personen:
1. Groß-Cantzler Graf Galowkin
2. Feld-Marschall Fürst Michaila Galitzin.
3. Feld-Marschall Fürst Wasili Dolgorukoi.
4. Feld-Marschal Fürst Trubetzkoi.
5. Fürst Dmitri Michalowitz Galitzin.
6. Fürst Wasili Luckitz Dolgorukoi.
7. Vice-Cantzler Baron von Osterman.
8. Fürst Iwan Fedorowitz Ramodanowski.
9. Fürst Alexe Cirkaskoi.
10. Paul Iwanowitz Jagusinski.
11. Grigore Petrowitz Czernischew.
12. Iwan Iliitz Dmitreew Mamonow.
13. Fürst Grigore Dmitrewitz Jusupow.
14. Semen Andreewitz Saltikow.
15. Andre Iwanowitz Uschakow.
16. Fürst Jurge Jürgewitz Trubetzkoi.
17. Fürst Iwan Baratinskoi.
18. Semen Iwanowitz Suckin.
19. Fürst Grigore Uruzow.
20. Michaila Gawrilowitz Galowkin.
21. Wasili Jakowlewitz Nowasilzow.

Sonst sind bey Hofe folgende Hohe Promotions vorgegangen: Ihro Kayserl. Maj. Oncle Wasili Fedarowitz Saltikow, ist von Ihro Majest. zum würcklichen Geheimen Rath und General-Gouverneur von Moscau, Simon Andreewitz Saltikow zum General und Ober-Hofmeister, der Herr Graf Leuwolde zum Ober-Hof-Marschall, der Herr Schapelow zum Hof-Marschall, die Herren Kaschelow und Birck zu Stallmeisters, die Herren Lapuchin, Balck, Fürst Kurakin, Fürst Galitzin, Peter Simonewitz Saltikow, und der Cammer-Herr Biron zugleich als Ritter des Hl. Alexander Newski zu Cammer-Herren, und die Herren Korf, Brilchin, Stresenow und Jusupow zu Cammer-Junckern allergnädigst ernennet worden.

St. Petersburg den 16. Martii.

Verwichen 28. passati ist der Herr Capitain Berings von der Marine aus Kamtschatka allhier zurück gekommen. Er ist auf eigenhändige Ordre Sr. Kayserl. Majest. Petri des Großen, Glorw. Andenckens, und auf confirmirten Befehl der Hochseel. Kayserin Catharina von dem Admiralitäts Collegio den 5 Febr. 1725 in einer ziemlich weitlauftigen Begleitung von theils Officiren, theils Gendarsisten, theils auch Matrosen und Soldaten dahin abgefertiget worden, und hat im Früh-Jahr 1727 zu

Ochotskoi an der änsersten Gräntze von Siberien das erste Fahrzeug bauen lassen. Damit ist er über das Penfinskische Meer nach Kamtschatka übergefahren, und hat in Kamtschatka auf dem Fluße desselben Nahmens im Früh-Jahr 1728 das zweite Fahrzeug bauen lassen. Wie nun seine precise Ordre gewesen, die Nord-Ostliche Gräntze dieses Landstrichs zu untersuchen, und zu sehen, ob einiger Meinung zufolge das Land mit dem Nordlichen Theile von America zusammen hange, oder ob eine freye Passage darzwischen zu Wasser anzutreffen sey, so hat er mit obgemeldeten Fahrzeugen noch in demselben Jahre seinen Cours gegen Nord-Ost angetreten, und biß auf den 67. Grad 19. Minuten Norder-Breite fortgesetzet, da er denn befunden, daß würcklich eine Nord-Ost Paßage daselbst sich befinde, dergestalt, daß man aus der Lena, dafern man von dem Eise in Norden nicht verhindert würde, zu Schiffe nach Kamtschatka, und so ferner nach Japan, China, und Ost-Indien gelangen könne; Gleich wie er auch von dortigen Landes-Einwohnern berichtet worden, daß schon vor 50 biß 60 Jahren ein Fahrzeug aus der Lena auf Kamtschatka angekommen sey. Sonst bekräftiget er die ehmahlige Nachricht von diesem Lande, daß es gegen Norden mit Siberien zusammen hange, hat auch außer seiner im Jahre 1728 eingeschickten Reise-Charte, welche von Tobolskoy biß an Ochotskoy erstrecket, noch eine andere gantz genaue Charte von dem Lande Kamtschatka und seinem See-Cours aufnehmen lassen, woraus zu sehen, daß es gegen Süden unterm 51. Grad Norder-Breite sich anfängt, und also biß zu dem 67. Grade gegen Norden ausläufft. Die Geographische Länge giebet er an von der Westlichen Küste, nach dem Meridiano von Tobolskoy zu rechnen, 85 Grad, und von der äussersten Nord-Ostlichen Gräntze nach eben demselben Meridiano 126 Grad, welches wenn es auf den allgemeinen Meridianum von denen Canarischen Insuln reduciret wird, von der einen Seite 173 und von der andern 214 Grad ausmachet. Ein mehreres von diesen neuen Entdeckungen soll künftig bey Gelegenheit gemeldet werden. Die Rückreise hat der Herr Capitaine Berings von Ochotskoy zu Ausgange des Augusti-Monaths im vorigen 1729 Jahre angetreten, und ist also 6 Monathe unterweges gewesen.

ILLUSTRATION I. Report of Bering's expedition in the *St Petersburgische Zeitung*, March 16, 1730. (Courtesy of the Library of the Academy of Science, Leningrad)

The following article about Bering's expedition appeared in the St. Petersburg newspapers shortly after he returned:

> On the 28th of last month Captain Bering of the navy returned here from Kamchatka. He had been dispatched there on 5 February 1725 by the Admiralty College on the handwritten order of His Imperial Majesty Peter the Great, of glorious memory, and on the confirming instructions of the late Empress Catherine, with a rather extensive retinue of officers, geodesists, as well as seamen and soldiers, and in the spring of 1727 had the first vessel built at Okhotsk, in the farthest reaches of Siberia. With this he sailed across the Penzhina Sea to Kamchatka and, in the spring of 1728, had a second vessel built in Kamchatka on the river of the same name. As his precise orders were to investigate the northeastern limits of this region and to see whether, as according to some opinions, the land were connected with the northern part of America, or whether an open water passage was to be found between them, he, in the same year, set his course with the aforementioned vessels toward the northeast, and continued to the latitude of 67 degrees, 19 minutes north, where he then judged the northeast passage was actually there, so that one could, if not hindered by ice in the north, travel by ship from the Lena to Kamchatka, and farther to Japan, China and the East Indies—just as he had been told by the local inhabitants, how 50 to 60 years ago a vessel had come to Kamchatka from the Lena. Moreover he confirmed the previous report about this land, that it is connected to Siberia towards the north, and also, in addition to his map dispatched in 1728, which extends from Tobolsk to Okhotsk, had another completely accurate map drawn of the land of Kamchatka and his sea route from which is seen that it begins at the south at 51 degrees north latitude and runs to 67 degrees north. He gives the geographical longitude of the west coast, reckoning from the meridian of Tobolsk, as 85 degrees, and the farthest northeastern limit is 126 degrees from the same meridian, which, if converted to the more common meridian of the Canary Islands, makes 173 degrees of the one side, and 214 degrees of the other. More about these new discoveries will be reported at a future occasion. Captain Bering set out on his return journey from Okhotsk at the end of the month of August in the previous year, 1729, and was thus six months under way.[64]

Peter Lauridsen found a 1730 Danish translation of this text published in a Copenhagen newspaper. He assumed that it was written by Bering or one of his close associates, and was sent to Copenhagen in a letter. He was not aware that the text was translated from the St. Petersburg newspaper. Scholars of Bering's expedition were unaware of this article, apparently, until it was identified in 1956 by a Soviet scholar, Vadim Grekov, as the earliest printed report on Bering's expedition.[65] The text was translated and printed in several European newspapers in the eighteenth century.[66]

The content of the article—its statement of Peter's instructions, the dating of events, the longitude and latitude readings—suggests that the text was based on information from Bering, or at least from one of his senior officers, Aleksei Chirikov or Martin Spanberg, who returned to St. Petersburg with Bering. But there are striking differences between the newspaper report and Bering's own "Short Account" of his expedition dated 30 April 1730, which was submitted to the Empress Anna.[67] The newspaper asserts Bering "judged the northeast passage was actually there, so that one could, if not hindered by ice in the north, travel by ship from the Lena to Kamchatka, and farther to Japan, China and the East Indies." In his "Short Account" Bering makes no claim for the discovery of a passage—in fact the term "northeast passage" is not even used! The newspaper further emphasizes the northeast passage by asserting that "he had been told by the local inhabitants, how 50 to 60 years ago a vessel had come to Kamchatka from the Lena." Bering does not include this information in his "Short Account" of the expedition either.

There is convincing evidence that Joseph Nicolas Delisle was involved in the content of the article and that the information for it came from Bering himself. The text indicates Bering sailed to 67° 19' north. The western longitude of Kamchatka is given as 85° and the eastern extremity of Siberia as 123° (from Tobolsk), figures which do not agree with Bering's "Short Account" or the later maps based on the expedition.[68] Bering's figures for latitude and longitude were corrected after his return to St. Petersburg, and before the official accounts were submitted, indicating that the figures given in the newspaper article were supplied soon after Bering's return to St. Petersburg. The earlier figures, recorded in the newspaper, appear on a sketch map made by Delisle, based on a conversation he had with Bering[69] (Map V). Delisle wrote to Maurepas on 25 June 1730 that he had met Bering and had discussed the expedition with him.[70] Delisle's map is good evidence that his conversation with Bering took place shortly after Bering returned to St. Petersburg in March 1730. An indication at point "E" on the Delisle map, with its statement that this is the point where ice often prevents passage around the cape, corresponds with the statement in the newspaper that the northeast passage can be made "unless ice prevents it."

Delisle was not alone when he met with Bering, for Delisle needed an interpreter in conversations with Bering, a function Gerhard Friedrich Müller said he performed.[71] Müller's known interest in Bering's expedition and his position as editor of the St. Petersburg newspaper make a strong argument for naming him as the writer of the article. Whether he wrote the article alone, based on the conversation he interpreted between Bering and Delisle, or whether Delisle had a part in the writing of the article and Müller translated it, can not be known without further information.

The article has been cited as an official statement about the expedition.[72]

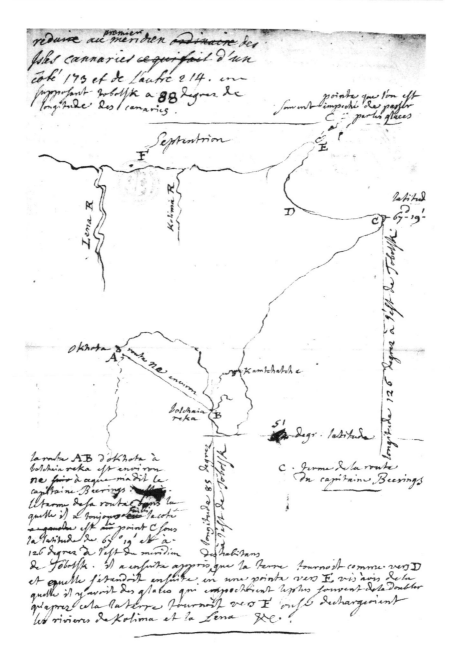

MAP V. Joseph Nicolas Delisle's sketch map. (Courtesy of the Archives Nationale, Paris)

While the newspaper did print government laws and notices, this assumption seems questionable in view of the state of the government at the time. Peter II died of smallpox in January 1730; he had not named a successor. In the resulting confusion the crown was offered to Anne of Courland (Anna Ivanovna, reigned 1730-40). The intention was to establish a limited monarchy in Russia, but once Anna arrived she rejected the limitations placed on her in favor of autocratic rule.[73]

The court in Moscow was preparing for her coronation when Bering returned from his expedition. In order to have approval from Moscow, the article would have had to have been written, sent from St. Petersburg to Moscow, approved, returned, set in type, proofread, printed, and prepared for distribution to the public—all within just over two weeks. If the article had official approval, therefore, it is likely that it received it only from the Admiralty Office in St. Petersburg.[74] The stress placed on the northeast passage in the article is apparent. This emphasis had a long-range effect on the view of the expedition, for it was incorporated into what was the first extensive account of the expedition printed in western Europe.[75]

Without an understanding of the picture Peter the Great had of the geography of northeastern Asia, it could be assumed that Bering was ordered to explore the mainland of Siberia to see if it was connected to America or not—the old question posed by the earliest Witsen map. This assumption dominates much of the literature on the first Bering expedition, and persists to this day.[76] The question of what map Bering received with his orders is important for understanding the Bering expedition. The map given to Bering was one made in Germany, based on Russian information. A number of maps made prior to Bering's expedition, reproduced in a collection edited by Aleksei V. Efimov, are good documentary evidence that Peter the Great did not believe that the mainland of Asia was joined to America.[77]

In recent studies of Bering's First Kamchatka Expedition a Soviet scholar, Boris P. Polevoi, and an American, Raymond H. Fisher, have argued that the map given to Bering was one titled "Kamtzedalie oder Jedso," made by Johann Baptist Homann (1633-1724)[78] (Map VI). These two scholars have argued that Peter the Great wanted Bering to search for a route to America along the land shown to the east on the Homann map. That Homann made the map given to Bering seems certain. Homann had made maps for the Russians and was rewarded for doing so. However, it seems questionable that the map given to Bering was the Homann map titled "Kamtzedalie oder Jedso."

In a letter of 17 June 1723 Homann wrote that he had made the map of Kamchatka ("Kamtzedalie oder Jedso") some years earlier. This information is especially important because the Homann maps are updated and are extremely rare.[79] In the same letter Homann said he had been asked to change the title of his general map of Russia from "Moscowitisch" to "Russisch" by an eminent

MAP VI. Homann's first map of Kamchatka. (Courtesy of Princeton University Library)

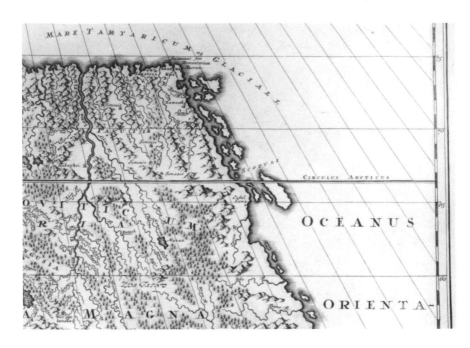

MAP VII. Cartouche and northeastern portion of Homann's map of Muscovy. (Courtesy of the James Ford Bell Library)

Russian.[80] He said that he had done this a short time earlier. Homann sent his correspondent a copy of his new map of the Russian empire. The map titled "Generalis totius Imperii Moscovitici" is based on the Ides map of 1704. The "Generalis totius Imperii Russorum" map is much changed in the northeastern part of Siberia. It is this latter conception of northeastern Siberia—shown on a map already completed in the summer of 1723—which Bering received with his instructions[81] (Maps VII and VIII).

With this conception of the geography of northeastern Siberia, Bering's instructions are clear: he was to explore the land noted as "incognita" on the map, because the northern part of it was unknown and some believed that this land joined to America. If Bering found the land did join to America, he was to follow its coast to see if he could locate a European harbor or ship. During his voyage Bering followed and mapped the coast. He was led not north, as indicated by Homann's map, but much farther to the east.[82] During his voyage he was usually, but not always, in sight of land.

By August 8, Bering encountered Chukchi people and inquired of them about the geography of the land. The Chukchi replied that, very near the place they were, the land went to the west for a long way.[83] To the question of whether there was any promontory from their land into the sea, the Chukchi replied that there was none. When they were asked whether there were islands or a land in the sea, the Chukchi answered that there was an island (St. Lawrence Island, to which the Russians later sailed) but no land. Bering continued his voyage through the strait separating Asia and America.

Shortly after this, when land was no longer in sight, Bering called a sea-council (a standard practice in the Russian navy) and asked his senior officers to present in writing their opinions about the future of the voyage. Martin Spanberg restated Bering's question: "In your oral request of the 13th of the present month your excellency deigned to ask: Because we have reached 65° 30' of the northern region and according to our opinion and the Chukchi's report we have arrived opposite the extreme end and have passed east of the land, what more needs to be done? Do we go farther. . . ."[84] Spanberg's recommendation was that they should sail north until 16 August. If they could not reach 66° north latitude, they should return to Kamchatka for the winter. Aleksei Chirikov also restated Bering's question, adding "The land of the aforesaid nos, about which the opinion has been that it is joined with America, is separated by the sea."[85] Chirikov recommended returning to the land they had been following and going along it unless ice prevented them from doing so or "if the coast does not lead away to the west toward the mouth of the Kolyma River."[86] If the land again turned north, by 25 August they would have to look for some place "where it will be possible to spend the winter, particularly across from the Chukotskii Nos, on land where according to the account obtained from the Chukchi through Petr Tatarinov, there is a forest."[87] Chirikov specifically states that they

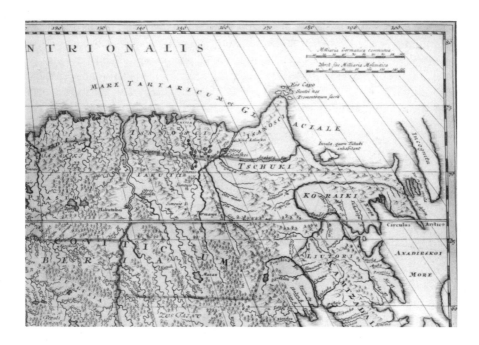

MAP VIII. Cartouche and northeastern portion of Homann's map of Russia. (Courtesy of the James Ford Bell Library)

should not follow the land if it turned toward the Kolyma River, a place known to the Russians because of trade. Obviously the expedition was not trying to sail around northeastern Siberia, or this is exactly the route Chirikov would have suggested. Instead, Chirikov advocated continuing along the land only if it went toward the north again. In this Chirikov was apparently visualizing a far northern hook of land that might connect the area they were exploring with America.[88] And the fact that he referred to a land thought to be "across from" the Chukchi Peninsula indicates that he did not believe that this land to the west was the one they were supposed to be following.

Spanberg and Chirikov both accepted the statement that they had passed east of the land they were sent to explore. As Chirikov stated, they believed that the nos was part of the mainland of Asia. The expedition had been given a specific assignment by Peter the Great. They were to explore the "incognita" land. They were convinced that they had gone east of the land and it was part of the mainland of Asia. The fault—if any—was in following Peter's orders precisely. Those who thought Bering was to search for the eastern portion of a northeast passage criticized him for not going west to the Kolyma River.[89] Others despaired that he did not discover America on either of his two voyages through the narrow strait separating Asia from America.[90]

The newspaper article, which was the first report of Bering's expedition, incorporated the true purpose of the expedition by stating: "Moreover he has confirmed the previous report about this land, that it is connected to Siberia towards the north." The "incognita" land was part of Asia, not America. But that message was lost in the emphasis on a potential northeast passage. The importance of Bering's expedition, for Delisle and probably for Müller, was not that Bering had returned with an accurate map of the areas he had explored. Their orientation and education were western European, with its long emphasis on a possible sea passage to the East. Both of them had studied a book that indicated Russians were already making regular voyages around the northeastern corner of Asia. Surely the question was asked of Bering whether a sea voyage around northeastern Siberia was possible. Bering would have answered that it was, if ice did not obstruct the way. Bering had heard reports of such a voyage made earlier.[91]

Bering had not explored that far north. To make the voyage from the Lena River to Kamchatka one would have to sail around Sviatoi Nos (Holy Cape) which appears on the Homann map. This modest promontory became, on Delisle's sketch map and in the maps prepared for the Bering expedition, a huge promontory. The shape and size of this promontory are reflections of the difference in projection and the extension eastward of the cape. Bering had discovered that northeastern Siberia stretched much further to the east than had previously been known[92] (Maps IX and X).

Delisle asked Bering if there were any indications of land to the east during

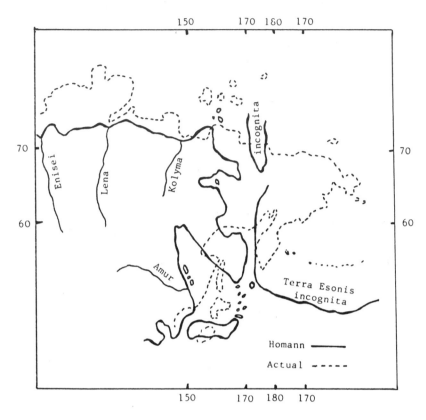

MAP IX. Comparison of Homann's map with a modern map. After Sandler, *Johann Baptista Homann,* 1886.

the voyage. Near the end of the northward course, Bering replied, there were signs of land—winds coming off land to the east, birds flying eastward, trees floating in the sea that were larger than those growing on the Siberian coast— which had been noted. Bering did not go in search of this land, he said, because he had strict orders to follow the coast he was sent to explore.[93] He was to go to America only if the land he was exploring *joined to America.* Chirikov was also aware of land east of Chukchi Peninsula, as his answer to Bering's question indicated. Chirikov did not recommend looking for this land. He suggested only that they go to it if they had to winter in the north. The importance of this land was not that it was there to be discovered, but that it had wood on it.[94] Spanberg may have sighted the North American continent during the passage through the strait. At least this is indicated by a statement on a map made later by Delisle.[95] The purpose of the First Kamchatka Expedition was not to "discover" land east of the Chukchi Peninsula. They had been assigned a specific task: to find out whether the "incognita" land on Homann's map was part of America. It was not. Bering, Chirikov, and Spanberg were all convinced they had accomplished what they had been sent out to do.[96]

Gerhard Friedrich Müller's first publication about Bering was short, almost casual—a news item. The more detailed account of Bering's expedition promised in the newspaper did not materialize in the near future.[97] Instead of being printed in Russia, Bering's "Short Account" of the First Kamchatka Expedition was printed for the first time in France, as part of a history of China. Bering's map also appeared with the text. This was in 1735, five years after the expedition.[98] Bering was already engaged in the Second Kamchatka Expedition; Müller was also. The newspaper article that Bering, Müller, and Delisle had created in 1730 was also sent to France, for its statement about the northeast passage was incorporated into the French printing of Bering's "Short Account."[99] In this way,

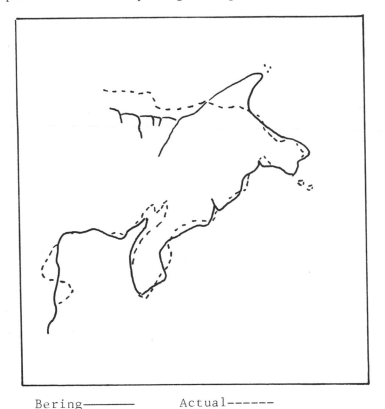

Bering————   Actual——————

MAP X. Comparison of Bering's map with a modern map.

the purpose of the First Kamchatka Expedition was stated to be a search for a northeast passage. The newspaper article therefore had an impact far greater than Bering, Müller, and Delisle—or anyone else—could have dreamed.

II. THE REBUTTALS

In the period from 1730 until the printing of his account in the *Sammlung russischer Geschichte* in 1758, Gerhard Friedrich Müller's writings on the two Bering expeditions were rebuttals of accounts that were printed in western Europe. Placing these publications in the context of Müller's life in this period will help one to understand them in terms of their purpose and content, and will also establish Müller's qualifications to write the formal history of the expeditions.

Why did Müller, a young, rising star in the administration of the Academy of Sciences in 1730, decide two years later to undertake a long journey to Siberia as a member of Bering's Second Kamchatka Expedition? In March of 1730, the same month that Bering had returned to St. Petersburg, Müller applied for promotion to the rank of professor, along with four other academicians. At the time Müller was disliked and distrusted by some members of the academy, who considered him a spy for Schumacher in the quarrels which plagued the academy. Not surprisingly, the other promotions were supported by the academy's conference of senior professors; Müller's was not. President Blumentrost promoted Müller in spite of this lack of support.[1] The lack of support also may have been the result of the growing emphasis within the academy on sciences, particularly on mathematics, rather than of a personal dislike for Müller.[2] The academy itself was suffering at the time from internal dissensions and a perceived lack of interest and support from the government in Moscow. The gymnasium operated by the academy had dropped from an enrollment of 112 in 1727 to 74 in 1729; by 1731 the university did not have a single student.[3] It was expected that conditions within the academy would improve when the court returned to St. Petersburg in 1730, but they did not.

In May of 1730, Müller asked permission to journey to Herford, to take care of some matters relating to the death of his father in 1729. This request was embellished in negotiations with Schumacher to become a journey on behalf of the academy—Müller was to visit England, Holland, and Germany in order to buy books for the academy, to foster relations with scholars, and to encourage some of them to become foreign members of the Russian Academy of Sciences, and additionally to seek out other potential members for the academy.[4] He was, in addition, charged with refuting any unfavorable impressions about the academy that he encountered.[5]

On 2 August 1730, Müller left St. Petersburg with his "best friends," the four other newly promoted professors of the academy, who accompanied him as far as Kronstadt. He went to London, where he spent a busy 2 1/2 months.[6] While in London, he met Sir Hans Sloane, President of the Royal Society. Sloane became a foreign member of the Russian academy in 1733. Müller, who attended a meeting of the Royal Society on 22 October, was invited shortly afterwards to join it, which he did. From London Müller traveled to Rotterdam, The Hague, Amsterdam, Leiden, and Utrecht before going to Leipzig and then to Herford early in 1731, where he remained for three months. Müller apparently carried out all his charges on behalf of the academy faithfully.[7]

When he returned to St. Petersburg on 2 August 1731, therefore, he could hardly have been prepared for the reception he received. Schumacher's attitude toward him had changed from warm friendship to antagonism. Schumacher had broken into his writing desk and had taken letters he had written to Müller.[8] There were disputes over Müller's expenses. The reasons for this change are not clear. There are several possibilities. In January 1731 Schumacher had written a letter to Müller urging him to cut short his travels and return to St. Petersburg in order to become tutor to the niece of the Empress. The position was filled by someone else; this has been cited as the cause of the first break between the two men.[9] Since Müller states specifically that Schumacher had broken into his writing desk and taken letters, it may be that Schumacher himself had been criticized for allowing his young protégé too much freedom in acting on behalf of the academy, and was destroying evidence. At least part of the later arguments over expenses related to the question of whether Müller was indeed an official representative of the academy. And it could be that Schumacher felt threatened by Müller's success on the journey, and acted out of jealousy. Or it may simply have been a personal matter; in any case, Müller wrote: "At that time my hopes of becoming Schumacher's son-in-law and successor were extinguished."[10]

In his history of the Academy of Sciences, written much later, Müller contradicts his own earlier statement about the time of Schumacher's turning on him by stating that "Schumacher's hatred for me began in 1732, when the Senate ordered the professors to examine the academic organization created by Schumacher."[11] At this time Müller expressed his opinions openly, criticizing Schumacher.

There is another possibility, although the evidence in support of it is only circumstantial. During his visit to England, where interest in the northeast passage was extremely high, Müller no doubt had shared his ideas about the potential northeast passage with people there. Müller had met Bering, who had explored the farthest reaches of Siberia and had sailed unknown seas. Two Englishmen, Richard Ensel and George Morison, had participated in the voyage.[12] Müller discussed Engelbert Kaempfer's *History of Japan* with Sir Hans Sloane; the map in that work showing the far northern areas of Kamchatka was undoubtedly also discussed[13] (Map XI). All of this may have nothing whatever to do with a proposal later made by John Elton, but there is a likelihood that it did. Elton, a ship's officer in the British merchant marine, presented Prince Antiokh Kantemir, the Russian minister in London, with a proposal offering his services to search for a northern passage from Arkhangelsk via Novaia Zemlia to Japan, India, and America.[14] In 1731, British relations with Russia were reestablished after many years; Elton's proposal was made in December of 1732. The Prince was apparently at least intrigued and somewhat uncertain about what course of action to follow, for Elton joined Russian service in 1733 and became involved in trade to Persia rather than in northern voyages.[15] It is possible that Müller's visit to London stirred an unwelcome interest in Russia's northern explorations.

Whatever had happened, the young Müller had obviously got into trouble somehow. He said: "I deemed it necessary to enter upon another learned field—that was Russian history, which I intended not only to study industriously myself but also to make known in compositions from the best sources."[16] At the same time Müller was embarking on his career as a historian he was also involved in preparations for the Second Kamchatka Expedition.[17]

*   *   *

When Vitus Bering presented his maps and logbook for the First Kamchatka Expedition he also submitted a proposal for further explorations, as well as recommendations for the development and administration of eastern Siberia.[18] Dated 30 April 1730, the proposals for a second expedition consist of five short paragraphs. In the first paragraph Bering recorded his reasons for believing land could be found near the east coast of Kamchatka (smaller waves in the sea, the presence of trees drifted on shore that did not grow in Kamchatka) and proposed searching for this land. He suggested in the second paragraph that a ship should be built in Kamchatka, rather than at Okhotsk, as it would be cheaper and easier. In his third paragraph Bering recommended searching for a route from Okhotsk or Kamchatka to the Amur River and the islands of Japan, reasoning that " . . .if the possibility of carrying on trade with Japan permits, no small profit may develop for the Russian empire in the future." The fourth paragraph consisted of an estimate of the costs of the expedition. In the final paragraph Bering proposed, "If it is considered desirable, it is possible to explore unhindered the northern lands or the coast of Siberia from the mouth of the Ob River to the Enisei and from there to the Lena River in boats or by land because these lands are under the high authority of the Russian empire."[19]

Bering's proposals were discussed by the Admiralty College, the Academy of Sciences, and a committee of the Senate, and were given preliminary approval in May 1731. Though Bering's proposals were accepted, the expedition took shape slowly. On 17 April 1732, the official order for the expedition, with Bering

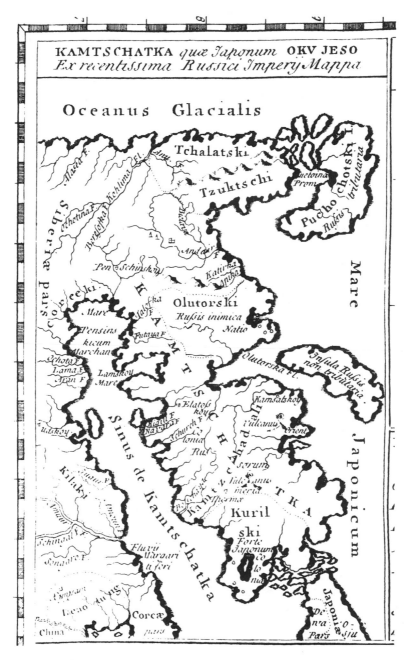

MAP XI. From Engelbert Kaempfer, *Historia Imperii Japonici* . . . vol. I., pl. VIII, 1727. (Courtesy of the James Ford Bell Library)

named as head, was made by the Senate; the following month a general outline of the plan of the expedition was announced. The purposes and results of the expedition were to be kept secret unless permission was obtained to disseminate them, and all participants in the expedition were to sign an oath to that effect. The Senate's report to Empress Anna on the expedition was not issued until 28 December 1732.[20] A committee of the Admiralty College and the Senate worked on the proposals for the expedition as well, until March 1733.[21]

By this time the simple paragraphs Bering had originally submitted had expanded beyond recognition. Three men in particular enlarged upon and supported Bering's proposals: Andrei Ostermann, a member of Anna's cabinet; Count Nikolai F. Golovin, of the Admiralty; and Ivan K. Kirilov, Senior Secretary of the Administrative Senate and head of the Geodetic Service.[22] Ostermann was instrumental in obtaining and maintaining support for the expedition. Golovin had an active part in the planning—he proposed that the ships for the Second Expedition be sent via the Cape of Good Hope to Kamchatka—a voyage of ten months rather than a journey of two years. Kirilov was, in the words of Gerhard Friedrich Müller, the "driving force" of the Second Kamchatka Expedition.[23] Kirilov was a cartographer, and he prepared the first atlas of Russia, which appeared in 1734.[24]

Kirilov's memorandum stated:

> *This sending of an important expedition, the like of which*
> *there has never been before, consists of various*
> *investigations: (1) to find out for certain whether it is*
> *possible to pass from the Arctic Ocean to the Kamchatka or*
> *Southern Ocean sea (I hope ultimately in light of the*
> *investigations of several people that this is so); (2) to*
> *reach from Kamchatka the very shores of America at some*
> *unknown place about 45 degrees of longitude ; (3) to*
> *go from Kamchatka to Japan, between which the distance is*
> *only ten degrees of north latitude; (4) on that voyage and*
> *everywhere to search for new lands and islands not yet*
> *conquered and to bring them under subjection; (5) to search*
> *for metals and minerals; (6) to make various astronomical*
> *observations both on land and sea and to find accurate*
> *longitude and latitude; (7) to write a history of the old*
> *and the new, as well as natural history, and other*
> *matters.*[25]

Müller was directly involved in the preparations for the Second Kamchatka Expedition. He served as translator in conversations between Joseph Nicolas Delisle, the academy's geographer, and Vitus Bering.[26] Delisle prepared a map for the expedition in 1731 (Map XII). It was based on maps of his brother

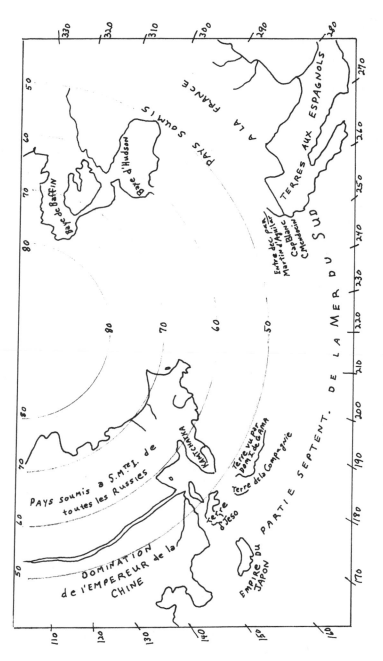

MAP XII. Joseph Nicolas Delisle's manuscript "Carte dressee en 1731, pour servir a la recherche des terres et des mers situees au nord de la Mer du sud." Redrawn after Bagrow, *A History of Russian Cartography.*

Guillaume and, in addition, Delisle stated he used Chinese and Dutch maps, as well as the maps prepared to accompany Engelbert Kaempfer's *History of Japan*.[27] On it Delisle included Jeso, States Island, and Company Land as well as Gama Land. The Delisle map was later considered by the members of the expedition to be a major cause of their difficulties. For its time, it was based on the best (though certainly inadequate) knowledge of the North Pacific. Delisle also wrote a memoir to accompany the map, noting three possible routes for the expedition to follow: eastward from the point Bering reached on his first voyage, to America in the north; eastward from the part of Kamchatka where Bering noted signs of land on his first voyage; southward from Kamchatka toward the land of "Dom Jean de Gama."[28]

Müller was involved in the proposals for the expedition in another way. After Kirilov wrote his memorandum for the expedition, he had it translated into German for presentation to Ernst-Johann Biron, the favorite of Empress Anna. Kirilov had chosen a bad translator, however. Bering suggested that Kirilov have the translation redone by Müller. "In that way," Müller wrote later, "I got to know Kirilov, whose acquaintance did not remain without consequences."[29] It is important to emphasize that Kirilov's memorandum cited as the first goal of the expedition "to find out for certain whether it was possible to pass from the Arctic Ocean to the Kamchatka or Southern Ocean . . . ," which was not the primary thrust of Bering's proposals.[30] Müller's later writings about the expedition reflect this emphasis on the geographical question about the possibility of this passage, as will be indicated in the notes to the translation. The portion of the Kirilov memorandum relating to the writing of "a history of the old as well as the new" (point seven) would have appealed to Müller, who had already decided to devote himself to the study of history. In addition, Müller taught geography to six students who were going on the expedition.[31]

Two members of the Academy of Sciences, Johann Georg Gmelin and Louis Delisle de la Croyère, had been selected to go with Bering on behalf of the academy. Gmelin was to study the natural history of the areas explored; de la Croyère was charged with making the necessary astronomical observations. The academicians were offered double salary for the expedition; they were given permission to purchase materials at the academy's expense, and they were given the right to private quarters and were promised Bering's assistance in making other journeys as well as freedom from his authority.[32] For Müller, who was under Schumacher's cloud, the prospect of his friends' travels undoubtedly appeared attractive. Then, in the winter of 1732-1733, Gmelin became ill "in the region of the liver" and withdrew as a participant in the expedition.[33]

Müller records: "Captain Commander Bering, with whom I had close relations, had aroused in me the desire for this journey even before there was any hope for me to go."[34] Bering reported this interest to Kirilov, who told Müller to apply for Gmelin's place. Müller did so and was accepted. He wrote: "I was glad, because in this way I was removed from the confused condition of the academy for a long time and, far from the hatred and hostility, I could enjoy a quiet peace, dependent only on myself. I never had cause to regret my decision, not even during my serious illness which I suffered in Siberia."[35] Müller was "to describe the history of those peoples" encountered during the expedition. Thus the historian Müller came to make his long Siberian journey, one which would have major consequences for the writing of Siberian history. Gmelin had a sudden recovery from his illness, which Müller ascribed to Gmelin's drinking two bottles of Rhine wine, and he, too, traveled to Siberia.

The academic contingent left St. Petersburg on 8 August 1733 and reached Tobolsk in January 1734.[36] Bering was waiting for them there, as de la Croyère and the other surveyors had the instruments necessary for the mapping of the arctic coasts with them. Müller and Gmelin visited Tomsk, Eniseisk, and Krasnoiarsk, and arrived in Irkutsk on 8 March 1735. They investigated the region around Lake Baikal and went to Kiakhta, the trading town on the Chinese border. They spent part of the winter of 1735-36 in Irkutsk. In the archives there Müller discovered the report of Semen Dezhnev's voyage from the Lena to Kamchatka in 1648.[37] They continued to Ilimsk and in the spring traveled down the Lena River. In September they rejoined Bering at Iakutsk. That winter Müller was ill and also had trouble with his eyes, a condition he attributed to working in poorly lighted archives.[38]

While Gmelin and Müller were having dinner with Bering one evening in November 1736, Gmelin's house burned down. The fire destroyed many of his natural history specimens. Müller and Gmelin had protested to Bering about their quarters, but since the naval officers had arrived first and had appropriated the better houses, Bering did nothing in response. Müller and Gmelin found their relationship with Bering increasingly strained as the winter passed, and felt that Bering's manner was arrogant and dictatorial. Bering's chief concern was for the naval contingent of the expedition, not the academic, and the complaints from the young Müller and Gmelin about housing, supplies, and transportation were not well received.[39] Bering himself was under pressure because of the cost of the expedition and the time it was taking.[40] The two academicians decided not to travel on to Okhotsk with Bering. Instead, they sent a student, Stepan Krasheninnikov, on a journey to Kamchatka to begin studies and preparations for their own arrival later. Houses were to be built, information gathered, and a botanical garden established. Before Krasheninnikov departed, Müller compiled the data he had obtained about Kamchatka from his archival work and summarized it for Krasheninnikov's use.[41]

During the winter of 1737-38, in Irkutsk, Müller tried to arrange for transportation to Iakutsk and from there to Kamchatka, without success. With no apparent hope for making the journey the following summer, in May 1738 Müller and Gmelin petitioned to be relieved of further responsibilities for the

Kamchatka expedition.[42]

Georg Wilhelm Steller, naturalist and mineralogist, was selected to replace Gmelin for the Kamchatka expedition.[43] Steller began his journey to Siberia in January of 1738, joining Müller and Gmelin in Eniseisk the following January. To prepare him for his Kamchatka journey, Müller and Gmelin gave him the same instructions they had given to Krasheninnikov, plus a copy of the geographical and historical reports Müller had compiled from the archives. The historian Johann Eberhard Fischer, Müller's replacement, was to assist Müller in further Siberian research.[44]

Müller received the decree recalling him to St. Petersburg in March 1739. His journey home was lengthened when he got pneumonia in Turinsk in the winter of 1742. The following summer he recuperated in the Ural Mountains, at Verkhoturie. He married the woman who nursed him during his illness. After ten years of travel, by his own account a journey of some 24,000 miles, Müller returned to St. Petersburg on 14 February 1743.[45]

*　　*　　*

To that time very little was known in western Europe about the Second Kamchatka Expedition. The First Kamchatka Expedition, as noted in Chapter I, had been reported in western Europe. By 1743 nothing had been published about the difficult explorations of the arctic coasts. The only news of the Second Kamchatka Expedition published in western Europe was a report of the voyage led by Martin Spanberg to Japan. A report of the Spanberg expedition had been received in St. Petersburg in January 1740. Information from the report appeared on a map printed in Amsterdam in 1740.[46] The legend published with the map indicated that the text was based on information received from Mr. Swartz, a representative of Holland in St. Petersburg, through a letter dated 13/24 (Old Style and New Style) January 1740.

The report states that Spanberg discovered thirty-four islands, where the Russians met friendly people but were unable to talk to them. These islanders had plenty of gold. Their money bore inscriptions that were thought to be either Japanese or Chinese. The map was based on one made by "Jean Kyrilow" which had been published in 1734.[47] Jeso, Company Land, and De Gama Land are shown on the map. A similar report of Spanberg's voyage was printed in the *Gazette de France*[48] of 27 February 1740, and a report about it was included in the *London Magazine*, which asserts that Spanberg discovered thirty-four islands "from whence it is thought they may sail to Japan, China, and so round to the East Indies, Persia, &c. which will greatly increase the trade and Commerce of Muscovy."[49] Nothing had then been published about the voyages of Bering or Chirikov.

On 16 November 1743 a report on Bering's voyage was published in the

Gazette de France. It stated:

> Captain Bering, who went to make an attempt to find out
> whether one could go to America by way of the Arctic Sea was
> wrecked on the coast of an island, and the captain with the
> larger part of the crew died here. Steller, the botanist of
> the academy, and several sailors were fortunate enough to
> resist the disease and from the wreck of the big boat built
> a smaller one, on which they returned to Kamchatka. Steller
> says that he met Captain Tscherikov, who told him that he
> had been on the coast of some unknown country whose
> inhabitants resemble the Americans, and after losing several
> soldiers and sailors, he had to give it up.[50]

An article in the *Gentleman's Magazine* also cited Steller as its source.[51]

Besides being inaccurate, there was the question of the origin of this account. "Steller says" suggests that the information was received from Steller, who was at the time still in Siberia. Steller learned of the newspaper accounts from a letter written by his brother Augustin, which reached Steller at Iakutsk on 13 March 1745.[52] Augustin congratulated his brother because the newspaper accounts made it appear that Steller had saved the remnants of Bering's crew and had built the ship for their escape from the island; this worried Steller. It appeared to him to be the work of his enemies, who were discrediting him and making it appear he had broken the oath of secrecy about the expedition. He responded: "I should like very much to know who has been making me out a sailor and a windbag. My desire is to fill gaps in the realm of science, not vacant space in the newspapers."[53] Steller was concerned, understandably, that these reports could be taken as evidence that he had broken his pledge of secrecy.

In the concerns about the provision of information to western Europe about the expedition, the members of the Academy of Sciences were obviously suspect. Because of their relationships with western Europeans, it was natural to look to the members of the academy as the sources of the leaks. The academy, planned as the apex of the educational system in Russia, was seen by officialdom as an enclave of foreign influence in Russia. And the value of the academy to Russia was questioned.[54]

Müller had been caught up in the conflicts within the Academy of Sciences soon after his return from Siberia; it did not help him that, as a member of the Second Kamchatka Expedition, he could come under suspicion of providing information to western European correspondents. The academy at the time of his return was in considerable disarray. Leonhard Euler, its most prominent member, had left it in 1741, for Prussia. Three other members left soon afterwards.[55] Schumacher, Müller's old enemy, had been accused of embezzling academy funds, and Andrei K. Nartov, who had been in the service of Peter the

Great, had been put in charge of the academy on a temporary basis. Nartov was called "a mechanic" because of his work in the laboratory of the academy. The investigation of the charges against Schumacher lasted from October 1742 until December 1743; in that time Nartov managed to turn the academicians against him so completely that Schumacher, by comparison, seemed preferable to them. Schumacher was reinstated in his old position in December 1743.[56] For Müller, Schumacher's continued animosity toward him seemed incomprehensible. He later wrote to a colleague, "Who could have thought that during so long a journey and so great an interval, his hostility toward me would not subside?"[57] Müller had brought the academy a huge collection of Siberian materials, described by J. L. Black as follows:

> His completed and catalogued collections included
> forty-two books of documents on the history and geography of
> Siberia, four books of chronicles, ten books of descriptions
> of Siberia prepared by Müller himself and three compiled by
> his students overseen by him, and a large quantity of maps,
> drawings, and city plans. Furthermore, he delivered
> fourteen thick files of reports, documents, letters, orders,
> and other communications between his group and St.
> Petersburg between 1733 and 1743.[58]

His experience qualified him as a knowledgeable scholar in Siberian geography. In 1744, when he saw some of the maps prepared for the academy's Russian *Atlas*, to be published in 1745, he made a number of suggestions for their improvement.[59] Müller's recommendations were not well received. Therefore Müller began work on his own maps—a general map of Russia and a map of Siberia. Since some information on these maps originated from the Second Kamchatka Expedition, when Müller presented them to the academy for approval on 3 March 1746, the academy determined that government permission was required before they could be published. Instead of permission, on 7 April 1746, the academy received orders to turn in all maps relating to the Second Kamchatka Expedition, and especially, any materials relating to Steller.[60] The concern about leaks was not without foundation, since maps containing information from the expeditions were published by the Homann firm in Germany in 1746 and a similar map appeared in Paris the same year.[61] It was suspected, apparently, that Steller might have been involved in the publishing of these maps.

Steller had received his recall from Siberia at the same time he received the letter from his brother Augustin. Steller had troubles with government officials in Siberia (these are noted in Müller's account, beginning on p. 127.) and an order had been issued for his arrest. Thus Steller's return journey from Siberia was prolonged when he was first arrested, then released, and then re-arrested to be taken part way back to Siberia to face charges. Then, on his return for the second time Steller got a fever, and he died in Tiumen on 12 November 1746. The news reached the academy on 8 December 1746; nobody thought to notify Steller's family, and his brother Augustin learned of the death only through the accounts which lamented the loss of the great naturalist.[62]

Augustin's attempts to get further information were unsuccessful.[63] In anger, he turned to his friend Justi, a writer, who prepared a biography of Steller based on the information Augustin supplied him.[64] This appeared in several papers. The article criticizes Russian authorities and questions the circumstances surrounding Steller's death. As Stejneger, Steller's biographer, indicates, "The article winds up with a severe criticism of the Russian authorities for their attitude toward Steller's death and the circumstances leading up to it, hinting that his tragic ending may have been the result of the machinations of his enemies, and challenging the authorities to divulge the facts."[65] The article was reprinted several times.

The reply to this article came as a short biography of Steller published in Frankfurt in 1748, based on a text written in Russia.[66] This biography consisted of only thirty-eight pages. The first twenty pages describe Steller's life before coming to Russia and only four pages—20 to 24—describe Steller's experiences on the voyage with Bering. This short section, however, indicates that the writer had access to factual information about the voyage, perhaps from Steller's journal. For example, it indicates that when Steller reached America he had six hours on land to pursue his researches in natural history, while the sailors took on fresh water. Huts and other evidence of the inhabitants were discovered, but the people themselves had run away at the arrival of such a large ship, said the writer. Steller collected as many plants as he could. During the difficult return voyage they met people from an island, but the translators the Russians had with them could not understand a word of the language these people spoke. After this they met with many violent storms and winds that drove them about in the sea. At last the ship was wrecked on an island, where Bering died on 8 December. The 46 surviving men built five huts for themselves for the winter, and ate sea animals, including sea otters and sea cows, for food. Pieces of their wrecked ship were carried onto the land, and from this wreckage the survivors built a small ship and made their way back to Kamchatka, where they arrived on 26 August 1742.

It was an error in the newspapers, according to the pamphlet, to say that Steller built or led the ship. The writer indicated that the rumors that Steller did not die, or that his enemies had something to do with his death, were wrong. Steller no doubt had some enemies; he was, the writer noted, a very suspicious man and once he had conceived a suspicion, he retained it for a long time. But that did not mean that anyone had caused Steller harm. He died of a fever, in the presence of Dr. Lau, at Tiumen.[67] That the biography served its purpose is not likely; it is rare and little known and was so, apparently, at the time it was printed. It was, however, the first—though very brief—official factual report on the voyage of Bering to America published from Russian sources.[68] The author of this publication was probably Müller.[69]

*　　*　　*

Russian attempts to keep accounts of the Second Kamchatka Expedition secret had not been entirely successful. In 1747, a Dane, Peder von Haven, published a book titled *Nye og forbedrede efterraetningar om det Russiske rige.* Inserted in volume two of this work is a summary of Bering's first expedition, a short statement about Spanberg's voyage to Japan, and a report on Bering's voyage to America.[70] Haven visited Russia for the first time in 1736, as a secretary and pastor to his countryman, Peter Bredal, who had served in the Russian Navy since 1703. Haven left Russia in 1739, and returned again in 1743. This time he remained in Russia until 1746, as chaplain to a Danish diplomatic mission in St. Petersburg. While there, he obtained official documents about the Bering voyage written by Sven Waxell, the first officer of Bering's ship. Presumably he got these from Martin Spanberg, who left Siberia without permission in 1745 and returned to St. Petersburg. For this Spanberg was court-martialed and sentenced to death—a sentence which was reduced to a lowering in rank for three months. Spanberg was assisted with his case by the Danish ambassador in St. Petersburg and it was during this time, presumably, that Haven met him and obtained the documents on which his report was based.[71] The work, however, was little known in Denmark and even less so outside of that country.[72]

There were other accounts of the Second Kamchatka Expedition which were much more widely known. One of these appeared in England in 1748, in Campbell's collection of travels.[73] Campbell, a Scot, had determined to update a collection of travel literature first published in 1705 by John Harris.[74] Campbell published a text of the first expedition, which he said was an original copy of Bering's journal, and he also published a new version of the Bering map.[75] It seems certain this material had been obtained by Lord Hyndford, who was the British minister in London beginning in 1744. Hyndford had been instructed to obtain material on the Russian explorations when he went to Russia, and three years later he wrote to the Earl of Chesterfield:

> *I have in consequence of my first instructions been*
> *endeavouring to learn, what discoveries this court has made*
> *to the north-east of Russia, and I have been so lucky, as to*
> *procure a copy of the journal and map of the famous Captain*
> *Bering, who took a survey of the coast of Kamchatka and of*
> *the islands towards Japan, which I hope to be able to send*
> *your Lordship by the next courier, but this must be kept a*

42

secret, for, if Czernischew [the Russian minister in London]
comes to the knowledge of it, some people here may be sent
to finish their days in that country . . . .[76]

The account Hyndford wanted was of the Second Kamchatka Expedition; what he received was the report on the first. This appeared in Campbell's publication together with a letter, dated 10 December 1746, from Leonhard Euler, then in Berlin.[77] Euler indicated that during the Second Kamchatka Expedition Bering believed he had sailed along a great land, which began 50 German miles east of Kamchatka (Bering Island) and extended to California. This led Euler to conclude that a northwest passage—at least, one through North America to the Pacific Ocean—was not likely. If it did exist, Euler stated, the passage would lead through North America into the northern seas near Kamchatka, and thus would not be useful for navigation. Euler later indicated concern that this letter had been published.[78] Arthur Dobbs, the great proponent of the northwest passage, responded to Euler's letter by maintaining that the account of Bering's voyage had proved nothing, since there were no indications of latitude and longitude in it. Further, Dobbs argued, it was likely that Bering had reached an *island*, not the mainland of America.[79]

There was still another unauthorized report on the Second Kamchatka Expedition, this one more directly associated with Müller. It was written by his friend and traveling companion Johann Georg Gmelin. In 1747 Gmelin had signed a new four-year contract with the academy. This contract specified that Gmelin had permission to visit Germany. He did so, with his friends Mikhail Vasilevich Lomonosov and Gerhard Friedrich Müller acting as guarantors for him. Once Gmelin returned to Germany and obtained a position at the University of Tübingen in 1749, however, he elected not to return to Russia.[80] This, of course, caused great financial hardship for Müller and Lomonosov. Word was received that Gmelin intended to publish a book based on his travels in Siberia. The publication had not been authorized by the Russian government and it was a clear violation of Gmelin's oath not to publish anything about the expedition without permission. On 22 October/2 November, 1751, Johann D. Schumacher wrote to Leonhard Euler in Berlin, stating he feared Gmelin would bring misfortune upon himself by the publication. "It would be better," wrote Schumacher, "to suppress this work. Nothing can be published about the Kamchatka Expedition without first consulting the academy."[81]

Gmelin acknowledged his oath about the expedition in the introduction to his book, stating, "The least of that is known to me, and I would commit a punishable offense, if I would make known to the world the little that is known to me about the sea voyages, without the highest permission."[82] Gmelin's book is a very detailed diary of his travels, including a strong condemnation of the Russian administration in Siberia. It appeared in four volumes between 1751 and 1752. Readers of it in the Russian Academy of Sciences found much in Gmelin's book that was "excessive, indecent, and suspicious," and, not surprisingly, the work was banned in Russia.[83]

The introduction to his work contains a commentary on Russian reasons for exploring the North Pacific. Gmelin traced this interest to a visit Peter the Great made to the French Académie des Sciences in 1717. Gmelin also described the possible routes the Russians could use in these explorations.[84] After that he said nothing whatever in his book about the Bering voyages. He did, however, make a rather extensive commentary on the Russian efforts in surveying and mapping the arctic coasts of Siberia.[85] This part of Gmelin's text was later translated into English and published in 1780 in William Coxe's *Account of the Russian Discoveries*.[86]

The academy was concerned about Gmelin's breach of contract. Attempts were made to suppress the publication and there were threats about possible consequences.[87] In his introduction Gmelin stated he could not divulge the "important geographical results" of the explorations. He did not discuss either the Spanberg expedition to Japan or the voyages to America. He confined his report to the northern explorations. A rebuttal to Gmelin's publication was considered by the academy, but Lomonosov and Müller were reluctant to prepare one.[88] In the end, the academy decided to counter Gmelin's publication with a history of Siberia. Johann Eberhard Fischer was charged with this work. It was completed in 1757, but not published until 1768.[89]

The maps and writings of another academy member who left Russia led directly to the publication of Müller's account of the Bering expeditions. This man was Joseph Nicolas Delisle, who has been the subject of several studies, in which he has been portrayed in characterizations ranging from an incompetent or a procrastinator to a French espionage agent.[90] Whatever else Delisle may have been, one thing is certain: his loyalties remained with France in spite of over 20 years of employment with the Russian Academy of Sciences.[91]

In 1726, when Delisle accepted his first appointment with the academy, he intended to remain in Russia for four years. He obtained a leave of absence from his position with the French Académie des Sciences to take the position in Russia, where he was to work as an astronomer and help with an astronomical observatory.[92] Delisle was a member of the foremost French family of geographers, and his appointment to the academy was supported by Ivan K. Kirilov, the Russian cartographer.[93] Once Delisle began his work in Russia, however, relations between Delisle and Kirilov were soon strained. Delisle insisted on obtaining new astronomical observations to verify or correct Russian mapping; he insisted that maps should not be published until this was done. The Russian observations had been painstakingly gathered over many years—since at least 1720.[94] The delay caused by Delisle was a source of annoyance and was seen as procrastination on Delisle's part.

Delisle entered Russian service under a set of conditions worked out in July, 1725, with Prince Boris Kurakin, the Russian ambassador extraordinary to France.[95] At the end of four years Delisle was free to extend his contract with Russia as long as he wanted to, under the same conditions. He was granted the right to share his astronomical observations with the Académie des Sciences. The French hoped to profit by Delisle's service in Russia. The Comte de Maurepas, on behalf of the Ministry of the Marine, agreed to permit Delisle to leave France on the express condition that in doing so Delisle would be engaged in work that would benefit geographical efforts in France. Delisle began to work on Russian maps soon after his arrival in Russia, and in December, 1726, Catherine I ordered the Senate to deliver all maps made by the *geodesists* (land surveyors) to the academy.[96] Delisle began his practice of copying these and sending them to France.[97]

On 25 June 1730 Delisle wrote to the Comte de Maurepas about the expedition of Vitus Bering, stating that he had met Bering and had seen his journal. Delisle stated that he hoped to send materials about the Bering expedition soon.[98] In this Delisle was apparently successful, as Bering's "Short Account" was first published in Paris in 1735 as part of a description of China by Jean Baptiste Du Halde. Müller gave only an abstract of the First Kamchatka Expedition in his account of Bering's expeditions, since the full report had been published previously.[99] There is little evidence to indicate that Delisle got into trouble in the early 1730s for sending this material to France.[100] Delisle was a participant in the academy's preparations for the Second Kamchatka Expedition. He consulted maps from the First Kamchatka Expedition in preparing a map for the use of the Second Kamchatka Expedition; he had Bering's journal; he discussed the expeditions with Bering.[101] The situation changed with the decision to keep matters relating to the Second Kamchatka Expedition secret. In 1744 a map dedicated to the Comte de Maurepas appeared in Paris[102] (Map XIII). The map included information from the Second Kamchatka Expedition, and showed the route of Chirikov and Delisle de la Croyère to America. Similar maps, as noted previously, also appeared in Germany in 1746 (Map XIV). Delisle had corresponded with the mapmakers who produced one of these maps for the Homann firm.[103] Although all evidence pointed to Delisle, Müller was questioned about a possible connection to the map publication, and his maps were taken from him.[104] Delisle's contract with the academy was not renewed and in 1747 Delisle returned to France. All members of the Russian academy were forbidden to correspond with him.

In April of 1750 Delisle presented a memoir to the Académie des Sciences in which he discussed Russian explorations in the North Pacific in connection with the geography of North America as it was assumed to exist on the basis of the voyage of one Admiral de Fonte. The memoir and two maps were published in 1752 (Maps XV and XVI). They were received with great consternation in

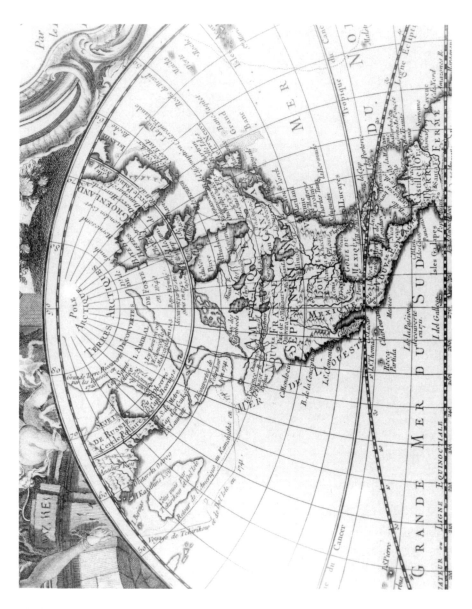

MAP XIII. A portion of Georges-Louis la Rouge's "Mappe monde nouvelle," 1744. (Courtesy of the Elmer E. Rasmuson Library)

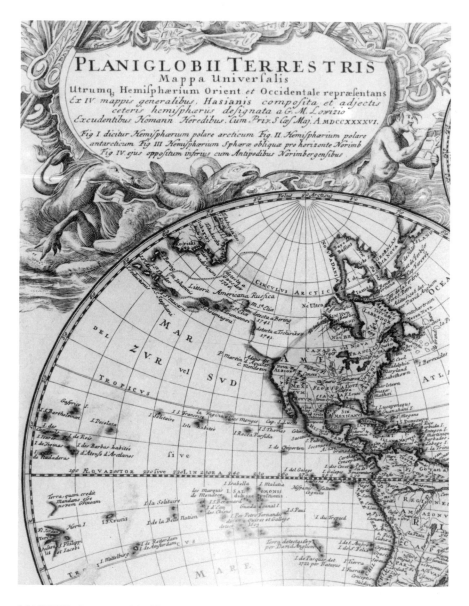

MAP XIV. A portion of the Hasius map published by the Homann firm in 1746. (Courtesy of the Kenneth Spencer Research Library, University of Kansas)

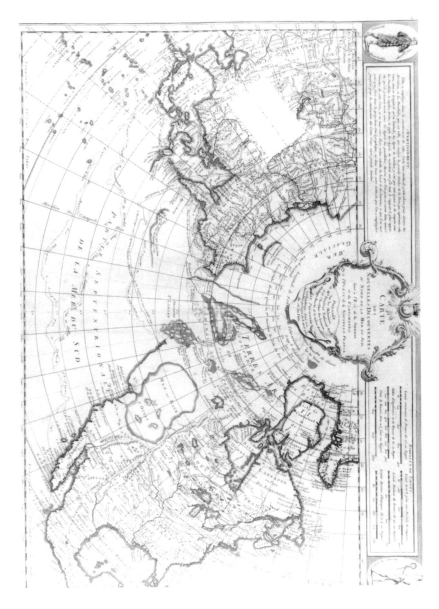

MAP XV. The Joseph Nicolas Delisle map of 1750, published in Paris in 1752. (Courtesy of the Elmer E. Rasmuson Library)

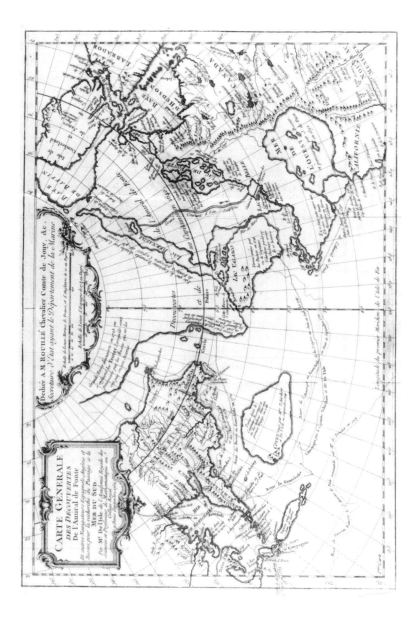

MAP XVI. The Joseph Nicolas Delisle map of 1752, published by his *Nouvelles cartes des decouvertes de l'Amiral de Fonte*, 1753. (Courtesy of the Elmer E. Rasmuson Library)

Russia.[105] They not only represented a breach in the secrecy which was supposed to be maintained about the expedition, but worse—they misrepresented the results of the expedition completely. According to Delisle's maps, Bering sailed only as far eastward as the island on which the ship was wrecked—he never reached America. The route to America is portrayed as the route of Chirikov and Delisle de la Croyère, as if the two were of equal importance in the voyage. And Delisle took a great deal of credit for initiating the expedition.[106]

The Delisle publications were especially disturbing in that they connected the de Fonte account to the Russian expedition. The report of the dubious de Fonte voyage was contained in a letter of Admiral Bartholomew de Fonte, who, in 1640, was supposed to have sailed north from Peru in search of a northwest passage with four Spanish ships. At about 53° north latitude, a river was discovered; de Fonte sailed north and east through the North American continent until he met a ship from Boston. An English translation of this letter had been printed in the *Monthly Miscellany* of 1708 for April and June. The text of it was republished by Arthur Dobbs in 1744.[107] Dobbs claimed to have found supporting evidence for the veracity of the voyage in New England. The de Fonte account was influential in the sending of the British eighteenth-century expeditions in search of northern sea passages.[108]

Why would Delisle attempt this link between the Russian discoveries and the report of a seventeenth-century voyage that was at the very least suspicious? One possibility is simply that Delisle had no other "new" information about the Russian discoveries.[109] During the latter years of his employment in Russia, care had been taken that he should not obtain this information; indeed, when he left Russia in 1747, there was not much information available to the academy. Delisle, after 20 years in Russia, had no more information than what had already been published—some of it as early as 1744. So, in order to publish something new about the expedition, he had to devise another tactic, which was to compare the findings of the Russian explorers with the de Fonte account.[110]

On the other hand, there were serious people who upheld the truth of the de Fonte account. With almost no information about the area in which the voyage supposedly took place, it was almost impossible to prove or disprove the accuracy of the account. In his study of the maps of North America, Delisle may have become convinced of the truth of the de Fonte account. Even after a Spaniard had investigated the voyage and declared it extremely dubious, in 1757, there were many who still believed in the voyage, particularly as the Spanish rebuttal was not translated into English.[111] One American who believed in the de Fonte voyage was Benjamin Franklin, who, in 1762, indicated that errors in it were the fault of the translation.[112]

Finally, Delisle may have prepared his map and publication as part of an effort to raise French interest in Canada. If Canada was the location of a passage for trade to the Pacific, it would be worth French efforts to retain it and to keep the British from taking it over. This concern with French overseas interest related directly to Delisle's friend in the Ministry of the Marine, the Comte de Maurepas.[113]

Delisle's publications could not remain unanswered, in the opinion of the academy and the Russian government. Müller was assigned the task of refuting them "promptly and secretly."[114]

This assignment was the turning point in restoring Müller to a leading position in the Academy of Sciences. Prior to this Müller's experiences in the academy following his return from the Siberian journey had been his personal "time of troubles." As noted earlier, the academy was filled with internal dissensions. Müller had apparently hoped to avoid these by recommending the establishment of a new department, located in Moscow, for studying history and geography. His proposal was rejected in 1746 and Müller was instructed to devote himself to the writing of his history of Siberia. When the department was founded in 1748, it was in St. Petersburg rather than in Moscow. Müller was head of the department. He was soon in conflict with his colleague, Professor Fischer, and with the Historical Assembly, the advisory board established to oversee the Historical Department.[115]

Müller's historical writings had also caused him trouble. In 1749, when he was asked to prepare a lecture to be delivered at a public meeting, Müller chose the subject of the origins of the Russian state. The lecture brought him into sharp conflict with Lomonosov, who, justifiably, felt that the lecture could cause difficulty for the academy because of its emphasis on the Scandinavians in early Russian history. A committee of the academy began an investigation of Müller in October, 1749. The report was issued in June of 1750. In this report Lomonosov stated, "In a public meeting there should be nothing said that could be an affront to a Russian audience which might produce grumblings and hatred against the academy. But I judge that they, on hearing in this dissertation of their new origins, founded on guesses, their naming by the Finns, the contempt for their ancient history, and the new information about the constant defeats, enslavements, and conquests by the Swedes over the Russians, they will certainly and rightly be dissatisfied not only with Mr. Müller but with the entire academy and its directors."[116] In September, 1750, copies of the published lecture Müller never delivered were destroyed; in October Müller was reduced to the rank of adjunct in the academy and his salary was cut by two-thirds. His rank and salary were returned to him in February of 1751. This "Normanist" controversy has continued to this day.[117]

Müller had also encountered difficulties with his more extensive work, the *Description of Siberia*. Müller had quarrels with the Historical Assembly over its content. For example, the Historical Assembly felt that Ermak, the cossack who led Russian expansion into Siberia, was portrayed in too brutal a fashion.

51

In the end, much of what Müller had written about Ermak did not appear in the first part of the *Description*, published in 1750.[118] Müller hoped that another part of the *Description* would appear in the *Commentarii* of the academy. Instead of receiving an acceptance of his work, however, Müller was told that it would not be published and that "It has been noticed that in the first volume of the Siberian history which is already printed, the greater part of the book is nothing but a copy from official records, and otherwise the book' would not have the proper size . . ."[119] The problems reflected deep issues, both philosophical and personal. What was the purpose of writing a country's history? Could Müller write Russian history properly? Was he loyal?

Concerns about Müller's loyalty had been raised in 1746 with respect to the Second Kamchatka Expedition. Because of fears that Müller would send unauthorized maps to western Europeans, his maps had been confiscated and he was forbidden to make others of Siberia. Although Müller had signed a permanent contract with the academy in November of 1747 and had become a Russian citizen in January, 1748, his enemies still found reasons to be concerned about his loyalty. His good friend Gmelin had left the academy in 1747, and had not returned to Russia in spite of a promise to do so. Delisle's relations with the academy were severed the same year. In October, 1748, Müller was accused of corresponding with Delisle and of providing him with materials belonging to the academy. Müller was placed under house arrest while an investigation was held and his papers were examined. In November he was cleared of the accusations against him. But the charge of corresponding with Delisle was raised again in the 1750 investigation concerning Müller's lecture on the origins of the Russian state.[120] In the investigation Müller was accused of pretending to be ill during the Second Kamchatka Expedition in order to avoid going to Kamchatka with Bering. Müller undoubtedly welcomed the opportunity to write a rebuttal to Delisle's map and memoir.

The rebuttal, *Lettre d'un officier de la marine russienne a' un seigneur de la cour*, was written by Müller in one month.[121] His source for it was the journal of Sven Waxell, the leader of Bering's crew after Bering's death in 1741.[122] Müller wrote the short rebuttal in the first person, as if it were written by an officer (Waxell) who had been with Bering on the expedition. He criticized Delisle and his brother, Delisle de la Croyère, sharply in the text. He deprecated Delisle's contributions to the publication of Russian maps, noting, ". . . I heard frequent complaints of Mr. de l'Isle's dilatoriness of his work, and of his excuses . . . ."[123] Müller then went on to discuss the First Kamchatka Expedition briefly and indicated that Bering was right in believing that Asia and America were not connected. Bering had not *proved* this, however, by sailing north as far as he had. Rather, "a member of the academy" had proved it by finding in the archives an account of a voyage around Chukotskii Nos; here Müller is referring to his own discovery of the record of Dezhnev's voyage. Delisle's map was made only after another expedition was already planned. Delisle therefore did not "incite" the Russians to undertake another expedition, as claimed in the memoir. Whether Delisle's map did "more good, or harm to the expedition" is questionable.

Müller's severest criticisms were directed against Delisle's account of the Bering voyage. He wrote, "Nothing can be more foreign to the purpose, and at the same time more jejune, than the narrative Mr. de l'Isle has thought fit to give us of Mr. Bering's voyage itself."[124] He was indignant at Delisle's implication that all Bering did was to sail a short distance to the east before being shipwrecked on the island. He next gave a summary of the voyages of Spanberg, Bering, Chirikov, and of the arctic explorers. Müller went on to discuss the importance of the explorations, which were "to find a shorter cut to the Indies." This, Müller wrote, would be an advantage "were not one obliged to go through a severe winter of three or four months by the way . . . ."[125] He concluded that "the nearest way to the East-Indies is to be found only on our maps and globes."[126]

Müller next raised questions about the authenticity of the de Fonte account.[127] He cited the lack of a Spanish original, errors in chronology, and the fact that the voyage was not mentioned in English collections of voyages as reasons to believe that the de Fonte account was false. Müller concluded with a further criticism of Delisle for linking de la Croyère's name in the map equally to Chirikov's, since de la Croyère was "no more than an idle spectator . . . ."[128]

In the English translation of the *Lettre* a commentary on it by Arthur Dobbs is included.[129] Dobbs admits that there are questions about the authenticity of the de Fonte account, but he also raises questions about the Russian discoveries. Dobbs wrote, "[there is] . . . no reason to believe that any of the places the Russians had been to were part of the American Continent."[130] Rather, he said, they were probably on a large island. Müller's response to the Dobbs commentary is given in the translation provided here.

Müller's short *Lettre* was only a rebuttal to Delisle's writings. A full narrative of the explorations was needed and Müller undertook the writing of one. He had a map prepared to accompany the narrative. The map was completed in 1754 and a few copies of it were printed in that year. In 1758, the year the narrative was published in volume three of Müller's *Sammlung russischer Geschichte*, the map, with a few minor alterations from the first impression, was also printed. Both the map and the narrative were printed in Russian as well.

Müller's narrative was soon translated into English and French. It became, and has remained, a standard source for its subject. Müller's narrative did not please those who believed in navigable northern sea passages. Müller's map, with its large, solid "turtle head" of land extending westward from North America, made any northern passage appear more difficult, for it would be necessary to sail around it in order to reach Japan, China, or the East Indies.[131] One of the academy's most important members, Mikhail Lomonosov, advocated further explorations for a navigable sea route north from Russia.[132] The Russians sent Captain Vasilii I. Chichagov on expeditions in 1765 and 1766 to try to sail north from Spitsbergen to Kamchatka, but he was forced to winter in Spitsbergen and lost many of his crew. No accounts of Chichagov's explorations were published at the time.[133]

Western European commentators criticized Müller and the Russians for the accounts of explorations that were published; they also accused them of withholding information about the explorations. In 1765 the Swiss geographer Samuel Engel published his *Memoires et observations geographiques,* in which he compared the writings of many authors on northern explorations, including Delisle, Dobbs, de Fonte, Du Halde, Gmelin, Krasheninnikov, Müller (both the *Lettre* and the narrative of Bering's voyages), Strahlenberg, and Witsen. Engel, a firm believer in northern sea passages, concluded that Müller's writings had been changed against his will in order to conceal the failings of the Russian Navy.[134]

Müller's response to Engel was published much later, in 1773, in a journal published by his friend Anton Friedrich Busching.[135] In a letter to Busching, Müller stated that the western coast of America was not solid land, as he had believed at the time his map was prepared. Further explorations had shown that there were many islands in the region between Kamchatka and America. But he criticized Engel for campaigning for the northern voyages and because he ". . . takes advantage of everything that will support his position."[136] In 1777 Engel was even more merciless in his published accusations against Müller. This time he charged that Müller had voluntarily concealed information about the Russian explorations in order to keep his position of power and influence within the academy.[137] About the northeast passage Engel wrote: "Russia has no reason to seek this passage, because it has already found it."[138] In addition, he asserted that "Whatever happens in the Russian Empire is a secret of state."[139] The question of how Müller used his sources and which ones he had available to him in the writing of his narrative was forcibly raised; the answer to this question is presented in the translation which follows.

From the time Müller wrote his account of the Bering expeditions to the present, the prevailing assumption about the purpose of the First Kamchatka Expedition was that Peter the Great sent Bering to determine whether the mainland of Asia was joined to America. This question was of importance to the persistent hope of finding a sea passage from western Europe to the Pacific Ocean. The arctic explorations during the Second Kamchatka Expedition were seen as a continuation of the search for this same passage.

Müller's accounts of the expeditions were instrumental in setting this interpretation firmly in the literature, beginning with his newspaper article in the *St. Petersburgische Zeitung,* discussed in Chapter I. Was this Müller's intention in his writings, or does it reflect the assumptions of the readers? In the *Lettre,* Müller says that Bering's instructions directed him ". . . to reconnoitre the furthest northern part of the eastern coasts of Siberia, and to see whether in any part they joined with America."[140] (See the texts of the instructions, pp. 17, 69.) Müller indicates that Bering, at the northern point of his first voyage "concluded that there could be no continent, by which Asia and America were joined, and that, having thus executed his commission, he returned."[141] In this, Müller states that Bering is looking for a *continent*, not a sea passage, and he further goes on to add that although Bering was right that there was a separation, he was wrong in stating that the coast went directly westward. Instead, the coast went westward first for a short distance and then turned to the northeast and formed the great promontory to the northeast. This was the most northern point of Asia. Bering would have had to sail to this point, according to Müller, in order to prove that no land extended from this promontory to America. In the same *Lettre*, Müller noted that "Captain Bering, sensible of the deficiency of his first discoveries, had offered himself to prosecute them, and so did his lieutenants, for which they were all rewarded by a higher rank."[142] This comment is the earliest source for the belief that the First Kamchatka Expedition had failed to achieve its purpose, and that Bering—and Spanberg and Chirikov as well—undertook a second expedition to redeem their careers and reputations. The record, as given in the *Lettre*, is not clear.

Müller prefaced his account of the Bering expeditions in the *Sammlung russischer Geschichte* with a commentary on records of seventeenth- and early eighteenth-century Russian explorations, which he had collected during his archival research in Siberia. Müller had found the account of the Semen Dezhnev voyage of 1648 from the Kolyma River around the northeastern point of Asia to Kamchatka. Dezhnev's voyage proved that Asia was not joined to America. But this, Müller said, had been forgotten.[143] Because of this, Müller stressed the importance of his discovery of the account of Dezhnev's voyage, asserting that "such a noteworthy event might perhaps have always remained secret, in spite of the traces of it encountered in the reports of the inhabitants, if I had not had the luck, in the year 1736 during my stay in Iakutsk, to discover in the city archives there written documents, in which this voyage is described with details that leave no remaining doubts."[144] This can be read as evidence that Müller's archival work succeeded where Bering's voyage failed, and by implication, that Bering was trying to sail around northeastern Asia.

But the account of the Dezhnev voyage was not the only report of interest in this respect, for Müller also recorded accounts of the Chukchi. He wrote about the Chukchi land and noted that there is an island in the sea near it; and "beyond the island is a great continent, which can barely be seen from it, and that only on clear days. In calm weather one can row over the sea from the island to the continent in one day. People live there who are similar to the Chukchi in all things, yet speak their own language."[145] Therefore, Müller concluded that there is a separation between Asia and America and " . . . that the same consists only of a small strait, and that one or more islands lie in the strait, through which the crossing from one part of the world to the other is facilitated, so that the inhabitants of each have had knowledge of the other part since ancient times."[146] There is no suggestion that all of this was "forgotten" as well.

Finally, in the translation that follows Müller makes two comments about the First Kamchatka Expedition that are relevant. He says that Bering "directed his course to the northeast, as the coasts of Kamchatka (which he generally had in view) led him. His main endeavor was to describe these coasts as accurately as possible on a map, in which he succeeded fairly well—at least we still have no better map of the area than his." Then further, at the time of the planning of the Second Kamchatka Expedition, "The purpose of the first journey was not brought up for discussion again because it was considered already completed." The case is made instead, that Bering was supposed to make an accurate map, which he did. The purpose accords with the purpose described in Chapter I.

What Müller wrote about the Bering expeditions was subject to interpretation by readers, some of whom were convinced beforehand that the purpose of the Russian explorations was to discover a northeast passage and thereby to gain an advantage in the lucrative trade in the east. Müller had no hopes for such a passage. In the text translated here Müller specified his reasons for concluding that no northeast passage is possible, at least for use in trade. The realities, he emphasized, were that the northern passage could not be used, not because of a land barrier but because of the climate and ice of the North. As a geographer he put the passage on his map, in accordance with the Dezhnev voyage, and as a historian he did not slight his discovery of this account. In spite of his strong declarations about the impossibility of ships from western Europe using the passage, his readers—at least those who were confirmed in their fixation with northern passages—refused to accept his evaluation and insisted that he had concealed information about the two Bering expeditions.

Müller continued to do research on the Russian voyages after Bering's time but he did not publish the results of this research.[147] Perhaps he was tired of academic battles. Or, perhaps he was happier in his archives. He got his wish to work in the archives in Moscow; this was his occupation in 1783, the year of his death.

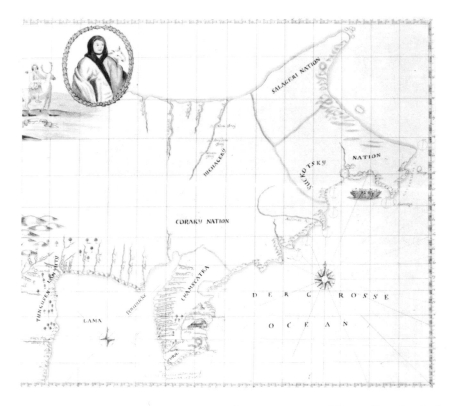

MAP XVII. Eastern portion (much reduced) of a manuscript map of Bering's First Kamchatka Expedition. (Courtesy of the James Ford Bell Library)

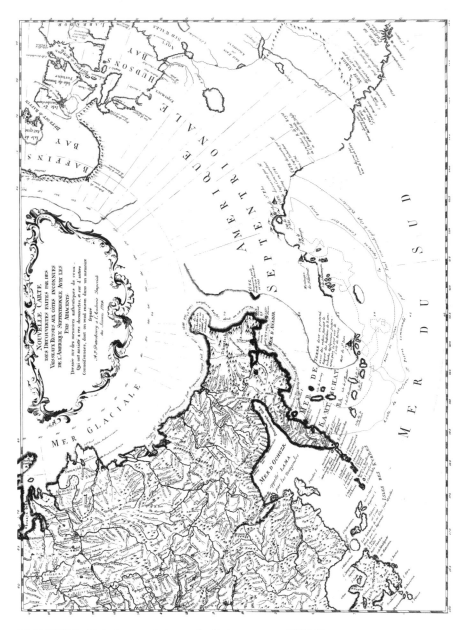

MAP XVIII. Müller's map relating to the Bering voyages of 1728-29.

MAP XIX. Portion of Müller's map relating to the Bering voyages of 1728-29.

$\mathcal{N}$.° XXV, 16, B.   C8-4∫

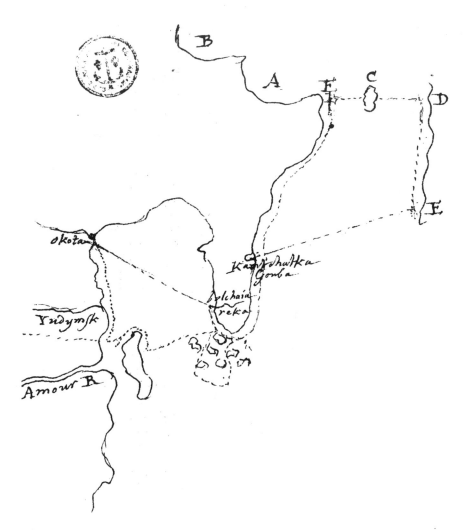

MAP XX. Sketch map of Gvozdev's voyage. (Courtesy of the Archives National, Paris)

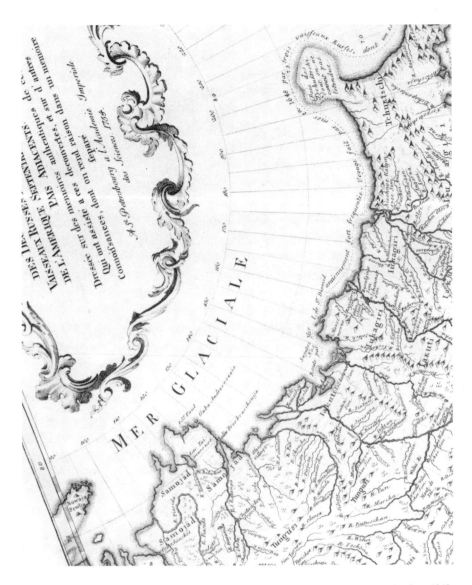

MAP XXI. Arctic coast, from Müller. For modern maps of these explorations, see Ianikov, 1949.

MAP XXII. Kamchatka to Japan, from Müller. For a modern map of Spanberg's voyage, see Lensen, 1959.

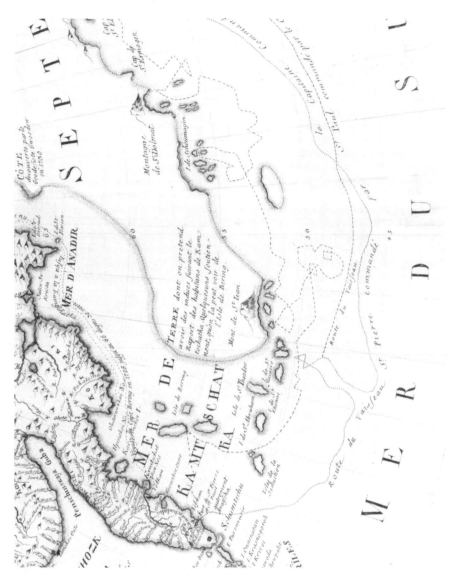

MAP XXIII. Routes of Bering and Chirikov, from Müller. For modern maps see Golder, 1922 and Lebedev, 1951.

VOYAGES

FROM

ASIA to *AMERICA.*

THE Czar, *Peter the Great*, being curious to know whether *Afia* and *America* were contiguous, or feperated by a wide or narrow channel of the fea, wrote the following inftructions with his own hand, and ordered the chief Admiral Count *Fedor Matfewitfch Apraxin*, to fee them carried into execution.

I. *One or two Boats with decks to be built at* Kamtfchatka, *or at any other convenient place, with which*

II. *Enquiry fhould be made in relation to the northerly coafts, to fee whether they were not contiguous with* America, *fince their end was not known. And this done, they fhould*

III. *See whether they could not fomewhere find an harbour belonging to* Europeans, *or an* European *fhip. They fhould likewife fet apart fome men, who were to enquire after the name and fituation of the coafts difcovered. Of all this an exact journal fhould be kept, with which they fhould return to* Peterfburg.

The Emprefs *Catharine*, as fhe endeavoured in all points to execute moft precifely the plans of her deceafed hufband, in a manner began her reign with an order for the expedition to *Kamtfchatka*.

Vitus Bering, at that time Captain of a fhip, was nominated commander of this expedition, and two Lieutenants, *Martin Spangberg*, and *Alexei Tfchirikow*, were his affiftants, together with other fea officers of inferior rank ; they alfo had fome along with them that

B   underftood

ILLUSTRATION II. Title page from the first English translation of Müller's *Voyages*, published in 1761. (Courtesy of the James Ford Bell Library)

III. THE TRANSLATION

As background to the translation, please note the following:

The Text. The original text for this translation appeared in the *Sammlung russischer Geschichte*, volume III, pp. 111-304, in 1758. The Academy of Sciences, the publisher and printer of it, also issued a Russian translation that year (see bibliography). Müller wrote in German and translators rendered his text into Russian. Müller checked the Russian translation before it was published. The German text translated here is the original text; some comparisons to the Russian translation were made.

In addition to his account of the Bering expeditions Müller also collected reports of earlier Russian explorations in Siberia and included them in the *Sammlung* as well. The text relating to these cases is either translated or summarized in the footnotes.

The Map. The map made to accompany Müller's account of the Bering expeditions exists in French and Russian editions printed in 1754. The French map was revised slightly and a second issue of it appeared in 1758. The map reproduced in this book is a copy from the French printing of 1754. The map maker, Ivan Truskott, was a member of the Geographical Department of the Academy of Sciences. Because Müller supervised the preparation of the map and determined its content, the map is ascribed to him.

The full map is reproduced in a much-reduced size on page 58. In addition, sections of the map have been reproduced in larger size to aid the reader in following the text.

Format. All of the text given in the translation, including material in parentheses, is Müller's. His footnotes have been inserted into the body of the translation and are indicated by brackets. Punctuation has been changed only when it seemed essential or to conform to modern usage. Some long sentences were broken up and paragraphing was added, again in conformity with modern practice. Section headings, identified by Roman numerals, were added.

Chronology. All dates have been given according to the Julian calendar (Old Style). In the eighteenth century these dates were eleven days behind the Gregorian calendar of western Europe (New Style). Müller also uses dates taken from the ships' logs. This explains what may appear to be slight discrepancies in the dating of some events, as the nautical day began at noon.

Names. If possible, the modern English spelling of geographical and personal names has been supplied. In those cases where identifications could not be made, Müller's spelling has been retained. When these are place names, they often appear on the early maps referred to in the text. The one departure from modern geographical nomenclature is in the use of "Icy Sea" rather than Arctic Ocean or the more specific designations of Kara Sea, Laptev Sea, East Siberian Sea, and Chukchi Sea. "Icy Sea" reflects an attitude toward the northern seas as well as the state of knowledge about them at the time of the explorations.

Terminology. A glossary of terms is provided on page 141. The terms are defined in footnotes when they first appear in the text and are repeated in the glossary.

Footnotes. The footnotes attempt to assist the reader, through explanations, identifications, and additional information. Special efforts were made to identify and, often, quote the sources Müller used in writing his narrative. These quotations are from English translations of the ships' logs and of the accounts of participants in the expeditions. There is no extensive English-language account of the explorations of the arctic coast undertaken during the Second Kamchatka Expedition, and the footnoting to this section of the translation has been supplemented by information from the detailed book on this subject by G.V. Ianikov, *Velikaia severnaia ekspeditsiia*, published in Moscow in 1949. See Terence Armstrong's publication on this subject listed in the bibliography; unfortunately it was not received until after the work on this section was completed. The journals of the voyages to Japan have not been published, and the footnotes to this section are to secondary works in English.

Style. In the preface to the 1761 translation of Müller's narrative, the editor, Thomas Jefferys, stated, "The reader will find the Style of this Recital to be very unaffected and simple, being only a plain Translation of Memoirs of Voyages collected from the Original Manuscripts, containing the Discoveries made . . . " (p. vii). This is the intent of the present translation as well. If the text is unclear in the translation, it probably is unclear in the original German also.

In preparing the translation, extensive use was made of the two English translations (1761 and 1764) which are, however, incomplete and, at times, extremely complex. The comparison of the two eighteenth-century translations with the German original revealed some changes indicating that the 1764 translation is superior to the earlier one. In addition, the changes suggest that Müller may have corresponded with the publisher and editor, Jefferys, about the translation.

Müller's sources. Although Müller spent ten years in Siberia and discussed Russian explorations with individuals who had firsthand experience in the explorations, Müller was not a participant in the voyages he described. He wrote a history, not a journal of his own experiences. The identification of the sources used by Müller, therefore, is important, particularly in view of the charges made that, either voluntarily or under duress, he omitted important material from his narrative. As will be seen, the evidence in the citations to his sources indicates that he had access to the records he needed to write his history and used them as he saw fit.

Müller gave only a shortened account of the First Kamchatka Expedition, he said, because the account of it had already been printed. This was Bering's "Short Account," which appeared in the many editions of Du Halde's *Descrip-*

tion of China. In addition to this source, Müller also had the account of the expedition written by Midshipman Peter Chaplin. Müller included details about the expedition from Chaplin, as the footnotes indicate. For the period between the two Bering expeditions Müller had his own research and the information gathered for Krasheninnikov's *Description of Kamchatka*, which Müller had edited for publication in 1755.

In writing about the Second Kamchatka Expedition Müller used many sources. For descriptions of the explorations and mapping of the arctic coasts he had the accounts of the explorers, which indicates the cooperation of the Admiralty College, to which these reports were submitted. Müller had reports of both Spanberg and Walton about the voyages to Japan. He had Chirikov's reports on the voyage to America. He had Steller's journal of his voyage to America with Bering. Above all, Müller used the journal of Sven Waxell. Müller also cited the ships' logs and maps. "I compare the various accounts as best I can," he wrote in his narrative. His problem was not a lack of sources.

Nature of the sources. Although he had ships' logs and official reports of the naval officers about the expeditions, Müller did not choose to print these documents undigested. Perhaps the criticism that the first volume of his Siberian history was only "a collection of official documents" had persuaded him to write a narrative rather than to publish official records of the expeditions. He used the official documents but did not reproduce them.

Two of the sources he used extensively were journals of Bering's voyage to America. One, the journal of Georg Wilhelm Steller, was full of natural history; it was also sharply critical of the Russian Navy officers. Steller, whose journal was published later in the eighteenth century, continually criticized the officers and berated them for not taking his advice (which was often wrong). Steller's was not an unbiased account of Bering's voyage.

Müller used another journal, written by Sven Waxell, as his main source for Bering's voyage, and indeed for other parts of his narrative, as the footnotes indicate. Waxell's account was not published until the twentieth century, so for nearly two centuries this source Müller used remained unknown. Waxell had prepared his account for publication. Why did Müller elect not to publish Waxell's account as it was written? For one reason, Waxell participated only in the Second Kamchatka Expedition and then only in the voyage of Bering to America. He had almost no information about the arctic explorations. Waxell was not an unbiased reporter, either. He emphasized his own part in the expedition. Waxell was convinced that he had "spoken" to the Americans through the vocabulary included in a dubious travel account by Baron de Lahontan—something Müller (and Steller as well) could not accept. Waxell was as vehement in his criticism of "intellectuals" as Steller was in his criticism of navy officers.

The comparison of the records of Waxell and Steller about the voyage to

America provides two very different views of the same voyage. In writing his text, Müller picks his way between them and takes something from each. Müller does, however, depend heavily on Waxell, for the arrangement of his account as well as its content. In view of the time span in which Müller's work was written, this is not surprising. Following the publication of his *Lettre* in 1753, Müller began to write an extensive account of the explorations undertaken before Bering, the First Kamchatka Expedition, the explorations prior to the Second Kamchatka Expedition, and the Second Kamchatka Expedition itself. The map intended to accompany his text was completed in 1754; Müller's narrative was not. What he had written and researched had consumed an enormous amount of time, undoubtedly, for a man who was doing many other things as well. At the end Müller came—willingly or not—to depend more and more heavily on Waxell for parts of his narrative.

Müller as a historian. Müller had been censured for remarks against Delisle and Delisle de la Croyére in his 1753 *Lettre*. He responded to this at the end of his narrative of the expeditions. Müller also went out of his way to soften his criticism of Delisle's map, stating that the problem was that it influenced the voyage to America, while it should properly have been used in connection with the voyages to Japan. He even tried to reconcile the sighting of the Land of Jeso by earlier explorers on the basis of an earthquake which could have broken that land into islands. Even though Müller cited and refuted the ideas of contemporary geographers, he did so with restraint. In short, Müller tried very hard to avoid conflict with his contemporaries. That does not mean he succeeded. He did succeed, however in writing an invaluable account of some of the most important events in the history of geographical explorations.

THE TRANSLATION

I: FIRST KAMCHATKA EXPEDITION

The long-standing question was anything but forgotten.[1] The emperor remembered it perfectly when he drafted, with his own hand, the instructions governing the investigation, and entrusted to General-Admiral Count Fedor Matseevitch Apraksin[2] the responsibility for the execution of the orders.

According to the contents of this imperial command:

1. one or two decked vessels should be built in Kamchatka or at some other convenient place, with which

2. the northern coasts[3] should be explored to determine whether, since the end of these coasts is not known, they are connected with America. And if this is the case

3. an attempt should be made to determine whether a harbor belonging to Europeans or a European ship could be found somewhere. Likewise, men should be sent out to ask about the land, to gather information about the name and nature of the coasts that have been discovered. An accurate journal of all these matters should be kept and brought back to St. Petersburg.

The noble Empress Catherine always tried carefully to observe the useful projects and orders of her late husband.[4] It is reasonable to say that she actually began her glorious reign carrying out the order just mentioned. An expedition established by that order took place as soon as possible. This was the so-called First Kamchatka Expedition, which we will briefly consider here. [The fourth part of Du Halde's *Description . . . de la Chine* also contains an account of this journey.][5]

Vitus Bering, at that time a captain, was appointed leader of the expedition, and two lieutenants, Martin Spanberg[6] and Aleksei Chirikov,[7] were appointed his assistants. Besides other seamen of lower rank they had men with them who were experienced in shipbuilding. They left St. Petersburg on 5 February 1725.[8] On 16 March they reached Tobolsk, the capital of Siberia, where they remained until 16 May both to wait for a suitable season to travel by river, as well as to take with them the various craftsmen and materials essential for their journey.[9] The following summer was spent in travel on the Irtysh, Ob, Ket, Enisei, Tungus, and Ilim rivers. After this they found it necessary to winter at Ilimsk. In the meantime they procured the provisions needed for a longer journey.

In the spring of 1726 they came down the Lena River to Iakutsk.[10] Lieutenant Spanberg immediately went on ahead via the Aldan, Maia, and Iudoma rivers with part of the provisions and the heavy ship materials.[11] Captain Bering followed overland with another part of the provisions, transported by horses.[12] Lieutenant Chirikov remained at Iakutsk so that he could bring the rest of the provisions by land. The supplies had to be divided up this way because of the exceedingly difficult route between Iakutsk and Okhotsk, which was impassable in summer by wagon or in winter by sled. The reason for that is the mountainous and morassy terrain. In addition the country is uninhabited, except in the vicinity of Iakutsk.

Lieutenant Spanberg's journey was as unfortunate as Captain Bering's was fortunate, since Spanberg did not reach Iudoma Cross,[13] his destination, but instead was frozen in on the Iudoma River at the mouth of the Gorbei, a small tributary. On 4 November he set out on foot to bring the most essential ship materials to Iudoma Cross and Okhotsk.[14] He suffered such terrible hunger on the way that he was forced to eat leather sacks, reins, and shoes for food. He finally arrived at Okhotsk on 1 January 1727. In the beginning of February he returned to the Iudoma to retrieve the remainder of his load. But since even this was still not enough, a third party was sent out from Okhotsk with horses and finally managed to transport everything successfully.[15] Then, on 30 July, Lieutenant Chirikov, with the last of the provisions, arrived from Iakutsk.[16]

In the meantime a ship, which was named the *Fortune*,[17] had been built at Okhotsk and on 30 June it sailed under the command of Lieutenant Spanberg to transport the most essential ship materials and the carpenters to Bolsheretsk. Spanberg's ship returned together with an old vessel which remained from the year 1716, when navigation between Okhotsk and Kamchatka began.[18]

On 21 August Captain Bering and Lieutenant Chirikov began their voyage. They arrived at the mouth of the Bolshaia River on 2 September, and left Bolsheretsk the following winter with Lieutenant Spanberg for Nizhne-Kamchatsk *ostrog*,[19] where the carpenters had preceded them in summer to fell trees for the ships. They carried with them—a tedious, slow-moving process using the dog sleds[20] available there—all the provisions and materials they believed were necessary.[21]

On 4 April 1728, a ship resembling the packet-boats used in the Baltic was laid out at Nizhne-Kamchatsk ostrog, and was later launched under the name of the messenger Gabriel.[22] Once all the equipment and food needed to support 40 men for a year had been taken on board, they did not wish to delay the voyage ahead of them and, thus, the fulfillment of the main purpose of their journey.[23]

To this end, Captain Bering sailed from the mouth of the Kamchatka River into the sea on 20 July of the said year. He directed his course to the northeast, as the coasts of Kamchatka (which he generally had in view) led him. His main endeavor was to describe these coasts as accurately as possible on a map, in which he succeeded fairly well—at least, we still have no better map of the area than his to which to refer.[24] On 8 August when the ship was at 64°30′ north latitude, eight Chukchi men rowed out from the shore in a small leather boat (*baidar*, from sealskins) to learn the purpose of this voyage. Bering's men spoke with these people through a Koriak interpreter and invited them to come aboard.[25] At first only one man approached the ship, swimming with the help of two inflated sealskins attached to a pole; then the entire boat followed. The captain asked them about the situation of the coasts which lay ahead and was told that he would soon find a turn to the west.[26] Whether or not he asked about islands or coasts across from the one being followed is not mentioned in the captain's account, of which the present narrative is an abstract. One may almost believe that this was not thought of, since our mariners had no knowledge of what had happened formerly, and consequently could not have suspected that land was so near.[27] They heard of an island that was supposed to lie ahead not far from the mainland.[28] This they named St. Lawrence because they sailed past it on 10 August, the Feast Day of St. Lawrence, seeing nothing more on it than the huts of Chukchi fishermen.[29]

Finally, on 15 August they came to a promontory at 67°18′ north latitude after which the coast extended westward just as the Chukchi had said earlier. From this the captain drew the quite reasonable conclusion that he had now reached the extreme northeast end of Asia. He was of the opinion that from there the coast must extend continuously toward the west; this being so, the land could not possibly be connected with America. Consequently he believed he had satisfied the orders given to him.[30] Therefore he proposed to his officers and the other seamen that it was time to "think about their return voyage." He said that if they chose to sail farther north, he feared they would meet unforeseen ice and they could become entangled in it, without being able easily to break free. The usual thick fogs of fall, which had appeared a few times already, could limit visibility. And if a contrary wind should arise, it could become almost impossible to get back to Kamchatka that summer. Also, it was not advisable to spend the winter in this area, because several things made it too dangerous: the well-known lack of wood throughout the entire region extending toward the Icy Sea, the still-wild inhabitants of this territory who were not yet subject to Russian sovereignty, and steep cliffs, found everywhere on the coast, between which no inlets or harbors were known would make this far too dangerous.[31]

It must be admitted that the circumstance upon which the captain based his decision was false. For it was learned later that this was the same promontory the inhabitants of Anadyr ostrog call Serdtse Kamen, because of a heart-shaped rock found on it.[32] And although the land beyond this promontory turns toward the west, this bend makes only a large bay, in the innermost inlet of which, as the cossack Popov reported, the rock Matkol is located.[33] Here, however, the coast resumes its previous direction toward the north and northeast until, at 70° or more north latitude, the actual Chukotskii Nos appears as a great peninsula, where it could first be said with justification that the two parts of the world are not connected.[34] But who on the ship at that time could have known all of this? Indeed, the truly genuine knowledge of the Chukchi land and the promontory named for it was only made possible thanks to my geographic research, conducted at Iakutsk in 1736 and 1737.[35] It is sufficient that they made no error in the main matter: Asia really is separated from America by a channel connecting the Icy Sea with the Southern Ocean.

The return journey proceeded without remarkable incidents other than that on 20 August 40 Chukchi rowed out to the ship in four baidars and brought reindeer meat, fish, fresh water, foxskins, white stone-foxes,[36] and walrus tusks as presents for which they received in exchange needles, flints, iron, and such things. On the 29th they cast anchor off the coast of Kamchatka in foggy, stormy weather. But since the rope broke the following morning as the men were weighing anchor, they had to abandon the anchor.[37] On 20 September they returned to the Kamchatka River, followed it upstream, and wintered once again at Nizhne-Kamchatsk ostrog.[38]

From the inhabitants of Kamchatka our sea officers often heard reports and opinions that were important enough to note, because according to them there must be a land nearby toward the east, which their duty required them to discover and afterwards to follow its coasts.[39] During their voyage they themselves had not noticed the great and high waves usually found in the open sea; they had seen pine trees floating in the sea which do not grow in Kamchatka.[40] They heard of other such signs of a nearby land, which have already been cited in the proper place.[41] Some people even insisted they had seen this nearby land from the heights along Kamchatka's coast when the weather was clear.[42]

Now the captain did not want to neglect what these exciting signs held and suggested following them up by yet another voyage. Therefore he made the decision, that if such were to be done the return voyage should not be to Kamchatka, but rather immediately to Okhotsk.[43] So he left the second time on 5 June 1729. But a violent wind from the ENE prevented him from getting further than 200 versts from the coasts, by his calculation. And since he found no land during this time, he turned back and sailed around the southern tip of Kamchatka, [This was named Cape Oskoi. Perhaps Oskoi originates from the Russian *uznoi*, that is, southern.] recording the true position and shape of it on his map.[44] He sailed to the mouth of the Bolshaia River, from which he continued on to Okhotsk, arriving on 23 July.

On 29 July he left on horseback from Okhotsk for Iudoma Cross. There he found a few small vessels—rafts that had been built—and went by them down the Iudoma, Maia, and Aldan rivers. At Belskaia Crossing, a portage from the Aldan at the mouth of the Belaia River, he once again got horses from the local Iakuts. He rode to Iakutsk, arrived on 29 August, and departed again on 10 September to continue his journey by river, intending to travel up the Lena as far as possible. Heavy drifting ice forced him to stop at Peledun *sloboda*[45] on 10

October. The delay only lasted until the twenty-ninth when he continued his journey by sled. He proceeded to Tobolsk from 10 to 25 January and returned to St. Petersburg on 1 March 1730.[46]

Shortly before this an error had slipped into the geographies in foreign countries: Kamchatka was shown as if it were one with the Land of Jeso, and consequently extended south to the vicinity of Japan. Two maps published in Holland shortly after Peter the Great's death gave rise to this misconception. ["Carte nouvelle de tout l'Empire de la Grand Russie dans l'Etat ou il s'est trouvé á la mort de Pierre le Grand" and "La Russie Asiatique tirée de la Carte donnée par Ordre du feu Czar." There is also a Homann map, engraved according to these.][47] These maps were trusted as if they were based on the latest experience. Swedish officers, imprisoned in Siberia, confirmed the error in notes to Abulgasi Bayadur Khan's history of Tartary. [*Histoire Genéalogique des Tatars*, p. 109.][48] Therefore Scheuchzer also accepted this theory when he published Kaempfer's history of Japan. [*Histoire du Japon*, by Mr. Kaempfer, vol. I. *Discours preliminaire*, p. xvii and Table 8.][49] Mr. Strahlenberg seems to have given new weight to this in his commentary. [*Nordliche und ostliche Theil von Europa und Asia*. Einleitung, p. 31 and the map.][50] Mr. de la Martiniere [*Dictionnaire Géographique*, vol. V. Article on Kamchatka.][51] followed with his approval, as did Mr. Bellin [*Histoire du Japon* by P. Charlevoix, Vol. II, p 493 and the map.][52], who added a new error, implying that there was a customary sea route from the mouth of the Lena River to Kamchatka,[53] which route was supposedly used for trade with Kamchatka. The blame for this misconception rests not so much with Mr. Bellin but with the author of the notes to Abulgasi because he mentioned the error first. [*Histoire Genéalogique*, p. 108.][54]

Bering, who had rounded the southern tip of Kamchatka at 51° north latitude, informed us better. His map was sent to Paris and incorporated in Du Halde's—or rather d'Anville's—atlas.[55] Then Father Castel took this opportunity to contradict Mr. Bellin. ["Dissertation sur la celebre terre de Kamtschatka," in *Mémoires de Trévoux*, July, 1737, pp. 1156ff.] Bellin defended this error, [*Mémoires de Trévoux*, August 1737, pp. 2389ff.] in the belief that the Bering map in Du Halde, by Mr. d'Anville, was made only according to that of Captain Bering's report,[56] which Bellin felt could well have been mistaken. But it could not be more certain that Captain Bering himself made this map. Mr. Ivan Kirilov, senior secretary of the Senate and, later, counselor of state, had included the essence of it in his general map of Russia even before Du Halde's work was published. Kirilov's map was already completed in 1732 and was printed for the public in 1734.[57] Therefore Mr. d'Anville could not have been mistaken. If Mr. Bellin had only read what Father Du Halde [*Description de la Chine*, IV, p. 561.] testified about how the map came into his hands, he would easily have been convinced to the contrary.[58]

II. EVENTS BETWEEN THE TWO BERING EXPEDITIONS

During the time that Captain Bering completed his final voyage from the Kamchatka River eastward, once again a Japanese vessel was driven onto the Kamchatka coast. It ran aground in July 1729 near the Kasat stream at the south of Avacha Bay. A *piatidesiatnik* (leader of 50 cossacks) by the name of Andrei Shtinnikov[59] arrived there with some of the Kamchadals just as the Japanese had moved their belongings from the ship to land. Shtinnikov received some presents from the Japanese, but that did not satisfy him. After spending two days with the Japanese, he stole away during the night, and he and his companions hid nearby to see how the Japanese would react. Just as the Japanese had rejoiced greatly when Shtinnikov arrived, they grieved much when he left. They wanted to find other inhabitants; they boarded their boat and proceeded along the coast. Then Shtinnikov ordered the Kamchadals to follow them in a baidar and to shoot all but two. The Kamchadals carried out his orders. There had been a total of seventeen Japanese people in all; of them only two survived: an old man and a boy of 11. Then Shtinnikov seized all their goods and had their ship broken into pieces so that he could use its iron. He brought the two Japanese with him to Verkhne-Kamchatsk ostrog as both prisoners of war and slaves. Such cruelty to shipwrecked foreigners could not remain unpunished.[60] After an investigation Shtinnikov got the noose as his reward.[61] The Japanese were brought to Iakutsk in 1731, from there to Tobolsk, and on to St. Petersburg in 1732.

Here they were first instructed for some time in the Russian language and the principles of the Christian religion. They became Christians. One took the baptismal name "Cosmos," the other "Damian." Previously their names had been "Sosa" and "Gonsa."[62] Then they were sent to the Academy of Sciences by order of the Senate. They took students, who could already speak and write Japanese fairly well by the time that the teachers died in 1736 and 1739.[63] They called the city of their birth "Satzina." Kaempfer writes this name as "Satzuma." Maps following the Portuguese pronunciation have "Saxuma."[64] It is a city and region on the southern coast of Ximo Island, which is generally called "Kiusiu."[65] Sosa had been a merchant. Gonsa's father had served as a navigator with the Japanese fleet, and the son had chosen the same career. They called their ship *Wakaschimar*. It was laded with cotton and silk goods, rice, and paper. Since they were headed for Osaka, the commander of Satzma, Inatzdare-Osim-Nokam, had given them the rice and paper, the first should serve as the needed sustenance of the residents, because rice does not grow there, and the second for recording public transactions. However, they never reached Osaka, but were hit by a storm and, after six months of being driven about at sea, they were finally stranded along the coast of Kamchatka on 8 July. The Japanese called the capital of their empire Kio, which lies on the Edogawa River, which there is over a verst wide.[66] It flows into the sea not far from there. They called the King of Japan Osama. There were similar accounts, which they gave under questioning and which were written down, but they are not included here as they are not to our purpose.

It was mentioned previously that the cossack leader Afanasii Shestakov from Iakutsk proposed to the Senate several times that he subject the rebellious Chukchi to the payment of tribute.[67] The result of his proposal is recounted now because it had not a little influence in the history of navigation. Shestakov wanted to rout not only the Chukchi, but also the Koriaks, who inhabited the Siberian coast of Penzhina Bay and both coasts of the northern part of Kamchatka and had, up to then, often rebelled. He wanted to search for the land across from Chukotskii Nos and demand that its inhabitants submit to Russia. He wanted to make another attempt to discover the alleged land in the Ice Sea.[68] And finally he also included the Shantar and Kurile Islands in his proposed investigations.

The eloquence with which he presented his proposals to high and low alike and the probability that through them much good could come won him approval. He was named head of a special expedition, which was supposed to accomplish everything mentioned above.[69] He received a navigator named Jacob Gens, an assistant navigator, Ivan Fedorov, a geodesist, Mikhail Gvozdev, an assayer named Gerdebol, and 10 seamen from the Admiralty College in St. Petersburg.[70] At Catherineburg he was supplied with a small cannon, mortars, and their accessories. Dmitrii Pavlutskii, a captain in the Siberian dragoon regiment in Tobolsk, was ordered to join him. Together they were to command 400 cossacks, as well as to have jurisdiction over all the cossacks stationed at the ostrogs and *zimovyes*[71] along their route through Iakutsk areas.[72]

In June 1727 Shestakov left St. Petersburg to return to Siberia. He waited at Tobolsk until 28 November, wintered in the upper Lena region, and proceeded to Iakutsk in the summer of 1728. Here a major disagreement arose between Shestakov and Pavlutskii which presumably gave cause for them to separate even though both aimed at the performance of a common goal.[73] Shestakov went to Okhotsk in 1729, and there appropriated ships for his own use—the vessels in which Captain Bering had come back from Kamchatka shortly before.[74]

Then on 1 September he sent out one of the ships, namely the *Gabriel*, with his cousin, the nobleman Ivan Shestakov, to go to the Uda River and from there to Kamchatka, investigating and describing all islands encountered en route.[75] Shestakov himself set out for Tauisk ostrog in the other ship, the *Fortune*,[76] but had the misfortune to suffer shipwreck on the way and to see the greater part of his crew perish in the sea. He and four others barely managed to save themselves in a small boat.[77] On 30 September he sent a cossack, Ivan Ostafev, with some of the Koriak elders from Tauisk ostrog, ahead of him along the coast. They had orders to proceed to the Penzhina River and, by favorable promises, to convince the rebellious Koriaks living along this route to submit. In the beginning of December he followed with the remaining men he had with him, caught up with Ostafev on the way and successfully came to within a two days' journey of the Penzhina River, where he met an exceedingly large swarm of Chukchi, who were approaching to fight the Koriaks. As small as the number of men accompanying Shestakov was—Russians, Okhotsk Tungus, Lamuts, and Koriaks together numbered a total of about 150—this did not prevent him from risking a battle with the Chukchi. This decision had an unfortunate outcome: Shestakov was struck by an enemy arrow so that he fell to the ground. Those who did not die with him fled. This battle took place 14 March 1730 at the Egach stream, which empties into Penzhina Bay between the rivers Paren and Penzhina.[78]

Three days before this unfortunate event Shestakov had sent an order to Tauisk ostrog, directing the cossack Trifon Krupischev[79] to go to Bolsheretsk ostrog in a seaworthy vessel, from there to sail round the southern tip of Kamchatka and put in at Nizhne-Kamchatsk ostrog. Furthermore, he was to continue his voyage in the same vessel until he reached the Anadyr River and then invite the inhabitants of the large land lying opposite to pay tribute to Russia. If the geodesist Gvozdev wanted to accompany them, Krupischev was to take him on the vessel and show him all good will.[80] There is no information about what happened afterwards. We know only that in 1730 the geodesist Gvozdev actually was on a foreign coast not far from the Chukchi land between 65° and 66° north latitude. This coast lay opposite the Chukchi's land. It is also known that Gvozdev found people with whom he could not speak for lack of a translator.[81]

While this happened, the nobleman Ivan Shestakov had sailed to Kamchatka in the ship *Gabriel* and reached Bolsheretsk on 19 September 1729. Although he had been ordered to go to the Uda River, that was not possible because of an adverse, severe storm. The following summer he made the voyage to the Uda, came to Uda ostrog, and found the people who had been sent there by Chief Shestakov,[82] who had built a useless ship. Shestakov then sailed back toward Kamchatka, seeing various islands both on the route out and back, and finally returned to Okhotsk. I regret that I cannot present the particular circumstances of this voyage here for lack of a journal kept during the voyage. In a report which the nobleman Shestakov submitted to the chancellery at Iakutsk on 23 October 1730, however, the days on which various events happened are noted; we will add these here as proof.[83]

16 June	1730	Departure from the Bolshaia River.
16 July	"	Arrival at the Uda River.
19 July	"	Arrival at Uda ostrog.
28 July	"	Departure from there.

13 August	1730	Arrival at Bolshaia River.
20 August	"	Departure from there.
5 September	"	Arrival at Okhotsk.

Just at the time Shestakov came back to Okhotsk, the navigator Jacob Gens [84] received an order from Captain Pavlutskii, who had meanwhile come from Iakutsk to Nizhne-Kolymsk zimovye, or ostrog, by the usual land route. The order stated that although Pavlutskii had received word from Anadyr ostrog of the cossack chief Shestakov's death, the expedition would continue without hindrance. The navigator Gens should round Kamchatka to Anadyrsk in one of the vessels Captain Bering left behind at Okhotsk. Captain Pavlutskii would also set out for Anadyrsk shortly afterwards, etc. [85]

Following his orders, Gens took the ship *Gabriel* and sailed to Kamchatka. On 20 July 1731 he stood at the mouth of the Kamchatka River, preparing to continue his voyage to the Anadyr River, when the report was delivered to him that a rebellious mob of Kamchadals had gone to Nizhne-Kamchatsk ostrog on the same day, killed most of the Russians there, and set fire to the houses of the inhabitants. [86] The few surviving Russians took refuge in their vessel. [87] Gens sent some men to bring the Kamchadals under control again, which then followed. [88] Thus the sea voyage to the Anadyr River was left undone.

Meanwhile Captain Pavlutskii arrived at Anadyr ostrog on 3 September 1730. From there he campaigned against the rebellious Chukchi during the following summer. I have collected not only written reports of this campaign, but also oral accounts of people who were there, which are noteworthy because they provide various details, and especially because they describe the geography of those areas.

On 12 March 1731 Pavlutskii marched with 215 Russians, 160 Koriaks, and 60 Iukagirs. [89] The route was via the sources of the Uboina, Belaia, and Tscherna rivers, which flow into the Anadyr, where they turned due north toward the Icy Sea. The source of the Anadyr River remained to the left of the route. Nothing is known of other rivers they might have crossed for there was no one who could indicate or name them. Since it was difficult to cover more than 10 versts per day and the men had to rest occasionally, two months passed before Pavlutskii reached the Icy Sea at a place where a sizable river, of which no one knew the name, empties into the Icy Sea. [90] For 14 days he traveled eastward along the coast, mostly over the ice, without noticing the mouths of rivers because of the great distance from land. Finally they saw a host of Chukchi approaching who seemed ready to engage in battle against our men. Through interpreters Pavlutskii called on them to submit to Russia. Since they would not hear of it, however, Pavlutskii did not hesitate to attack them as the enemy, having the good fortune to rout them completely. This happened on 7 June. [91]

After resting for eight days, Pavlutskii continued his journey; at the end of June he came to two rivers, the mouths of which at the Icy Sea, are about a day's journey distant from each other. At the second of these rivers a second battle took place on 30 June (oral reports say on the Feast of Peter and Paul) which ended just as successfully as the first.[92]

After they rested three days, they continued on to Chukotskii Nos and planned to make their way to the Anadyr Sea across it when for a third time they were approached by a host of Chukchi, who had assembled from both seas. Thus on 14 July the third engagement took place there, in which the defeat on the side of the enemy was greater than the advantage on the Russian side, because the Chukchi, nonetheless, would not agree to submit, nor to pay tribute.[93] Among the spoils, things were found which had belonged to the cossack chief and had been lost at the battle near Egach stream. Therefore Shestakov was avenged fairly well, especially since not more than three Russians, one Iukagir, and five Koriaks were killed in all three encounters. We are assured that among the enemy's dead from the last battle one was found with two holes in his upper lip at each side of his mouth through which teeth carved from walrus tusks had been inserted.[94]

Now Pavlutskii crossed Chukotskii Nos in triumph. He had to cross considerable mountains and spent 10 days under way before he reached the coast again. From there he had a part of his men proceed by sea in baidars. But he himself stayed on land with the greatest part of his men and followed the coast, which there extends toward the southeast, so that he had word from the baidars every evening; on the seventh day they came by sea to the mouth of a river, and 12 days later they reached the mouth of another, from which, after an interval of 10 versts, a promontory runs towards the east far into the sea. This is mountainous at first, but farther out it ends in a plain across which one cannot see. This promontory is probably the one that caused Captain Bering to turn back. Among the mountains on it is one the inhabitants of Anadyr ostrog call Serdtse Kamen, as was mentioned previously. From here Pavlutskii turned inland along the route he had taken on the journey out, and he returned to Anadyrsk 21 October.[95]

I shall ignore the other accomplishments of this worthy man who later became major, then lieutenant-colonel, and who ultimately died at Iakutsk as voevoda,[96] because they do not pertain to the present purpose. Instead I turn to the so-called Second Kamchatka Expedition, which surpasses all preceding ones in importance, and therefore deserves to be described in so much more detail.

III. BEGINNING OF THE SECOND KAMCHATKA EXPEDITION

Captain Bering himself made the proposals for the expedition,[97] and he, as well as lieutenants Spanberg and Chirikov, declared they would gladly make a second journey to Kamchatka to undertake the remaining discoveries which were to be made in those seas. In connection with this the captain was promoted to captain-commander and the two lieutenants to captain at the beginning of 1732. The object of the first journey did not come under discussion again because it was considered already completed.[98] Instead of this, orders were given to make voyages east to the continent of America as well as south to Japan, and at the same time to discover, if possible, the northern passage through the Icy Sea, so often attempted by the English and Hollanders.[99] The Senate, the Admiralty College, and the Academy of Sciences jointly partici-pated in the preparations,[100] and Mr. Kirilov, at that time senior secretary of the Senate and, later, counselor of state, pressed the affair, so that it soon became reality.

The first imperial command promulgated about the expedition was sent from the Administrative Senate to the Senate on 17 April 1732. The Senate required the Academy of Sciences to report to them all information known to that time about Kamchatka and the neighboring lands and waters. The academy assigned this responsibility to Mr. Delisle, who accordingly prepared a map showing Kamchatka; the Land of Jeso, as it was described on the ship *Castricom*; States Island; Company Land; Japan; and the coast seen by a Spanish captain, Don Juan de Gama.[101] To accompany this map, Mr. Delisle prepared a written ac-count describing earlier discoveries and proposing various ways and means of making new ones.[102] Therefore, after he returned to Paris, his memory was at fault if he said, in a memoir delivered to the Academy of Sciences at Paris in 1750, that he had already completed the said map and account in 1731, as if they inspired the new Kamchatka expedition.[103]

After the map and the accompanying report were delivered to the Senate by the Academy of Sciences, the order followed that a professor of the academy should be appointed to accompany Captain Commander Bering on the in-tended journey, to determine through astronomical observations the exact posi-tion of newly discovered lands and to observe what might be found noteworthy in the realm of natural history in the way of animals, plants, and minerals. Fortunately for the sciences, two professors at the academy volunteered for the expedition, namely, Johann Georg Gmelin,[104] professor of chemistry and natural history, and Louis Delisle de la Croyère,[105] professor of astronomy, and, on nomination by the academy, they were appointed by the Senate. Then, in the beginning of 1733, I also offered my services to describe the civil history of Siberia, the antiquities, the manners and customs of the people, and the events of the journey, which likewise was approved by the Senate. It can truthfully be said that such a hard and tedious expedition could scarcely have been under-taken by participants with better spirit and pleasure than these. For there was no lack of any kind of encouragement, no shortage of anything that might in any way contribute to the assigned tasks.[106]

Because of the various voyages to be made, the Admiralty College assigned the following naval officers to Captain Commander Bering: lieutenants Peter Lassenius, William Walton, Dmitrii Laptev, Egor Endaurov, Dmitrii Ovtsyn, Sven Waxell, Vasilii Pronchishchev, and Michael Plautin, and the midshipman Alexander Schelting.[107] Three of these were assigned to the discovery of the northern passage: namely one would go from the Ob to the Enisei, another would sail from the Lena westward until he also entered the Enisei, and the third would sail from the Lena eastward around Chukotskii Nos, to try to reach Kamchatka.[108] The Admiralty College directly supervised the voyage from Arkhangelsk to the Ob, employing three lieutenants, Muravev, Malygin, and Skuratov. The remaining sea officers were assigned to the ships which the captain commander and captains Spanberg and Chirikov commanded. One officer was supposed to lead a special ship since the orders stipulated that four ships should put out to sea from Kamchatka.

After 21 February 1733 Captain Spanberg was sent ahead of the main contingent with one detachment and the heaviest equipment. Captain Commander Bering began his journey at St. Petersburg on 18 April, traveling from Tver to Kazan by water and then to Tobolsk by way of Catherineburg.[109] Our academy travelers followed this same route when they began their journey on 8 August of the same year, and in January 1734 caught up with the captain commander at Tobolsk. Bering traveled to Irkutsk via Tara, Tomsk, and Krasnoiarsk, from where he went to the Lena and navigated along this river to Iakutsk. Captain Chirikov, on the other hand, traveled from Tobolsk in the summer of 1734 on the Irtysh, Ob, Ket, Tunguska, and Ilim rivers to Ilimsk, and reached Iakutsk only the following year.

Meanwhile, in order to employ themselves usefully during the time of shipbuilding at Okhotsk, our academy travelers took various tours and short excursions, which benefited geography and natural history in no small measure. Professor de la Croyère traveled by water with Captain Chirikov, left him at the mouth of the Ilim River, and continued on to Irkutsk and from there to Selenginsk, Nerchinsk, and the Argun River by way of Lake Baikal. Professor Gmelin and I, however, traveled up the Irtysh to Ust-Kamenogorsk *krepost*';[110] we went to Irkutsk via Kolivano-Voskresenskii *zavod*,[111] Kuznetsk, Eniseisk, Tomsk, and Krasnoiarsk. From there we also visited the regions beyond Lake Baikal; we spent the summer of 1735 on this latter part of our journey. In the spring of 1736 we gathered again in the upper region of the Lena River. De la Croyère went straight on to Iakutsk without stopping anywhere. Gmelin and I again passed the entire summer in river travel to gain that much more time for our own occupations.

The captain commander was still at Iakutsk and from there saw to the transportation to Okhotsk of the provisions;[112] Captain Spanberg continued with the shipbuilding at Okhotsk. But neither had much luck in their dealings, for everything proceeded so slowly that no one could predict when the voyage to

Kamchatka would begin. We did not wish to lie idle, but rather thought of new travels to occupy ourselves. A fire at Iakutsk robbed Professor Gmelin of all his travel observations of which the loss of those made on the Lena the summer before was especially unfortunate, since copies of his earlier observations had already been sent to St. Petersburg. I believe this fire prompted him to travel again up the Lena River in the summer of 1737. De la Croyère traveled the Lena to Schigani, Siktak, and the Olenek River. Because of my poor health, I was obliged to accompany Mr. Gmelin so that I could have help from him.[113] This illness was the reason I did not return to Iakutsk afterwards. Rather, an order arrived from the Senate, which released me from continuing on the voyage to Kamchatka. Instead, I was instructed to travel through other areas of Siberia— places I had not visited or had seen too briefly on the journey out—in order that all of Siberia could be described in greater detail. Gmelin also asked for his recall and received permission for it. Fortunately, while we were waiting at Iakutsk we had sent a student, Stepan Krasheninnikov,[114] to Kamchatka in order to make various preparations for our arrival. Thus we could hope that he would perform what was necessary in Kamchatka. Later, in 1738, the adjunct Georg Wilhelm Steller,[115] who was sent by the Academy of Sciences to assist Professor Gmelin, joined us. He expressed such a strong desire to go to Kamchatka and from there to go to sea, that we could not help but grant his request. Everything that was supposed to be done in Kamchatka for the sciences was taken care of with much skill by him.

IV. EXPLORATION OF THE ICY SEA

During this time, while the preparations were underway for the main work of the expedition, various voyages were made along the coasts of the Icy Sea to find out whether Kamchatka could be reached by this route. First, Lieutenant Muravev was assigned the voyage from Arkhangelsk to the Ob.[116] The first summer, 1734, he got no further than the Pechora River, and he wintered at Pustozersk ostrog.[117] The following summer he sailed through Vaigach Strait with Vaigach Island to his left and the mainland to his right. The Russian *promyshlenniki*[118] who go out to Novaia Zemlia to catch walrus, seals, stone-foxes (*pestsi*),[119] and white bears, call this passage Iugor Shar. The other passage between Vaigach Island and Novaia Zemlia was not explored.[120] From there he came again to an open sea, called Karskoe More, after the Kara River which flows into a bay in this sea.

The route this far has been known since the beginning of the last century. The inhabitants of Arkhangelsk, Kholmogory, Mezen, and Pustozersk ostrog sail to Novaia Zemlia almost annually to catch walrus, seals, and white bears.[121] Formerly voyages had been made along this route by sea to Siberia, that is to say, to the Ob River and to Mangazeia.[122] This was done in the following manner: Mutnaia is the name of a river, which together with the Kara River, flows into the same bay.[123] They traveled up this for eight days until they reached a lake, its source. They crossed the lake in one day. Then the little boats, or *kaiuks*, used for this voyage were hauled overland 200 fathoms or, according to other accounts, three versts, to another lake. A river known as the Selenaia or, according to the Russian *Atlas*, the Tylowka, flows out of this lake into the bay of the Ob River.[124] So that they would not be too heavy, the boats had to be unloaded for the portage and the goods were carried overland. Since this crossing requires a great deal of work, especially hauling the boats, various vessels generally made this journey together, so the people could give each other a helping hand. Once they reached the Selenaia, the boats were carried along with the current. But this river has many shallows. The boats that rode too deeply in the water had to be unloaded again in such places and the goods carried overland. In this way 10 days generally passed before they reached the bay of the Ob River. From there some went to Obdorsk gorodok[125] to trade with the Samoyeds.[126] The majority, however, turned into the bay of the Taz River so that they came to the site of the former city Mangazeia. The return journey was made in the same way, for it is hardly likely that these people sailed around the large cape (which is called Iamal by the Samoyeds) stretching from the Kara River northward to over 73° north latitude, and there are no reports of it.[127]

In 1735 Lieutenant Muravev sailed along this cape to 72°30′ north latitude.[128] Lieutenants Malygin and Skuratov continued the voyage.[129] They sailed around Cape Iamal and came to the bay of the Ob River, so that the route was thus seen as fully discovered and completed. This was done in 1738.[130]

In this same year Lieutenant Ovtsyn and the fleet master Ivan Koshelev began the voyage from the Ob to the Enisei River with two vessels built at Tobolsk.[131] At first the lieutenant was alone and had only one vessel, the double shallop *Tobol*,[132] 70 feet long by 15 wide, which was built so narrow in comparison to its length so it could pass between ice floes more easily. The first summer Ovtsyn reached just under 70° north latitude in this vessel, but because it was late in the season, he was forced to return to Beresov.[133] The following summer he got only as far as 69°, at which latitude the bay of the Taz River merges with the bay of the Ob.[134] The third summer he turned back at 72°30′ because of heavy ice, and he doubted whether it was reasonable to hope for a passage in the Icy Sea.[135] At that time the Admiralty College sent Master Koshelev to assist him. Koshelev built a ship's boat, the *Ob-Postman*, and joined the lieutenant.[136] Then in 1738 both ships not only succeeded in sailing around Cape Matsol,[137] which lies to the east of the bay of the Ob River, but also entered the Enisei without further difficulty.[138]

The ship's boat from this last voyage[139] was used on another journey that same summer. Under the command of the navigator Fedor Minin it was to meet the ship bound from the Lena to the Enisei. But this voyage was not successful.[140] Minin had to steer north to 73°15' before he could turn east, because the mainland projected so far.[141] When he reached the region where the Piasida River flows into the sea, he was forced to turn back because of the great ice floes, which allowed no passage.[142]

The same fate awaited the vessel sent out from Iakutsk, the double shallop called *Iakutsk*, which had the task of discovering the mouth of the Enisei River.[143] It had been built at Iakutsk and Lieutenant Pronchishchev commanded it himself. After he had left from Iakutsk 27 June 1735, he got no further than the mouth of the Olenek River that summer; a few versts up the river he found a Russian village where he wintered.[144] The following summer he went further, passing by the Anabara and Khatanga rivers, and reached not quite to the mouth of the Taimura River. Here he found a row of islands in front of him, stretching northwest from the continent far into the sea.[145] Ice was everywhere between the islands, and it did not seem possible to pass through. Pronchish-chev believed that if he followed these islands to the north, he would eventually find open sea where they ended. But this was not the case. When he reached 77°25', he found such solid ice before him that he was forced to abandon all hope of continuing. He, as well as his wife who had accompanied him on this voyage out of love, were already very ill when they set out from the winter camp. Their illness worsened daily. Pronchishchev, who returned to the Olenek River on 29 August, died a few hours later, and his wife followed him in death. He left behind a reputation as an extremely skillful and hard-working officer, whose loss was regretted by everyone.[146]

In 1738 Lieutenant Khariton Laptev was sent from St. Petersburg to replace him; he had orders to describe the coasts by land if he were unable to get through by sea.[147] That is what he did, and it proved to be one of the chief benefits of his expedition,[148] for in the voyage he undertook in 1739, he faced the same difficulties that had forced Pronchishchev to return.

Now follows the last voyage in the Icy Sea: it was made from the mouth of the Lena eastward in order to discover a route by sea to Kamchatka. Lieutenant Lassenius was the leader of it. His vessel was the boat *Irkutsk*, which had been built at Iakutsk, just as the former vessel had been.[149] He began his journey on 30 June 1735 from Iakutsk. On 7 August he left the mouth of the Lena—or actually Bykovskii Mys—for the open sea,[150] but on the fourteenth of the same month he found it necessary to seek a harbor for wintering, because of the unfavorable winds, fog, and drift ice, along with a heavy snowfall. A suitable harbor was not found until 19 August, when Lassenius entered the Kyrlak River[151] (which flows into the Icy Sea between the Lena and Iana rivers), where this voyage ended.

Several old Iakut dwellings stood along this river a verst from its mouth. Near them Lassenius had a large barracks built with various compartments where he planned to spend the winter with his men.[152] However, a deadly attack of scurvy overcame him and most of his men so that of the fifty-two people who had left Iakutsk on the ship, except for six men the lieutenant had sent with a report to the captain commander on 14 October,[153] only the priest, the assistant navigator Rtishchev and seven men of the company remained alive. Lassenius was the first to die, on 19 December. Besides him, one other person died that month. In January there were seven deaths, in February twelve, in March fourteen, and in April three.[154] In May no more died. Some of the lieutenant's subordinates had accused him of high treason during his lifetime.[155] They had taken his command from him, and transferred authority to the second mate, Rtishchev. Once this was known at Iakutsk, Captain Commander Bering dispatched the assistant navigator Shcherbinin with fourteen men to that place, with the order that both the accused and his accusers should return to Iakutsk. But all these men were already dead when Shcherbinin reached the Kyrlak on 9 June. Rtishchev still had to defend himself. Therefore, he left for Iakutsk with the seven other survivors on 11 June. During this wintering the sun was seen for the last time on 6 November and showed itself again for the first time on 10 January. The ice on the Kyrlak began to break up on 29 May. According to Lieutenant Lassenius's observations the latitude of the place was 71°28′. His successor, however, recorded it as 71°11′.

This successor was Dmitrii Laptev, who left Iakutsk with a new company and provisions at the beginning of the summer of 1736.[156] When he arrived at the mouth of the Lena the sea was still full of ice. But a narrow channel sufficient for small canoes to pass through was found between the ice and the coasts. The lieutenant used this means, and thus reached the Kyrlak River, where the ship was anchored, but he was not able to depart from there before 5 August.[157] The provisions remained back at the mouth of the Lena. Consequently, his first task was to retrieve them. Then on 15 August he began his appointed voyage, in order to sooner reach the promontory, called Sviatoi Nos,[158] projecting far into the sea between the Iana and Indigirka rivers — or, more correctly, between the Chendon and Khroma rivers. Because the sea then appeared to be free of ice, he took a course to the northeast but, after 48 hours he found so much solid ice in front of him in the east and north that he gave up all hope of going further.[159] He called the required council, at which it was unanimously decided to return to the Lena. In the meantime the vessel had been so surrounded by ice that it had open water at only four points of the compass, to the southwest. Nevertheless, they succeeded in reaching the mouth of the Lena on 23 August, continued up the river in September and set up winter quarters at the mouth of the Chotycz-tach stream because of the masses of ice coming toward them. Here, too, severe cases of scurvy began to appear among the ship's crew. But they treated the disease with a decoction made from the needles of the dwarf cedar trees[160] growing there, and (according to the custom of that country) frozen fish, which, raw and frozen as they are, are cut small and eaten. In this way, together with active work and exercise, most of the men remained healthy, and the sick recovered.

Our academy travelers were at Iakutsk when, at the beginning of 1737, a report arrived from Lieutenant Laptev himself about this twice unsuccessful voyage.[161] The instructions from the Senate to Captain Commander Bering indicated that a second voyage should be attempted if the first could not be completed successfully. And should this also encounter obstacles, the commanding officer was to go to St. Petersburg to report to the Senate and the Admiralty College about his voyages.[162] Two voyages had been made in vain, but Lieutenant Laptev had led only one of them, so Bering was uncertain about what to do. Those same instructions directed Bering to consult with the professors on the Kamchatka Expedition in doubtful cases. This was done. His judgement, and ours, was that it would be best to leave the decision to the Senate.[163] At that time I had already gathered some reports from the archives at Iakutsk about earlier voyages through the Icy Sea, some of which are included at the beginning of this paper.[164] I put all of these in order and added other reports about present conditions in the Icy Sea, which I had likewise gathered at Iakutsk from people who had experience in the Icy Sea. So that the common good might thereby be served in case any further attempt should be made, I gave my writings to the captain commander, who sent them to St. Petersburg, where excerpts were included in the St. Petersburg *Notes* in 1742.[165]

As a result Bering sent Lieutenant Laptev an order to return to Iakutsk with the boat *Irkutsk* and the entire crew.[166] He came, and set out for St. Petersburg; from there he was sent back to Siberia in 1738. They wanted to make another attempt to determine whether the voyage, which had really taken place many years earlier according to the accounts I had discovered, might be possible now. In case the lieutenant should meet with insurmountable obstacles, he was ordered to follow the coasts by land, and to prepare a detailed description as well as a map of these.

It must be admitted that this talented and energetic officer spared no effort to conscientiously carry out the orders he had received, even if it did not go completely according to plan. In the spring of 1739, he met the first open water at Iakutsk, boarded his former ship, and left in it for the Icy Sea. On 29 July he sailed into the sea. He reached Sviatoi Nos on 15 August and the mouths of the Indigirka at the end of the month. The winter was already so severe at this place that the ship was frozen in on 1 September. Laptev would have entered one of the mouths of the Indigirka if they had not been too shallow for his ship. A storm tore the ship free and drove it far out to sea, where it was frozen in again on 9 September about 60 versts from land. The crew thought only to transport the ship's supplies and provisions to the shore, which was done. The ship itself was abandoned to its fate, as nothing else could be done.[167] After Laptev spent the winter on the Indigirka River, the following summer he went along the coasts to the Kolyma River in a small vessel. To follow the coasts any further, either by land or by sea, was not advisable because of the Chukchi. Instead, Laptev went overland to Anadyrsk and from there to the mouth of the Anadyr River. With that his expedition ended.[168] No others have been undertaken through the Icy Sea in the region.

The benefit from all these efforts was this: on one hand, knowledge of the geography of these regions increased considerably. On the other hand, the impossibility of a navigation through the Icy Sea, as the English and Dutch had attempted formerly in order to find a shorter route to the Indies, was revealed in such a decisive way, that in my opinion nobody will so easily think of attempting such a voyage in the future. In order to put this important truth in the strongest light, I will add the following considerations.

First, if such a navigation were to be useful, it would have to be completed in one summer. But we have seen that a ship cannot even go from Arkhangelsk to the Ob and from there to the Enisei in one summer. Four to five years passed before a single such voyage succeeded even once. And have the Dutch and English not encountered unending difficulties during their voyages through Vaigach Strait?

Next, one would have to be able to say with certainty that no areas remained where either land or islands would prevent the passage. But how can this be claimed for the area between the Piasida and Khatanga? For there a row of islands stretches very far into the sea from the mainland, itself situated very far to the north. These islands obstruct the passage from both directions. Jelmerland,[169] which Hasius[170] placed on his map of Russia as if, according to old reports, it had been discovered in 1664, apparently does not exist; through the same reports he connected Novaia Zemlia to Siberia. But these islands, considering their effect, can fully substitute for that land.

This is also true of the gigantic stationary icebergs found in the Icy Sea. These also raise some doubt against the opinion of those who want to make a voyage through the open sea near the North Pole rather than along the coasts. It is true the voyage would be much shorter. But would the obstructions perhaps not remain the very same? For if the said icebergs remain immovable, like those found near Greenland and Spitzbergen, something must be blocking the movement the winds and the sea would otherwise cause. This can be the case through the fact that either the ice stretches to the North Pole in one solid mass or that under the pole or near it there is land, on the gently sloping bank of which the great icebergs are firmly fixed, since they go much deeper under the water than above it. In 1676 Captain Wood strongly asserted the probability of a northern passage near the North Pole before he began his voyage; the passage appeared to be quite impossible after his voyage convinced him of all the difficulties of it.[171]

In the description of the oldest voyages through the Icy Sea, given previously, I could nowhere find, with certainty, the big land which is reported to be found in the Icy Sea; from this, however, it does not follow that there is none. The American coast, which lies opposite the land of the Chukchi, could stretch far enough to the north and west without our knowing it.[172] If this is so, it, together with the mountains of ice attached to it, would lie directly in the way of those who wanted to pass near the pole.

Even the passage along the coasts no longer promises the same success it offered one hundred and more years ago. The general observation that the water in the sea is decreasing applies here too. Along the coasts of the Icy Sea wood washed ashore can be seen at heights that can now be reached by neither tide nor wave. Near the mouth of the Iana River, not far to the west, there is supposed to be an old *koch'*, about five versts away from the current seashore. From this, it is to be concluded that the coasts are exceptionally flat, which is also confirmed through the oral accounts of people who have often been on the Icy Sea. Such a change is not at all advantageous for navigation, since this is generally made between the land and the ice through a channel that is not very wide and becomes ever more shallow the longer it is. As early as 1709 *shitiki*[173] could barely pass between the rivers Indigirka and Kolyma, though these vessels are smaller than the former *kochi* and do not ride so deep in the water; I have a written testimony of this. Were one to build the vessels smaller and flatter, they would certainly be good for such shallow places, but since steep cliffs project into the sea in some places, such vessels would perform less service here, not to mention that small vessels are totally incompatible with the purpose of the voyage.

Likewise there are other obstacles which ships, especially foreign ships, meet, if they want to make this voyage. When, in our time, voyages were to be made through the Icy Sea, people were dispatched to all the rivers emptying into that sea who were to erect markers of piled wood at the mouths of the rivers to guide mariners when they arrived in those areas. At various places along the coasts storehouses were set up, from which food could be taken in case of need. All the pagans living in the area were advised of the voyage and ordered to respond quickly to the first call for help. Foreign ships cannot count on such advantages. The foreigners must almost place extraordinary confidence in their own strength, which, however, can fail only too easily. Anything they do not bring with them, they cannot expect there. And even if it could be hoped that the people there would not refuse assistance to foreign ships, these people are seldom encountered along the coasts, but instead prefer to go up the rivers, where they enjoy more advantageous hunting.

And what sad consequences ensue, when a European ship (like Heemskerk at Novaia Zemlia)[174] is forced to winter? The lifestyle and diet of European mariners do not adapt at all to such a wintering. Brandy, salt meat, and biscuit are no remedy for scurvy. And the lack of exercise, which always ensues if a mariner has nothing to do outside his hut, is even more harmful.

For such cases, the lifestyle of the Russians from Arkhangelsk, who spend almost every winter on Novaia Zemlia without ill effects, can serve as a model. They imitate the Samoyeds by frequently drinking fresh reindeer blood. Their brandy, which they bring on the voyage, is consumed before they reach the coast of Novaia Zemlia. They know nothing of salted or dried food, but live on the fresh game they catch, especially wild reindeer. Hunting requires constant movement. Therefore, no one stays in his hut even one day, unless an exceptionally severe storm or deep snow prevents him from going out. Not to mention that these people are supplied with good, warm furs which the European mariners lack. These are, in my opinion, reasons enough to prevent other countries from such enterprises in the future. Indeed, Father Castel (Dissertation sur la celebre Terre de Kamtschatka et sur celle d'Yeco in *Mémoires de Trévoux* 1737, July, p. 1169.)[175] already had such thoughts, but they were without sufficient proof. We would have remained in continual uncertainty had we not been led from it by the voyages through the Icy Sea related above.

V. THE VOYAGES TO JAPAN

We continue, and come to the main undertaking of the Second Kamchatka Expedition, which consisted of the voyages to be made towards the east and south from Okhotsk and Kamchatka. Captain Spanberg had already arrived at Iakutsk in the month of June, 1734, and had continued on with the same vessel he had used to travel on the Aldan, Maia, and Iudoma rivers, in order to reach Iudoma Cross before winter, if possible. However, he was frozen in more than 150 versts from this place, and he decided to proceed on foot with a few men to Iudoma Cross and Okhotsk.[176] Now in order that Spanberg might not lack things most necessary for him there, the captain commander sent 100 horses to that place in the spring of 1735, each loaded with five *puds* of flour, as was the local custom. After that they endeavored to convey the ship materials and provisions for the next year's voyages from Iakutsk to Iudoma Cross, some of which had arrived with the captain commander, some in vessels built at Iakutsk and at the mouth of the Maia River. In the summer of 1736 Captain Chirikov had charge of this; the following winter he traveled from that place to Okhotsk.[177] In the summer of 1737, 33,000 puds of provisions and materials were brought by Lieutenant Waxell along this same route to Iudoma Cross, but the transport from there was made overland in the winter to the Urak River, where storehouses were established and new vessels were built. With the first open water, when this river—which otherwise is very shallow in summer—was swelled very high, the provisions on hand there were conveyed to Okhotsk. The place on the upper Urak River from which the vessels left was named Urakskoe Plotbishche.[178] It is about halfway between Iudoma Cross and Okhotsk. With its windings the river runs about 200 versts to the sea. Because of the river's strong current the distance can be traversed in 17 hours, without the help of oars.[179]

During this time Captain Spanberg had two vessels built at Okhotsk for the voyage he was commanded to make to Japan—a hooker, named the *Archangel Michael*,[180] and a double-sloop, named the *Hope*.[181] At the end of summer, 1737, these were completely finished. Captain Commander Bering, who came to Okhotsk in the same summer, had two more packet-boats built for the American voyage and two supply vessels built which would be used only as far as Kamchatka. These were completed in the summer of 1740, and the two packet-boats were assigned the names *St. Peter* and *St. Paul*.[182] Meanwhile the transport of provisions from Iakutsk to Iudoma Cross, and from there to Okhotsk, went on continually. It was very helpful that, at the request of the captain commander, the Admiralty College had sent two lieutenants of the fleet to Siberia in 1738, namely Vasilii Larionov and Gabriel Tolbuchin — the former to Iakutsk, the latter to Irkutsk—who took care of the needs of the Kamchatka expedition.[183]

Thus, in 1738 they could begin the voyage to Japan. Captain Spanberg commanded the hooker, the *Archangel Michael*, and Lieutenant Walton[184] the double-sloop, the *Hope*. The boat *Gabriel*, from the first Kamchatka voyage, was added to these and was entrusted to the command of Midshipman Schelting.[185] With these three vessels Captain Spanberg set sail from Okhotsk about the middle of June, 1738. He could not sail earlier because the sea was full of ice until then. And even at this time of year he had great difficulty getting through the ice. He steered first to Kamchatka, entered the Bolshaia River, and made preparations for his future winter quarters. After a short stay there he directed his course to the Kurile Islands, and went along them to the southwest as far as 46° north latitude. The arrival of late fall pressed him to return to Kamchatka, which he did, with the intention of going to sea earlier the next summer to complete the voyage.[186] During the wintering at Bolsheretsk ostrog, Captain Spanberg built a little birchwood yacht, or decked shallop, with 24 oars, which he named the *Bolshaia River*, to better serve the exploration of the islands, if perhaps the hooker and the double-sloop could not be used conveniently between them.[187]

On 22 May 1739 the voyage, with all four vessels, was begun again. They waited for one another at the first of the Kurile Islands, where the captain gave his subordinate officers the necessary orders of conduct, and the signals were agreed upon. This done, on 1 June they sailed and initially held their course to the southeast to about 47° north latitude without encountering land, and then to the southwest, so that they could reach the Kurile Islands again, which they did. On 14 June there was a violent storm together with a thick fog. Because of it Lieutenant Walton in the double-sloop was separated from Captain Spanberg, and although they searched for each other for two days and fired off various cannons as signals, they did not rejoin each other again during the course of the voyage.[188] Each continued his voyage for himself. They both touched at Japan in different places and, after their return, gave the following reports to the captain commander.

On 18 June Captain Spanberg anchored in 25 fathoms at the land of Japan, where he calculated himself to be at 38°41′ north latitude.[189] A great many Japanese vessels were seen, and on the land some villages, and, standing in the fields, grain of a kind they could not recognize. Fairly high woods were seen in the distance. Two Japanese vessels came rowing toward them; these remained lying off at a distance of from 30 to 40 fathoms with their oars at rest, and would not come closer. Beckoned to come closer, they replied with corresponding signs, and gave them to understand that the captain and his people should come to the land. But Captain Spanberg guarded himself carefully against this; indeed he did not remain long in one place, so that he would not be overtaken unexpectedly, but held sometimes again to sea, and sometimes he started back toward land again, as the circumstances appeared to require.[190]

On 20 June they again saw many Japanese vessels, each occupied by from 10 to 12 men. On the 22nd the captain anchored in another place, at 38°25′ north latitude.[191] Men from two fishing boats came on board there, who exchanged fresh fish, rice, large tobacco leaves, salted gherkins, and other trifles for various Russian goods with which the ship's people were supplied. Cloth and cloth- ing,[192] and also blue glass beads, seemed to be the most acceptable to the Japanese. On the contrary, they did not ask for cotton and silk goods, or mirrors, knives, scissors, nails, and other similar implements which the crew showed them, because they had all of these in their own land. They were very polite and were reasonable in their prices.

The crew received some oblong, four-cornered, gold coins from them, of the same kind that Kaempfer described and portrayed.[193] They are not as bright in color as the Dutch ducats, and are somewhat lighter than these. I had the opportunity to see one of them and, in comparison with a Dutch ducat, I noted a difference in weight of two grains.

The following day they saw 79 of the same kind of fishing boats near at hand.[194] All of them were flat at the rudder and very pointed in front. Their width was 4-1/2 to 5 feet; their length about 24 feet. In the middle of each was a deck, on which stood a little hearth. The rudder could be taken in and laid in the vessel, if it was not being used. Some had two rudders, both at the back, one on each side, which were bent quite crooked. The oars were used while stand- ing. They were also supplied with little four-pronged iron anchors. Spanberg's crew noticed that on these and other Japanese vessels, brass was used for the nails and clamps, instead of iron as we use.

Junks are another kind of vessel which are used for trade to the islands situated nearby and even for a great distance along the coast. These are much larger than the former vessels, built with a point at the stern as well as in front; they carry more people and sail well, although mostly only before the wind.[195] Therefore, at sea they are easily driven out of their course by contrary winds and weather, when—because of their inexperience in the art of navigation—the people do not know how to help themselves, but simply submit to fate. Junks of that kind have been driven off their course more than once to the coast of Kamchatka.

The Japanese are mostly small in stature, brownish in appearance, with black eyes and flat noses. Adult males shave their hair from the forehead to the crown; the remaining hair is combed smooth and made shiny with glue, and is tied together at the neck and wrapped up with paper. The young boys differ from them by a shaved spot in the middle of the crown, which is one and a half to two inches big, around which the hair is dressed in other respects like that of the adults.[196] Their clothes are long and wide, of the style of European dressing gowns. They do not wear real trousers; instead of these the lower part of their bodies is wrapped in linen cloth.[197]

Before the captain left this place, a large boat came to the ship in which, in addition to the workers, sat four men who, to judge by their embroidered clothes and other appearances, seemed to be of high rank. The captain invited them to his cabin. At the entrance they bowed down to the ground with their hands folded together over their heads and remained kneeling until the captain urged them to rise. They were entertained with brandy and food, which seemed to please them. When the captain showed them a sea-chart of those areas, as well as a globe, they immediately recognized their land, the name of which they pronounced Niphon. They also pointed with their fingers on the sea-chart to the islands Matsmai and Sado, as well as to the capes Songar and Noto.[198] In leaving they again bowed to the ground and expressed gratitude as well as they could, for what they had eaten. That same day the fishing boats from before came again, and brought various trifles to sell, which they exchanged for Russian goods.

By this time Captain Spanberg had no doubt that the main purpose of his voyage—which was the discovery of the true situation of Japan in relation to the land of Kamchatka—had been fulfilled. Therefore, after the elapse of some days he began the return voyage, in which he made observations about some islands, seen before, which he was obliged to sail past again. I cannot help mentioning this, but I refer for further details to the map made of his voyage, which is contained in the Russian *Atlas*.[199]

He sailed toward the northeast, and came on 3 July to a great island at 43°50′ north latitude,[200] at which he anchored in the depth of 30 fathoms, and sent his birch yacht with a boat to the land, to try to find fresh water. But they could not find a landing place because of the steep cliffs, which made up the coast itself. Therefore he sailed to another spot, from which the boat was again sent to land; 13 barrels of good, fresh water were brought on board. Birch, fir, and other kinds of trees that the Russian crew did not know, grew on the island. They saw people who dispersed as soon as they caught sight of the Russians. They found leather boats and sledge bottoms made in Kurile and Kamchatka style. That induced the captain to sail in closer, and to anchor in a bay with a sandy bottom at eight fathoms. In this bay lay a village. The captain sent a shallop to it; of the inhabitants, eight men were brought on board the ship.

The appearance and the stature of the people were like the Kurilians and they spoke the same language. A main difference consisted in this—that they had fairly long hair over their whole bodies. The middle-aged men had black beards, and the old men were entirely gray. Some wore silver rings in their ears. Their garments were of silk cloth of various colors, and reached to their feet, which they left bare. The crew gave them brandy to drink and presented them with various trifles, which they accepted with thanks. When they saw a live cock on the ship they fell to their knees, clapped their hands to the ground as if for the presents they had received. After that the captain put them again on land.

On 9 July Captain Spanberg sailed away from this island again and explored the position of the other islands situated near there in order to put them with certainty on his map. This was not done without danger and hardship. Sometimes they had only three or four fathoms of water. Many men on the ship became sick, and several died shortly thereafter.[201] On 23 July he came by a southwesterly course to the island of Matsmai,[202] at 41°22′ north latitude, where he met three large Japanese junks which he prepared to fight, in case they should attack him. As a precaution, he would neither prepare to land nor drop anchor, but rather proceeded on the return voyage to Kamchatka on 25 June. On 15 August he arrived at the mouth of the Bolshaia River, which he entered in order to allow his people to rest a little. He sailed again on 20 August. When he arrived back at Okhotsk on the 29th, he found Lieutenant Walton already there before him, out of whose report the most remarkable things will be cited now.[203]

After Walton became separated in the fog and storm from Captain Spanberg, whom he tried in vain to rejoin, Walton decided to search, without loss of time, for the land of Japan, which he sighted two days later, on the 16th, at 38°17′ north latitude.[204] At that time he was situated, according to his calculation, 11°45′ west from the first Kurile island. He sailed further to the south, to 33°48′ north latitude, mostly following the coasts, and observed the following: on 17 June, when he was near the land, 39 Japanese vessels of the size of galleys came into view, which appeared to have put to sea from one harbor, but which soon dispersed to various places. These had upright sails of cotton fabric, some blue and white striped, others entirely white. Walton followed one of them in order to look around for a harbor, and came before a great market town, or city, where he anchored in 30 fathoms.[205] On the 19th a Japanese vessel with 18 people on it came to the Russian ship. Because the people seemed very polite and, through signs, gave Walton to understand that they could come to land, the lieutenant sent the assistant navigator, Lev Kazimirov, and the quartermaster, Vereshchagin, to land in a boat with six armed soldiers, and he gave them two empty casks to fill with fresh water. At the same time he supplied them with things they should present to the Japanese in order to win their friendship.[206]

When they approached the shore, over a hundred small vessels came towards them and crowded the boat so hard, that they could scarcely use their oars. The Japanese rowers were naked to the waist. They showed pieces of gold, of which they had not a few, as a sign, apparently, that they desired to have trade with the foreign guests. Meanwhile the boat landed and the little vessels remained behind at some distance. An innumerable crowd of people was on the shore. They all bowed to the newcomers. Obligingly, the two empty water casks were taken on shore, filled with water, and brought back again to the boat.

In the meantime, the assistant navigator and the quartermaster went on land with four soldiers, and two soldiers remained as a guard at the boat. The city consisted of approximately 1500 houses, partly wood and partly stone, which occupied a space of about three versts along the coast. Kazimirov proceeded to the house into which he had seen his casks carried. At the door he was received in an exceedingly friendly manner by the owner himself, taken into a room, and entertained with wine from a china vessel and similarly with sweets served in china containers. The sweets consisted of grapes, apples, oranges, and little radishes preserved in sugar. From this house he went to another, where he was treated the same way, and besides was served cooked rice to eat. The same happened to the quartermaster and the soldiers who were present. Kazimirov gave glass beads and trifles to his benefactors and to the people who had attended to his casks. After that he went around the city a little and noted great cleanliness and order everywhere, in the houses and in the streets. In some houses there were small shops, in which chiefly cotton material was sold. In their haste they did not notice silk material.[207] Horses, cows, and poultry were abundant. The field crops there were wheat and peas.

When Kazimirov returned to his boat again he saw two men with swords in hand. Indeed, one of them held two swords in his hands.[208] This roused fear in him, so he hurried back to his ship as fast as he could.

Over a hundred small Japanese vessels, each occupied by 15 men, followed the boat to observe the ship close at hand. Among them was one in which rode a distinguished man who had a rope thrown to the boat, so his little vessel could be drawn up to the ship. He came onto the ship. From his beautiful silk clothing and the deference which the people in his retinue showed to him, they concluded that he was the commander of this place. He presented a vessel of wine to Lieutenant Walton, which the latter brought with him to Okhotsk. The wine was dark brown in color, fairly strong and not unpleasant in taste, only somewhat sour.[209] Perhaps it suffered damage at sea from the warm weather.[210] The lieutenant returned this politeness with other presents. He entertained both his guest and the retinue with food and drink, in the course of which it was noted that the Russian brandy did not taste bad to the Japanese. At the same time the ship's people carried on a little trade with the Japanese. Everything that the Russians had, even old shirts, stockings, etc., suited the Japanese. They paid for it with their copper coins, which, like the Chinese coins, have a square hole in the middle, and are strung on a string. Finally, with testimonies of his friendship and gratitude, the distinguished man returned to the city. Walton observed meanwhile, that the little vessels which ringed the ship became ever more numerous. He believed he was no longer safe enough.[211] After firing a cannon as a farewell, he raised his anchor and stood again to the sea.

On 22 June he again reached land, and cast anchor in 23 fathoms. The anchor did not hold so they raised it again. They looked around them, to see whether there might not be a better opportunity to land elsewhere. But the coast was steep and rocky everywhere. At one place they noticed that vessels, which were not small, had been drawn up on land for lack of a harbor. Therefore Walton returned to the place where he had not succeeded in anchoring previously.[212] There some small vessels came to him at the ship; he gave them to understand that he was in need of water. Immediately the Japanese took the casks that they were given into their vessels, carried them to land, and brought them back filled with fresh water. They also showed our people a written paper, which was taken as an order by virtue of which they were bound to give all possible assistance to strangers. It seemed as if the Japanese wanted to make the lieutenant understand that he should come nearer to land; there was a harbor, into which the ship could be taken by towing; they would be helpful in that. But before Walton decided on that a boat came from land with orders which forbade the people any more communication. In the boat was a man who was taken for a soldier because he had a sword at his side and a pistol in his hand. Therefore this Japanese boat was called a guard boat in the report of Lieutenant Walton.[213]

The next day they lay at anchor, near land, in 20 fathoms at another place, where the bottom consisted of coarse sand and shells. In the great heat of summer they could not supply themselves with enough fresh water. Besides, this always provided new opportunities to gather reports from the land. Therefore on 24 June Walton sent the second gunner Yuri Alexandrov, with a crew, to the coast in a boat. There was also an apprentice in surgery, named Ivan Diagilev, in the crew. Alexandrov indeed found no water, but he saw Japanese who went about in white linen smocks. The horses of the country were dark brown and black. He brought an orange tree, pearl shells, and a branch of a pine tree back with him. The apprentice Diagilev, however, gathered herbs, and supplied himself especially with fir tree buds, from which they subsequently cooked drinks for the sick on board the ship.[214]

Afterwards Walton sailed for awhile along the coasts of Japan, and also made a voyage quite far toward the east, in order to see whether he could not discover land or islands, which did not happen; so he turned back toward Kamchatka and reached the Bolshaia River on 23 July. There he remained until 7 August, in order to wait for Captain Spanberg if possible. But in the meanwhile the latter did not come, so he set off on the voyage to Okhotsk, which he reached on 21 August.

It is not necessary to make special mention of the third vessel, which the midshipman Schelting led. It shared the same lot as the captain, since it was not separated from him on the voyage. Spanberg, as well as Walton, prepared maps of their voyages, from which were composed those which appear in print in the Russian *Atlas*.[215]

After his return Spanberg received permission from the captain commander to winter at Iakutsk, and after that to travel to St. Petersburg, in order to make his own account of his performance to the Senate and the Admiralty College. In the meanwhile the discoveries made by him were reported to St. Petersburg. Initially these were well received and the result was that the order of the captain commander with regard to the return journey of Captain Spanberg to St. Petersburg was confirmed;[216] yet the opinions soon changed.[217] The proofs that Spanberg had been in Japan were regarded as not convincing. Kirilov's general map of Russia, after the example of Strahlenberg, presented Japan almost under the same meridian as Kamchatka.[218] According to Spanberg's and Walton's courses and observations, on the other hand, it should be placed from 11 to 12 degrees more to the west. It was believed that Spanberg could have taken the coasts of Korea for Japan.[219] It was thought beneficial that he should attempt a second voyage. In addition, two Russian youths who had learned the Japanese language from the Japanese who had come to St. Petersburg in 1732 would serve as translators.[220]

Spanberg received this order in the month of July, 1740, at Kirensk ostrog, when he was already on his journey to St. Petersburg. He proceeded back to Iakutsk, and from there to Okhotsk, where he met the captain commander only briefly, because everything was finally in readiness for Bering's own intended voyage. In the meanwhile, not only was the suitable season for the voyage to Japan past for this year, but also a vessel was lacking, because one of those which Spanberg had used on his first voyage, on account of certain preparations, had been sent to Kamchatka by the captain commander.[221] They had to build a new one, and that was done in the winter under the supervision of Captain Spanberg, who remained at Okhotsk.[222]

In the summer of 1741 he went to sea with it.[223] But the vessel was soon leaking so much that they could barely reach the coasts of Kamchatka. The cause was ascribed to the hurried building of the vessel and the fact that the wood had not had enough time to dry. It did not help that they repaired the ship at the mouth of the Bolshaia River and that Spanberg spent the winter at Bolsheretsk on account of this; for when he sailed again on 23 May 1742[224] he had barely passed the first Kurile island when water penetrated the ship again, without the men being able to prevent it or to close up all the leaky places.[225] With matters in such a shape, Spanberg still did not want to return without any discoveries. He therefore sent out Midshipman Schelting to inquire about the regions of the sea as far as the mouth of the Amur River. But this also did not have the desired success.[226] In short, the whole second voyage of Captain Spanberg was accompanied by nothing but calamities, and all three vessels returned unsuccessfully to Okhotsk.

One has cause to explain this as a natural consequence of the duress with which the second voyage was undertaken. The first voyage was made voluntarily. Everyone worked for his honor. Because of this, many a crisis was overcome which, with less courage, perhaps would have placed obstacles in the way. Now, however, all problems were felt with full force, and it may well be that, with this altered nature, the ability, absolutely necessary in such cases, to find in time the means by which they could avoid or prevent difficulties, was lacking.[227]

Still, be that as it may. With that the voyage to Japan was ended. Gradually the arguments increased that our sailors had not missed their destination the first time.[228] And at present nobody doubts it any more, since the most famous French geographers, such as the Messrs. d'Anville, Buache, and Bellin, accepted in their maps as great or even a somewhat greater difference of longitude between Kamchatka and Japan as Spanberg and Walton.[229]

VI. TO KAMCHATKA

The expedition of Captain Spanberg to Japan in 1738 had so denuded the main detachment at Okhotsk of provisions that two years passed before it could be adequately resupplied.[230] During this time two new vessels, namely the packet-boats St. Peter and St. Paul, which really were designated for the intended American discoveries, were built at Okhotsk.[231] In the fall of 1739 the captain commander had sent the navigator, Ivan Elagin, to Kamchatka ahead of him, with one of the vessels which had been with Captain Spanberg, to investigate the eastern coast of this land to the Bay of Avacha, where all the necessary conveniences for a harbor were said to exist, and at the same time to build storehouses and barracks so that they could stay there in the winter time.[232] After that, in the spring of 1740, Professor Delisle de la Croyère and Adjunct Steller[233] came to Okhotsk. At the same time Fleet Lieutenant Ivan Chikhachev and Fleet Master Sofron Khitrov (who soon afterwards was made lieutenant) also arrived from St. Petersburg to replace other sick and dismissed officers.[234]

Now, as nothing more was lacking, it was decided to cross over to Kamchatka that same summer. The departure was delayed, however, until 4 September.[235] The captain commander led the packet-boat *St. Peter* and Captain Chirikov the packet-boat *St. Paul*. Two other ships were loaded with provisions.[236] De la Croyère and Steller had a separate vessel for themselves and their provisions, with which they followed the rest of the squadron on 8 September.[237] When the packet-boats arrived at the mouth of the Bolshaia River on 20 September, the captain commander ordered the storeships to enter it. The voyage of de la Croyère and Steller was finished here, because they had proposed to make observations and investigations at Bolsheretsk ostrog.[238] However, the captain commander and Captain Chirikov, who found the entrance too shallow for their ships, continued further the next day, and went around the southern point of Kamchatka to the harbor at Avacha.[239]

From the danger that he encountered as they crossed the strait between this point and the first Kurile Islands, the commander saw how necessary a precaution it had been to leave the storeships back at the Bolshaia River. In the middle of the straits, which they estimated to be 1 $1/2$ German miles wide and a half mile long, lies a great stone reef over which rolling waves run.[240] This can be passed on both sides, but the southern passage, because it is wider, is preferred to the northern. Though the wind with which the captain commander thought to come through the straits was favorable and strong, that helped him little, because at the same time a strong tide which he had not seen earlier, being unacquainted with these waters, came toward him.[241] For a whole hour, it could not be observed by the coasts that the ship had progressed even a little farther.[242] The waves, which were very high, beat over the ship's stern, and a boat which had a tow rope of 40 fathoms was often slammed against the ship with great force; indeed, once it was almost thrown on board with the waves. They had bottom at from 10 to 12 fathoms. When the ship dropped to the depth with the waves, however, they figured barely three fathoms to the bottom.[243] The wind was so strong that they could set no more than the foresail and main topsail. In this case there was nothing to do but to hold the ship exactly before the wind, straight against the current, because if they had turned even a little they would have been in danger between the waves.[244] Besides, the previously noted rocky reef was very near, of which they had to be wary, in order not to be wrecked on it. When the violence of the tide abated somewhat the ship began to advance a little and, finally, after the straits lay completely behind, they saw they were free of all further impediments. This, however, only happened to the captain commander, whereas Chirikov, who came through an hour and a half later, encountered no difficulty.

It was 26 September when the said straits were passed. The next day they arrived in front of the Bay of Avacha; since a thick fog arose exactly at that same time which prevented them from seeing the entrance, they were forced to go to sea again. They then suffered from heavy storms in which the boat that had been towed behind the ship was lost. Probably it had been more than a little damaged earlier, because the waves of the strait had often thrown it against the ship. Finally, on 6 October both packet-boats succeeded in entering the bay and harbor of Avacha, where they then spent the following winter.

This bay has the name of the Avacha River (or really, in the Kamchatka pronunciation, Suaatscha),[245] which flows into the bay on the western side. It is almost circular, and is approximately 20 versts in diameter. The entrance may be about 300 to 400 fathoms wide. It extends toward the southeast, and is so deep that the largest ships could enter it. The bay itself is also of a considerable depth.[246] Three natural divisions in the bay—Niakina, Katovaia, and Tareinaia guba—could serve equally well as harbors, differing only in size.[247] The navigator Elagin, however, had chosen the first—the smallest—as the harbor for the packet-boats, and had built the prescribed storehouses, houses, and barracks there. In addition, a church[248] dedicated to the Holy Apostles Peter and Paul was built while the captain commander wintered there.[249] On that account, and because the packet-boats were called the *St. Peter* and the *St. Paul*, the place received the name Petropavlovsk from the captain commander.

An officer, who in forty years had sailed all quarters of the globe and who was with the expedition at that time, gave testimony that this harbor is the best place for shipping that he has seen in his lifetime.[250] It can conveniently hold 20 ships, is protected from all winds, has a soft sand bottom and a depth of 14 to 18 feet, so that even larger ships than the packet-boats could lie in it.[251] Good and wholesome water is found nearby, particularly from the Avacha River, which they much preferred to some other rivers and streams there that arose out of bogs. From the entrance of the bay to the harbor one steers by the NNW and NW by N. One has 8, 9, 10, and 11 fathoms of water and a secure passage over a sandy bottom, except about three versts in front of the harbor, where some sunken rocks lie in the middle of the channel, of which one had to be wary as there is only 9 feet of water.[252] The maximum rise of the water, at the time of the new or full moon when the tide increases the most, amounts to 5 feet 8 inches English measure according to the observations they made themselves.

During the wintering at Petropavlovsk every effort was made to transport there the provisions that had been brought to Bolsheretsk.[253] However, they could not quite bring that off. The distance between the two places amounts to 212 versts. Because there are no horses in Kamchatka, dogs had to be used in relays, and sometimes they had to be fetched from 400 to 500 versts distance for that.[254] They had to have eight to ten times as many dogs as horses, for in Russia 40 puds can be hauled by a horse on winter roads; in Kamchatka this load would be hauled by not less than eight to ten dogs. The Kamchadals were not used to such relays and were not accustomed to being so far from their homes.[255]

98

This produced many obstacles.[256] But the Russians had been aware of these difficulties earlier, and had made sure that a good number of reindeer had been bought up at Anadyr ostrog and driven to Avacha. These went to good pasture and were eaten during the winter; also, dried fish in abundance were obtained from the Kamchadals, so that half portions from the usual sea provisions could be saved.[257] However in the spring of the following year, 1741, the captain commander ordered one of the ships remaining back at Bolsheretsk to come later with the provisions remaining there. The ship reached the harbor of Petropavlovsk successfully before Bering went to sea, and its cargo was delivered partly to the ships that were ready to put to sea and partly to the storehouses there.

When the roads began to get better Professor de la Croyère and Adjunct Steller came to Petropavlovsk, in order to assist in the appointed American discoveries. The captain commander took the latter with him[258] while the former joined Captain Chirikov.

VII. SELECTION OF THE ROUTE

Now the course that should be held for the impending voyage had to be determined. To decide this, the captain commander called all the officers together for a council, and he also invited Professor de la Croyère. Each one should express his opinion; the best of all was to be chosen. Now the signs of a nearby land towards the east were known to everyone. Through the whole winter the officers had given their opinion that they must hold the course to the east, or somewhat northerly. Only the Delisle map, which was presented by the academy to the Senate, as I mentioned above, was not in harmony with this.[259] The Senate had given the Delisle map to the captain commander, in order that he might direct himself according to it.[260] De la Croyère also had a copy of it, which he brought along to the council meeting. There was no land shown towards the east. On the contrary, on this map there was a coast southeast from Avacha under the forty-sixth to forty-seventh degrees of latitude, which was supposed to extend about fifteen degrees from the west to the east; it was shown in such a manner as if it had only been seen from the southern side. Near it were the words: "Terres vues par Dom Jean de Gama [land seen by Don Jean Gama]."[261] Accordingly they decided in the sea council that if such a coast was really to be found in the area (as they believed, because the author of the map would not have represented anything on uncertain ground) then that land might extend toward the north far enough and consequently would be found much more easily.[262] It was also decided to run easterly toward the southeast by south to the same land and, having discovered it, to let its coasts be used as a guide towards the north and east;[263] if they did not find it at forty-six degrees, they would change the course and sail to the east and east by north until they discovered land, which they would follow between north and east, or between north and west, to the sixty-fifth degree of latitude, and, in general, would arrange the voyage so they could come back to Avacha in the month of September.[264]

Because this decision was held by the mariners who were with the expedition to be the cause of all the disasters they had on the voyage, it is necessary to dwell on it a little. It is not known who Jean de Gama was, or even when the discovery attributed to him took place. All that is known is that the Royal Portuguese cosmographer Teixeira[265] published a map in 1649, on which under the latitude of 44 to 45 degrees, at 10 to 12 degrees northeast of Japan, are shown a great many islands and a coast running toward the east with the annotation: "Terre vule par Jean de Gama Indien en allant de la Chine a' la nouvelle Espagne [land seen by John de Gama the Indian, in going from China to New Spain]"[266] (*Considerations Geographiques et Physiques* by Mr. Buache, p. 128).[267] The discovery took place either at the same time as that of the Dutch ship *Castricom*, or still earlier, and the position of the Land of Gama, as it was described on the Teixeira map, appears not to be different from the Company Land discovered by the same ship, the *Castricom*.[268] Our mariners believe that they were misled to a useless navigation by the Delisle map.[269] This is true in respect to the voyage to America, which certainly was very much delayed through it. But the mistake lies only in this, that Mr. Delisle put the Land of Gama too far to the east and granted it a place among the American discoveries, when it should have been among the Japanese or Jeso. Had this latter been the case, they would have entrusted the same investigation to Captain Spanberg; and there would have been no mistake if equally as little of it had been discovered as Jeso, States Island, and Company Land. It may indeed be that the Land of Gama or Company Land met with exactly the same fate as the Land of Jeso[270] without our having to be astonished by it. By the way, one notices that the Land of Gama is now either no longer accepted by the geographers or is made so small and placed so near Japan and Company Land that there hardly remains any difference between it and Company Land. For that one needs only to examine the newest maps of Messrs. d'Anville, Bellin, Green, Buache, and even Delisle himself.[271]

Afterwards what remained for the dispatch of the voyage was arranged, and particularly the supplying of the ships with as much provisions as they could hold; then on 4 June 1741 both ships set out on the voyage.[272] They steered the agreed-upon course towards the SE by S until the 12th of the same month, when they found themselves under the forty-sixth degree of latitude. Nothing more was needed to convince them of the nonexistence of the Land of Gama.[273] They went with a northern course as far as fifty degrees, and, when they wished to take a course from there eastward to discover the mainland of America, Captain Chirikov was driven away from the course of the captain commander in a violent storm and fog on the twentieth.[274]

VIII. CHIRIKOV'S VOYAGE

This was the first disaster for our seafarers. Through it the ships were robbed of the mutual assistance which they should have had from each other,
an intention which gave rise to the furnishing of two ships and ordering them in
the instructions never to separate from each other.[275] The captain commander
indeed did his utmost to search for Chirikov. He circled between 50 and 51
degrees for three days, and sailed back toward the southeast as far as 45 degrees:
but it all was futile.[276] Chirikov had taken an easterly course at the latitude of 48
degrees,[277] which course the captain commander first began on 25 June under 45
degrees.[278] Thus they did not meet with each other again; nevertheless, they
made discoveries which concur exactly with each other.

Nothing special happened until 18 July, when the captain commander, after he
steered more and more northerly,[279] got sight of the mainland of America under
the latitude of 58°28′ and, after the reckoning, believed he had traversed 50
degrees of longitude from Avacha.[280] Captain Chirikov had arrived at the same
coast three days earlier, namely on 15 July, in 56° latitude, and had, according to
his calculation, 60 degrees difference from Avacha.[281] Both, however, could have
erred somewhat in the difference of longitude; for if one compares the return
journey with the voyage out, it appears the captain commander had been under
60 and Captain Chirikov under 65 degrees of longitude from Avacha to the
coast of America. Now, the longitude from Petropavlovsk in the bay of Avacha,
determined by astronomical observations, is 176°12′0″ from the first meridian,
taken from Ferro Island. Consequently the longitudes of the aforesaid coasts of
America amount to 236° for the first place and 241° for the second. If these
places are considered with respect to the nearest known regions of California,
there is between Cape Blanco, the most northerly region of California, and the
place where Captain Chirikov was, a difference of only 13 degrees latitude and
not more than 5 degrees longitude, as a matter of fact a modest distance, which
well deserves to be investigated, especially as the doubtful discoveries of Admiral
de Fonte are attributed to this region.[282] At the time, however, our seafarers had
no information about it.

Where Captain Chirikov was, the coast was steep and rocky, without any
islands.[283] Therefore he did not dare come near to the land but rather anchored
at some distance. Because he wanted to investigate the land and because he
needed fresh water, he sent the mate Abraham Dementiev and 10 of his best
men to shore with the large longboat,[284] after furnishing them with provisions
for some days, with good guns and sidearms, even with a metal[285] cannon and
accessories, and with formal instructions on how they should behave in various

101

events and how they should indicate the same through signals.

They saw the boat rowed into the bay behind a little promontory. They concluded that it reached land successfully, because the signals were given as had been ordered in that same case.[286] A few days passed without the boat coming back. The signals, however, continued on.[287] They got the idea that the boat might have suffered damage in the landing and could not come back to the ship again without being repaired. Therefore, it was decided to send the small longboat to land with the boatswain Sidor Savelev, and three men[288] (another account says six men)[289] among whom were carpenters and a caulker, well armed and supplied with the necessary materials. This happened on 21 July.[290] Savelev had orders to present himself again immediately to the commander with Dementiev—if he had performed the necessary assistance to the boat—or alone. However, neither of the two took place.[291] In the meanwhile they saw a heavy smoke continually rising from the shore.

The next day two vessels came rowing from the land towards the ship. One was larger than the other. When they saw them at a distance they believed it was Dementiev and Savelev with the two longboats. In this opinion, Captain Chirikov ordered all the people to come on deck in order to make preparations for departure.[292] However, these were Americans who in the distance could not be differentiated at sight; they stopped rowing, probably for the reason that they saw many people on the deck; they stood up and shouted "*agai, agai*," with loud voices and hastily turned back to the land.[293] If it is true that the Americans became shy because of the number of Russians and that they previously had believed they could master the ship themselves as there were no or few more people on it, it would have been better if Chirikov had kept his people hidden. The Americans would perhaps have come onto the ship. They might have seized them and their vessels and could have exchanged them and their vessels for the Russians and the Russian longboats on the land. But the joy over the supposed return of Dementiev and Savelev was too great to use such caution, which would only occur to someone after reflection.[294]

Now they gradually lost hopes of seeing their ship comrades returned from the land.[295] They had no boats in the ship and because of the rocky coasts, they dared not go nearer to the land with the ship itself. Rather, because a strong west wind began to blow and the ship lay at anchor without any protection toward the open sea, they had to raise the anchor and go to sea again in order not to be driven onto the coasts.[296] Nevertheless, Chirikov circled around in the same region a couple of days and when the weather became milder, he again sailed to the place where his people landed.[297] It must be said in his praise, that he was unwilling to forsake his countrymen on a so-distant coast, and among wild people. But as they neither saw nor heard from them, after the prescribed council with the rest of the sea officers it was decided unanimously to start out on the return voyage to Kamchatka, which was done on 27 July.[298]

IX. BERING

In the meantime, as this happened to Captain Chirikov, Captain Bering attempted to get more detailed information about the coast which he had sighted,[299] and to provide himself there with fresh water. The land had terribly high mountains which were covered with snow. He sailed nearer toward it, but because nothing but slight variable winds were blowing, he could not reach it earlier than 20 July, when he anchored in a depth of 22 fathoms with a soft, clay bottom at a fairly large island not far from the mainland.[300] A point of land which projects into the sea there was named St. Elias Cape, because it was Elias' day.[301] Another point of land, which afterwards appeared towards the west opposite the first, received the name of St. Hermogenes.[302] Between these was a bay, which offered protection, if perhaps their circumstances would cause them to seek a harbor.

For this reason the captain commander sent Fleet Master Khitrov with some armed men to investigate the said bay;[303] at the same time another boat, in which the adjunct Steller traveled, was sent for water.[304] Khitrov found a convenient anchorage between some islands in the bay, where they could lie safely in all winds.[305] But the case did not arise that they needed to use it. On an island he found some empty huts, about which it was presumed that the inhabitants of the mainland kept them there to use for fishing. These huts were made of wood, covered with smooth wooden boards, and the boards were carved in some places, from which it may be concluded that the inhabitants might not be quite so wild and uncivilized as the North Americans are usually described to be.[306] In one hut he found a box made of poplar wood, a hollow earthen ball in which a stone rattled, like a toy for children, and a whetstone on which it appeared that copper knives had been sharpened.[307] So necessity teaches making use of one metal for another. Has one not found also in Siberia at the head of the Enisei River all kinds of cutting tools made of copper, whereas none of iron have been found in the old pagan graves, a proof that the use of copper has been older in those regions than of iron?[308]

From Steller's observations I will mention only the chief.[309] He found a cellar and, in it, a supply of smoked salmon and sweet leaves[310] (*Sphondilium foliolis pinnatifidis* Linn. *Hort. Cliff*. 103) that had been prepared for eating in exactly the way as in Kamchatka. Ropes and all kinds of household utensils also lay in it. He came to a place where the Americans had eaten shortly before, at noon, but when they caught sight of him they had run away.[311] He found an arrow there and a wooden tool to make fire, made in the same way as in Kamchatka[312] (namely a board with various holes, and with it a stick of which one end is put into the holes and the other is turned back and forth quickly between the hands, until the wood burns in the holes, when a tinder is ready to catch the fire and share it further) which the Americans in their flight had left behind them.

On a somewhat distant and forested hill a fire burned, which presumably the people had started there themselves. Steller had a mind to go so far, but a steep cliff blocked the approach.[313] However, he gathered herbs and brought so many of them with him to the ship that he needed a fairly long time to describe them. The descriptions were afterwards used by Gmelin in the *Flora Siberica*.[314] He regretted nothing so much as that he did not have more time permitted to him to look around the American coast; the whole stay lasted only six hours.[315] As soon as they had taken the fresh water, he had to be content to return to the ship.[316]

The ship's people who had gotten the water related that they had found two fireplaces where fire had burned just previously, also hewn wood and paths where men had traveled through the grass. They had seen five red foxes, which went along quite tamely and were not in the least afraid of the arriving strangers. The men brought smoked fish on board with them, which looked like big carp and tasted very good. They had found a hut dug out of the earth, which perhaps is the same as what Steller called a cellar.[317] I compare the reports coming from the various sources as well as I can. It cannot be avoided that occasionally a little difference should be evident.

After they had provided themselves with sufficient water[318] they wanted to show the Americans that they had no reason to flee from their unknown guests. They sent some presents to land for them—a piece of green-glazed linen, two iron kettles, two knives, 20 large coral beads, and a pound of Circassian tobacco leaves[319]—these were things which they believed would be to the taste of the people, and which they carried into the aforesaid huts.

The next day, 21 July, it was decided to go to sea again,[320] and it was also decided to take the course along the coasts as far as 65° north latitude before their departure for Avacha, if their position would allow it. How impossible did they find this attempt? Not only could they sail no further north, but they also had to sail continually more to the south, because the coasts ran towards the southwest. Moreover, the many islands which surrounded the mainland almost everywhere were a continual obstacle.[321] Whenever they believed they were sailing safely, land was seen ahead and on both sides; therefore they were forced to turn around several times, in order to search for another, open passage. At times it happened that, in the night, with the same wind and weather, they sometimes sailed in a heavy, rough sea, sometimes in quiet water, and if this lasted some hours, they came once again among great waves, where the ship could scarcely be governed.[322] What else could this indicate, than that during the calm weather they had located a sheltered passage between the islands, which they had not noticed in the gloomy night?

Some days passed without sighting land when, on 27 July, about midnight, they came to a depth of 20 fathoms.[323] Because it was completely dark, they could not know whether it was a sandbank, or whether they had to be wary of a mainland or an island. They tried to steer now here, now there. Everywhere, however, they found less water. They did not dare to cast anchor because of the strong wind and high waves. Moreover, it was to be feared that they might still be too far from land, or too close to it. Finally it was decided to sail at random towards the south, which succeeded so well that they again reached a safe sea after the depth of 20 fathoms had continued for some hours.[324]

An island which they discovered on 30 July, in foggy weather, was named *Tumannoi Ostrov*, that is, Foggy Island. They arrived at it in 7 or 8 fathoms, and cast the anchor with great haste.[325] But when it cleared they were more than a verst from it. The whole month of August went by with similar events. The ship's crew began to be affected strongly by scurvy, which especially affected the captain commander.[326]

Because fresh water was reduced to a small quantity, they ran toward the north on 29 August and immediately discovered the mainland again, as a broken coast;[327] before it, however, were many islands, among which they anchored.[328] These islands lie in 55°25′ north latitude. They were named Shumagin's Islands, because the first of the ship's crew who died on this voyage, and who was buried there, bore that name.[329] On 30 August the navigator Andreas Hesselberg was sent to the largest island, in order to seek fresh water. He did not remain long, and brought two samples of water which indeed were not perceived as being very good because they tasted somewhat salty, but because there was no time to lose and they thought it was better to have this water than none at all, as they could at least use it to cook (for drinking, however, the remaining supplies could perhaps suffice through careful expenditure), preparations were made to bring on board as much of this water as they could.[330] They took it out of a pond. Steller warned against this, and believed that the seawater flowed into this pond at the time of the tide, and ran out again at the time of the ebb.[331] But in this he could have been mistaken, because it would have been far saltier through repeated mixing with the seawater.[332] Still, be that as it may. Steller afterwards ascribed to this reason all the evil consequences, by which, through the spread of scurvy and other sicknesses, many of the ship's crew became mortally ill.[333]

X. KHITROV

The ship did not lie very securely.[334] Any southern wind might be capable of tearing it loose, and to the north they had nothing but rocks and cliffs in front of them. Therefore they did not dare to lie long at anchor in this spot. But, since during the previous night a fire had been seen toward the north-northeast on a small island,[335] and Fleet Master Khitrov (the officer having the watch at the time) suggested "that while they hauled water with the longboat, the small boat could be sent in order to inquire about the people who made the fire," thus, on account of this assumption, the stay at this place was lengthened. Because of his sickness, the captain commander no longer left his cabin, and Lieutenant Waxell commanded the ship.

The latter did not want to run the risk, in the uncertainty in which the ship lay, of allowing the small boat to go far from him:[336] "Because he believed it was doubtful, if they should be forced by a worse wind to seek the open sea, whether they would be able to aid the people sent out, if they were hindered by contrary and strong winds from returning to the ship." But, as Khitrov persisted in his idea and entered it in the ship's log, Waxell presented the matter to the captain commander for a decision[337] and received the reply: "If Khitrov has the desire to undertake this inquiry they should allow him permission for it, and also to take some of the ship's people with him, whom he could choose himself."[338]

A man of courage, like Khitrov, rejoiced over this opportunity offered to him. He took five men with him, among whom was a Chukchi translator.[339] All were well armed. Some little things were given to them which they were to distribute to the people they might encounter. On 30 August at about noon they got to an island which was estimated to be about three German miles from the ship.[340] There was still fire in the fireplaces, but the people were no longer there. Otherwise they found nothing noteworthy on the island. After midday Khitrov wanted to return to the ship, but a strong contrary wind forced him to take refuge at another island lying to the side—by which he barely saved his life— because the strong and large waves would have swallowed up the small boat or the crew would have been washed off of it. That this did not happen, however, was thanks to a flat sail which Khitrov set in this danger, and sailed with it straight into the waves.[341] With great luck it happened that as one large wave filled the boat entirely with water, another threw it, with all the crew, onto the land.

Immediately after his arrival on this island Khitrov ordered a great fire to be made, partly to dry and warm themselves, partly to give notice to those on the ship so that they might come to their aid. But exactly at that time the wind increased so much that the ship had first to be taken to safety. For that reason they raised the anchor and kept themselves behind another island.[342] In the meanwhile it had gotten dark, and Khitrov, who indeed saw the ship leave but could not know where it had gone, nor what those aboard had decided,[343] fell with his companions into great distress and grief.

This continued until 2 September, when the storm finally lessened. Since Khitrov had not come back that same day, the next morning the large longboat was sent to him with the order that if the smaller boat had been somewhat damaged he should leave it and should come back on board again with the larger one — indeed the little boat had suffered so much damage when it was thrown onto the land by the waves that they did not dare to venture out to sea

106

in it again. It remained on the island, and Khitrov came back to the ship with the large longboat.[344]

Preparations were immediately made to raise the anchor and to go to sea again. However, because of the strong adverse winds they could not go far, but rather towards evening had to seek safety between the islands. So it went until 4 September. Indeed, they went on; but the continuing strong and contrary wind forced them to turn back to the former anchoring place.[345] A violent storm continued all night long.

The next morning they heard a loud cry from men on one of the islands, and also saw a fire burning there.[346] Soon afterwards two Americans came rowing toward the ship in separate canoes which were shaped like those used in Greenland and Davis Strait; they remained, however, at some distance.[347] They knew the calumets, which the North American people were in the habit of using if they wished to express their friendly sentiments. These people held the same in their hands. These were sticks, to which falcon's feathers were bound at one end.[348] The people, through words as well as through their behavior, appeared to invite our seafarers to land; by the same token the latter tried to entice the Americans to the ship, through beckoning and presents which they threw to them.[349] However, the Americans would not allow themselves to be persuaded, but rather turned back to their island.

XI. WAXELL AND STELLER

It was decided to pay them a visit on land. They let the large longboat into the water, in which Lieutenant Waxell and Steller, with a company of nine men, all well provided with arms, went to the island. They found the shore covered with large and sharp rocks, because of which they did not dare to come nearer than three fathoms, especially because the weather was becoming stormy.[350] First they tried to invite the Americans (nine of whom stood on the shore) to the boat through friendly signs and showing them various presents. But this was not successful, and the Americans, on the other hand, invited our Russians to the land; so Waxell ordered three men from his company, among whom was a Chukchi or Koriak translator, to get out and after that to fasten the boat by a rope to the rocks.

It has been noted everywhere that the Chukchi and Koriak interpreters did not understand the speech of these people.[351] But nevertheless they served very well as leaders, because they were bold and were seen by the Americans as similar to themselves.[352] The whole conversation consisted here only of gestures and signs, which showed all friendly intentions on both sides. The Americans wanted to do well by the Russians and gave them whale meat, the only provisions they had with them. They appeared to be there only because of the whale fishing, because our people saw on the coast the same number of canoes as men; on the other hand, there were no huts or women from which it was concluded that their real dwellings were on the mainland.

The canoes were shaped like those they had seen previously; they were completely covered with sealskins and were only large enough to hold one man. In the middle there is a round opening, in which the American, who binds the leather so tightly around his body that not a drop of water can get in, sits. Only one oar, which is paddle-shaped on both ends, is used with it. And thus he travels not only between the islands, which are often situated four or five miles from one another, but also risks himself in the open sea, and in powerful waves which do him no harm even if they sometimes cover him. The agility with which these people are known to keep their balance in such small and long canoes is to be wondered at. They travel so easily in them that it seems as though no effort is required from them.[353]

No bows and arrows or other weapons, of which our Russians had to be fearful, were seen among these Americans.[354] They therefore remained a fairly long time on land and walked around with the Americans; nevertheless, as they were ordered, they did not go out of sight of the longboat.

In the meanwhile, one of the Americans seized enough courage to come to Lieutenant Waxell in the boat.[355] He seemed to be the oldest and most distinguished of them. Waxell gave him a cup of brandy to drink. That was for him, however, an unknown and disagreeable drink. He spit the brandy out again immediately and cried loudly, as if he complained to his countrymen how badly they treated him.[356] There was no remedy remaining to appease him.[357] They wanted to give him needles, glass beads, an iron kettle, tobacco pipes, etc., but he accepted nothing. He desired only to return to the island and they did not think it was good to stop him. On the other hand, Waxell called to his countrymen who were on the land that they should come back.[358]

This did not please the Americans. They made an attempt to keep all three with them. Finally they let the two Russians go, and held only the translator.[359] Some of them took the rope by which the longboat was fastened to the land, and pulled on it as hard as they could. Probably they thought the boat would be drawn on land as easily as their little canoes, or they wished that it would be wrecked between the rocks on the shore.[360] In order to prevent this, Waxell had the rope cut. The translator shouted that they should not abandon him. The urging and beckoning from the boat that the Americans should let him go did not help. Because of this Waxell fired two muskets which, as it only was done with the purpose of frightening them, had the desired effect. Because of the unaccustomed noise, which was augmented even more by the echo from a nearby mountain, all the Americans fell to the ground as if completely dazed, and the translator escaped from their hands.[361] Soon afterwards they recovered from their stupor, made very angry gestures and shouts, and made them to understand that no one should come to the land.[362] At the same time night fell; it was stormy weather and the ship lay a few versts away. Therefore Waxell did not think it advisable to test these people further.

I have said previously that they had noticed no bows and arrows among the Americans. That does not prove that they use none, but rather strengthens the conjecture that at this time they had been only whale fishing, for which such weapons were not used. Only one man had a knife hanging at his side, which to our people appeared noteworthy because of its remarkable design. It was eight inches long and instead of being pointed, was very wide and thick.[363] One cannot guess what the purpose of it was.

Their outer clothing consisted of whale guts, their trousers of sealskins, and their hats were made of the hides of sea lions, which in Kamchatka are called sivucha, and were decorated with various feathers, especially hawks' feathers. They had their noses plugged with grass, which they sometimes removed; then much moisture flowed out, which they licked up with their tongues.

Some of their faces were painted red and some various colors, and they were of various forms, as with the Europeans. Some had flat noses like the Kalmucks. All were pretty tall in stature.[364] It is to be supposed that their food consists mainly of the sea animals which are caught in the waters there. These are the whales, the sea cows (manati), the sea lions (sivucha), the sea bears (koti), the sea beaver—or more often the sea otter (*Lutrae marinae*), and the seals. They also saw them eat roots, which they pulled out of the ground and, before use, only barely shook the earth off.[365] More about their circumstances was not noticed, or at least was not written down.[366]

What further might be added consists of this—that someone asserted he had made himself, to some extent, intelligible to these people through the list of words which Lahontan added to his *Description of North America*,[367] because, if he spoke the words 'water' or 'wood' from the same list, the people had pointed to areas of the land where these were present. But I think this could well have happened by chance, or the gestures which were made with the words might have contributed to their understanding, because Lahontan does not belong among the conscientious and reliable travel writers. And even if he were, the distance between the lands is too great for one and the same language to be spoken in them. Not to mention that a European (especially a Frenchman) could scarcely have comprehended and written the words of such a language so that they could be understood again by another people, who otherwise have almost the same speech.[368]

Lieutenant Waxell thus returned to the ship and, the next morning, made preparations for departure, when seven of the Americans seen the day before came in the same number of canoes, which they brought near to the ship. Two men rose up in the canoes, held themselves by the rope ladders of the ship, and handed over two of their hats and an image of a man carved out of bone, which the crew took to be an idol. The usual peace sign, the calumet, was also again presented to them. It consisted of a five-foot-long stick, on which various feathers without any order were bound at the upper and thinner end.[369] From this it is seen that resemblance of the calumet to Mercury's staff, as the American travel descriptions present, is not absolutely necessary.[370] Presents were given to them in return, and they would certainly have come onto the ship, if a strong wind had not begun to blow, because of which they were prompted to return most hastily to the land. After their return to land they stood in a crowd and raised a great shouting which lasted almost a quarter of an hour. Soon afterwards our people got under sail. And as they passed by the island on which the Americans were, these shouted again as loud as they could, which equally as well might be taken as a friendly indication that they wanted to wish our people a successful voyage as for cheers of joy that they were rid of their foreign guests.[371]

XII. RETURN

They steered mostly southward, in order to get away from the land, and also as there was no other course to hold, because the wind blew from the west and west southwest.[372] From this time on until late fall, when the voyage was finished, the wind seldom alternated other than between WSW and WNW, so they had reason to believe that at this time of the year the western winds blow almost continually in these areas. If an easterly wind arose, it did not last more than a few hours and then was immediately westerly again.[373] Now this was a great obstacle to the speed of their return voyage.[374] Besides, the weather was so continuously foggy that sometimes they did not see the sun by day or the stars at night for two or three weeks. Therefore no observations of latitude could be made; consequently, the ship's positions could not be corrected. It is easy to imagine what anxiety this must have caused our seafarers, who groped around in long uncertainty on an unknown sea. In his account of this voyage, an officer who was there expressed himself about it: "I do not know if there can be a more unpleasant and grim way of living in the world, than sailing on an unknown sea. I speak from experience and can truthfully say that I did not get many peaceful hours of sleep during the five months I was on this voyage and saw no land, because I was in constant fear and uncertainty."[375]

They sailed mostly in adverse winds and in storms until 24 September, when they again came in sight of land, which consisted of very high mountains and many islands lying before them at a fair distance.[376] There they calculated their latitude to be 51°27′ north and their longitude 21°39′ from Petropavlovsk at Avacha. Because it was the day of the conception of St. John the Baptist, one of the highest mountains on the coast was given the name St. John's Mountain.[377]

Subsequently they believed the position of the coast was determined exactly, because they attributed it to be 52°30′ north latitude; this is contradicted, however, in the report of Captain Chirikov, who was also at this coast and declared it to be 51°12′, as we will learn in its place.

Nothing further happened here, since they did not dare to go closer to the coast because of a strong south wind. Rather, it was thought advisable to tack against the wind, which soon afterwards turned into a severe storm from the west and drove the ship back very far to the southeast. The storm lasted continually for 17 days—there are very few examples of the same. At least, the navigator Andreas Hesselberg (who has been mentioned already), a man who had served at sea in various parts of the world for 50 years, professed that he had never experienced such a long, incessantly violent storm.[378] During this time they carried as little sail as they could, in order not to be driven too far off the course. How far they were driven back can be taken in some measure from this: they found themselves at the latitude of 48°18′ on 12 October when the storm subsided.[379] That, however, is only to be understood from the ship's reckoning, because the continually dark weather did not permit making an observation.

Many men on the ship had become sick earlier, but now the attacks of scurvy lasted longer and appeared more frequently.[380] Seldom a day passed when no one died of it.[381] And there were barely enough healthy men remaining to manage the ship.[382]

In these circumstances, it was difficult to decide whether they should try to get back to Kamchatka or seek a harbor on the American coast and winter there. The latter seemed to be required by the general distress, the late season, the lack of fresh water, and, in addition, the very long distance from Petropavlovsk.[383] The former, however, was resolved on in a ship's council.[384] As the wind was favorable, they sailed again toward the north, and after 15 October, toward the west. They passed by an island which they should have seen on their voyage out, given the way the ship's course is shown on the map.[385] Indeed, Steller reported in one account that land had been seen in the same area on the voyage out.[386] But the ship's logbooks contain nothing about it, and it is hard to believe that they would have sought so far for land if they had found it much closer earlier. It is much more likely that a mistake, which can creep in only too easily in an unknown sea, had been made in the determination of the course on the map, or that the island had been concealed in fog on the voyage out. This island was named after St. Macarius; the others, which followed in the west, received the names St. Stephan, St. Theodore, and St. Abraham.[387]

Two islands to which they came on 29 and 30 October were left without names, because they resembled the first two Kurile Islands in their position, size, and other external features, and for which these were taken.[388] For that reason they took their course toward the north, but, as later times showed, would have needed to continue toward the west for only a couple of days to come to Avacha

111

harbor.[389] Therefore, I call these islands the Seduction Islands (Isles de la Seduction).[390] The seduction caused by them, however, had the worst conclusion.

Then, as the long-hoped-for Kamchatka coast was not revealed to the west, there was, consequently, so late in the year, no hope of a harbor, and the crew, notwithstanding their need, misery, and sickness, had to work constantly in the cold and wet; everyone fell into despair because of it.[391] It went so far that the sailors who were to attend the rudder had to be led to that place by two other sick ones, who could still walk a little. If one was no longer capable of sitting and steering, another—in not better condition—came to his place. They did not dare to set many sails, because in case of an emergency there was no one to take them in again. Also, the sails were already so thin and worn that any strong wind would have torn them to pieces; and, among other reasons, they were not in condition because of the lack of able men.[392]

The continual rains now began to turn to hail and snow.[393] The nights became ever longer and darker, and with that risk increased because they could not for a moment be certain about the safety of the ship. At the same time an almost complete lack of fresh water developed. The few people who were on their feet could no longer endure so much work. They excused themselves with this impossibility and wished for themselves only an early death—which they saw as inevitable—and much preferable to such a miserable life.[394]

The ship remained for a few days without any government. It lay like a log on the water and was left naked to the winds and waves, wherever these wanted to drive it. No strictness could have been used against the despairing crew. It was far better that the lieutenant in command urged the men with kindness: "They should not despair so completely of God's help, but on the contrary, they should use their remaining strength for the rescue of all, which perhaps was nearer than they believed."[395] Thus some allowed themselves to be persuaded to remain on deck and they resolved to work as long as it was possible for them.[396]

This was the condition of the ship when, early in the morning of 4 November, they began to sail toward the west without knowing in what latitude they were or how far they might still be from Kamchatka.[397] How could they know this, since it had not been possible to take observations in such a long time? Consequently the ship's reckoning, since it remained so long without correction, must have daily increased in uncertainty.[398] However, a westerly course was the only one by which they could still hope to get back to Kamchatka. And how glad they were soon after that when, at eight o'clock in the morning, they were able to see land![399]

They tried to come near it. However, it still lay far off, for at the beginning they saw only mountaintops which were covered with snow. And, although they could have reached it, night fell, during which it was advisable to heave to, in order not to put the ship in danger. For this reason, during the night as much sail was set as was necessary to keep from going to the land.[400] The next morning, however, they saw that most of the ropes on the starboard side of the ship were split. Nothing more was lacking to make the misfortune complete. Because, since almost all the men were sick, nobody could remedy this evil.[401]

Lieutenant Waxell, who gave a report of this to the captain commander, received an order to call all the higher and lower officers together and deliberate, which was done.[402] They deliberated. They took into consideration the imminent danger to all that the ship would be unfit for a further voyage because of its bad rigging. They knew that the ropes still remaining were just as fragile. They heard some tearing in the course of their council.[403] The lack of water and the sickness of the crew increased continually and, as before, the constant dampness caused great discomfort. The cold was now painful and the late season promised no relief from it, rather threatened an increase in the same. From all of this a resolution followed: to go to the land they had sighted[404] and try at least to save their lives there.[405] Perhaps the ship could be taken to safety, but if this was not possible, they should leave their further destiny to Providence.

Immediately they steered toward the land, though only with a few sails because of the weakness of the masts. The wind was northerly and they sailed WSW and SW. The lead showed a depth of 37 fathoms and a sand bottom.[406] A couple of hours later, at 5 o'clock in the evening, the lead gave them a depth of 12 fathoms and still the same bottom. At that time an anchor was cast, with which they let out three-fourths of the rope. At six o'clock the rope was torn to pieces. Huge waves drove the ship onto a reef, where it struck heavily twice, although by the lead the depth was still found to be five fathoms. At the same time the waves repeatedly beat over the ship with such intensity that the whole ship shook from it. They let the second anchor fall, the rope of which was torn immediately, before they could notice that the anchor had set in the bottom.[407] In all of this it was particularly fortunate that no other anchor was ready.[408] They would have also, in the distress in which they found themselves, cast and lost the last anchor. A great wave pitched the ship off the reef, even as they were going to make still another anchor ready.[409]

All at once they came to calm water and lay at anchor in 4 $1/2$ fathoms with sandy bottom, some 300 fathoms from land. The following day they saw what luck the delay had given them, and how miraculously merciful Providence had led them to this—though highly dangerous, nevertheless the only place where they could find their salvation. The coast was surrounded everywhere by high cliffs protruding far into the sea, except for this place, where it was possible to land. It appeared that the hidden reef over which the ship had come had formerly made up the coast, and had been torn off from it, perhaps by an earthquake. It stretched lengthwise in front of the coast. Through it was a narrow channel to the land, the same that our mariners had met with so fortunately. Had they come only about 20 fathoms more to the north or south, the ship would certainly have been wrecked and in the dark night there would have been nothing to save them.[410]

XIII. BERING ISLAND

Since they had to winter there, their first concern was to look about the land, in order to search for the most convenient place for this. After having a little rest till midday, the completely exhausted crew got the boat into the water, but not without great effort. On 6 November, at one o'clock in the afternoon, Lieutenant Waxell and Adjunct Steller went onto the land, which was entirely covered with snow.[411] A stream rushing down from a mountain and falling into the sea not far from the landing place was still not frozen and carried clear, good water. They saw, however, no forest and not even firewood, other than what the sea had washed ashore. And this was already covered with snow and not easy to find. What could be used to build houses or barracks? Where could they put the sick?[412] How could they protect themselves from the cold? Necessity is the mother of invention. Near the said stream lay many sandhills between which fairly deep holes were found. They decided to clear the bottom of these somewhat and cover them over with sails, so they could at least live in them long enough to find enough driftwood to be able to build huts from, however bad they might be. Toward evening Lieutenant Waxell and Steller went back and reported what they had seen to the captain commander.[413]

It was decided to send to the land early the next morning as many men as were still on their feet, so that they could first of all make some suitable holes between the sandhills to house the sick. This happened. On 8 November they began to bring the sick onto land.[414] Some died, however, as soon as they came to the open air on the deck, others during the time they were on deck, others in the boat, and still others as soon as they were brought on land.

How eagerly the blue foxes, which live there in great numbers, rushed toward the corpses! It was noticed that they were not scared away by the men, as if, as it seemed, they now walked on this land for the first time. Therefore, they were not fearful in the least and did not run away, if someone approached them. It was difficult to keep them from the dead bodies. Some of these, already given Last Rites, had their hands and feet eaten before they could be buried in the earth.[415] This circumstance gave further cause to expect that this land must be an island. And in reality it was one, the certainty of which was later demonstrated by further experiences.

On 9 November Captain Commander Bering, fully protected from the outer air, was brought to land on a litter (which consisted of two poles connected by ropes) carried by four men. A special cave had been readied for him.[416] The putting ashore of the sick continued every day. But every day some also died, who had to be buried. None of those who had become bedridden on the ship

114

recovered from it.[417] These were, however, chiefly those whose indifference and despair over it had contributed much to the spread of the illness so far with them.

Because this evil takes its beginning as a weakness over the whole body, making everyone lazy and sullen, entirely depressing the mind and gradually causing a shortness of breath with the least exercise, the sick person prefers to lie still rather than move around. This, however, is his ruin. For this is followed by aching in all the limbs and swelling of the feet; the face turns completely yellow and the body is full of blue spots. The mouth and the gums bleed, and all the teeth become loose. Then the sick person generally does not care to move, but becomes equally indifferent to life or death. Gradually all of these stages of the illness and the accompanying effects were seen on the ship. Some of the sick people were observed to be subject to a terrible anxiety, so that any noise and clamor (which on a ship is unavoidable) immediately put them in great fear. Yet many ate with good appetites, not believing themselves to be as sick as they in fact were. For when the order was issued that the sick should be brought on land they were very happy—they stood up, put on their clothes, and believed they would now soon recover. However, when they came from their beds (which were in the lower part of the ship where the air was damp and filled with many strange particles) to the deck into the open air outside, that was their end.[418]

They handled it well who did not allow the sickness to overpower them into constantly lying in bed, and who forced themselves to remain as much as possible on their feet and in motion. They had their lively dispositions to thank that they had not lost heart. Such served their fellow men excellently by their example and by constant encouragement. This was noted especially among the officers, who were constantly employed in things relating to the command and had to spend most of their time on deck so that nothing would be neglected. They always had a great deal of exercise.[419] They could not lose heart, because they had Steller with them. Steller was a doctor who at the same time ministered to the spirit; he cheered everyone with his lively and agreeable company.[420]

But all this did not help the captain commander. His age and his constitution caused him to have more of an inclination toward rest than toward motion. Near the end he became mistrustful, and viewed everyone as an enemy; even Steller, of whom he had formerly been very fond, dared not come into his presence.[421]

Waxell and Khitrov remained fairly healthy as long as they were at sea. They remained on the ship the longest, both because they wanted to convey everything to the land first and because they had various conveniences on the ship. This, however, made them very ill. Was it the lack of movement, or did the vapors of the sick rising from the hold have this effect? In a few days they were so sick that on 21 November they had to be carried off the ship. They were brought to land like the others. Since experience had already taught that they must be careful in leaving the ship and entering the open air, the sick were wrapped up carefully, and were not allowed to partake of the open air freely until they were gradually accustomed to it. Afterwards both regained their former health, though Khitrov later than Waxell.

The captain commander died on 8 December, and had the honor that the island was named Bering Island after him. He was a Dane by birth and had already in his youth traveled to the East and West Indies,[422] when he was enticed by the great inclination of the immortal Emperor Peter the Great toward maritime affairs to seek his fortune in Russia. I have somewhere found that he had been a lieutenant in 1707, and in 1710 a captain lieutenant in the Russian fleet. When he became captain I cannot exactly determine, because he served with this same rank in the Kronstadt fleet from its first beginning and was present at all the undertakings at sea in the Swedish war at that time. He combined the skill proper to his office with long experience, which made him especially deserving of such an extraordinary business as the discoveries that were twice entrusted to him.[423] It is to be lamented that he had to end his life in such an unfortunate way. One could say that his still-living body was half buried, because the sand continually rolled down the sides of the hole in which he lay, and covered his feet. In the end he no longer permitted it to be cleared away. He felt some warmth from it, he said, which otherwise was lacking in other parts of his body. And thus the sand heaped up to his stomach; so that after his death they had to first scrape the sand away in order to bury him in a proper way in the earth.[424]

XIV. CHIRIKOV

Such adverse fortune befell not only this ship; Captain Chirikov, on his part, had not less to suffer. We have already learned how on 27 July he set out from that most distant American coast on his return voyage. It was in every respect accompanied with exactly the same accidents as the captain commander's voyage was. Always contrary winds; always obstacles from coasts and islands which they lamented most sorrowfully not to have discovered on the outward voyage.[425] Indeed, he had still an additional inconvenience, namely this—that he could nowhere supply himself with fresh water because of the loss of his two longboats.

On 20 September, at the latitude of 51°12', he came to a coast which appears to have been none other than the one the captain commander arrived at four days later.[426] This coast was so surrounded by reefs—the tops of which projected out of the water—that they had to take all pains to escape a danger which, in going closer, would have been inevitable. They were compelled to cast the anchor 200 fathoms from it.[427] Twenty-one of the inhabitants of the island came rowing toward them, each in his own leather canoe, acting in a friendly way as if they wanted to help our people, and at the same time amazed at the ship, which they could not look at enough. However, no one could talk with them.[428] They also did not dare to stop, because the anchor rope was torn to pieces on the reefs, and they sought only to reach the open sea again, which although they succeeded still was of little advantage on the voyage because of the continual adverse winds.[429]

As the supply of fresh water began to decrease, they thought to help themselves by distilling sea water. In this way they removed the salt from it, but a peculiar bitterness remained. Yet there was no other remedy than mixing the distilled sea water equally with the remaining fresh water and distributing this in small portions so it would last all the longer.[430] What a joy whenever it rained in such distress! For then they refreshed themselves with the collected rain water and had no qualms about the sails, out of which it was pressed.[431]

One will easily imagine that at the same time this condition promoted scurvy,[432] by which on Chirikov's ship not a few of them were snatched away. The captain himself lay continuously sick after 20 September. On 26 September the constable Joseph Kachikov died; on 6 October Lieutenant Chikhachev; on 7 October Lieutenant Plautin.[433] Finally, on 8 October the land of Kamchatka came into view, and on the ninth they entered the Bay of Avacha. On the tenth de la Croyère, who had already been sick for a long time, wanted to go to land; when he came on deck, however, he fell dead.[434] From the total of 70 men who had made up the whole ship's company, gradually 21 died. The navigator Elagin, the only officer still healthy, brought the ship back to Petropavlovsk on the eleventh, after it had spent more than four months on this voyage.[435]

The following spring Captain Chirikov, who meanwhile had recovered from his sickness, sailed about in the sea[436] in order that he might come across the captain commander, and after that sailed to Okhotsk; from there he traveled to Iakutsk and waited for further orders from St. Petersburg. He had to stay some time at Eniseisk. When he returned to St. Petersburg he was appointed captain commander. However, he died soon thereafter,[437] and earned the renown he won with everyone, that he had been so able and energetic a seaman; indeed he had also possessed a great deal of honesty and fear of God, and therefore his memory would not easily pass into oblivion for those who knew him.

XV. THE WINTERING

We return to Bering Island, where shortly before the death of the captain commander the company had the additional misfortune to lose their chief comfort and hope, the only means by which they, in their opinion, could be delivered from their predicament—that is, the ship.[438] It lay at anchor, as we have already seen, toward an open sea. There was nobody left on it as a guard, because they needed the few men who were still on their feet for nursing the sick and for other duties. When, on the night of 28 to 29 November, a severe storm arose out of the east southeast, the anchor rope tore and the ship was thrown onto the land not far from the spot where our people lay in the hollows, and filled with sand to a depth of eight to nine feet.[439] The bottom or the sides had to have been badly damaged at the same time, because they observed that the sea water came in from below with the tide and ran out again with the ebb. Thus much of the flour, groats, and salt was lost, because most of it was still in the ship and, although they saved some of it, little by little, at low tide, it still had received much damage.[440] Was this not, however, an extraordinary stroke of luck that the ship was thrown on land, rather than being driven out to sea? In the latter case would not the people have had to remain for all their lives on this desert island, because no wood grew on it from which they could have built a new vessel?[441] Thus, hope still remained if the ship itself could not be made serviceable again, to build a smaller one out of its wreckage in order to return to Kamchatka. However, no one thought of that at the time. They yielded themselves to their fate and were only intent on preserving their lives as long as possible, for which purpose the following preparations were made.

First, it was necessary to explore the land where they were—whether it was a mainland or an island, because at the outset they could not know this immediately.[442] They saw rocky mountains in front of them, which seemed to indicate the former, and as a matter of fact, this island may indeed have formerly been a part of the mainland, from which it had been separated sometime by earthquakes. They wanted to know whether inhabitants might not be found, from whom they could get help. It was important to learn if woodlands might be in the distance, and what in the way of animals and other works of Nature the land offered. Because our unfortunates inhabited the eastern shore of the island, people were first sent toward the north and south who went as far as the high rocks projecting into the sea would permit them.[443] Some came back in two days, others in three. Their unanimous report was that they had not met men anywhere, not even a trace of them.[444] Everywhere along the coast, however, they had found many sea beavers, namely, the same as in Kamchatka are called beaver which really should be called sea otters (*Lutra marina Marggravii, Brasiliensium Jaga s. Carigueibeiu*).[445] Farther inland they had seen a great many arctic foxes, both blue and white, which had been not in the least shy, from which it was concluded that these animals had never seen any men before.[446] After this, people were sent inland. Some 12 to 15 versts from the coast they came to a high mountain, and saw toward the west an open sea, as they had in view toward the east.[447] Now they were convinced that they were on an island. Forests were nowhere to be seen. During the winter they found driftwood so seldom that they barely had enough to burn, for they had to search it out laboriously from under the snow.[448] But as the snow left there was no further lack of it, a proof that a wooded land from which the wood was washed ashore must be close at hand.

The greatest width of the island was estimated to be some 20 versts; its length, however, stretching from the southeast to the northwest, was not exactly investigated. Since it lies in the same latitude as the mouth of the Kamchatka River, the distance between the two was calculated, during the succeeding voyage, as 30 German miles.[449] Everywhere there were many high mountains and cliffs, between which, in the valleys, high grass grew and there was usually good, fresh water. Low bushes grew along some of the little streams; however, because the branches were no more than a finger thick they were not useful.[450] They tried to see if a place could be found somewhere on the coast where a ship could anchor, safe from the winds, but none was discovered. The tide rose from seven to eight feet. They noticed no land animals except the arctic foxes, and more blue ones than white. Their hair was not as soft as that of the Siberian foxes, which perhaps can be blamed on the difference in food and air.[451]

Prudence required an estimate to be made of how large the food supply was and how long they would last with it. Accordingly, they adjusted the distribution of the portions, which, although about 30 people died of sickness on the island, were by and by so small that no one could have lived on them if the flesh of the sea animals had not proved useful in this scarcity.[452] Eight hundred pounds of flour were reserved for use on the future voyage, if they should be lucky enough to put into condition a vessel with which they could return to Kamchatka.[453] Here the rank of a person did not matter. Officers and commons received equal portions,[454] and they all ate together, though in different companies, the same way as they lived separated from each other in the hollows. Therefore no real command could be followed according to the prescribed rules. Because, even though immediately after the captain commander's death Lieutenant Waxell took command, he did not dare to punish anyone out of fear that they might repay him in a forceful way.[455]

Concerning the sea animals which served as food: at the beginning they had none other than the beavers mentioned above, whose flesh, however, especially that of the male, was found distasteful, very hard, and tough as leather, so that they could barely chew it. They had to cut it into very small pieces that could simply be swallowed.[456] One beaver may provide about 40 to 50 pounds of pure flesh. The entrails and intestines were mostly used as food for the sick. Steller has accurately described some of these sea animals; the treatise is inserted in the *Commentaries* of the Academy of Sciences.[457] In it he presents the meat of the beaver as a remedy against scurvy and asserts that if they recovered from the sickness they had it to thank for their health. But how many of the sick, who ate the beaver meat, also died? The sickness lasted long enough that one can ascribe the eventual recovery from it to other causes.[458] They killed a great multitude of beaver also when they no longer needed the flesh as food, because of their beautiful skins, for every one of which the Chinese at the Kiakhta border usually pay a price of from 80 to 100 rubles.[459] That was a comfort for our shipwrecked crew. They collected nearly 900 of these skins, which were divided among everyone. But here nobody was luckier than Steller. As a doctor he received many skins as presents, and many others he acquired from those who, in the uncertainty over whether they would ever again meet with men, did not value these goods. His share alone is said to have amounted to nearly 300 beaver skins, which he brought back to Kamchatka and Siberia.[460] The animals indeed, gradually learned to flee their pursuers.[461] Often however, animals were found asleep or as they mated. In the latter case they were so beside themselves with lust that it required little effort or skill to kill them.

It also happened that a dead whale was thrown onto the island by the sea at the beginning of winter, which, although they had to go five versts for it, caused great joy among our people. It was nearly eight fathoms long, and perhaps might have been floating in the sea a long while, because the fat was already somewhat sour. But that did not prevent its use. Our people called the whale their storehouse because if other animals were lacking they could always be sure of it. The fat was cut in little square pieces and boiled a long time in water, by which most of the fluid train oil was separated from it. Whatever hard or sinewy parts then remaining were, like the flesh, swallowed whole.[462] Then, toward spring, the sea brought them another whale which was fresher than the previous one, and it was used in the same way.

The beaver disappeared in March. Instead another animal appeared, which in Kamchatka is called a sea cat (koti morskie) because of the long hair which projects on both sides of its mouth, as with cats.[463] Dampier, on his voyage on the other side of the equator, encountered it frequently and described it, giving it the name of sea bear.[464] The western coast of the island was, so to speak, covered with them. These animals keep together in families so that a male, who generally has from 15 to 20 wives, cares for these and all his children at sea as well as on land, until they begin their own households. The largest weigh from 18 to 20 puds, that is, about 800 pounds. It is a very wild and aggressive animal which is difficult to approach. They killed no more than was absolutely necessary, for the flesh has a very repugnant, rank taste[465] and the skins are hardly good for anything, except those of the very young and unborn (viporoshiki), which are in some measure suitable as furs.[466] Mostly they were killed while they slept, because in the springtime the oldest, glutted with fat, spend a few months sleeping without taking any food at all, like the true bears in winter.[467]

When these took their leave at the end of May, for some time the crew had no other sustenance than the seals.[468] There were not only the usual ones here, but also the larger species which in Kamchatka are called lakhtak.[469] They are as big as an ox, and weigh about 800 pounds. But as the flesh is disgusting in taste and the men were soon tired of it, it was lucky that sometimes they could catch young sea lions, from which they had so much better sustenance.

The sea lions are the animals which are called sivucha in Kamchatka. They are twice as big as the largest sea bears, and weigh from 36 to 40 puds, that is, about 1600 pounds. Their short yellow hair differentiates them from the rest of the sea animals. They pursue the sea bears; this is surely the reason that the sea bears so frequently take refuge on the coasts. The sea lions seldom go there; they post themselves mostly on big reefs and cliffs which lie in the sea at some distance from the coast and which, to all appearances, were thrown up there from the land by earthquakes. There these animals raise such a terrible roar that it can be heard at a distance of 3 to 4 versts. All other animals flee as soon as a sea lion appears. Their strong and grim appearance reveals their aggressiveness. Therefore our ship's company did not like to attack them.[470] They killed only a few of the old sleeping ones; the young ones, whose flesh was found especially tasty, were killed more often. Dampier had described them before Steller.[471] The similarity with a lion consists only in the somewhat long upright hair, which grows around the neck of the male.[472]

Lastly, they also sometimes ate the flesh of the animal which in Russian, as well as in Dutch and English, is called the sea cow (*korova morskaia*); the Spanish call it the *manati*, and French the *lamentin*.[473] One would think that the similarity to a cow must be very great, if the different people and travelers (who most certainly could have known nothing of each other) saw it, because they were accustomed to giving a name to an unknown thing at first sight. But this similarity consists in nothing more than the snout, which I suspect was the only part they caught sight of at first,[474] because there are neither horns, nor protruding ears, nor feet, nor anything else that resembles a cow to see. It is an animal like the seal, only tremendously bigger. There are two fins in the front part of its body, which it uses for swimming. Between them the females have two teats for nursing their young. This nature of the parts, which is somewhat similar to the human (especially because the mothers can use the fins to hold their young to the teats) is the reason for the Spanish name manati; i.e., an animal with hands, for the Spaniards compared the fins to human hands. It was called lamentin by the French because it does not usually cry loudly, but more or less only whines or sighs.[475] Christopher Columbus is said to have taken it for the Siren of the ancients. When it swims in the sea, a part of the back generally rises out of the water, which is said to appear like an overturned boat floating on the sea.[476] It is found not only in these waters, but rather in all the seas around Asia, Africa, and America. Therefore many travelers, such as Lopez, Dampier, Kolb, Atkins, and Labat have mentioned it,[477] but they commonly contradict one another, which also has given occasion for the many errors in the natural histories of Clusius, Johnston, Raius, Klein, Artedi, Linnaeus and others—to remedy all this Steller's description is hardly sufficient.[478] A particular species of this animal dwells in the Amazon River in South America, of which Mr. de la Condamine gives a report in his book of travels.[479]

In the Tübingen *Berichten von gelehrten Sachen* of 1752, p. 74, in connection with the *Historia quadrupedum* of Mr. Klein,[480] a sea animal which appears both in the Icy Sea and in the Okhotsk and Kamchatka seas and which is called by the Russians there *beluga* (because of its white skin) is held to be the same as the sea cow or manati.[481] Here, however, one cannot agree with the author. The sea animal beluga, which is indeed to be differentiated from the beluga fish, which lives in the Volga, and also in the Iaik, Don, and Dnieper (in the Donau[482] this fish is called the sturgeon), is indeed not fully known; some features, however, which have been told to me, are sufficient to make its difference from the manati clear.[483] The former has a white skin, from which the name originates; the latter, a black skin. The former has thin hair over its whole body; the latter is entirely smooth. The former feeds on fish; the latter on grass. The former sometimes comes to the Okhotsk Sea, namely in the region of the Uda River, because in this river the fish seek safety for themselves from the sea (which gives the inhabitants of Uda ostrog a rich fishery); however, one hears nothing about the manati in the same area. And is the same not shown also by the difference in the Russian names, both of which are commonly used in the same area, for example, in Kamchatka and at Anadyr ostrog, where the inhabitants know both animals? This is all the more necessary to remember, as it appears that my one-time traveling companion, the deceased Professor Gmelin, is the author of the article in the Tübingen scholarly papers; in view of his great knowledge of natural history, other teachers of this science could easily follow him.[484] Through it, however, an error, which had a quite innocent origin, was propagated. For Gmelin it was only an error of memory. If he had been less overloaded with work, he could have easily revised this from his own travel observations, because in these are found the same and still more details, as I have already shown. He described the beluga as an animal that has feet and a tail similar to the seal. It is supposed to be from 15 to 20 feet long, and is from three to four feet thick. It has teeth like a cow. The skin is very white, and is described by some people as scaled, by others as smooth. According to some reports it is said to have no hair; according to others, which deserve more confidence, the hair is said to be so thin that the white skin shines through strongly all over it. And that is logical because the animal gets its name from the white color. At the nape of the neck there are two air holes, like those of whales, out of which it spouts water a few fathoms high. Under the skin, which is said to be as thick as the strongest oxhide, there is blubber from two to three thumbs thick. A tough flesh follows after that which is similar to the color and smell of seal flesh and therefore was not eaten except in the most extreme emergencies. It eats all species of fish. It is said to travel in crowds and the little young ones are carried on their backs. One never sees it on the land, nor even close to the shore. It has to be most wary of shallow places, and because of that does not go up the rivers. It is the most numerous at the mouth of the Enisei River. Mr. Gmelin has written these reports at Eniseisk and Turukhansk, just as I wrote mine down at Iakutsk.[485] The famous Witsen (*Noord en Oost Tartarye*, second edition, p. 955)[486] recounts that the beluga usually come into the rivers Mezen and Iaesma (the latter of which joins with the former at its mouth) with the tide and return to sea with the ebb. At that time the fishermen are said to lie in wait for these animals. They stretch a net made of strong and thick rope from 200 to 300 fathoms long across the Iaesma River. The beluga entangle themselves in it when they try to return, and are killed with spears. They are said to be two to three fathoms long, and give 2 1/2 tons of train oil. If the catch is good, a ship of 200 tons can get its whole load in two days. Thus indicated Witsen. I have also been assured that beluga carrying their young on their backs have been seen at times in the Dvina near Arkhangelsk, indeed even at Kholmogory. The blow holes could have produced the idea that it is a species of whale; the white skin, however, that it is the same species called whitefish by members of the Greenland expedition. (*Albus piscis cetaceus raii.* G. Anderson's *Nachrichten von groenland*, p. 224).[487] One can believe as he wishes; the matter deserves to be more closely investigated and it is really to be wished that a lover of natural history at Arkhangelsk might remove all doubts with an exact description of the beluga.

I return to my purpose of reporting how useful the manati was to our ship's company for their sustenance. The caught animals were three to four fathoms long from the nose to the end of the tail and weighed 200 puds, or 8,000 pounds. One of them provided enough to live on for 14 days.[488] Moreover the flesh was very tasty, like the best beef; indeed, that of the young animals was like veal.[489] The sick men felt noticeably better if they ate the manati rather than the disgusting and hard beaver flesh. But it required effort to catch an animal. They never came on the land, but rather only near the coast to eat the sea grass that grows on the coast, or was thrown out by the sea. This good diet may have contributed much to the fact that its flesh was not of a disagreeable taste as with the others, which ate fish. The young ones, which nonetheless weighed about 1200 pounds or more, were occasionally left high and dry between the rocks when the water ran off at low tide. That was a good opportunity to kill them. The old ones, however, which were more cautious and went away at the right time with the ebb, could not be caught in any other way than with harpoons on which long ropes were fastened. Many a time the ropes broke and the animal escaped before it could be struck a second time. As a rule this animal was seen in the winter as well as in summer. The crew melted out the fat, with which it was covered, like the bacon of hogs, from three to four fingers thick, and used it like butter. Several barrels full of the meat were salted as ship's provisions, which did excellent service on the return voyage.[490]

XVI. RETURN TO KAMCHATKA

As the month of March neared its end and the ground was becoming free from snow, Lieutenant Waxell called together the remaining people from the crew of the ship, of which there were 45, to confer and to make a decision about how the return voyage could best be accomplished. Here the lowest sailor had the same right to give his opinion as the commanding officer. Therefore various opinions were given, which, when they were not acceptable, first had to be refuted with reasons and cleared out of the way in order to make room for the one which was the surest and most suitable.[491] For example, some believed they should make a deck out of sailcloth for the open ship's boat, and otherwise put it in condition of seaworthiness. They should have six people sail straight west in it, in order to make the state of affairs on the island known to people found in Kamchatka, and to ask for help from there. That might indeed have been possible in calm weather, but who could guarantee that during this voyage a storm would not arise, and bury the boat with the people between the waves? Was it certain that they would find Captain Chirikov or another seagoing vessel that could help them in Kamchatka? Would those remaining on the island not be in terrible doubt? Should they in the meanwhile put their hands in their laps and run the risk of spending still another winter on the island? That was a painful thought! Finally they thought it would be more advantageous to immediately seize upon a means which promised more certainty and by which everyone could be helped at one time.[492]

Some of them wanted to consider this—that they should make an effort to take the ship from the beach back into deep water and to repair it where it was damaged, so that it could be used on the voyage.[493] But how was that possible? The ship lay with its bottom buried in nine feet of sand. They did not know whether it still had a bottom, or whether this was in pieces. Assuming, however, it were whole, some 40 men would not be enough to get the ship afloat. And where would they get beams, in order to bring the ship out of the sand?[494] To dig a canal from the ship to the sea, as some suggested, in order to bring it into deep water, was not possible because the shore where the ship lay consisted of quicksand which upon digging would fill in immediately, to say nothing of the piles of sand that would be washed up again with the incoming tide every time and thereby defeat the work.[495]

Therefore Waxell and Khitrov presented a proposal to break up the ship and to build a smaller vessel from its wood, in which everyone, with as much food as was necessary for 14 days, had a place. That way those who had suffered together would be rescued together from their distress. Should any new misfortune develop, they could remain together and no one would reproach the other. This was chosen unanimously, and a document was drawn up, which everyone confirmed with his signature.[496] But it did not lack opposition later, since some wanted no hand in breaking up a ship that had been built at the expense of the crown; but the opponents had to settle for the previous goal, because they were outvoted in a new council meeting.[497] In the beginning of the month of April they made a start at unrigging and breaking up the wreck, a task which lasted the whole month through, and at which the officers were always the first on the job, in order that the common man be all the more encouraged to industry by their example.[498]

Now the greatest difficulty was in who should direct the shipbuilding, for they lacked a ship's carpenter,[499] three of whom had set out on the voyage, but died on the island. Fortunately, a Siberian cossack born at Krasnoiarsk named Sava Starodubsov, who had been employed as a worker by a shipbuilder at Okhotsk, volunteered to direct the work if only they would give him the proportions of the vessel. And in fact the cossack kept his word as well as they could have wished. For this he was, after his return, favored by the Eniseisk provincial chancellery with *syn boiarskii*, which is the lowest rank of Siberian nobility. On 6 May a vessel of a length of 40 feet at the keel, a breadth of 13 feet and a depth of 6 1/2 feet was laid out.[500] At the end of the same month all stem posts were put in, so that at the beginning of June they could begin to hang these with planks on the exterior as well as the interior.[501] It was covered, and it received a mast, a cabin at the back and forward a kitchen, and on each side four oars. For caulking there was no lack of hemp and old tackle. Because the stock of tar was not sufficient they helped themselves in the following manner.[502] They took a new anchor rope which had never been in the water, cut it in pieces a foot long, unraveled the strands from each other, and with them filled a large copper kettle for which they made a tight-fitting lid with a hole in the middle. Then they took a wooden vessel, made for it a similar perforated lid and buried this up to the lid in the earth. On it they overturned the copper kettle so that cover and cover and hole and hole came together. They filled earth around the kettle far enough so that no fire could penetrate the wooden vessel. Next the kettle, which was now inverted, and more than half of which was above ground, was surrounded with fire. The tar found in the rope melted from the heat and collected in the wooden vessel below. By this means they received enough so that the bottom part of the vessel could be tarred. The upper part was smeared with melted tallow.[503] They built a canoe in exactly this way, which could hold about eight to ten men; and, while all this was happening, masts, sails, ropes, anchors, water casks, and sea provisions were provided and everything put in ready condition.[504]

At the end of the month of July there was nothing left to do but to make the slides on which the vessel could be let into the water.[505] These were about 25 fathoms long, for the vessel could not be laid out very near the sea because of the quite high tide. It was let down from the stocks on 10 August and was named the *St. Peter*, after the packet-boat from whose wood it was built. One could call it a one-masted hooker because in its rigging it came closest to this kind of vessel.[506] A quantity of cannon balls and grape-shot, and all the iron-work remaining from the former ship had to serve as ballast. The mast was set; the tackle, sails, and accompanying oars were properly prepared. Fortunately, there was continual calm at this time, without which they would have had trouble. The ship was launched where there was open sea for half of the com-pass, from NNW to SSE. If a storm had arisen it could easily have been beached on the coast. It drew five feet. They could have loaded it deeper, but this was enough for the intended purpose.[507]

After everyone had gotten on board, they put away from land toward evening on 16 August.[508] The previous ship's boat was towed by a rope, though only as a trial, to see if they could keep it with them. If that could not be done, they would set it adrift. The reefs and other shallow places were passed over by warping. They found four, five, seven, and nine fathoms water. Afterwards the oars were used. When they came by this means some two German miles from land, a slight north wind began to blow, with which they continued the voyage. It was surprising that the vessel sailed so well, and turned so easily. It could not have sailed much better had it been built by a real master.[509] The following noon, they had in view, at a distance of two miles toward north by east, the southeast-ern point of Bering Island, to which they gave the name Cape Manati. The sea cows noted previously, which were more numerous there than in other places, were the reason for the name. The latitude of this cape is 54°55′ or about 55° north, whereas the place of the wintering was observed to be almost under 56°. In the morning of 18 August they encountered a strong adverse wind from the southwest, because of which it was decided to cut away the large boat so that its burden could not damage the little vessel.[510] The same day about noon the vessel began to leak considerably. Two pumps were not sufficient to draw out the water. They had to use buckets to help bail the water out through the large hatchways. Many cannon balls, much grape-shot, and other heavy things were thrown into the sea to lighten the vessel, and to discover the place where it leaked. It was discovered, and the further entry of the water was controlled, though not entirely, as well as it could be. Afterwards they had to use only one pump, and even this not constantly. On 25 August they came into sight of the land of Kamchatka,[511] whereupon on 26 August they entered the Bay of Avacha safely, and on the 27th they entered into Petropavlovsk harbor.

What joy this produced in our seafarers will easily be imagined by everyone.[512] All the hardship and danger that they had been so repeatedly exposed to was now over. They came to a full supply depot that Captain Chirikov had left behind.[513] They wintered also there, after they had tried to return to Okhotsk that same fall with this very vessel, which the contrary and strong winds did not permit.[514]

Meanwhile, the vessel was put into condition in Petropavlovsk so that it could again go under sail in May of the following year, 1743, and could take the whole command back to Okhotsk.[515] From there Waxell himself proceeded to Iakutsk and further, after he wintered there, to Eniseisk, where, on his arrival there in October, 1744, he met Captain Chirikov because the latter had received an order from the Senate to remain in an inexpensive place, until a decision about the continuation or abolition of the Kamchatka voyages was made. In such a way Waxell remained also at Eniseisk, and when Chirikov got an order in 1745 to travel to St. Petersburg, Waxell took command over the mariners there in his stead. He did not come to St. Petersburg with them until the month of January, 1749, which time one can take as the end of the Second Kamchatka Expedition—so that it had lasted nearly 16 years.[516]

Concerning the academy's travelers: Gmelin and I, after we had traveled through all parts of Siberia, came back to St. Petersburg on 15 February 1743. Steller, however, who still remained in Kamchatka after Waxell because he desired to carry out still more investigations in natural history, did not enjoy this luck.[517] He became absorbed, indeed with good intention, but without need, in things that were not part of his duty.[518] This brought a judgment down on his head at the provincial chancellery in Irkutsk upon his return. A report about it was delivered to the ruling Senate at St. Petersburg. Steller justified himself so perfectly at Irkutsk that the vice-governor there granted him permission to continue his journey.[519] There came to St. Petersburg, however, the report of his journey through Tobolsk, the same of which he had been acquitted in Irkutsk.[520] The Senate sent a ukase to meet him, that he should travel back to Irkutsk. Yet, soon after the report was delivered from Irkutsk, another ukase was sent to cancel the first order. Meanwhile the first ukase had found Steller at Solikamsk; he had already been escorted back to Tara. And it was here that the second ukase reached him.[521] Without stopping, he set out on the return journey via Tobolsk, but he got no farther than Tiumen, where he died of a high fever in the presence of a surgeon named Lau, who had been with the Kamchatka expedition.[522] These true circumstances are reported of necessity, because in foreign lands many falsehoods have circulated; indeed, even his death has been called into doubt.[523] He was born on 10 March 1709 at Winsheim in Franconia. His industry and skill would still have been of great use to the scholarly world, if it had pleased divine Providence to give him a longer life.

In the year 1747 Gmelin returned to Tübingen, in his native Germany, where he died on 20 May 1755 as professor of botany and chemistry—likewise no small loss to the scholarly world, because his many observations collected in Siberia were still far from being put into order and written out. I cannot add more to his fame. One might ascribe my praise to the known friendship between us. I will say only that he was born 11 August 1709 at Tübingen that he already was *Licentiatus Medicinae* in 1727, and in the same year also obtained the doctorate; he came to St. Petersburg for the academy; he already had provided various scholarly papers for the *Commentaries* of the academy before his journey to Siberia, and he shared his scholarship even more after his return by special public papers. This is enough to make his memory unforgettable to all who value true merit.[524]

Since that time, nothing further has been attempted in those seas by special imperial order—though after Bering's voyage became known certain individuals have made voyages to Bering Island and other islands situated nearby.[525] The lucrative beaver hunt has enticed the people there, and they never come back without good profit. This has brought considerable income to the royal treasury through the customs duties—in view of which the commanders at Iakutsk, at Okhotsk, and in Kamchatka have themselves encouraged the merchants and promyshlenniki in this.[526] And, indeed, the commanders have allowed these people the use of the little *Peter*; thus, this vessel has also provided much service.

As a matter of fact, a vessel like this one, or even smaller,[527] must be used if they want to visit the islands situated there for the sake of hunting beaver. Our seafarers reflected on this when they still were on the island. Their opinion is: a place should be selected for landing where there are no rocks; but where, on the contrary, a sandy coast reaches shallowly into the sea as is generally the case. There, one would run in towards the land with the tide and fasten the vessel to the coast; when the ebb falls, it will remain standing on dry sand after the water recedes. Afterwards, with the following high tide, one can draw it still higher on the land and thus it will be secure from all danger. Such places, where they can land in this way, they would like to have found on the western side of Bering Island. On the contrary, there is around the whole island, as will be remembered, no harbor or bay known where a vessel can lie at anchor without fearing that it might either founder on the rocks or be driven onto the beach and stuck in sand by strong winds.

XVII. COMMENTARY ON PUBLICATIONS

It is necessary to mention a letter published in Berlin in 1753, which recounted this same voyage under the title: *Lettre d'un Officier de la Marine Russienne à un Seigneur de la Cour*.[528] When Mr. Delisle presented the Kamchatka discoveries as well as some ascribed to Admiral de Fonte on a map at Paris in 1752[529] and accompanied it with a printed explanation [*Explication de la Carte des nouvelles découvertes au Nord de la Mer du Sud*. Paris, 1752.], the author of the letter was instructed to give his opinion of it.[530] He found that Mr. Delisle had very inadequate reports from which he had compiled his map. He discovered various errors and falsehoods in it and in the explanation. He noted how groundlessly the author wished to claim the honor for the discoveries for himself and his brother, Mr. Delisle de la Croyère, who had died in Kamchatka.[531]

He reported all this truthfully. The letter was first published separately and afterwards, with the correction of some printing errors, was incorporated into volume 13 of the *Nouvelle Bibliotheque Germanique*. There was a German translation of it in Berlin and an English translation in London, the latter of which was accompanied by commentaries of Mr. Arthur Dobbs, the great promoter of northern voyages.[532] Everyone was pleased to read the true circumstances about a voyage, for which all of Europe had already waited a long time with desire. Some, however, reprimanded the author for writing with a bitterness which should be removed from the refutations. (*Considerations* of Mr. Buache p. 51.[533] A good criticism must be instructive and without personalities. He finds the first quality in the letter in question and would have wished to see in it equally the second. *Mémoires de Trévoux* 1754. May p. 185. Edit. de Holl.[534] Mr. Buache censures rather clearly, although in indirect terms, the part of the writing which is unduly contentious, that it is even to the point of being able to pass as a satire.) This is one of the reasons why I make notice of the letter: for I believe the author deserves to be pardoned from this accusation. His intention was in no way to offend the laws of well-being. He had no hostility toward Mr. Delisle. He saw it necessary, however, were he to follow his conscience and not suppress the truth, to say the complete opposite of what Mr. Delisle had alleged. Should he not have done this? In such cases I think the blame should be apportioned only to those who give occasion for conflict. But it comes to the wording. Indeed that is the whole difficulty. Why should a man weigh his words, if he believes that he had no reason for it? The author wrote a letter. Who does not know that one usually writes such with more freedom and frankness than in public writings? Still, the author himself wished that some passages might have been omitted before his letter appeared in print without his prior knowledge. Among these he numbers especially those which apply to a deceased person, who cannot defend himself—I mean Professor Delisle de la Croyère, who was with the expedition.[535] And that is fair.

Another reason to mention the letter here is this: it contains the first news which was made known from Russia about the Kamchatka discoveries.[536] Everything in the letter was composed very quickly; it was written in haste.[537] Therefore many small differences will be encountered, which one will notice in things concerning the voyages in comparison to the reports given here. In other respects the conclusion that one must trust a man who passes as an eyewitness more than one who only gathers foreign reports has much strength. Here, however, this does not matter. The author of the letter recognizes his error; he declares that he never will contradict the reports related here.[538]

Some of the observations at hand, which occur in the letter and which agree with the story recounted here, give me yet a third reason, and some additions are still possible. For example, in the printing in the *Nouvelle Bibliotheque Germanique*, page 68, is the advice that the eastern sea, at least in the areas where Bering and Chirikov traveled, should not have the name Pacific Ocean (*Mare Pacificum*).[539] The surveyors who were in Kamchatka and made a map of this land introduced this abuse and it has even stolen into the new Russian *Atlas* printed by the academy. Thus the reminder is necessary, although it is not to be feared that responsible geographers, to whom it is known to which area of the world the name of Pacific Ocean really belongs, will follow such an example.

Page 75. A conjecture that America formerly was joined to the land of the Chukchi, and was perhaps separated from it by earthquake or flood.[540] From this, the author wishes to make a conclusion about the inhabitants of America: what can be most closely and surely explained by this is the great similarity of the North American peoples to the Siberian in their manners, diet, clothing, indeed in almost all customs, and even in religion, which presumes an association between them since antiquity, which could not have passed more easily than if both parts were connected.

Page 79. Doubt about the honesty of the report of the alleged voyage of Admiral de Fonte.[541] Indeed, Mr. Arthur Dobbs had objected against it here and there, but whether the honesty of the report is thereby demonstrated is left undecided. Mr. Dobbs himself wavers and believes the summary of the de Fonte voyage sent into the world is at the least suspicious, because a map cannot be appropriately made on the basis of it.[542] That is enough. Other famous geographers, such as d'Anville, Bellin, Green,[543] etc., appear to be of the same opinion because they concede just as little place to the discoveries of the Spanish admiral on their maps.

Page 84. A proposal to name the part of North America discovered by the Russian ships New Russia, after the example of other peoples.[544] On this occasion, I cannot help noting that Mr. Buache (*Considerations*, p. 55) does the author of the letter wrong, if he thinks that the author only shows the discoveries of Admiral de Fonte to be erroneous in order to make the claim of the Russians to the land discovered by them that much stronger.[545] What must Messrs. d'Anville and Bellin, and other such skeptics, have as intentions?

Page 86. The introduction of unfairness whenever the discoveries of the ship *Castricom* in respect to the land of Jeso were preferred to those of Captain Spanberg.[546] On this, indeed, Mr. Buache explained (p. 54) that he did not prefer the Dutch discoveries to the Russian; rather he wished to combine both with each other: but one sees how his combination is procured.[547] He approves only those islands indicated by Spanberg which are called Nadeschda. The Three Sisters, Zitronnoi, Selanoi, and Kunashir islands are said to be part of the land of Jeso. Spanberg is said to have been misled by bays and steep cliffs into transforming connected land into islands.[548] On the other hand, Mr. Buache cannot imagine that the Dutch might have taken a number of neighboring islands for a connected land (p. 123ff.)[549] Why? Is the description of the voyage of the ship *Castricom* perhaps so detailed that it precludes all error? Is it perhaps easier to regard a connected land as islands, than neighboring islands as a connected land? What happened here to the promised impartiality? Even if my assumed proposition[550] that Jeso received a different shape since the voyage of the Dutch has found no approval, there are still other arguments ready for the certainty of the Spanberg discoveries and the inadequacy of the observations of the ship *Castricom*, which I will indicate below.

Finally, something must still be said about a map of the new Kamchatka discovery which has recently appeared at the Academy of Sciences. It was made under my supervision.[551] I must therefore give an account of the reasons why I have represented certain countries in a particular way, and not otherwise, on it. The engraving is: "Nouvelle Carte des Decouvertes faites par les Vaisseaux Russieus aux côtes inconnues de l'Amerique Septentrionale avec les pais adjacents: dressée sur des memoires authentiques de ceux qui ont assisté a ces Decouvertes et sur d'autres connoissances dont on rend raison dans un Memoire separé." S. Petersbourg a l'Academie Imperiale des Sciences, 1758. Some of the first prints bear the date 1754.[552] And, in fact, the map was prepared and engraved in that year. I have, however, revised it once again this year, improved it in some places, and changed the date, so the succeeding printings differ from the former.[553] The *Memoir* relating to the engraving is none other than this treatise. I will begin from the western side.

That part of Siberia which is found on the map is a copy of a new map of Siberia which I have had corrected according to my own observations and descriptions made in that territory, but which is still not engraved. A very great difference from the Siberian maps in the Russian *Atlas* will be observed. In that nobody erred. It was done only for the improvement of the Russian *Atlas* that I undertook this work myself.[554]

The coasts of the Icy Sea are laid out according to the voyages described previously.[555] Since, however, the drawing of the coasts from Arkhangelsk to the Ob—which also includes much that is new—would not be suitable here, that will follow on another occasion. The alleged islands in the Icy Sea have not been put on because of their uncertainty, which I have dealt with extensively above.[556] For what use are propositions which any contradiction can destroy again? Even if one cannot give incontestable proofs for everything in geography, the probability of a thing must be very great before one presents it on a map. The island and the great land opposite the mouth of the Kolyma, for which Messrs. Delisle and Buache have declared themselves as patron saints, run beyond the little island of Kopai, close to the solid land which is introduced in their stead.[557] I have also omitted the whale fishery represented on the general map of the Russian *Atlas*. This invention of the engraver, simply intended to fill up an empty space, has already misled many to believe that real ships go whaling in the same area (Mr. Buache *Considerat.*, p. 4, note b).[558]

A new shape has been given to Chukotskii Nos. Whoever reads carefully what was quoted about it previously will easily find the reasons.[559] The Strahlenberg map had something similar, but it represents the nos as much too small.[560] First, the strength of the people is on the nos. The real home of the Chukchi is there, whence they spread only occasionally toward the south and west. There is a narrow isthmus, over which they go by foot frequently from the Kolyma toward the Anadyr Sea. Consequently it must be that this nos extends still much farther beyond this isthmus. I am afraid it is still made too small. Therefore the outline is only indicated with dots, in order to show the uncertainty.

I could have put islands around Chukotskii Nos, if the reports received from there were only in agreement enough, and had not, on the contrary, left a fear of erring in their definition.[561] As for Puchotzkoi Island, which is found on those maps from Holland after the death of Peter the Great and is also found on the Strahlenberg map, one sees that the island could find no place, as the name is entirely unknown in Siberia, unless it should be called Chukotskii.[562]

Anadyr ostrog and the course of the Anadyr River lie a good deal more northerly than on the earlier maps, according to me.[563] As my justification for this I can only cite the observations of the surveyors of latitude taken at Anadyr ostrog, which came to 66°09′ north latitude. And it also conforms to the position of the adjoining Penzhina Sea, because the distance between the Anadyr ostrog and the mouth of the Penzhina River was found by the same surveyors to be not much more than 200 versts. In addition, it was necessary for the Penzhina Sea to extend farther towards the north than on previous maps, on account of the many large rivers emptying into it, of which only the principal ones could be shown on the map.[564] In other respects these coasts never have been properly described. Both Kamchatka expeditions could almost be charged with the fault that they did not pay attention to such subsidiary matters, but only busied themselves with their principal work.

An error occurred in the determination of the position of Okhotsk on this map, which I report so that it will not be copied. After my return from Siberia, when I was making the new map, no astronomical observations from Okhotsk had yet arrived. It seemed to me that in the travel route measured and described by compass from Iakutsk to that place, shown in the Russian *Atlas*, the distance between both places is two degrees too great in longitude. I therefore had Okhotsk moved two degrees to the west, until I could get solid confirmation of it. The observations came after that. They were compared, calculated, and incorporated into the third part of the new St. Petersburg *Commentaries*.[565] My supposition was only half confirmed. The true longitude of Okhotsk is 160°59′ 15″; the latitude is 59°20′.[566] What is mistaken in this map is to be attributed to the rather too exact following of my first map, and neglecting to use the determination in the *Commentaries*.

As has already been said concerning the coast between Okhotsk and the Amur River, in my opinion it must not extend toward the south, as shown on all earlier maps, but rather toward the southwest from Okhotsk to the Uda River and toward the southeast from the Uda to the Amur.[567] The coast is also represented in this way on the present map. Observations of the latitude were made at Uda ostrog; at one time it was found to be 55°10′ north latitude and at another time 55°27′ north latitude. Thence the mean is concluded to be 55°18′ north latitude. My reasons for presenting the coast in the area in the said manner are based on the measured and geodetically described distances from Iakutsk and Uda ostrog (which better coincide with my accepted theses), on the multitude of rivers entering the sea between Okhotsk and Uda ostrog, and on the distances between them indicated by the people who were knowledgeable about the area. For if the coast from Okhotsk takes a course toward the southwest, the rivers will be longer, they will have more room, and the distance between them will be closer to the truth. It depends on whether my conjecture, which I believe is reliable, will be confirmed through future experience. This much is certain—that the areas there deserve a true investigation, because they are known to us almost only from hearsay.

As has been said about them, the Shantar Islands are constituted in such a way that one can easily remove them.[568] They are therefore indicated on the map only, as it were, approximately, without expending the effort to make the position agree with my description. Such a description may be drafted as diligently as possible but can hardly agree with nature. In the future, whoever carefully navigates the sea there will undoubtedly find the position, size, and number of islands entirely different.

Because the island which lies opposite the mouth of the Amur River, like all coasts and lands belonging to China, is taken from Du Halde's map, the author is not in the least responsible if there should be mistakes in it. But it may be supposed that the Chinese maps of this area are not free from errors, because no Jesuit went there and because the Mandarins Khan Kang-hsi had sent to describe the island gave little effort to it (Du Halde, vol. IV, p. 14).[569] There may well still be much to discover there if a voyage were organized for that purpose.

I come again to the land of Jeso, or rather to the island, which lies in the middle between Kamchatka and Japan. The geographers foster many different opinions about it; sometimes they believe the land joins with Japan, sometimes with America, sometimes with eastern Tatary; sometimes they consider it to be Kamchatka, sometimes they make one, sometimes more, islands of it—these various opinions, I say, allow little to hope for from the old discoveries. Usually they rely on the account of the ship *Castricom*, as printed in the collection of Thévenot,[570] as the third part of the *Voyages au Nord*[571] and in P. Charlevoix, *Hist. du Japon* (Vol. II, p. 494).[572] I cannot bring myself to accept the account, as Mr. Buache does, as decisive. It contains far too little of a proper sea journal. It would conclude from nothing that the leader of the ship gave effort to learn to truly know the land that he saw or the sea that he sailed. No calculation of longitude is noted anywhere, though it is unbelievable that the skipper should not have taken notice of the same. Therefore it is generally believed that the course of the *Castricom* was held mostly toward the north, and most maps show Jeso nearly under the same meridian with the northern coast of Japan, which is an error that only Mr. d'Anville has corrected in some measure on his map of Asia.[573] The account of the ship *Breskes*, which went with the *Castricom* for the discovery of Jeso, has far more exact observations. But they are little known and therefore have not yet been used by anyone in geography; for though it seems likely that Mr. d'Anville had known something of them (because his placement of Jeso comes nearest to the one given in the relation of the ship *Breskes*), the opposite can be supposed from other particulars. Mr. d'Anville built much on probabilities. These have caused him to consider Jeso, States Island, and Company Land as one with the Jeso Islands, from Japan to the island Nadeschda. They have also misled him to connect various places from the relation of the *Castricom*, for example, Blydenberg, Tamari Aniwa, Cape Aniwa, etc., with eastern Tatary and to place Cape Patience, which is generally considered to be the northern point of Jeso, on the southern point of the island of Sakhalin Ula, about which it cannot easily be decided whether he is right or wrong.[574] One will be eager to become better informed about what the report of the ship *Breskes* contains. It is found in Witsen (*Noord en Oost Tartarye*, ed. 2, p. 138).[575] Because of its rarity I will insert all of it here: "The ship *Breskes*, which put to sea in the year 1643, together with the ship *Castricom*, for the discovery of Tatary, and was driven away from the latter onto the east coast of Japan, also—and indeed alone—discovered the land of Jeso. It was in the month of June, as she sailed through the strait which separates the land of Jeso from Japan. This happened in the latitude of 41°50′ north and in the longitude of 164°48′ east. On the cape which was discovered first, eight or ten cliffs appeared, like sails, and from these a great reef stretched a mile into the sea. They saw little vessels (*prawen*). The rowers had an oar in each hand, which they used alternately, striking into the water with one, then another. They traveled very swiftly. They were an intelligent people. They had black, long, rough beards, and their faces were brown; in the front of their heads they had long hair about three fingers wide; their hair was cut off in the back. It was observed that they folded their hands together over their heads as a sign of thankfulness. They were dressed in bearskins. Their weapons were arrows and bows. From there the ship sailed far to the east and the sailors caught many cod in the sea. At the latitude of 43°04′ they again saw land. At 44°04′ vessels came to the ship; the people on them were strong in body and intelligent in their dealings. They had women with them, brown in color, whose lips and hands were colored blue. These wore their hair around their heads cut about three fingers below their ears, and had the appearance of young men. The people took much pleasure in drinking brandy. Some of these people wore clothes of the Japanese fashion. Some had crosses on their coats. In addition to arrows and bows, they had swords (*houwers*) made like those in Japan. The sheaths of the swords were decorated with little pieces of gold, the blades (de plaet) with a silver edge, and the sheaths with foliage. Their belts, from which the swords hung, were decorated with silver. They wore silver rings and Nuremberg corals in their ears. They had sealskins, beaverskins and some Indian cloth. Their vessels were hollowed out from a tree and had no sails (*vlerken*). At 43°45′ they again discovered land, as also at 44°12′ north and 167°21′ east longitude. The land that they saw was high. Moreover, they found many islands and broken land. A little farther north they observed many seals and a kind of grass that floated in the sea. At 45°12′ north latitude and 169°36′ east longitude land appeared at a distance, as if it were islands; as they came nearer to it they found that it was a mainland covered with snow in many places. They went to the land. It was deserted, however. Beautiful fresh water flows in a valley not far from the coast. Nearby they found low shrubs, cherry trees, wood sorrel, wild cabbage, leeks, and stinging nettle. They did not see either people or animals, except for a fox. High mountains appeared at 46°15′ latitude and 172°16′ and also at 172°53′ longitude. Likewise land was discovered at 47°08′ and 173°53′ but was not set foot on. This land is situated, according to the journal kept by the ship *Breskes*, 12° more easterly than the easternmost point of Japan, which lies at 38°04′. The difference of latitude is 9°38′; direction NE by E and SW by W."[576]

From this it follows that the position of the alleged land of Jeso is the very same as the islands represented on our map. Therefore one can think as he will, even justly take any position, for it can hardly be proved by the voyages of the *Breskes* or of the *Castricom* that all the land encountered by these ships was united.[577] Matsmai is taken as a separate island by Messrs. Delisle and Buache without regard to many accounts, especially those of the missionaries to Japan and even of the ship *Castricom*, which are contrary to this opinion.[578] With this part already granted, why would one not recognize something similar about the islands Kunashir, Urup, Figuroi, Zitronnoi, etc.? The existence of the island of Nadeschda is not denied.[579] But if the voyages of the *Castricom* and *Breskes* retain their attested value and all the land that they saw is considered contiguous, then this cannot be. One sees also that the voyages are mentioned by Messrs. Delisle and Buache to prove too much, and consequently nothing at all. It is also not proof on their behalf that the Europeans in Japan have heard the land of Jeso described as a large continuous land. One remembers the report given previously that the inhabitants of these islands were named with the common name Jeso by all the Japanese.[580] This could have given rise to the misunderstanding. The people of the *Castricom* and *Breskes* brought preconceived opinions with them. Thus they believed that all the land they saw was one and the same island. Thereby they may have been prevented from accurate examinations of the areas between—the bays and inlets—they observed, which were probably straits between the islands. Thus it is not even necessary to accept a radical change as has been hypothesized to help explain the present condition of those regions.[581] It is conceivable enough that an error of this kind could have been produced and copied. May I refer to the opinion of burgomaster Witsen, whose words are these (*Noord en Oost Tartarye*, ed. 2, p. 866): "Van Keulen indicates on his map that Jeso is contiguous to Tatary, about which nothing previously could be said with certainty, though I am quite sure that Jeso surely is divided into islands."[582] Such testimonies serve at least for this: that one should not indict an opinion for being far too bold. Here, by the way, the same order and names of the islands are retained as they, following Captain Spanberg's voyage, appear in the Russian *Atlas*, without using the oral reports cited previously.[583] The comparison of these with the former can best be done by further investigations made in these regions, which it is hoped will not be left undone, in order to remove all remaining doubts concerning the land of Jeso.

Japan is set up according to the model of Messrs. d'Anville ("Carte d'Asie")[584] and Bellin (in the *Histoire Générale des Voyages*, vol. X, or in the German translation, in volume XI).[585] Indeed, Father Charlevoix (*Hist. du Japon*, vol. I, p. 4)[586] says this empire lies, according to a new map, corrected by the astronomical observations of the Jesuits in China, between 157 and 175 degrees of longitude. But that is an obvious error from which it would follow, contrary to experience, that one would have to sail directly to the south from Kamchatka to Japan.

My corrections for Kamchatka, just as all previous ones, will be seen in comparing it with the preceding map. In general Kamchatka now appears a good deal longer than before, because the Penzhina gulf takes up a greater length toward the north. On the Kirilov map the Penzhina River flows into the western side—on the map in the Russian *Atlas* into the eastern side—of the bay.[587] Here the river flows into the far north corner of it. Almost all rivers have received a different position, and many a corrected spelling. The most remarkable mistakes were in the Olutora and Tigil, or Kigil, rivers, by which the former was placed two degrees too southerly, the latter, however, just as much too northerly. There is not even one degree of latitude left between the mouths of both. The difference should amount to five degrees. Since these rivers are among the principal ones of the country; since they are often visited by the inhabitants of both the Russian ostrogs on the Kamchatka River; since the route from the Penzhina River to the Tigil and from this to the rivers Kamchatka, Bolshaia Reka, etc., has been described by surveyors; since finally it is exactly known in Kamchatka which of these rivers falling from it on both sides into the sea lie across from each other—thus no uncertainty or doubt can occur here. People travel from Anadyr ostrog to the Kamchatka River and pass the Olutora River half way. It must be about 61° in latitude. Then the mouth of the Kamchatka River is at 56° or somewhat more northerly. About the Tigil, however, one knows for certain that its mouth lies under the same latitude as the mouth of the Kamchatka.

Astronomical observations have been made at Bolsheretsk ostrog and in the harbor of Petropavlovsk, according to which:

	Latitude	Longitude[588]
Bolsheretsk ostrog is	52°54'30"	174°10'
Petropavlovsk Harbor is	53°01'20"	176°12'30"

Other observations of the latitude are:

at the mouth of the Bolshaia River, 52°54'

at the southern point of Kamchatka 51°03'

This may be enough about Kamchatka for the present.

Now the part of the map remains which reveals the American discoveries: I can be very brief about it, since I have not found it necessary to compare the map with the accompanying reports, because it was not drawn according to these but rather according to maps which were prepared on both ships, as well as they were consistent with one another. I also do not have to account for it, if differences are noted in some places between them in the description and the map. My work in this has been no more than to connect together by dots, according to probability, the coast seen at various places.[589] The author of the account mentioned previously has already recommended this. Mr. Buache, who earlier had taken the coast sighted between 51 and 52 degrees of latitude and the twenty-first degree of longitude from Avacha (Mr. Delisle says, incorrectly, 12°)[590] for a separate land, or island, has followed the same advice in his newest maps.[591] And in general he has been successful, except for the various coasts not known to him, which should be connected.

But it could be the same case here as that which gave us so many opportunities to talk about Jeso, so that caution requires us not to rely too much on conjecture, but to leave the confirmation of it to a future investigation.[592]

I have deemed it proper, following the example of Messrs. Delisle and Buache, to connect the Russian discoveries with the American regions already known. For that purpose it was necessary to be guided by a map of America, the accuracy of which could not be denied. I chose one of Mr. Green's because it came to hand during the course of the work.[593] The known regions of America have been produced, therefore, according to it. If astronomical observations had been set up on our ships, as was the intention, the distance between the newly discovered and previously known regions could have been determined with more certainty. For lack of them, it was based solely on the ship's reckonings, and one would not insist upon them, should some future navigations show a difference from the present determination.

Consequently, until that time we may be allowed to show doubt also about the judgment of Mr. Dobbs. He will accept nothing of that land seen by our people as a continent, unless it is confirmed through new discoveries. Everything should be represented as a vast island. ("It can't," are his words, "without a

137

further discovery be considered otherwise than an island of considerable extent.")[594] In that case the hoped-for northwest passage from Hudson Bay to the Southern Sea, in our opinion, is more difficult and almost loses its probability. But I have reported the grounds for maintaining that the land of America extends as far as the neighborhood of the Chukchi land.[595] I should wish that Mr. Dobbs were right; Russia would lose nothing by that. It would get its future possessions even more incontestibly, because no European could boast of ever having had knowledge of this great island. On the contrary, regarding the northwest passage—which is to be desired for certainly more than one reason—the enterprises of the English could be supported more conveniently. But the opposite opinion still appears to me to have the most probability.

Why the Western Sea of Mr. Guillaume Delisle and the pretended discoveries of Admiral de Fonte do not appear here needs no additional explanation than that already given.[596] I believe it is always more fair to leave an empty space remaining for future discoveries, than to fill it up with such uncertainties. Here, also, a new voyage is needed if one wants to be convinced with reason of the truth or falsity of these things.

Finally, if my readers find nothing, either on the map or in the description from the pertinent report of Mr. de Guignes, which he collected from Chinese writings and presented to the Paris Académie des belles lettres in 1752, and some of which he also incorporated into the *Journal des Scavans* for the month of December of the same year,[597] I excuse myself on account of the judgment of a greater connoisseur of the Chinese language and history, the famous Father Gaubil of Peking.[598] One cannot doubt the skill and sincerity of this man. He has demonstrated this in many writings which have brought honor to him and to his fatherland, his order, and to our academy, of which he is a member. He has dealings with a Chinese man whose industrious efforts have earned much praise. His judgment must thus have total conviction as its basis. The same however, is so little favored in the report of Mr. de Guignes, that it even declares it to be empty fables. The love of truth and my own justification obliges me to add here some words of Father Gaubil in a letter of 23 November 1755 to the illustrious president of our academy: "We have seen here," the same says, "the maps of Messrs. Delisle and Buache on the discoveries of the Russians in America. A Frenchman named Mr. de Guignes, who studies Chinese at Peking, believes he has discovered in the Chinese books a voyage of the Chinese from China to California in America in the year 458.[599] He has had a map made of this voyage and has read various memoirs on it at the Académies des Inscriptions and Belles Lettres. I believe that the voyage is a fable, and I wrote my reasons to Mr. de Guignes himself in response to one of his letters, where he detailed his discovery to me." Now it falls on Mr. de Guignes to share with the world his objections against Father Gaubil.

Allow me to conclude with a general observation. We see that the result of all this is that although, indeed, much has been done, much still remains to be done. Should we not be allowed to hope to bring such an important enterprise to its completion? After the example of Peter the Great, Russia's most worthy rulers seek their greatest glory in promoting the sciences. They are striving not only to make them more familiar and thus more pleasant to their subjects. They also share with other nations what, through their organization and at their expense, promotes the expansion of the sciences themselves. No fame is more lasting than this. In this way a prince establishes memorials for himself that time cannot ruin nor accident destroy. The First Kamchatka Expedition raises such a monument to Peter the Great, its founder. It also glorifies the radiant time of the high and mighty Elizabeth, because of the Second Kamchatka Expedition, which terminated under her rule and about which, by her order, what happened was made known for the use of the whole world. Such a fortunate monarch, who has the opportunity to show herself in such a light! Our great Empress has still more to hope for. She can grant completion to the initial discoveries. She can give an entire quarter of the globe a new appearance. She can banish the darkness with which a great part of a science is veiled. A future voyage in the Kamchatka and American waters cannot be more arduous. The trail is broken. One knows the means and difficulties by experience. It is only a question of a suitable arrangement of the existing circumstances; thus a desirable conclusion of the matter is not to be doubted. Without question everyone to whom the advancement of the sciences is dear will wish with me that this will be done soon.

G. F. Müller

GLOSSARY

Adjunct—the rank below professor in the Academy of Sciences.

Cossacks—"a social rather than an ethnic class" (Krasheninnikov, 1972, x). These men served the government "in return for certain privileges (e.g. tax exemption)" (Gibson, 1969, p. 4). See also Armstrong, 1965, pp. 21-5.

Fathom, land—one sazhen or seven feet (English).

Fathom, sea—six feet (English).

Geodesist—a land surveyor; mapper.

Gorodok—a small town.

Iasak—taxes or tribute paid in furs.

Krepost—fortress.

Mile, German—four nautical miles or 4.61 English statute miles. Golder, 1922, II, 11.

Navy ranks:
    General Admiral
    Captain Commander
    Captain (First, Second, and Third Rank)
    Fleet Lieutenant (Captain Lieutenant)
    Fleet Master
    Navigator, Quartermaster
    Assistant Navigator
    Boatswain

Also used:

Master—the commanding officer of a smaller ship used in exploration.

Mate—"When the word mate is used without qualification it always denotes. . .the one upon whom the command of the vessel would fall in the event of a death or disability of the captain." Kerchove, p. 143.

Nos—a cape. Coxe, 1803, xiii. Literally, "nose." See also Fisher, 1981, p. 221, for a discussion of the use of the term in the seventeenth century as cape or peninsula.

Ostrog—a palisaded fort.

Piatidesiatnik—leader of 50 men.

Promyshlenniki—fur hunters and traders, generally, who worked for the state, though at times they also engaged in other trade, for example in ivory. See Fisher, 1981, p. 43.

Pud—40 Russian pounds; 36 pounds avoirdupois.

Russian settlements (principal places only, described by Chaplin and Krasheninnikov. See maps also):

Bolsheretsk—founded in 1700. In 1727 there were about 15 households; in 1737-40 Krasheninnikov reported some 30 buildings there, including a storehouse, buildings to hold iasak and hostages, a church, a tavern, and a distillery.

Eniseisk—administrative center, founded in 1619.

Iakutsk—administrative center of northeastern Siberia, founded in 1632. At the time of the First Kamchatka Expedition there were about 300 houses in the town.

Irkutsk—founded in 1651. An administrative center and key for conducting Russian trade with China.

Nizhne (Lower) Kamchatsk ostrog—founded in 1701. In 1728 there were 15 houses and a church. The place was destroyed by a rebellion of the Kamchadals in 1731 but was quickly rebuilt, and in 1738-39 Krasheninnikov reported there were 39 houses plus a church, a chapel, buildings for storing iasak and ammunition, plus a tavern and a distillery.

Okhotsk—port on the Sea of Okhotsk, founded in 1647. At the time of the First Kamchatka Expedition there were only 11 houses there, built of logs, according to Chaplin. By 1738 there were 19 households, with some 70 to 85 Russians.

Petropavlovsk—(Harbor of St. Peter and St. Paul). Port established on Avacha Bay in 1740.

Tobolsk—administrative center, founded in 1587.

Tomsk—administrative center, founded in 1604.

Verkhne (Upper) Kamchatsk ostrog—founded 1697. There were 17 households at the time of the First Kamchatka Expedition; in 1738 Krasheninnikov indicated that there were 22 houses, plus a church, a tavern, and a distillery.

Verkhoturye—founded in 1598, in the Ural Mountains. The gateway to Siberia.

Sazhen—seven feet (English).

Siberian people mentioned in the text:

Chukchi—two branches, the nomadic or "reindeer" Chukchi and the coast dwellers, who hunted marine animals and fish. On Bering's map a northern branch of these people is called "Shelagi."

Iakuts— these people were incorporated into the Russian empire in the seventeenth century; they raised horses and cattle and they also hunted and fished. In the north they kept reindeer.

Iukagir—these people lived in small clan or tribal groups in the eighteenth century; they were hunters and fishermen.

Kalmucks—the ancestors of this people originated in Central Asia; they were nomadic and semi-nomadic herders.

Kamchadals (Itelmensy)—inhabitants of the Kamchatka Peninsula, who lived by fishing and hunting marine animals.

Kurilians—in the eighteenth century, these people lived in southern Kamchatka, as well as in Sakhalin and the Kurile Islands.

Koriaks—two branches; some were reindeer herders and the others were settled coastal dwellers who lived by fishing and hunting marine animals.

Lamut—nomadic people who kept reindeer and also hunted. Also, Okhotsk Tungus.

Okhotsk Tungus—see Lamut.

Samoyeds—general name for people who spoke the Samoyed language.

Sloboda—a settlement exempted from normal taxes and work obligations.

Sviatoi Nos—Holy Cape.

Syn boiarskii—the lowest rank of nobility. Originally it was hereditary; later the rank was conferred on those considered worthy of noble rank in Siberia.

Train oil—oil from whales or other marine animals.

Verst—500 sazhens; 0.663 of a statute mile.

Vessels:

Baidar (Umiak)—wooden-framed boat covered with sealskins. The kind used by the Chukchi for fishing held from seven to nine men.

Canoe—the kayak, a boat with a wooden frame covered with sealskins, usually held from one to three men.

Hooker—a general name for a fishing vessel. The *Archangel Michael*, used on Spanberg's voyage to Japan, was described by Müller and Waxell as a hooker. Barratt (1981, p. 35) described it as a one-masted brigantine.

Kaiuk—small boat used in transporting goods by rivers in the north; it was hauled overland on portages.

Koch—one-masted vessel used by the Russians in northern seas; it could carry up to 40 people. See Fisher, 1981, pp. 161-69.

Longboat—a ship's boat, carried on board. The *St. Peter* and *St. Paul* each had two longboats, a larger and a smaller. These were equipped with a mast, sails, and oars.

Packet boat—a ship for carrying passengers and goods. The *Gabriel* was constructed in the style of the packet boats used in the Baltic, according to Müller, and had forty-four men on board. The *Gabriel* was 60 feet long by $27\frac{1}{2}$ feet wide.

Shallop—light, open vessel with oars and sails, used chiefly in exploring rivers. Here "double" or reinforced vessel with small draft, because of icy conditions in the northern seas.

Shitiki—small boats held together by thongs; they could be easily disassembled for portaging. See Fisher, 1981, p.13.

Sloop—*The Hope*, Walton's ship on the voyage to Japan, the *St. Peter*, Bering's ship, and the *St. Paul*, Chirikov's ship, are all described as double (reinforced) sloops. They were 80 feet long by 20 feet wide, carried two masts and were brig-rigged. Golder, 1922, I, p. 34.

Voevoda—a military governor.

Zavod—mine.

Zimovye—winter quarters.

FOOTNOTES

Chapter I

I1—The controversy about the expeditions is discussed in Raymond H. Fisher, *Bering's Voyages: Whither and Why* (Seattle: University of Washington Press, 1977).

I2—For a biography of Müller as a historian, see J.L. Black, G.F. *Müller and the Imperial Russian Academy of Sciences, 1725-1783: First Steps in the Development of the Historical Sciences in Russia* (in press). Two other biographies are of special interest: one written by his contemporary, Anton Friedrich Büsching, in *Beytrage zu der Lebensgeschichte denkwurdiger Personen insonderheit gelehrten Manner*, III (Halle, 1785), pp. 1-160, and the biography written by an early historian of the Academy of Sciences, Petr Petrovich Pekarskii, *Istoriia imperatorskoi akademiia nauk v Peterburge*, 2 vols. (St. Petersburg: Imperatorskaia Akademiia nauk, 1870-73), I:308-430.

I3—A convenient listing of accounts available in English is found in Harry W. Nerhood, compiler, *To Russia and Return: An Annotated Bibliography of Travelers' English-Language Accounts of Russia from the Ninth Century to the Present* (Columbus: Ohio State University Press, 1968). For a selection from early travelers' reports with an excellent introduction, see Anthony Cross, editor, *Russia under Western Eyes, 1517-1825* (New York: St. Martin's Press, 1971).

I4—A description of the long search for a northwest passage is found in Ernest S. Dodge, *Northwest by Sea* (New York: Oxford University Press, 1961). On Cabot, see James A. Williamson, *The Cabot Voyages and Bristol Discovery under Henry VII*, Hakluyt Society, *Works*, 2nd series, CXX (London: Hakluyt Society, 1962).

I5—Early ideas about a river route are discussed in James D. Tracy, editor, *True Ocean Found: Paludanus's Letters on Dutch Voyages to the Kara Sea, 1595-1596* (Minneapolis: University of Minnesota Press, 1980). Herberstein's book appeared in many editions; an English translation is Sigismund von Herberstein, *Notes upon Russia*, translated by R.H. Major, 2 vols., Hakluyt Society, *Works*, 1st series, X (London: Hakluyt Society, 1851); XII (London: Hakluyt Society, 1852). The text on voyages in the "Frozen Sea" is found in volume II, pages 105-112.

I6—For the Muscovy Company, see T.S. Willan, *The Early History of the Russia Company, 1553-1603* (Manchester: Manchester University Press, 1956). See also M.S. Anderson, *Britain's Discovery of Russia, 1553-1815* (London: St. Martin's Press, 1958). The "discovery" is commented on by Richard Pipes in his introduction to a facsimile edition of Giles Fletcher, *Of the Russe Commonwealth, 1591* (Cambridge: Harvard University Press, 1966).

I7—A general survey is Leslie H. Neatby, *Discovery in Russian and Siberian Waters* (Athens: Ohio University Press, 1973); an earlier English work is James Burney, *Chronological History of Northeastern Voyages of Discovery*, first published in 1819 and reprinted (Amsterdam: Da Capo Press, 1969). A standard Russian text is Mikhail I. Belov, *Arkticheskoe moreplavanie s drevneishikh vremen do serediny XIX veka* (Moscow: Morskoi transport, 1956).

I8—For Barents, see Gerrit de Veer, *The Three Voyages of William Barents to the Arctic Regions (1594, 1595, 1596)*, 2nd ed., Hakluyt Society, *Works*, 1st series, XLIV (London: Hakluyt Society, 1876). On the Dutch involvement in early trade with Russia, see Paul Bushkovitch, *The Merchants of Moscow, 1580-1650* (Cambridge: Cambridge University Press, 1980), especially chapter 3.

I9—Fisher, *Bering's Voyages*, p. 9; Belov, *Arkticheskoe moreplavanie*, pp. 116, 118-19.

I10—See John Parker, *The Strait of Anian: An Exhibit of Three Maps in the James Ford Bell Library at the University of Minnesota, Portraying Sixteenth and Eighteenth Century Concepts of the Waterway between Asia and America, which is now known as the Bering Strait* (Minneapolis: The James Ford Bell Book Trust, 1956); Godfrey Sykes, "The Mythical Straits of Anian," *Bulletin of the American Geographical Society*, XLVII:3 (1915), pp. 167-71.

111—The theoretical geography is discussed by John K. Wright, "The Open Polar Sea," *Geographical Review*, XLIII (1953), pp. 338-65; early English hopes for northern navigation are described in E.G.R. Taylor, "The Northern Passages" in *The Great Age of Discovery*, edited by Arthur Percival Newton (London: University of London Press, 1932). Mercator's influence is cited on pages 202-204 of the latter work; his map was first made in 1569 and is reproduced here from a printing in 1595. For a brief biography see George Kish, "Gerardus Mercator," *Dictionary of Scientific Biography*, IX, pp. 309-310.

112—See Raymond H. Fisher, *The Russian Fur Trade, 1550-1700* (Berkeley, Los Angeles: University of California Press, 1943) and George V. Lantzeff and Richard A. Pierce, *Eastward to Empire: Exploration and Conquest on the Russian Open Frontier, to 1750* (Montreal: McGill-Queen's University Press, 1973).

113—[Nicolaas Corneliszoon Witsen] "A Letter, not long since written to the Publisher by an Experienced Person residing at Amsterdam, containing a true Description of Nova Zembla, together with an Intimation of the Advantage of its Shape and Position," *Philosophical Transactions*, X, No. 101 (London, 1674), p. 3.

114—"A Narrative of some Observations made upon several Voyages, Undertaken to Find a Way for Sailing about the North to the East-Indies, and for Returning the same Way from thence Hither; Together with Instructions Given by the Dutch East-India Company for the Discovery of the Famous Land of Jesso near Japan," *Philosophical Transactions*, X, No. 109 (London, 1674), pp. 197-207.

115—John A. Harrison, *Japan's Northern Frontier: A Preliminary Study in Colonization and Expansion with Special Reference to the Relations of Japan and Russia* (Gainesville: University of Florida Press, 1953), pp. 145-64, contains an appendix with a commentary and bibliography on "The Discovery of Yezo" which discusses the confusion about the area. The expedition of Vries is also the subject of P.F. von Siebold, *Geographical and Ethnographical Elucidations to the Discoveries of Maerten Gerrits Vries commander of the flute Castricum A.D. 1643 in the East and North of Japan* (London: Trubner & Co., 1859).

116—[Nicolaas Corneliszoon Witsen] "A Summary Relation of what hath been hitherto discovered in the Matter of the North-East Passage; Communicated by a good Hand," *Philosophical Transactions*, XI, No. 118 (London, 1675), p. 419.

117—*Ibid.*, p. 424.

118—John Harris, *Navigantium atque Itinerantium Bibliotheca: Or, A Compleat Collection of Voyages and Travels*, 2 vols. (London: T. Bennett [etc.], 1705), I:610-33. Quotation is from page 615.

119—Leo Bagrow, "The First Russian Maps of Siberia and Their Influence on the West-European Cartography of N.E. Asia," *Imago Mundi*, IX (1952), pp. 83-93; Johannes Keuning, "Nicolaas Witsen as a Cartographer," *Imago Mundi*, XI (1954), pp. 95-110.

120—Nicolaas Corneliszoon Witsen, *Noord en oost Tartarye*, 2 vols. (Amsterdam, 1692), II:542-43. Translation by Tracy Norris.

121—*Ibid.*, pp. 36, 468.

122—Fisher, *Bering's Voyages*, p. 64, note 56, indicates that Peter told Witsen about this during the visit. See also Boris P. Polevoi, "Petr Pervyi, Nikolai Vitsen i problema 'soshlasia li Amerika s Asiei' " *Strany i narody vostoka*, part VII, *Strany i narody basseina tikhogo okeana*, book 3, comp. and ed. Y.V. Maretin (Moscow: AN SSSR, 1975), pp. 19-32. In his "O kartax severnoi Azii N.K. Vitsena," *Izvestiia AN SSSR*, seriia geograficheskaia (Moscow, 1973), No. 2, pp. 124-33, Polevoi states that F.C. Saltykov was the person who told Witsen there was no "nos" in eastern Siberia connecting Asia with America (p. 130). In the 1705 edition of his *Noord en oost Tartarye* Witsen reports "One can consider going from the Enisei River to the Amur by way of the Lena, on the other hand with misgivings on account of the ice" (II:656).

123—In a letter of 1709, Witsen writes "The description of Isbrandts is composed by me, as it was published from papers that were very confusedly written in Hamburgish or Lower Saxon. He was my friend and is now deceased." Keuning, "Nicolaas Witsen," p. 107.

124—Evert Ysbrandszoon Ides, *Three Years Travels from Moscow over land to China*. (London: W. Freeman [etc.], 1706), p. 93.

125—For a short biography see George Kish, "Guillaume Delisle," *Dictionary of Scientific Biography*, IV (1971), pp. 22-25.

126—The maps are found in Guillaume Delisle, *Atlas nouveau, contenant toutes les parties du monde* (Amsterdam: J. Covens & C. Mortier). The first one is titled "Magnae Tartariae Tabula" and was completed in 1706. The second map is "Asia accurata in Imperia, Regna. Status & Populas divisa, ad Usum Ludovici XV Galliarum Regis." The legend on the latter map states it is based on information received from Peter the Great.

127—The question of whether Asia and America were joined remained the central issue for mapmakers, in spite of information available about the difficulties of sailing in the northern seas. In the early eighteenth century, western Europeans had very little information about the Pacific. In Japan, the Dutch had a trading center at Deshima but were kept in isolation; in China, Canton and the Portuguese Macao were the only areas known to Europeans. Marco Polo and medieval sources were still used by mapmakers. See Peter J. Marshall and Glyndwr Williams, *Great Map of Mankind: Perceptions of New Worlds in the Age of Enlightenment* (Cambridge: Harvard University Press, 1982).

128—Black, *G.F. Müller*, p. 12.

129—Members of the Academy met and discussed the ideas of Newton prior to the official opening. See Black, *G.F. Müller*, p. 14; Alexander Vucinich, *Science in Russian Culture: A History to 1860* (Stanford: Stanford University Press, 1963), p. 76.

130—For example, John Perry, an Englishman who served in Russia for many years and wrote a popular book based on his experiences there, reported great difficulties in obtaining his pay, and he left Russia under the protection of Charles Whitworth, the British ambassador to Russia. Perry blamed his problems on Peter's associates. Perry also stated that the mathematician Henry Farquaharson had difficulties in getting his salary. John Perry, *The State of Russia under the Present Czar* (London: Benjamin Tooke, 1716), pp. 57, 212.

131—J.G. Garrard, editor, *The Eighteenth Century in Russia* (Oxford: Clarendon Press, 1973), p. 28; Max J. Okenfuss, "Russian Students in Europe in the Age of Peter the Great," *ibid.*, pp. 131-45. For a description of the impact Peter the Great's visit had, see A.G. Cross, "British Knowledge of Russian Culture (1698-1801)," *Canadian-American Slavic Studies*, 13, No. 4 (Winter, 1979), pp. 412-14.

132—Valentin Boss, *Newton and Russia: The Early Influence, 1698-1796* (Cambridge: Harvard University Press, 1972) describes Peter the Great's visit to England in 1698, particularly in relation to the question of whether Peter met Isaac Newton (pp. 9-15). Boss noted the common assumption that Leibniz had "much to do" with the founding of the Academy of Sciences, and reminded his readers that "in this context it is worth recalling Peter's visit to the Royal Society in 1698. . ." (p. 93). A summary of Peter's visit is found in Ian Grey, "Peter the Great in England," *History Today*, VI (April, 1956), pp. 225-34.

133—The idea that Leibniz was the inspiration to Peter for the founding of the Academy was supported by Liselotte Richter, in *Leibniz und sein Russlandbild* (Berlin: Akademie-Verlag, 1946). An extract from a 1716 letter written to Peter by Leibniz is in Philip P. Wiener, editor, *Leibniz Selections* (New York: Charles Scribner's Sons, 1951), pp. 595-99. Leibniz, referring to the Royal Society of Prussia, wrote, "This Society which the King founded according to my plans, has been established on such a basis that it scarcely costs the King anything to maintain; this can not only happen but be realized with greater profit in the great empire of his Czarist Majesty, and become glorious by his renown" (p. 598). For a translation of the draft, see *A Source Book for Russian History from Early Times to 1917*, George Vernadsky, senior editor, vol. II (New Haven: Yale University Press, 1972), pp. 367-68.

134—Vucinich, *Science in Russian Culture*, pp. 65-67; Aleksandr I. Andreev, "Osnovanie Akademii nauk v Peterburge," in *Petr Velikii: Sbornik statei*, A. I. Andreev, editor (Moscow: AN SSSR, 1947), I:283-333. Peter's visit to the Académie des Sciences is discussed on pages 289-95.

135—Black, *G.F. Müller*, p. 11; Vucinich, *Science in Russian Culture*, pp. 67-8, and 71.

136—For the decree founding the Academy, see *A Source Book*, ed. Vernadsky, II:368-69.

137—Vucinich, *Science in Russian Culture*, p. 71.

138—*Ibid.*, p. 70.

139—J.L. Black, *Citizens for the Fatherland: Education, Educators, and Pedagogical Ideals in Eighteenth Century Russia* (Boulder: East European Quarterly, 1979), pp. 23-5.

140—See James Cracraft, "Feofan Prokopovich," in J.G. Garrard, editor, *The Eighteenth Century*, pp. 75-105. In a later article, Cracraft questioned how much of the writings ascribed to Prokopovich are really his. See Cracraft, "Did Feofan Prokopovich Really Write *Pravda Voli Monarshei?*" *Slavic Review*, XL (1981), pp. 173-93. A contemporary letter from an Englishman, Thomas Consett, states that the *Ecclesiastical Regulation* was by several "Divines from Kiof, and other places, who had a learned education abroad" (p. 177).

141—Vucinich, *Science in Russian Culture*, p. 72.

142—Black, G.F. *Müller*, p. 20.

143—Black, *Citizens*, p. 27; Iudif Kh. Kopelevich, *Osnovanie Peterburgskoi Akademii nauk* (Leningrad: Nauka, 1977), p.31.

144—On Schumacher's handling of the Academy, in the early years, see Black, G.F. *Müller*, pp. 17-20, 26-30.

145—*Ibid.*, pp. 28-9.

146—*Ibid.*, p. 22.

147—Carl Eichhorn, *Die Geschichte der "St. Petersburger Zeitung" 1727-1902* (St. Petersburg: Buchdruckerei der St. Petersburger Zeitung, 1902), p. 22.

148—*Materialy dlia istorii Imperatorskoi Akademiia nauk*, edited by M.I. Sukhomlinov, 10 vols. (St. Petersburg, 1885-1900), VI, pp. 168-9.

149—For Strahlenberg's comments on this work see his *An Historico-geographical Description of the North and Eastern Parts of Europe and Asia* (London: J.Brotherton [etc.], 1738), pp. vii-viii, 127-28.

150—*Materialy dlia istorii*, VI, p. 169.

151—Ebulgazî Bahadir Han, *A General History of the Turks, Mongols, and Tatars*, 2 vols. (London: J. and J. Knapton, 1729-30), II, pp. 663-64. In the French original of 1726, this text appears in volume 2, on pages 108-09.

152—For a short biography see Seymour L. Chapin, "Joseph Nicolas Delisle," *The Dictionary of Scientific Biography*, IV, pp. 22-25. More extensive biographies are Pekarskii, *Istoriia*, I:124-49 and Albert Isnard, "Joseph-Nicolas Delisle, sa biographie et sa collection de cartes géographique à la Bibliothèque Nationale," *Comité des travaux historiques et scientifiques, Bulletin de la Section de Géographie*, XXX (1915), pp. 34-164.

153—M.H. Omont, "Lettres de J.N. Delisle au Comte de Maurepas et à l'Abbé Bignon sur ses travaux géographiques en Russie (1726-1730)," *Comité des travaux historiques et scientifiques, Bulletin de la Section de Géographie*, XXXII (1917), p. 142.

154—The only extensive biography of Bering in English is the one written in the nineteenth century by a Dane, Peter Lauridsen, which was translated into English by Julius E. Olson as *Vitus Bering: The Discoverer of Bering Strait* (Chicago: S.C. Griggs, 1889). The most recent Russian-language biography is Vasilii Mikhailovich Pesatskii, *Vitus Bering* (Moscow: Nauka, 1982).

155—For example, the biography of Bering in the *Russkii biograficheskii slovar'*, ed. A.A. Pelovtsov, II (St. Petersburg: Akademie der Wissenschaften, 1900), pp. 740-742, states simply that there is no information about Bering from 1716 to 1723 (p. 741). Other biographers have not been successful in adding significantly to the knowledge of Bering's activities in this period.

156—Peder von Haven, *Reise in Russland* (Copenhagen: Gabriel Christian Rothe, 1744), pp. 474-75. Haven, a Dane, was in Russia from 1736 to 1739, as secretary and minister to Peter Bredal, a Dane who had served in the Russian Navy since 1703. For Haven see Bjorn Kornerup, "Peder v. Haven," *Dansk Biografisk Leksikon*, IX (1936), p. 478.

157—The French traveler Aubry de La Mottraye, who visited Russia in 1707, 1714, and again in 1726, wrote that Peter was trying to discover a northeast passage, without success, and had sent an expedition from Arkhangelsk in 1724. "But these Difficulties did not deter him; he ordered two other Ships to be built for the same Design, according to the Directions of Captain Barring, a British Subject; who set sail in the Year 1724 with a 100 men for a second Attempt." Aubry de La Mottraye, *Travels through Europe, Asia, and into parts of Africa of A. de la Mottraye*, 3 vols. (London: For the Author, 1723-32), III, p. 145.

158—Glynn Barratt, *Russia in Pacific Waters, 1715-1825: A Survey of the Origins of Russia's Naval Presence in the North and South Pacific* (Vancouver: University of British Columbia Press, 1981), p. 17.

159—Lauridsen, *Vitus Bering*, p. 202.

160—Karl von Baer, *Peters des Grossen Verdienste um die Erweiterung der geographischen Kenntnisse*, original edition 1872 (Osnabrück: Biblio Verlag, 1969), p.40. Baer said that on 5 August 1724 Peter told Apraksin that Bering was again in service, as a captain of the first rank. This oral notification was given by Apraksin to the Admiralty on 7 August, in Bering's presence.

161—This translation of the instructions accompanies the text of the "Short Account" printed in John Harris, *Navigantium atque Itinerantium Bibliotheca*, John Campbell, 2 vols. (London: T. Woodward [etc.], 1744-48), II, p. 1020. Campbell stated that he had an original copy of Bering's journal.

162—A modern English translation of Bering's "Short Account" of the expedition is found in Frank A. Golder, *Bering's Voyages: An Account of the Efforts of the Russians to Determine the Relation of Asia and America*, 2 vols., (New York: American Geographical Society, 1922), I, pp. 8-20.

163—*Ibid.*, I, p. 19.

164—This article appeared in the *St. Petersburgische Zeitung*, no. 22, of 16 March 1730. This rare work was made available to me by The Library of the Academy of Sciences of the USSR, Leningrad, for which I am extremely grateful. The translation given here was made by Paul Brashear, who at the time had not read either my dissertation or the present book and therefore translated it without any bias. There was an eighteenth century translation of the same article in *The Historical Register for the Year 1730*, XV, p. 60 (London: R. Nutt, 1730), which is reproduced and discussed in Urness, "Bering's First Expedition," pp. 155-64. Raymond H. Fisher translated the same article from the *Sanktpeterburgskiia Vedomosti* in *Bering's Voyages*, pp. 12-13.

165—Vadim I. Grekov, "Naibolee ranee pechatnoe izvestie o pervoe Kamchatskoi ekspeditsii (1725-30 gg.)," *Izvestiia AN SSSR, seriia geograficheskaia* (Moscow) No. 6 (November-December, 1956), pp. 108-12. The newspaper text on pages 108-9 was translated by Raymond H. Fisher in *Bering's Voyages*, pp. 12-13.

166—In addition to the English text cited in footnote 64, the article appeared in Danish, in *Nye Tidender om laerbe og curieuse Sager*, No. 17, 27 April 1730. Strahlenberg, the Swede who had been in Siberia earlier, was in Stockholm in 1730; he mentioned reading a report on the Bering expedition "in the common newspapers." Philip Johann Tabbert von Strahlenberg, *Das nord-und ostliche Theil von Europa und Asia* (Stockholm, 1730), p. 10. Friedrich Christian Weber, a Hanoverian minister to Russia during the reign of Peter the Great, incorporated the newspaper article in a revised edition of his book on Russia, *Das veranderte Russland*, 3 vols. in 1 (Frankfurt: Nicolai Forster und Sohnes, 1744), III, pp. 157-58. This is almost a verbatim printing of the newspaper article.

167—The "Short Account" was first published in Jean Baptiste Du Halde, *Description géographique, historique, chronologique, politique et physique de l'empire de la Chine*, 4 vols. (Paris: P.G. Mercier, 1735), IV, pp. 452-58, with a map. See also note 62.

168—The "Short Account" indicates that the turn-around point was at 67° 18'. The manuscript and printed copies of the map made by the expedition vary. See William H. Dall, "A Critical Review of Bering's First Expedition," *The National Geographic Magazine*, II (1890), pp. 111-169, and the commentary on it by General A.W. Greely, "The Cartography and Observations of Bering's First Voyage," *The National Geographic Magazine*, III, (1892), pp. 205-230.

169—This map is reproduced as a frontispiece to Frank A. Golder, *Russian Expansion on the Pacific, 1641-1850* (Cleveland: Arthur H. Clark Company, 1914), but the map is not discussed in the text of the book.

170—Omont, "Lettres," p. 162.

171—[Gerhard Friedrich Müller] *A Letter from a Russian Sea-Officer, to a Person of Distinction at the Court of St. Petersburgh* (London: A. Linde, 1754), p. 11.

172—Fisher, *Bering's Voyages*, p. 12; J.L. Black, "G.F. Müller and the Russian Academy of Sciences Contingent in the Second Kamchatka Expedition, 1733-1743," *Canadian Slavonic Papers*, XXXV, No. 2 (June, 1983), pp. 235-52. See page 237.

173—Prokopovich (the clergyman noted in the text) produced three writings on this subject. See James Cracraft, "The Succession Crisis of 1730: A View from the Inside," *Canadian-American Slavic Studies*, XII, No. 1 (Spring, 1978), pp. 60-85. About this, Prokopovich said the plan was "to bridle and indeed to abolish the autocracy" (p. 63).

174—It seems unlikely that Bering would have discussed the expedition with anyone before reporting to the Admiralty Office. Possibly Bering stressed the northeast passage theme as part of a plan to maintain secrecy about the expedition. On the matter of secrecy relating to it, see Fisher, *Bering's Voyages*, pp. 72-76. It seems likely that Delisle and Müller supplied the emphasis on the basis of their own view of the importance of the expedition.

175—The French text (Du Halde, *Description. . . de la Chine*, IV, p. 452) stated that "les nouvelles publiques" indicated that Bering had orders to go to Kamchatka, "afin d'examiner les frontieres de ce Pays-la" to determine if connected to America or not. The newspaper article was the "public news" referred to; without the Homann map showing the "incognita" land on it, readers assumed that the frontiers were part of northeastern Asia.

176—See, for example, Barratt, *Russia in Pacific Waters*, pp. 1-23.

177—Aleksei V. Efimov, editor, *Atlas geograficheskikh otkrytii v Sibiri i v severo-zapadnoi Amerike XVII-XVIII vv.* (Moscow: Nauka, 1964), especially maps 47 (1701), 48 (ca. 1700), 49 (between 1699 and 1715), and 50 (1713). See also Harry M. Majors, "Early Russian Knowledge of Alaska, 1701-1730," *Northwest Discovery: The Journal of Northwest History*, vol. 4, no. 2 (October, 1983), pp. 84-152.

178—Fisher, *Bering's Voyages*, pp. 68-71.

179—There are only two copies in North America of the Homann atlas with the title page dated 1716. Johann Baptist Homann, *Grosser Atlas uber die gantze Welt*, (Nuremberg: In Verlegung des Autoris, 1716). The table of contents for the copy in the National Map Collection, Public Archives of Canada, lists the "Maris Caspii & Kamtzadaliae tabulae" as map number 170. Apparently, however, this copy has the title page of the 1716 atlas and the table of contents and maps of the 1725 edition. The contents are not the same as the copy of the 1716 atlas in the Boston Public Library, and I am grateful to Dr. Mary Emily Miller for verifying this.

180—See Endel Warep, "Über einige Karten Russlands in J.B. Homanns Atlas vom Jahre 1725," in *Petermanns geographische Mitteilungen*, 107:4 (1963), pp. 308-11, with a map. The letter is to Johann Alexander Doderlein; the pertinent text is on p. 310.

181—It is difficult to date these maps with certainty. In Paris, Peter the Great gave the French geographer Guillaume Delisle two manuscipt maps on 17 June 1717, one of them a new map of the Caspian Sea. Kopelevich, *Osnovanie*, pp. 43-44. Presumably this was the map published with Homann's first Kamchatka map. In his study of Homann, Sandler dates the "Imperium Moscoviticum" map as prior to 1707 and both the first Kamchatka map and the "Imperium Russorum" map from the period 1716 to 1724. See Christian Sandler, *Johann Baptista Homann, Matthaus Seutter und ihre Landkarten.* (Amsterdam: Meridian Publishing, 196-. Reprinted from the original of 1886), pp. 58, 60-61.

182—See map IX, which is a redrawing of the Homann map on a modern map of eastern Siberia.

183—Fisher, *Bering's Voyages*, p. 81; the full text of the questions is on pages 81-82.

184—*Ibid.*, p. 83, giving the full text of Spanberg's reply. Note Spanberg says they "have passed *east* of the land. . . ." [Emphasis added.]

185—*Ibid.* Chirikov, too, believed they had sailed east of the "incognita" land of the Homann map, since he indicates the nos was separated by sea from America. The word is literally "nose," meaning promontory or cape; it was often used in the eighteenth century to mean "peninsula." *Ibid.*, p. 40, footnote 25.

186—*Ibid.* See also the discussion of this on pages 84-5.

187—*Ibid.*, p. 84.

188—Chirikov was recommending that they return to the land, presumed to be the east coast of the "incognita" land shown on the Homann map, and follow along it to be sure that it did not extend northeastward again toward America. The possible high northern land bridge was the reason that Müller was convinced that his discoveries of a report of Dezhnev's voyage, rather than Bering's expedition, proved there was no land connection between Asia and America. This is shown in Müller's commentary on the expedition.

189—For example, Glynn Barratt, in *Russia in Pacific Waters*, stated "Bering at least firmly believed that he had carried out his orders and was certain that he had discovered a strait. So he had; but he had failed to demonstrate the fact. Chirikov understood the nature of proof as he, apparently, had not" (p. 22). Barratt has seen Bering's expedition in the context of an attempt to discover a Strait of Anian for purposes of trade via a northeast passage.

190—Both on the voyage north through the strait and on the return four days later, the weather was cloudy, so America, which would have been visible on a clear day, was not sighted. Baer, in an early comment on this, noted "Ist das nicht Unglück?" Baer, *Peters des Grossen*, p. 45.

191—In the newspaper article about the expedition the statement is made that there were reports of such a voyage "50 or 60 years ago." This may have been an incorrectly dated reference to Dezhnev's voyage, which was made in 1648. See Raymond H. Fisher, *The Voyages of Semen Dezhnev in 1648: Bering's Precursor, with Selected Documents.* Hakluyt Society, *Works*, 2nd Series, no. 159, (London: Hakluyt Society, 1981).

192—Maps IX and X. The latter is a comparison of Bering's map and a modern map.

193—Omont, "Lettres," p. 161.

194—The wood was important if they were going to spend the winter in the north. Gvozdev "discovered" this land in 1732, but this discovery was little noted. See Fisher, *Bering's Voyages*, pp. 168-69.

195—See Delisle's "Carte générale des découvertes de l'Amiral de Fonte" dated 1752 in his *Nouvelles cartes des découvertes de l'Amiral de Fonte* (Paris, 1753). The legend states that this land was sighted by Spanberg in 1728. Compare this to Müller's map, which indicates that the land was discovered by Gvozdev in 1730 (the date Gvozdev's expedition began).

196—The council and the stating of opinions about the voyage were not taken lightly; as an example see the commentary in this book about the decision to break up the ship used in Bering's voyage of 1741-42. Both Chirikov and Spanberg put their opinions in writing; neither indicated a belief that the mission had not been accomplished.

197—In the issue of 26 March 1730, however, a report appeared about the arrival in Moscow of "a monk by the name of Ignatius Kozirewski," whose father and grandfather had served Peter the Great in Siberia. This monk had been with Bering on the expedition. Dall, "Notes," p. 761. In the years

1711-14 Kozirevski had orders to explore Kamchatka and nearby lands. Friedrich Christian Weber, a minister from Hanover who served in Russia from 1714 to 1721, cited the reports from Kozirevski as the reason Peter sent Bering on the expedition. Weber said, "The reason that he [Bering] was dispatched can be seen from the following curious account. . ." and then went on to give the report given in the newspaper. Weber, *Das veranderte Russland*. 3 vols. in 1 (Frankfurt: Nicolai Forster, 1744), III, p. 158. Kozirevski, according to this report, had orders from Peter the Great to explore "der Granzen des Landes und insonderheit der Nord-Ostlichen Houk Kamzatkoi Noss genannt" (the frontiers of the country and especially the northeastern hook named Kamchatka Nos). An incomplete text of this article was found in the Delisle manuscripts, translated by Golder in *Russian Expansion on the Pacific*, pp. 294-97.

I98—The "Short Account" appeared in several translations in western Europe but was not published in Russia until the mid-nineteenth century. By that time the belief that the expedition was sent to search for part of a northeast passage was firmly embedded in the literature.

I99—This same statement appeared in the numerous editions and translations of Du Halde's text. See Urness, "Bering's First Expedition," pp. 172-93.

Chapter II

II1—J.L. Black, *G.F. Müller and the Imperial Russian Academy of Sciences, 1725-1783: First Steps in the Development of the Historical Sciences in Russia*, (in press), p. 28; Petr Petrovich Pekarskii, *Istoriia imperatorskoi akademiia nauk v Peterburge*, 2 vols. (St. Petersburg: Imperatorskaia akademiia nauk, 1870-73), I, 312-13. For the general history of the academy, see Alexander Vucinich, *Science in Russian Culture: A History to 1860* (Stanford: Stanford University Press, 1963).

II2—Of the 16 original members of the academy, nearly half were skilled mathematicians. This group was greatly enhanced in 1727, when Leonhard Euler joined the academy. Vucinich, *Science in Russian Culture*, p. 78.

II3—*Ibid.*, pp. 78-79.

II4—He was especially to ask "scholars of jurisprudence, experienced physicians, and men familiar with the Eastern languages" (Black, *G.F. Müller*, pp. 30-31). The instructions are given in Iu. Kh. Kopelevich, "Pervaia zagranichnaia komandirovka peterburgskogo akademika (iz zapisakh G. F. Millera o evo puteshesshestvii 1730-1731 gg.)," *Voprosy istorii estestvoznaniia i tekniki*, no. 2 (1973), pp. 47-52.

II5—Kopelevich, "Pervaia," p. 48; *Materialy dlia istorii imperatorskoi akademiia nauk*, ed. M.I. Sukhomlinov. 10 vols. (St. Petersburg, 1885-1900). VI, pp. 202-03.

II6—Kopelevich, "Pervaia," pp. 49-51.

II7—Black, *G.F. Müller*, p. 35; *Materialy*, VI, pp. 37-39, 212-14.

II8—Pekarskii, *Istoriia*, I, p. 315.

II9—*Ibid.*, pp. 315-16.

II10—*Ibid.*, p. 318.

II11—Black, *G. F. Müller*, pp. 35-36; Pekarskii, *Istoriia*, I, p. 26.

II12—Both served in the navy with the rank of mate in the First Kamchatka Expedition according to Chaplin's journal, in William H. Dall, "Notes on an Original Manuscript Chart of Bering's Expedition of 1725-1730, and on an Original Manuscript Chart of his Second Expedition; Together with a Summary of a Journal of the First Expedition, kept by Peter Chaplin, and Now First Rendered into English from Bergh's Russian Version." *Report of the Superintendent of the U.S. Coast and Geodetic Survey Showing the Progress of the Work during the Fiscal Year Ending with June, 1890*. Appendix no. 19. Washington: Government Printing Office, 1891.

II13—Kopelevich, "Pervaia," p. 49.

II14—The text of this proposal is published in Aleksei V. Efimov, *Iz istorii russkikh ekspeditsii na tikhom okeane*, (Moscow, 1948), pp. 251-52.

II15—For more information on Elton, see Douglas K. Reading, *The Anglo-Russian Commercial Treaty of 1734*, (New Haven: Yale University Press, 1938), pp. 239-43, and Jonas Hanway, *An Historical Account of the British Trade over the Caspian Sea*, 4 vols. (London: Mr. Dodsley [etc.], 1753), I, viii, 13-70.

II16—Pekarskii, *Istoriia*, I, p. 318.

II17—It must be emphasized that the aspect of Müller's work considered throughout this text is only a small part of his contribution to historical studies. In addition to the biographical references cited, see Samuel H. Cross, "The Contribution of Gerhard Friedrich Müller to Russian Historiography, with some consideration of August Ludwig Schloezer." Ph.D. dissertation, Harvard University, 1916.

II18—The emphasis placed on the geographical discoveries of the two Bering expeditions obscures their effect on Russian settlement and administration of eastern Siberia. Bering's reports from the First Kamchatka Expedition contained many recommendations relating to the development of eastern Siberia. On the general subject, see James R. Gibson, *Feeding the Russian Fur Trade: Provisionment on the Okhotsk Seaboard and the Kamchatka Peninsula, 1639-1856* (Madison: University of Wisconsin Press, 1969). For an account of the effects of the First Kamchatka Expedition on Kamchatka, see Isaac Morris Schottenstein, "The Russian Conquest of Kamchatka, 1697-1731." Ph.D. dissertation, University of Wisconsin, 1969.

II19—Raymond H. Fisher, *Bering's Voyages: Whither and Why* (Seattle: University of Washington Press, 1977), pp. 112-13, as part of a chapter discussing the proposals. See also Frank A. Golder, *Bering's Voyages*, I, p. 26; Glynn Barratt, *Russia in Pacific Waters, 1715-1825* (Vancouver: University of British Columbia Press, 1981), pp. 28-31.

II20—The requirement of secrecy was stated in a Senate ukase of 2 May 1732. It was elaborated in the Senate report. Fisher, *Bering's Voyages*, p. 144. Chapter VI of this work, "The Second Kamchatka Expedition: Plans and Objectives," pp. 120-51, gives an excellent description of the development of the expedition.

II21—Barratt, *Russia in Pacific Waters*, pp. 28-31. The involvement of the Academy of Sciences is also discussed here.

II22—Fisher, *Bering's Voyages*, pp. 120-23; on Kirilov, see also Barratt, *Russia in Pacific Waters*, pp. 25-26.

II23—*Materialy*, VI, p. 253.

II24—On Kirilov, see Mariia G. Novlianskaia, *Ivan Kirilovich Kirilov: geograf XVIII veka* (Leningrad: Nauka, 1964) and Leo Bagrow, "Ivan Kirilov, Compiler of the First Russian Atlas." *Imago Mundi*, II (1938), pp. 78-82.

II25—Fisher, *Bering's Voyages*, p. 186. The memorandum is translated in this work on pages 184-87.

II26—Müller, A Letter from a Russian Sea-Officer, to a Person of Distinction at the Court of St. Petersburgh (London, A. Linde [etc.], 1754), p. 11.

II27—See Delisle's "Memoir presented to the Senate with map which Bering used in going to America," (p. 311) translated by Frank A. Golder, *Russian Expansion on the Pacific, 1641-1850* (Cleveland: Arthur H. Clark Company, 1914), pp. 302-13. Müller later stated "His map hurt the discoveries made from Kamchatka more than it helped." *Materialy*, VI, p. 254.

II28—Golder, *Russian Expansion*, pp. 302-13.

II29—*Materialy*, VII, p. 253.

II30—Fisher, *Bering's Voyages*, p. 186. Kirilov, however, goes on to stress the importance of the rivers in Siberia, and the sea route from Okhotsk, for trade. *Ibid.*, p. 187.

II31—Black, *G.F. Müller*, p. 70.

II32—*Ibid.*, p. 72.

II33—*Materialy*, VI, p. 270.

II34—*Ibid.*

II35—*Ibid.*, pp. 270-71.

II36—An account of Müller's part in this is found in J.L. Black, "G.F. Müller and the Russian Academy of Sciences Contingent in the Second Kamchatka Expedition, 1733-1743." *Canadian Slavonic Papers*, XXXV, no. 2 (June, 1983), pp. 235-52.

II37—See Raymond H. Fisher, *The Voyages of Semen Dezhnev in 1648: Bering's Precursor, with Selected Documents*. In Hakluyt Society, *Works*, 2nd Series, no. 159. (London: Hakluyt Society, 1981).

II38—The exact nature of Müller's health problems is not known; Büsching, in his *Beytrage*, III, comments on Müller's health at some length. He indicated (p. 44) that long after their return from Siberia both Gmelin and Müller suffered from a "schweren hypochondrischen Krankheit" which had been caused by their journey.

II39—Leonhard Stejneger, *Georg Wilhelm Steller: The Pioneer of Alaskan Natural History* (Cambridge: Harvard University Press, 1936), pp. 111-13.

II40—Bering had estimated the cost of the expedition at 12,000 or 13,000 roubles; more than 300,000 had already been spent. Barratt noted that, "An unhappy series of deliberate or unavoidable delays, slanders, and outbreaks of envenomed bickering marked the expedition's progress—or, more accurately, lack of it—in 1735-37 . . . ." (*Russia in Pacific Waters*, p. 33).

II41—Krasheninnikov spent the years 1737 to 1741 studying the natural history of Kamchatka. In addition to his own research, he also used Steller's in preparing his *Opisanie zemli Kamchatka*, published by the academy in 1755. A new edition and translation is *Explorations of Kamchatka: North Pacific Scimitar* by E.A.P. Crownhart-Vaughan, (Portland: Oregon Historical Society, 1972).

II42—Stejneger, *Georg Wilhelm Steller*, pp. 114-15.

II43—Steller was quite a contrast to Gmelin and Müller, who, as Stejneger puts it "went about primitive and sparsely populated Siberia in grand style." According to Gmelin, Steller did not trouble himself with clothing, food, or drink. He cooked everything himself and "that with so little circumstance that soup, vegetables, and meat were put into the same pot and boiled together . . . . He used no wig and no powder; any kind of shoe or boot suited him." Stejneger, *Georg Wilhelm Steller*, pp. 146-47.

II44—Fischer was supposed to travel with Steller, but on his way to Okhotsk he was denounced by a member of his escort and was returned to Iakutsk for trial. Though he was freed, he was unable to make the journey to Kamchatka. Stejneger, *Georg Wilhelm Steller*, pp. 247 note 32, pp. 449-50; Pekarskii, *Istoriia*, I, pp. 621-22.

II45—Büsching, *Beytrage*, III, p. 44, citing 31,362 versts or 4,480 German miles.

II46—The map is titled "l'Hemisphere septentrional pour voir plus distinctement les terres arctiques." The text of the letter is dated 13/24 (Old Style and New Style) January 1740. A copy of it appears in Guillaume Delisle's *Atlas nouveau, contenant toutes parties du monde* (Amsterdam: Covens et Mortier, [1741]).

II47—The map was from Kirilov's *Atlas*. Kirilov was not involved in providing the information on the map, for he died in 1737.

II48—A translation of this appears in Golder, *Russian Expansion*, pp. 330-33.

II49—*The London Magazine*, IX, (London: T. Astby, 1740), p. 155.

II50—Translated in Golder, *Russian Expansion*, pp. 212-13.

II51—This was published a month earlier than the *Gazette de France* article. Steller's role is less heroic: "Mr. Stoller, with the Assistance of some of his Companions, found Means to build, out of the ruins of their great Ship, a little Shallop in which himself, and 19 others, after running through a Thousand perilous Adventures, arrived at Kamschatka." *Gentleman's Magazine*, XIII, (London, 1743), p. 552.

II52—Stejneger, *Georg Wilhelm Steller*, p. 442.

II53—*Ibid*. This text was translated by Stejneger from the Justi biography of Steller; the same text appears in *Leben Herrn Georg Wilhelm Stellers* . . . . Both of these works are discussed in this chapter.

II54—For example, Count Christopher Manstein, a German who had been in Russia from 1736 to 1744, wrote, "The Academy is not so organized as to enable Russia to receive from it even the smallest benefit, because its members are not predominantly engaged in the study of languages, moral sciences, civil law, history, or practical geometry—the only sciences from which Russia could benefit. Instead, the Academy's staff works mostly in algebra, speculative geometry, and other fields of higher mathematics." Quoted in Vucinich, *Science in Russian Culture*, p. 85.

II55—Vucinich, *Science in Russian Culture*, pp. 82-89, describes the conflict between the members of the academy in this period, and notes, "It was also at this time that open suspicion was cast on foreign scholars as possible clandestine informers of various Western powers" (p. 84).

II56—*Ibid.*, pp. 83-4; Black, G.F. *Müller*, pp. 108-11.

II57—Samuel H. Cross, "The Contribution," p.118.

II58—Black, G.F. *Müller*, pp. 249-50.

II59—Aleksandr I. Andreev, "Trudy G.F. Millera o vtoroi kamchatskoi ekspeditsii." *Izvestiia*, VGO, XCI:1, (January-February, 1959), p. 3.

II60—Materialy, VI, p. 78.

II61—The University of Kansas Library has four different states of the Homann map. See Thomas E. Smith and Bradford L. Thomas, *Maps of the 16th to 19th Centuries in the University of Kansas Libraries* (Lawrence: University of Kansas Libraries, 1963), pp. 16-17. The map published in Paris was by Georges-Louis Le Rouge, titled "l'Amerique suivant Le R.P. Charlevoix Jte, Mr. De La Condamine et plusieurs autres Nouvelles Observations . . . ." See the discussion of Delisle on page 44.

II62—For a more extensive account see Stejneger, *Georg Wilhelm Steller*, pp. 472-88.

II63—*Ibid.*, pp. 490-91.

II64—Johann Heinrich Gottlob von Justi, "Zuverlassige Nachricht von dem merkwurdigen Leben und Reisen Herrn Georg Wilhelm Stollers, der Russisch Kaiserl. Akademie der Wissenschaften Adjuncti und Mitglieds." *Ergetzungen der vernunftigen Seele aus der Sittenlehre und der Gelehrsamkeit uberhaupt*, V:4 (October, 1747), pp. 362-84.

II65—Stejneger, *Georg Wilhelm Steller*, p. 491.

II66—The publication was *Leben Herrn Georg Wilhelm Stellers, gewesen Adjuncti der Kayserl. Academie der Wissenschaften zu St. Petersburg: worinnen die biszher bekannt gemachte Nachrichten Deselben Reisen, Entdeckungen, und Tode, Theils wiederleget, theils erganzet und verbeszert werden.* (Frankfurt, 1748).

II67—The details given are specific enough to suggest that the writer may have used Steller's journal. On 4 November 1742 Steller wrote a letter to Gmelin about the expedition, which Gmelin received in St. Petersburg in October of 1743. The text of the letter appears in Golder, *Bering's Voyages*, II, pp. 242-49. It does not contain enough information to be the source of the biography.

II68—This publication appears to be "official" in the sense that it was published in answer to the rumors that had been spread about Steller's death. A copy of this rare work is in the Lilly Rare Book Library at Indiana University.

II69—In *Georg Wilhelm Steller*, p. 492, Stejneger considers possible authors and concludes that Müller wrote the biography. If Müller did not write it, another member of the academy—perhaps Fischer or Gmelin—did.

II70—The text is the official report on the voyage of the *St. Peter*, submitted by Waxell to the Admiralty College. Haven's book was published in Copenhagen; the account appears on pages 17-43 of volume two. The academy was aware of this publication; see A. I. Andreev, "Trudy G.F. Millera," p. 5.

II71—For a biography of Haven, see Bjorn Konerup (A. Jantzen), "Peder v. Haven," in *Dansk Biografisk Lexikon*, IX, p. 478. Haven stated, "I got these rare writings from Captain Spanberg himself," in his *Reise udi Russland*, (Soroe: Jonas Lindgren, 1757), pp. 489-90.

II72—This text was translated by Golder in *Bering's Voyages*, I, pp. 270-81. Golder was unaware of Haven's eighteenth century printing of the text, which was subsequently translated by Leonhard Stejneger, "An Early Account of Bering's Voyages" in *The Geographical Review*, XXIV:4 (October, 1934), pp. 638-42, and compared to the Golder text.

II73—In John Harris, *Navigantium atque Itinerantium Bibliotheca, Or, A Complete Collection of Voyages and Travels*, edited by John Campbell, 2 vols. (London: T. Woodward [etc.], 1744-48), II, pp. 1016-22, with a map.

II74—Campbell was a dedicated proponent of the discovery of a Northwest Passage. See Glyndwr Williams, *The British Search for the Northwest Passage in the Eighteenth Century* (London: Longmans, 1962), pp. 92-4.

II75—"This Detail which we have given our Reader, is not barely copied from the Accounts that have been published in German, Low-Dutch, French, and other Languages, but hath been compared with a Copy of Captain Behring's original Journal . . . ." Harris, *Navigantium*, II, p. 1021. Unfortunately, Campbell did not publish the text itself, but translated it into the third person and added editorial comments. On this text see Urness, "Bering's First Expedition," pp. 186-90.

II76—Russkoe istoricheskoe obshchestvo, *Sbornik*, CIII (St. Petersburg: 1897), p. 452. On this see also Fisher, *Bering's Voyages*, pp. 181-82.

II77—The letter appeared in the *Philosophical Transactions* of the Royal Society; it is reprinted in Harris, *Navigantium*, II, p. 1024.

II78—In 1748 Euler wrote to Schumacher "It was very unpleasant for me to learn that H. Wettstein in England made public the letter I wrote to him about the newly discovered areas near America." Leonhard Euler, *Die Berliner und die Petersburger Akademie der Wissenschaften im Briefwechsel Leonhard Eulers*, 3 vols. (Berlin: Akademie-Verlag, 1959-76), II, p. 130.

II79—The response of Dobbs is summarized by Campbell in Harris, *Navigantium*, II, pp. 1025-28.

II80—On Gmelin's troubles with the academy, see Lothar A. Maier, "Die Krise der St. Peterburger Akademie der Wissenschaften nach der Thronbesteigung Elisabeth Petrovnas und die 'Affare Gmelin'" in *Jahrbuch fur Geschichte Osteuropas*, neue Folge, XXVII:3 (1979), pp. 353-73.

II81—Euler, *Die Berliner*, II, p. 259.

II82—Johann Georg Gmelin, *Reise durch Sibirien*, 4 vols. in 2, (Gottingen: Abram Vandenhoecks seel, Wittwe, 1751-52), I, sig. $++2^v—++3^r$.

II83—Pekarskii, *Istoriia*, I, p. 452.

II84—Gmelin, *Reise*, I, sig. +3 ff.

II85—*Ibid.*, II, pp. 410-41.

II86—William Coxe, *Account of the Russian Discoveries between Asia and America* (London: J. Nichols, 1780), pp. 304-310. In the 1803 edition of this work the text appears on pages 366-72.

II87—Maier, "Die Krise," pp. 371-72.

II88—Lomonosov and Müller were reluctant to write a rebuttal. Andreev, "Trudy G. F. Millera," p. 4.

II89—Pekarskii, *Istoriia*, I, pp. 366-68. The work is Johann Eberhard Fischer, *Sibirische Geschichte von der Entdeckung Sibiriens bis auf die Eroberung dieses Lands durch die russische Waffen*. (St. Petersburg: Akademie der Wissenschaften, 1768).

II90—Barratt, in *Russia in Pacific Waters*, p. 24, writes "Regrettably, he [Delisle] was a poor cartographer." Müller says "I cannot help thinking, that it was wrong in him to aspire at a perfection . . . yet, after all this scrupulous exactness of Mr. de l'Isle, and after the space of twelve years, so far was the work from being brought to any forwardness, that there was scarce the first outlines to be seen of it." *Letter*, p. 6. On Delisle as a spy, see O.M. Medushevskaya, "Cartographic Sources for the History of Russian Geographical Discoveries in the Pacific Ocean in the Second Half of the 18th Century." Trans. James R. Gibson, *The Canadian Cartographer*, IX:2 (December, 1972), pp. 99-121 and Lydia T. Black, "The Question of Maps: Exploration of the Bering Sea in the Eighteenth Century." *History and Archaeology Publications*, Series no. 25. Office of History and Archaeology, Alaska Division of Parks, November, 1979, pp. 6-50.

II91—See the biography by Albert Isnard, "Joseph-Nicolas Delisle, sa biographie et sa collection de cartes géographiques à la Bibliothèque Nationale," in Comité des travaux historiques et scientifiques. *Bulletin de la Section de Géographie*, XXX (1915), pp. 34-164, especially pp. 48-9.

II92—*Ibid.*, p. 38.

II93—Leo Bagrow, "Ivan Kirilov," p. 79.

II94—*Ibid.* Bagrow dates the earliest surveys from 1716. Henri Froidevaux, "Les études géographiques de Joseph-Nicolas Delisle sur l'Empire russe," in *La géographie*, XXXIII (January-May, 1920), pp. 219-228, dates the surveys from 1720 (p. 221), when the official order for compiling the maps was made by Peter the Great.

II95—Isnard, "Joseph-Nicolas Delisle," pp. 39-40.

II96—*Ibid.*, p.44.

II97—Lydia Black, "The Question of Maps," (p. 8) gives the number of maps copied by Delisle as 350; 195 maps sent by Delisle to France are described by Isnard, "Joseph-Nicolas Delisle," pp. 82-164.

II98—H. Omont, "Lettres de J.N. Delisle au Comte de Maurepas et à l'Abbé Bignon sur ses trauvaux géographiques en Russie (1726-1730)," (p. 162) in Comité des travaux historiques et scientifiques. *Bulletin de la Section de Géographie*, XXXII (1917), pp. 130-64.

II99—Müller states this in the translation itself.

II100—Isnard, "Joseph-Nicolas Delisle," pp. 47-8, gives this as the reason Delisle was under suspicion in Russia.

II101—Joseph-Nicolas Delisle, *Explication de la cartes des nouvelles decouvertes au nord de la Mer du Sud* (Paris: Desaint et Saillant, 1752), pp. 5-6.

II102—The map by Georges-Louis Le Rouge, was titled "Mappe monde nouvelle" and dated 1744.

II103—The mapmaker was Johann M. Hasius, or Hase; in a letter written in 1726 Delisle indicates that he had met him and was corresponding with him. Omont, "Lettres de J.N. Delisle," p.133.

II104—Andreev, "Trudy G.F. Millera," p.3. Müller had made a map showing the coast of America. His maps were returned to him in 1752.

II105—The map published in 1752 to accompany the *Explication* is titled "Carte des nouvelles découvertes au nord de la Mer du Sud . . . Dressée sur les mémoires de Mr. De l'Isle . . . par Philippe Buache." Map XVI.

II106—Delisle, *Explication*, p.6. *The Explication* was translated and published with Müller's *A Letter from a Russian Sea-Officer*, (London: A. Linde, 1754) on pages 53-71. Delisle writes that the second voyage was "to be made according to the plan which I had drawn up for it." (p. 63).

II107—Arthur Dobbs, *An Account of the Countries adjoining to Hudson's Bay, in the North Part of America*, (London: J. Robinson, 1744), pp. 123-28.

II108—See Glyndwr Williams, *The British Search*, particularly chapters VII and VIII.

II109—Since Delisle was presumably the source for the maps printed earlier in western Europe, he was under suspicion for his activities in copying Russian maps. He was not given access to more maps. Isnard, "Joseph-Nicolas Delisle," pp. 48-9.

II110—Many of the journals and maps had not been received by the Admiralty College at the time Delisle left Russia. Andreev, "Trudy G.F. Millera," p.5. Delisle also had financial difficulties on his return to France. He was an "expert" on the Russian explorations, no doubt anxious to prove his worth. Isnard, "Joseph-Nicolas Delisle," pp.50-52.

II111—See Glyndwr Williams, "An Eighteenth-Century Spanish Investigation into the Apocryphal Voyage of Admiral Fonte," in *Pacific Historical Review*, 30:4 (November, 1961), pp.319-27 for an account of how the authenticity of this voyage was refuted by a Spanish scholar in 1757.

II112—Williams, *The British Search*, pp. 152-53.

II113—Georges-Louis Le Rouge published a map dated 1744 which showed Bering's route (Map XIII). He dedicated his map to Comte de Maurepas, who supplied information for it; this information presumably came from Delisle. R. Oehme, "A French World Atlas of the 18th Century: The Atlas General of G.L. LeRouge," in *Imago Mundi*, 25 (Amsterdam: 1971), pp. 55-64, especially pp. 57-59.

II114—Andreev, "Trudy G.F. Millera," p. 6.

II115—Black, *G.F. Müller*, pp. 119, 128, 131-34.

II116—*Ibid.*, p. 155.

II117—D. Obolensky, "The Varangian-Russian controversy: The First Round," in Hugh Lloyd Jones, et.al., eds. *History & Imagination*, (New York: Holmes & Meier, 1981). pp. 232-42.

II118—Black, *G.F. Müller*, pp. 135-36.

II119—Cross, "Contribution," p. 142.

II120—On Müller's contract negotiations and the two investigations of him, see Black, *G.F. Müller*, pp.127-37, 144.

II121—Andreev, "Trudy G.F. Millera," p. 6. The text was printed in sixty pages, in a small octavo format.

II122—*Ibid.*, p. 8. That Müller used Waxell as his source for the *Letter* was first shown in 1940, in the Russian translation of the Waxell journal.

II123—Müller, *Letter*, p. 5.

II124—*Ibid.*, p. 14.

II125—*Ibid.*, p. 25.

II126—*Ibid.* Müller is reminding his readers that the theoretical routes traced on maps and globes are not shorter if in reality they cannot be used because of ice and weather conditions in the north.

II127—The text of "A Letter by Admiral Barthelemi de Fonte . . . " is printed in the English translation, following Müller's *Letter*, on pages 72-81.

II128—Müller, *Letter*, p. 31.

II129—Arthur Dobbs, "Observations upon the Russian Discoveries," is printed with Müller's *Letter*, on pages 35-51.

II130—Dobbs, "Observations," p. 47.

II131—See L. Breitfuss, "Early Maps of North-Eastern Asia and of the Lands around the North Pacific: Controversy between G.F. Müller and N. Delisle," in *Imago Mundi*, III (London, 1939), pp. 87-99.

II132—See V.A. Perevalov, *Lomonosov i arktika* (Moscow, Leningrad: Glavsevmorput, 1949).

II133—Peter Simon Pallas, *A Naturalist in Russia: Letters from Peter Simon Pallas to Thomas Pennant*, ed. Carol Urness (Minneapolis: University of Minnesota Press, 1967), pp. 118, 135. An account of Chichagov's expeditions, written by Müller, was published in Pallas's *Neue nordische Beytrage*, Vol. 5 (St. Petersburg: J.Z. Logan, 1793).

II134—Samuel Engel, *Memoires et observations geographiques et critiques sur la situation des pays septentrionaux de l'Asie et de l'Amerique* (Lausanne: Antoine Chapuis, 1765), pp. 228-29. For further commentary, see James R. Masterson and Helen Brower, *Bering's Successors, 1745-1780* (Seattle: University of Washington Press, 1948), pp. 14-16. This publication is a reprint of *Pacific Northwest Quarterly*, volume 38, numbers one and two. See also Peter Hoffmann, "Gerhard Friedrich Müller— Die Bedeutung seiner geographischen Arbeiten fur das Russlandbild des 18 Jahrhunderts." Ph.D. dissertation, Humboldt University, 1959, especially pp. 229-31.

II135—Müller's letter appears in *Anton Friedrich Büschings wochentliche Nachrichten von neuen Landcharten, geographischen, statistischen, und historischen Buchern*, 13 December 1773 (Berlin: Haude und Spener, 1773), pp. 401-08. Müller indicates that he had not responded to Engel earlier because of his reluctance to quarrel, his age, and his involvement in other writings.

II136—*Ibid.*, p. 407.

II137—Samuel Engel, *Geographische und kritische Nachrichten und Anmerkungen uber die Lage der nordlichen Gegenden von Asien und Amerika*, 2 vols. (Basel: Carl August Serini, 1777), II, p. 28.

II138—*Ibid.*, p. 119.

II139—*Ibid.*, p. 107.

II140—Müller, *Letter*, p. 7.

II141—*Ibid.*, p. 8.

II142—*Ibid.*, p. 12.

II143—Gerhard Friedrich Müller, *Sammlung russischer Geschichte* (St. Petersburg: Keyserl. Academie der Wissenschaften, 1758), III, p. 5.

II144—*Ibid.*, pp. 5-6.

II145—*Ibid.*, pp. 61-62.

II146—*Ibid.*, p. 65.

II147—Apparently Müller's research was published by "J.L.S." in the *Neue Nachrichten von denen neuentdekten Insuln in der See zwischen Asien und Amerika* (Hamburg und Leipzig: Friedrich Ludwig Gleditsch, 1776). For a commentary on the authorship of this work see Valerian Lada-Mocarski, *Bibliography of Books on Alaska published before 1868* (New Haven: Yale University Press, 1969), p. 98. In addition, see Leonhard Stejneger, "Who was J.L.S.?" in *The Library Quarterly*, vol. IV, no. 2, (April, 1934), pp. 334-40, where the case is made for J.L. Stavenhagen, an archivist who worked closely with Müller, as the author.

Translation

1—The English translation of 1764, which Müller may have corrected, differs from the 1761 (Illustration II) in stating the question was "whether Asia and America were contiguous to, or separated from each other . . . ." Contiguous here could mean "nearby" rather than "joined." The preliminary material for both English editions stresses the search for a northeast passage.

2— Apraksin, a close friend of Peter the Great, was president of the Admiralty College, the ruling body of the Russian Navy. He died in 1728, while Bering was on the expedition.

3—The "northerly coasts" indicated here were not, in my opinion, part of the mainland of Siberia. They were, rather, the coasts of land shown in the northeast on the Homann map. Two other eighteenth century versions of the instructions which are discussed in this book are significant for this interpretation. John Harris translated this portion of the instructions as "whether the Country towards the North, of which we have no distinct Knowledge, is a Part of America, or not." This text of the instructions is cited in Chapter I. The authenticity of this account is discussed in Chapter II. In the *Lettre* of 1753 Müller writes that Bering was "to reconnoitre the furthest northern part of the eastern coasts of Siberia, and to see whether in any part they joined with America." This translation is from the English edition of 1754; the German reads that Bering was to build boats and "mit solchem den aussersten nordlichen nordlichen Theil der Custen von Siberien gegen Osten zu untersuchen, und zu sehen, ob die Custen etwa an America stossen. . . ".

4—Catherine I, Peter the Great's widow, succeeded him and reigned from 1725 until her death in 1727.

5—Bering's "Short Account" of his expedition was first published in Jean Baptiste Du Halde, *Description géographique, historique, chronologique, politique et physique de l'empire de la Chine et de la Tartarie chinoise* (Paris, 1735) IV:452-458, with a map. For other editions, see the bibliography.

6—Martin Spanberg (1698-1761), a Dane by birth, was "illiterate, with a reckless audacity, rough, and exceedingly cruel, avaricious, and selfish, but strong in mind, body, and purpose, of great energy, and a good seaman," according to Bancroft, 1886, p. 50.

7—Aleksei Ilyich Chirikov (1703-1748), a Russian, attended both the Moscow School of Navigation and the St. Petersburg Naval Academy. "Before setting out on the expedition he was promoted to lieutenant, and gave evidence throughout the expedition of great courage and common sense." Bancroft, 1886, p. 49.

8—On 24 January Lieutenant Chirikov and Midshipman Peter Chaplin, together with "a surgeon, a geodesist, a garde marine officer, a quartermaster, clerk, 10 sailors, 2 ship carpenters, an officer with three marines, 4 calkers and sailmakers and several other workmen" left St. Petersburg. They had 25 wagons of supplies. Bering, Lieutenant Spanberg, two mates and three sailors left on 5 February. Dall, 1891, p. 761.

9—At Tobolsk, 34 more men were added to the company, including a monk, a commissar, petty officers, and soldiers. Chaplin says "They started their long journey with four barges and seven canoes." Dall, 1891, p. 761.

10—At this place Bering "obtained from the Voivod [voevoda or governor] the services of the monk Kozuireffski." Dall, 1891, p. 762. Ivan Kozyrevskii knew as much about Kamchatka as anyone; he had been there for more than two decades. He had been forced to become a monk in 1715 as a result of difficulties with the officials in Kamchatka. In 1713 he made a map which may have been used in preparing the Homann map; see Efimov, *Atlas*, no. 50; Fisher, 1977, p. 40. Bering not only consulted with Kozyrevskii, but took him along on the expedition.

11—He left in June with 13 barges and 204 people. Dall, 1891, p. 762.

12—There were 600 horses loaded with flour. Less than half of them reached Okhotsk in October, according to Chaplin. Dall, 1891, p. 762.

13—This was a landmark set up near the headwaters of the Iudoma River, beyond which navigation was not possible. Golder, 1922, I, p. 13.

14—Chaplin reports, "On the 21st of December a report from him [Spanberg] was received to the effect that his party was on the road with 90 sledges, having left a mate and 9 soldiers in charge of the barges; the next day 10 sledges of provisions, and twenty-four hours later 39 men with 37 sledges, were dispatched to his relief." Dall, 1891, p.762.

15—In February 90 men with dog sleds went with Spanberg back to get more supplies. Finally another group of men, with pack horses, brought the remaining supplies from the Iudoma River in May. Golder, 1922, I, p. 16.

16—Chirikov arrived on 3 July rather than 30 July; he brought 200 sacks of flour on 110 horses. Dall, 1891, p. 763; Golder, 1922, I, p. 16.

17—The name of this ship is not given in the "Short Account" of Bering's expedition; it is given by Chaplin. Dall, 1891, p. 762.

18—Chaplin says "This was the same vessel which made the first voyage from Okhotsk to Kamchatka in 1716." This statement, too, indicates that Müller was using Chaplin's journal of the First Kamchatka Expedition, for this information does not appear in Bering's "Short Account". Dall, 1891, p. 762. Nikifor Treska sailed the one-masted, sixty-foot-long vessel on that first crossing.

19—A palisaded fort.

20—The literal translation is "dog carts" or "dog vehicles."

21—Early in January, 1728, 78 sleds were sent to Upper Kamchatka Post; Bering and his company left Bolsheretsk on 14 January and arrived at the post there on 25 January. Bering spent seven weeks there while goods were being transported to Nizhne-Kamchatsk. Dall, 1891, p. 763; Golder, 1922, I, p. 17.

22—On 4 April, to celebrate beginning the ship, "Bering issued a bountiful allowance of wine to all hands." On 9 June the ship was named and launched; by 9 July everything needed was on board the vessel. Dall, 1891, p. 764. The ship was 60 feet long by 20 feet wide, with a draft of seven feet. Fisher, 1977, p. 117.

23—The crew consisted of a captain, 2 lieutenants, 1 2nd lieutenant, 1 physician, 1 quartermaster, 8 sailors, 1 saddler, 1 rope-maker, 5 carpenters, 1 bailiff, 2 cossacks, 9 soldiers, 6 servants, 1 drummer, and 2 interpreters. Lauridsen, 1889, p. 30.

24—See Map X.

25—"The interpreters said there was so much difference between the Kariak [sic] dialect and that of these Chukchi, so that they were not able to get from them all the information that would have been desirable." Dall, 1891, p. 766.

26—The text of this conversation was put in a memorandum signed by Bering, Chirikov, and Spanberg. It is translated in Fisher, 1977, pp. 81-82.

27—These are Müller's comments. From his study of early accounts of Siberia he concluded "there is a real separation between the two parts of the world, Asia and America; the same consists only of a small strait and one or more islands are situated in this strait, . . . so that the inhabitants of each have had knowledge of the other part since ancient times." Müller, 1758, p. 65; cf. Jefferys' translation, 1761, p. xxvii.

28—The Chukchi, during this interview, told the Russians about St. Lawrence Island. Golder, 1922, I, p. 18; Fisher, 1977, pp. 81-82.

29—The Russians took the boat to the island twice to try to find people, without success. They found only some dwellings. Golder, 1922, I, p. 18.

30—Golder's translation: "By August 15 [Old style] we came to latitude 67°18′ N. Lat. and turned back because the coast did not extend farther north and no land was near the Chukchi or East Cape and therefore it seemed to me that the instructions of His Imperial Majesty of illustrious and immortal memory had been carried out." (1922, I, pp. 18-19). Dall's translation: "On the 15th of August we arrived at the latitude of 67°18′ and I judged that we had clearly and fully carried out the instructions given by his Imperial Majesty of glorious and ever deserving memory, because the land no longer extended to the north. Neither from the Chukchi coast nor to the eastward could any extension of land be observed." (1890, p. 141). Harris: " . . . conceiving that he had now fully executed the Emperor's Orders, as he saw no Land, either to the North or to the East, he resolved to return . . . " (1748, p. 1020). The record of the council Bering held with Chirikov and Spanberg appears in Fisher, 1977, pp. 83-84; Golder, 1922, I, p. 19.

31—The quotation, although not direct, ends here in the original text. It should be remembered that there is a difference of eleven days in the dates in this journal because of the Russian calendar in the eighteenth century; the date was 26 August on the Gregorian calandar. All of the concerns cited by Bering are valid ones.

32—Serdtse means heart; kamen' means rock. See Map XIX. The question of its location is discussed in Fisher, 1977, pp. 99-101 and in Fisher, 1981. Its identity has not been established; it may have been a heart-shaped rock, cliff, or mountain.

33—Information taken from a deposition of Peter Popov, a cossack who attempted to bring the Chukchi under Russian control in 1711. Müller, 1758, p. 60; 1761, p. xxv.

34—This peninsula appears on Bering's map of the expedition; it is found in an area not explored by Bering, and the great "Chukotskii Nos" on the map is the result of placing the cape shown in this area on the Homann map on a new projection. Müller is arguing that Bering would have needed to reach the end of this nos to prove conclusively that no connection could exist between Asia and America.

35—Müller is pointing up the importance of his discovery in the winter of 1736-37, of the record of the voyage of Semen Ivanov Dezhnev, a cossack who sailed from the Kolyma River around the northeastern point of Asia to a place south of the Anadyr River in 1648. On Dezhnev, see Fisher, 1981.

36—The arctic fox. Krasheninnikov writes about Kamchatka: "Almost every kind of fox can be found here: red, fire-colored, the ones with a black band across the chest or a black chest and the rest of the body red, those with a black cross, chestnut, black, etc. Once in a while a white fox is found, but only rarely." (1972, p. 119).

37—This is found in the "Short Account" printed by Harris (1748, p. 1021) but not in the others printed in the eighteenth century. Chaplin reports the difficulty in more detail—on 31 August (nautical time): "At 10 p.m. the fore and main halyards gave way and the sails fell, becoming entangled with the rigging. On account of the high sea the rigging could not be slackened up, so they were obliged to let go the anchor in about 21 fathoms, a mile or less from shore." The next day the anchor cable broke. Dall, 1891, p. 768.

38—The date of the return was 2 September [Old Style], not 20 September as stated in the text. Golder, 1922, I, p. 20; Dall, 1891, p. 768.

39—This restatement of the purpose of the expedition does not suggest any search for a northeast passage, but rather the specific assignment to explore a land thought to lie near Kamchatka—in this case Bering would be looking for the "Company Land" on the Homann maps. See Map VI and Map VIII.

40—These observations are not cited in the "Short Account" of Bering, but were used by Bering as arguments in support of proposals for the Second Kamchatka Expedition. Golder, 1922, I, p. 26. Chaplin says that the belief in land to the east was supported by "the statements of the Chukchi and other circumstantial evidence." Dall, 1891, p. 769.

41—Some of the indications mentioned by Müller are reports of people living in a country to the east, certain "platters and other wooden vessels" that the Chukchi had obtained from these people, and the migration of birds to the east and back. Müller, 1758, pp. 65-68; 1761, pp. xxviii-xxix.

42—The land sighted from Kamchatka would have been the Commander Islands. During the wintering on Bering Island, where they were shipwrecked during the Second Kamchatka Expedition, Bering's men reported that they sighted the mainland of Kamchatka in clear weather.

43—This sentence is unclear. What Chaplin says is "Bering decided to make an attempt to investigate the matter before returning finally to Okhotsk." Dall, 1891, p. 769. Bering had decided to search for this land during the voyage from Kamchatka to Okhotsk.

44—The Gabriel sailed to the southeast from the Kamchatka River on 5 June. Gloomy and cloudy weather, with strong winds, began on 7 June and continued until 9 June when the search for land was given up. They returned to Kamchatka and followed the coast after that. Dall, 1891, p. 769.

45—A sloboda is a settlement exempted from normal taxes and work obligations.

46—The dates and route agree with those given in Golder, 1922, I, p. 20.

47—On the first map Amsterdam is indicated as the place of publication; there is no publisher or date on it. In a letter of 25 May 1729, Joseph Nicolas Delisle mentions this map, giving the full title of it and stating that it was based on the geographical work of Johann Philip von Strahlenberg. He also states that this map, in a reduced form, appears in the *Histoire générale [sic] des Tatars*, published in 1726 and in the new edition of the *Voyages du Nord*, with the statement that this was "donnée par ordre du feu Czar." Omont, 1915, pp. 141-42. The southern extent of Kamchatka on this map is at 38° N. See Map IV.

48—Ebulgâzî Bahadir Han, *Histoire genéalogique des Tatars*, 1726, I, p. 109. The text states that Kamchatka extends from 62° N.Lat. at Cape Sviatoi Nos southward to 41° N. Lat., near Japan. The Swedish prisoners of war were those taken at the Battle of Poltava in 1709; many of them, including Strahlenberg, were sent to Siberia. About the map in this book, Strahlenberg writes that it was much more accurate than other maps, "but would not have been so, if its author had not plowed with my heifer; i.e., made Use of my first Maps of this Part of the World, designed in 1714, and 1718, which I was obliged to leave behind me, in Russia." Strahlenberg, 1738, p. ix.

49—Johannes G. Scheuchzer, in his introduction to Kaempfer's *History of Japan*, notes that a map of Kamchatka has been added (plate VIII) "as I found it represented in a large map of the Russian Empire, made according to the latest information, the Russian Court had from those parts, and publish'd in Holland but a few months before . . . ." (p. xxi). Kamchatka is very close to Japan on this map. See Map XI.

50—In the English edition of 1738 this text is: "Now the Peninsula Jedso, or the country call'd Kamchatki, of which neither the Japonese and Chinese, nor we Europeans, have heretofore had any true information . . . ." (p. 32). On both the map in the English edition and the large one printed to accompany the German edition, the legend indicates "Terrae Kamtszatka alias Jedso" and the land extends southward to 42° N.

51—This article is found in volume III (1740), pp. 4-5 in the edition of Bruzen de la Martiniére, *Le Grand Dictionnaire* published in 10 volumes between 1726-1739. In the article Kamchatka is said to extend from 60° N. Lat. to 39° N. Lat.

52—There are several editions of the *Histoire du Japon* by Pierre Charlevoix, but one with the page and map citations given by Müller was not located. In volume V of the 1754 edition a translation of Scheuchzer's statement about Kamchatka appears on pages 25-28, with a commentary. There is no map. The writer referred to is Jacques Nicolas Bellin (1703-1772).

53—This statement appears earlier. For example, Scheuchzer wrote, "But those inhabitants of Siberia, who live about the River Lena, and along the Icy Ocean, commonly come with their Ships round Cape Suetoinos, and this they do to avoid falling into the hands of the Tschalatzki, and Tschutzki, two fierce and barbarous nations, possess'd of the North-East point of Siberia, and great enemies to the Russians." Kaempfer, 1727, I, p. xxii.

54—The text reads: "It has been believ'd till the present, that Asia was joined on the N.E. to North America, and that for this Reason it was impossible to sail from the Icy Sea into the eastern Ocean; but since the Discovery of the Country of Kamtzchatka, 'tis known for certain that America is not contiguous to Asia, for the Russian Ships coasting the firm Land, pass at present Cape Suetoi Nos, or Holy Cape, and go traffick with the Kamtzchadals upon the Coast of the eastern Sea, about the 50th Deg. of Latitude . . . ." Ebulgâzî Bahadir Han, 1730, II, pp. 663-64. The text was first published in 1726.

55—Jean Baptiste Bourguignon d'Anville, *Nouvel Atlas de la Chine*, La Haye, 1737. It also appeared in Du Halde's *Description. . .de la Chine*, IV, published in Paris in 1735, between pages 452 and 453

56—In this extensive article, Castel compares Bering's map with earlier maps, especially those of Kaempfer and Strahlenberg. He cites the report of Father Gerbillon, one of the interpreters between the Chinese and Russians during the 1689 negotiations leading up to the Treaty of Nerchinsk, that there were two chains of mountains. The more northern one, according to Gerbillon, extended far into the sea and was inaccessible to the Russians. Du Halde, 1735, IV, 198-99; 1736, IV, 186. Castel maintains that the more northern chain (the imaginary Cape Shelagi on Bering's map) joined to America. Since, according to Castel, "the timid" Bering had not explored this area, he should not have shown it with the end closed. Bellin responded that Bering's map was accurate. Müller, however, who also supported the accuracy of the map, follows this with the notation that Bering's report could be wrong.

57—Ivan Kirilov (1689-1737) was named by Peter the Great to organize the mapping of Russia. Kirilov was noted for his skills in surveying; he had studied at the School of Mathematics and Navigation. As part of his service in the navy, he continued his studies in London and Amsterdam. He joined the Civil Service and rose rapidly in its ranks, though he did not give up his work in cartography. He encouraged Joseph Nicolas Delisle's employment in Russia. The relationship between the two was difficult, almost from the beginning. Kirilov's *Atlas* was in print by 1734; very few copies of it were distributed. Bagrow, 1938.

58—Du Halde states that Bering had made a map of his expedition and that the map was sent to the King of Poland as a present. The King sent it to Du Halde, with permission to make whatever use of it he pleased. Du Halde, 1735, IV, p. 452.

59—A brief account of Shtinnikov's actions is found in Lensen, 1959, p. 41 and in Krasheninnikov, 1972, p. 320.

60—Lensen wrote, "As news of the robbery seeped out, local authorities vied with each other in conducting an investigation. The Japanese captives were freed and Shtinnikov thrown into jail until he agreed to split the booty with the officials." (1959, p. 41).

61—A later investigation, concluded in 1733, convicted Shtinnikov, together with several others. The concern was not only with the treatment of the Japanese who were shipwrecked, but also with a revolt that had broken out in 1730. Krasheninnikov, 1972, p. 320. As stated by Lantzeff and Pierce, "affairs in the northeastern regions had continued to be characterized by misrule and lawless behavior on the part of officials and subordinates and by native rebellion." (1973, p. 212).

62—In 1734 they were presented to the Empress Anna Ivanovna, who gave the order that they should be baptized. Lensen (1959, p.42) gives their name changes as Sozo to Kuzma Schulz; Gonzo to Demian Pomortsev.

63—Lensen (1959, p. 42) noted that the Japanese had two students, Petr Shenanykin and Andrei Fenev, but "the secrets of their tongue remained uncommunicated." Krasheninnikov (1972, p. 315) wrote that the two Japanese in St. Petersburg heard of Shtinnikov's fate and "had the satisfaction of learning that the scoundrel had received his just punishment."

64—See Kaempfer, 1727, I, Table VIII. The position shown on the map would be near the present city of Kanoya.

65—Kyushu Island.

66—"Kio, Miaco (the plan of which town abridg'd from a large Japanese map is represented in Tab. XXVII) signifies in Japanese a city. It is so-called by way of pre-eminence, being the residence of his holiness the Dairi, or Ecclesiastical hereditary Emperor, and on this account reckon'd the capital of the whole empire." Kaempfer, 1727, II, p. 484. The city of Kyoto on the Yodogawa River.

67—In his earlier mention of Shestakov (1758, p. 49; 1761, p. xxi) Müller wrote that Shestakov was in St. Petersburg in 1726, advocating several projects. He also made maps, one of which Müller received, though he did not make use of it unless supported by other records, because Shestakov "could neither read nor write, and merely from his Memory, or from the Accounts he had heard from others who could scarcely write, got the Situation of the Countries and Rivers marked upon Maps." (1761, p. xxi). Fisher (1977, p. 165) indicates reasons for believing that Shestakov was in St. Petersburg earlier—in 1725, at least. One example of Shestakov's mapping is reproduced in Golder, 1914, p. 111.

68—On Shestakov's map there is a "Bolshaia Zemlia" or big land, located opposite the mouth of the Kolyma River. The map is reproduced in Golder, 1914, p. 111.

69—Krasheninnikov (1972, p. 315): "They were ordered to explore and map the northern and southern coasts in great detail, to bring into submission, either voluntarily or by force, all the Koriaks and Chukchi . . . to establish settlements and build ostrogs in critical places, to explore the country further, and to organize trade with the neighboring peoples . . . ."

70—In addition, the Senate named him "commander-in-chief of the northeastern region." Lantzeff and Pierce, 1973, p. 211.

71—Winter quarters.

72—Accounts of the Shestakov and Pavlutskii expeditions can be found in the following: Fisher, 1977, pp. 164-68; Golder, 1914, pp. 153-58; Lantzeff and Pierce, 1973, pp. 211-12, 214.

73—Fisher (1977, p. 167): "Quarreling between Shestakov, who as an illiterate was jealous of his literate associates, and Pavlutskii, who claimed equal authority with Shestakov, hindered the efforts of the expedition."

74—They obtained the *Fortune* and the *Gabriel* from Bering and built two ships, the *Eastern Gabriel* and the *Lion*. Golder, 1914, p. 155; Lantzeff and Pierce, 1973, p. 211.

75—The *Gabriel* was to sail to the Uda River, explore the Shantar Islands there and continue to the Kurile Islands before going to Kamchatka. If time permitted, the ship was to be sent eastward in search of the "Big Land." Ivan Shestakov is cited as a nephew, rather than as a cousin, by Golder (1914, p. 155) and Lantzeff and Pierce (1973, p.212). Noblemen in Siberia at this time were usually of the lower nobility, originating as impoverished sons of boyars.

76—The *Fortune*, commanded by Shestakov's son Vasilii, was supposed to go to the Bolshaia River and then chart the Kurile Islands. It succeeded in reaching some of the northern islands, though the record is unclear. Lensen, 1959, p. 44.

77—Müller's sources were apparently incomplete. In the fall of 1729 Shestakov set sail in the *Eastern Gabriel*; the *Lion* was to follow. He intended to go to the Penzhina River but, because of contrary winds, landed at the Taui River instead. The *Eastern Gabriel* was wrecked in September 1730. Shestakov was already dead by then. The *Lion* did not meet up with the *Eastern Gabriel*; the ship was anchored at the Iana River. During the winter the Koriaks killed almost all the men and burned the ship. See Golder, 1914, pp. 156-57; Lantzeff and Pierce, 1973, pp. 211-12.

78—Krasheninnikov (1972, p. 315) wrote, "Shestakov was killed in 1730 by the Chukchi, large numbers of whom had come to attack the tributary reindeer Koriaks." In Golder's words (1914, p. 157): "The battle opened by the discharge of firearms by the Russians. It was immediately answered by a cloud of arrows from the Chukchi. Before the Russians could reload the Chukchi swept down on them in a mass . . . ."

79—This man has not been identified or mentioned in the usual sources, English or Russian, about Shestakov's expedition. Bancroft (1886, p. 38), evidently basing his information on Müller, has this man making a two-year voyage around Kamchatka and north to the Chukchi Peninsula.

80—The geodesist (land surveyor) was Mikhail Spiridonovich Gvozdev, who sailed on a voyage to America in 1732. See Map XX.

81—The text of Gvozdev's report on the voyage appears in Golder, 1922, I, pp. 22-24. That Müller had such incomplete information about this voyage is unfortunate; it was the earliest recorded Russian voyage to the mainland of America.

82—Afanasii Shestakov presumably sent these people to the area separately from the sea expeditions, but there does not seem to be any further information about this.

83—From Müller's research in the Iakutsk archives.

84—This name is "Hens" in Müller's text and is sometimes cited in that form in other sources; the more common form has been used here.

85—This is the order from Pavlutskii that resulted in the voyage of Gvozdev and Fedorov to America. There is a close similarity to the order given by Shestakov to the cossack Krupischev, as recorded by Müller.

86—Krasheninnikov (1972, p. 316) writes: "In order to regain their liberty, these people had for a long time been plotting to kill all the Russians in Kamchatka; but since the discovery of the Sea of Okhotsk route there were too many of them, because every year ships full of troops came to Kamchatka, and one expedition was immediately followed by another." After Bering had left, and the rest of the troops had embarked on the *Gabriel* to help Pavlutskii fight against the Chukchi, the Kamchadals revolted.

87—The Kamchadals attacked the few Russians left as soon as the others had set sail; because of winds the Russians dropped anchor almost immediately. When informed of the revolt by the survivors from Nizhne-Kamchatsk, the voyage to Anadyrsk was cancelled, and the Russians returned to put down the rebellion. Krasheninnikov, 1972, pp. 316-321.

88—Sixty men, led by Gens, came from the ship to Nizhne-Kamchatsk, calling on the Kamchadals to surrender. When they would not, Gens sent to the ship for a cannon, and on 26 July blew a hole in the wall around the ostrog. "Thirty men then surrendered, but others fought on, until a shot ignited the magazine, and the entire fort and all its rich content of furs blew up. Only four cossacks were killed in the struggle, but many were wounded, and the others were so enraged that they slaughtered all the prisoners." Lantzeff and Pierce, 1973, p. 213.

89—Lantzeff and Pierce (1973, p. 214): "Arriving in Anadyrsk on 3 September 1730, Pavlutskii was met by requests for aid from the Koriaks, who had suffered repeated raids from the Chukchi, in which hundreds of iasak-paying Koriaks were slain or forced to renew their earlier submission to the Chukchi, and in which entire herds of reindeer were driven off."

90—See Map XIX.

91—According to Lantzeff and Pierce (1973, p. 214) this occurred on 14 June when Pavlutskii "defeated seven hundred Chukchi, killing three hundred, with no Russian losses, and drove off forty thousand reindeer."

92—Lantzeff and Pierce (1973, p. 214): "On 30 June near Bering Strait, he met and put to flight a thousand Chukchi."

93—This battle is not reported in Lantzeff and Pierce; Krasheninnikov (1972, p. 315) states that Pavlutskii "fought several battles with the rebellious Chukchi, killed a great many of them, and for some time kept the Koriaks and the people who lived at Anadyrsk safe from their incursions."

94—None of the Siberian people decorated their faces in this way; Müller is pointing out that this was an American.

95—See Map XIX.

96—A military governor.

97—For the content of these, and a discussion, see Fisher, 1977, pp. 108-19; Golder, 1922, I, pp. 25-26.

98—This statement contradicts the thesis that the purpose of the First Kamchatka Expedition was to go to America, unless it was "completed" through the voyage of Gvozdev.

99—Bering put the exploration of the arctic coasts as point 5 in his proposals (Fisher, 1977, p. 113) and then suggested only the exploration between the Ob and the Lena rivers, not the coast eastward from the Lena River to Kamchatka (*Ibid.*, p. 118).

100—The proposals were approved by May 1731. A committee of the three institutions met often about the exploration until March 1733. Barratt, 1981, pp. 29-30.

101—See Map XII.

102—The text of this, in parallel French and English versions, is included in Golder, 1914, pp. 302-13.

103—Delisle, 1752, p. 6. Müller (1754, p. 11) translates this statement by Delisle: "In the year 1731, says he, I had the honor of laying before the Empress Anna, and the senate, this map of mine, in order to incite the Russians to prosecute their discoveries, wherein I also succeeded." See the commentary in Chapter II.

104—Johann Georg Gmelin was a doctor of medicine as well as a professor of chemistry and natural history.

105—The astronomer Louis Delisle de la Croyère was a brother to Joseph Nicholas Delisle.

106—The officers received a full year's payment in advance, and promotions. Barratt, 1981, p.31. The academy's participants were similarly rewarded for their services. Gmelin and Müller (Krasheninnikov, 1972, p. xxvii) "traveled with elaborate supplies of food and wine."

107—These are identified in the portions of the text relating to their actions.

108—Waxell (1952, p. 54) said: "Behind all this activity lay no other purpose than to serve mankind and promote geography, so that the world of learning might at long last be helped out of the dream by which it had so long, even till now, been lulled."

109—"A new city, begun in the year 1721 . . . and had the name given it, in honour to the late Empress Catherine." Several iron, tin, and steel works were located here. Jefferys, note to Müller, 1761, p. 9.

110—Fortress.

111—Mine. Silver and copper mines were opened here, in the Lesser Altai Mountains, in 1729. Stejneger, 1936, p. 435, note 23.

112—There were now some 800 people involved in the expedition during the wintering at Iakutsk in 1736-37. For the academy members, "This was their first protracted association with Bering and the proximity was not to their liking. The professors complained about their quarters ('not good enough even for students'), went over Bering's head to local officials, and generally made a nuisance of themselves." Black, 1983, p.245.

113—The German text (Müller, 1758, p.144) reads: "Ich befand mich meiner kranklichen Umstande halber genothiget, Herrn Gmelin zu begleiten, damit ich von ihm Hulfe haben konnte." The 1764 English translation (p. 61) reads: "I was obliged, on account of my ill state of health, to accompany M. Gmelin, in order to receive, *occasionally, the benefit of his assistance and advice.*" [emphasis added.]

114—Stepan Petrovich Krasheninnikov, at the age of 25, was sent to Kamchatka in 1737. The ship was wrecked just as it reached Kamchatka and he lost all his supplies. Krasheninnikov spent three years there, describing the country. His book about it was published in 1755, the year he died. See Krasheninnikov, 1972.

115—On Steller, see Chapter II and Stejneger, 1936.

116—Lieutenant Stepan Muravev and his assistant Lieutenant Mikhail Pavlov commanded two *kochi*, the *Expedition* and the *Ob*, used on this expedition. A koch was a single-masted, decked vessel with one sail and oars, which ranged in size up to 60 feet in length and 20 feet in width. For an excellent description and illustrations, see Fisher, 1981, pp. 161-69. Ianikov gives the dimensions as 52 1/2 by 14 by 8 feet. (1949, p. 27).

117—The two vessels left Arkhangelsk on 4 July; they sailed through Iugor Shar and in early August were near the Iamal Peninsula. They sailed along it to 72° 35′ N. Lat. Because of the lateness of the season and adverse winds they turned back, and sailed to the Pechora River, where they left their ships. They wintered at Pustozersk. Golder, 1914, pp. 232-33; Ianikov, 1949, pp. 28-32.

118—Fur hunters and traders.

119—Arctic fox.

120—Iugor Shar is the passage between Vaigach Island and the mainland; "the other passage" referred to is between Vaigach Island and Novaia Zemlia. It is called Kara Gate.

121—Novaia Zemlia was known to the Russians at least as early as the sixteenth century; whalers and hunters went there but no Russian settlements were established. It is named on sixteenth-century European maps. See, for example, the "Septentrionalium terrarum descriptio" of Gerardus Mercator (Map I).

122—Mangazeia was established by the Russians in 1601. The town was established by the government to control the fur trade as well as to serve as a fort in fights against the Samoyeds. For almost half a century it was an important and flourishing trade center; its later abandonment was caused by a number of factors, perhaps the most important of which was the eastward movement of the fur trade itself. Armstrong, 1965, pp. 17-20.

123—Mutnaia River does not appear on the maps in the Russian *Atlas* of 1745; however, there is a "Mutnoi Zaliv" or gulf. The Kara River is shown on the map, but there is no lake at its source.

124—The Selenia River does not appear on the maps in the 1745 Russian *Atlas*; the Tylowka, with a lake at its source, is shown. It flows into the Ob at approximately 70° N. Lat.

125—Gorodok—small town.

126—These traders continued south along the east side of the Iamal Peninsula to the Ob River, to trade with the Samoyeds, the nomadic reindeer herders, fishermen, and hunters who lived in the far north. This fur trade was a longstanding and profitable one: it is believed that Anika Stroganov, in the sixteenth century, obtained most of his wealth by sending agents to this area to deal directly, rather than through other intermediaries, with the Samoyeds. Lantzeff and Pierce, 1973, pp. 83-84.

127—Müller is referring to his own research in Siberian archives here; the fact that the portage route, which was not easy, was used rather than a sea route indicated the difficulty of the latter.

128—Although Muravev and Pavlov were ready to leave the mouth of the Peschora River on 1 June, because of ice they could not get under way until 29 June. To add to the difficulties, the two vessels were separated from each other. Muravev reached 73°04′ N. Lat., Pavlov 73°11′ N. Lat. With this second failure the two leaders fought and made accusations against each other. Golder, 1914, p. 233.

129—Müller omits the events between 1735 and 1738. Lieutenant Stepan G. Malygin took command in May, 1736, because of the problems between Muravev and Pavlov, who were reduced in rank. Muravev attempted the voyage once more in 1736. Two new kochi, the *First* and the *Second*, of the same size as the earlier ones but with a shallower draft, were built for Malygin, who wintered on the coast of the Iamal Peninsula near 70° N. Lat. During the summer of 1737, Malygin and his assistant, Aleksei Skuratov, sailed around the Iamal Peninsula. On 11 September they reached the Ob River, and sailed up it to Berezov. Golder, 1914, pp. 233-34; Ianikov, 1949, pp. 38-45.

130—In 1738 Skuratov completed a second voyage around the Iamal Peninsula, this time from east to west, as part of a voyage that ended in Arkhangelsk in the summer of 1739. The first accurate mapping of the Iamal Peninsula was completed. Golder, 1914, p. 234; Ianikov, 1949, pp. 45-47.

131—This was the successful conclusion to the attempts which were begun in 1734 by Lieutenant Dmitrii L. Ovtsyn. The voyages are discussed briefly by Golder, 1914, pp. 234-36; a complete account is given by Ianikov, 1949, pp. 49-64. Waxell (1952, p. 55) apparently knew nothing of the difficulties surrounding these voyages. He assumed there was one ship and "the purpose of her voyage was to try to reach the river Yenisei from the Ob, and she also accomplished her task, reaching the mouth of the Yenisei and sailing on against the current right up to the town of Yeniseisk."

132—Presumably the ship was reinforced with extra planking in order to make it stronger. Cf. Kerchove, 1961, p. 233 on "double."

133—Ovtsyn left Tobolsk on 14 May 1734 with 56 men as the ship's crew; he reached Obdorsk on 11 June, where he made advance preparations for his later wintering there. By 5 August he had reached 70°04′ N. Lat., where he turned back. Golder, 1914, pp. 234-235; Ianikov, 1949, pp. 51-53.

134—In 1735 Ovtsyn began his voyage on 29 May, but the weather and ice conditions were worse than the preceding year. On 10 July they reached the northern limit of their voyage at 68°40′ N. Lat. At the time only 17 men were capable of work—the rest were sick with scurvy and four had already died. Golder, 1914, p. 235; Ianikov, 1949, pp. 53-54.

135—Ovtsyn went to Tobolsk and St. Petersburg in the winter of 1735-36; he asked for better vessels, more officers and supplies. In the summer of 1736 he made another voyage on the *Tobol*, beginning on 23 May from Tobolsk. He left Obdorsk on 29 June and reached 72°40′ N. Lat. by 5 August; because of ice he could get no further and on 15 August he started the return voyage. Golder, 1914, p. 235; Ianikov, 1949, pp. 56-57.

136—The boat was 60 by 17 by 7 ¹/₂ feet deep. Koshelev left Tobolsk on 5 May 1737 and joined Ovtsyn on 5 June. Ovtsyn commanded the *Ob-Postman* and Koshelev the *Tobol* with a combined crew of 70 men. Golder, 1914, p.235; Ianikov, 1949, p.59.

137—A complete account is found in Ianikov, 1949, pp. 58-64.

138—They sailed from Obdorsk at the end of June; the northernmost land was passed on 6 August and they continued on the open sea to 74°02′ N. Lat., where they encountered ice. They turned eastward around Cape Matte-Sol (Tupoi Mys) and arrived at the mouth of the Enisei River on 31 August, continuing up it to Turukhansk (or Novaia Mangazeia). Ovtsyn was later arrested because of his association with the exiled Prince Dolgoruky, was reduced in rank, and went to join Bering on the expedition to America. Golder, 1914, pp. 235-236; Ianikov, 1949, pp. 59-63.

139—The *Ob-Postman*.

140—Minin was to sail from the Enisei around the Taimyr Peninsula to the mouth of the Khatanga River. He tried it three times, in 1738, 1739, and 1740, finally reaching 75°15′ N. Lat. Golder, 1914, pp. 236-37; Ianikov, 1949, pp. 65-75.

141—Near Dickson Island.

142—The mouth of the Piasina River is east of Dickson Island at about 74° N. Lat.; Minin did get north of it.

143—Golder (1914, p. 237) gives the dimensions as 70 by 16 by 6 ¹/₂ feet; Ianikov (1949, p. 76) indicates the dimensions were the same as those of the *Tobol*—70 by 15 by 7 feet. The assignment was to sail west from the Lena River around the Taimyr Peninsula to the Enisei.

144—Lieutenant Vasilii Pronchishchev, with his wife Maria and a crew of fifty men, could not get through the western side of the Lena Delta. It was mid-August by the time the *Iakutsk* got through the eastern side, and it was 25 August when the ship arrived at the Olenek River. The crew wintered at a small village made up of hunters and traders. Golder, 1914, p. 237; Ianikov, 1949, pp. 76-78.

145—Because of bad ice conditions, Pronchishchev could not leave the Olenek River until 3 August. He sailed to the mouth of the Anabara River, examined the area for mines, then continued west across Khatanga Bay. Turning northward along the Taimyr Peninsula, he reached Faddeia Bay by 18 August. Golder, 1914, pp. 237-38; Ianikov, 1949, pp. 78-80.

146—Accounts of this voyage are found in Coxe, 1803, pp. 369-371; Golder, 1914, p. 238; Ianikov, 1949, pp. 76-82. Coxe (p. 371) notes that a more complete account than that of Müller is found in Gmelin, 1752, II, pp. 427-434. This was published without permission, which caused Gmelin serious difficulties (see Chapter II).

147—Laptev left Iakutsk on 9 June 1739; he reached Khatanga Bay 6 August. On 21 August he reached 76°47′ N. Lat, the northernmost point of his voyage. He wintered at Khatanga Bay; the following summer, on 12 July, the *Iakutsk* again sailed north, reaching 75°30′ before it was caught in the ice. A leak was discovered on 13 August and the men abandoned the vessel, going over the ice to safety on shore. Golder, 1914, pp. 239-40; Ianikov, 1949, pp. 87-89.

148—After the loss of the *Iakutsk*, the work of exploring and mapping the Taimyr Peninsula was continued by men using dog teams. Semen Chelyuskin, in particular, accomplished much of the mapping, which continued to 1742. Golder, 1914, pp. 240-41.

149—Lieutenant Peter Lassenius commanded the *Irkutsk*, which was 60 by 18 by 6 ¹/₂ feet, and carried a crew of 55 men. Golder, 1914, p.242; Ianikov, 1949, p. 104.

150—Up to this point he was sailing with Pronchishchev, but here they separated, with Pronchishchev heading west. "Buikowskoi Muis" is found in the Russian *Atlas* of 1745; it is near Stolb Island. Ianikov, 1949, p. 106.

151—This river is shown on the Russian *Atlas*, and on Müller's map; it is the Kharandakh River.

152—The barracks was 77 feet long by 21 feet wide, and 6 feet high. It was divided into four compartments, and had a kitchen and a bath. Golder, 1914, p. 242.

153—These men went to Irkutsk; Bering by this time was in Iakutsk, so the report was delayed. When Bering received word about the situation, he sent help immediately. Golder, 1914, p. 242.

154—The totals here suggest that Lassenius was not counted in the 52 men, but rather had a crew of 52 under him.

155—According to Stejneger (1936, pp. 330, 449) the person who denounced Lassenius was Boris Roselius. The "slovo i dielo" denunciation could be given by a person of any rank against another; once this was done in public it was the duty of those present to arrest both parties immediately, to be sent to St. Petersburg for trial.

156—With a crew of 43 men, Laptev was ordered to take the *Irkutsk* and continue the explorations. Golder, 1914, pp. 242-43. On Laptev, see Ianikov, 1949, pp. 107-29.

157—The *Irkutsk* had to be put into condition to sail. Golder, 1914, p. 243.

158—This name was also given to the nos at the far northeastern point of Siberia.

159—At 73°16' N. Lat.

160—The prostrate nut pine, *Pinus cembra*, was used as a remedy for scurvy. Golder, 1922, I, p. 262.

161—Laptev had gone to Iakutsk to consult with Bering, but Bering had already gone to Okhotsk. The academy contingent was still in Iakutsk. Golder, 1914, p. 243.

162—Laptev sent a report to Bering. At the same time he left for St. Petersburg to report to the Admiralty College in person. Golder, 1914, p. 243.

163—It appears that Müller is attempting to claim unwarranted importance for the academy contingent in making this decision about the northern explorations. While en route to St. Petersburg, Laptev received an order from the Admiralty College to attempt the voyage again. He was close to St. Petersburg, so he did continue there. By doing so, he missed the sailing season of 1737, which was a mild one. Golder, 1914, p. 243.

164—These are not included in this translation; they can be found in Müller, 1761, pp. i-xliii as *A Summary of Voyages made by the Russians on the Frozen Sea.*

165—This was published as "Information about the Northern Sea Passage" in the *Notes to the St. Petersburg Gazette*. Fisher, 1981, pp. 4-5.

166—Müller's documents did not, as he is implying, influence the decision to have Laptev make another voyage. In view of the results it may have been a fortunate thing for Müller.

167—About the loss of the ship and the subsequent transfer of provisions to land, Golder (1914, p. 240) indicated: "Discouraged, suffering from cold and dampness, the men sickened, lost hope, and almost prayed that death would come. Laptev did all he could to put life into the men, and succeeded in leading them back to their winter quarters, where several died soon after their arrival."

168—On Laptev's expedition, see Ianikov, 1949, pp. 107-29.

169—Name given to the presumed extension of land connecting the eastern part of Novaia Zemlia with the mainland. For an example of this cartography, see Weber, 1723, map.

170—"Johann Matthias Hase or Haase or Hasius (1684-1742) was a professor of mathematics in Wittenberg and a collaborator of Homann's publishing house." Bagrow, 1975, p. 245, footnote 43.

171—See commentary on Wood's voyage in Chapter I.

172—For an example of this idea, see Map XVI.

173—These were small boats which could be disassembled for crossing over land, since they were held together by thongs. Fisher, 1981, p. 13.

174—Jacob van Heemskerk sailed from Amsterdam with Willem Barents in the spring of 1596 in search of a northeast passage. Their ship was frozen in somewhere beyond the northern point of Novaia Zemlia. A wooden house was built for wintering there. Because of ice conditions, they could not leave the island until June of 1597; Barents died on the return voyage and Heemskerk returned to Amsterdam with most of the men, in November, 1597. Tracy, 1980, pp. 25-26.

175—In this section of his article Castel cites the same difficulties Müller gives—the distance, the weather, the lack of supplies, and the sparse population.

176—According to Waxell (1952, p. 63) this journey was made on *lyshi*, or skis. He wrote, "*Lyshi* are long thin boards that are tied under the soles of the feet to prevent their sinking into the snow."

177—Waxell (1952, pp. 66-67) states that the country between Iudoma Cross and Okhotsk "is a complete wilderness." Therefore men on foot, each pulling a long narrow sled called a *narte*, were the mainstay of the transport system as far as the Urak River. The men, harnessed to their sleds, made this round trip between Iudoma Cross and the Urak River 15 times in 16 months.

178—Urak Landing, the place on the Urak River where Bering's men built storehouses and dwellings for themselves. It was about 40 miles from Iudoma Cross. See Gibson, 1969, pp. 80 (map) and 81.

179—They built small boats, Waxell (1952, p.68) said, because "even with suitable craft, navigation of the Urak is tolerably dangerous: it has a dreadfully strong current, many small rocks and large rapids." He traveled down the river twice in journeys of under 17 hours each time.

180—This one-masted ship was 60 feet long and 18 feet wide, and had a crew of sixty-seven. Lensen, 1959, pp. 48-49.

181—The *Hope* (in Russian *Nadezhda*) was three-masted, 70 by 18 feet, and carried a crew of forty-six. Lensen, 1959, p. 49.

182—On the voyage to Kamchatka, Waxell commanded the *St. Peter*, Chirikov the *St. Paul*. Waxell, 1952, p. 92. The ships were 80 feet by 20 feet, with two masts. Golder, 1914, p. 178.

183—Bering was sharply criticized because the expedition was not proceeding rapidly enough to suit the Admiralty College, which was advised by the Senate "to look into the Kamchatka expedition to see if it can be brought to a head, so that from now on the treasury should not be emptied in vain." Golder, 1914, pp. 177-78.

184—William Walton was an Englishman who had joined the Russian Navy only two years earlier.

185—Aleksei Schelting "was an illegitimate son of contre-admiral Petrovski, a Hollander. He was twenty-five years of age and had been attached to the fleet only two years." Bancroft, 1886, p. 51.

186—Spanberg had gotten a late start on the voyage; the ships were separated from each other in the autumn fogs and provisions were running low. Waxell, 1952, p. 76; Lensen, 1959, p. 49.

187—Waxell notes, "This little craft had been most useful to Spanberg . . . He had her with him throughout the entire Japanese voyage." Waxell, 1952, p. 77. This vessel is also called the *Bolsheretsk*. See Barratt, 1981, p. 35.

188—It is suggested that this happened because " . . . Walton, like other subordinate commanders of his day, wished to do some exploring on his own." Lensen, 1959, p. 50. See also Golder, 1914, pp. 222-23.

189—This was the east coast of Iwate Prefecture. Hirabayashi, 1957, p. 323. This area is presently included in Rikuchu National Coastal Park. Barratt, 1981, p. 36.

190—Spanberg's instructions carried specific warnings against being captured by the Japanese. Lensen, 1959, p. 47.

191—Sendai Bay (Ajishima, Ojika County). Hirabayashi, 1957, p. 323. Waxell(1952, p. 81) noted that "Captain Spanberg, however, would not let his men go ashore, and on that point I consider his conduct to have been right." He went on to criticize Walton for letting his men go ashore.

192—"Laken" in Müller's text. The kind of cloth is not specified.

193—Kaempfer, 1727, I, plate XIX. This is Müller's comment; it is not in Waxell's account.

194—The number of these fishing boats, together with the 800 or more men in them, made the Russians somewhat nervous about their safety. Lensen, 1959, p. 52.

195—Waxell's (1952, p. 83) comment about junks is simply: "They sail well, but like to wait for a fair wind."

196—A Japanese account of the Russians reports: "Their appearance resembled that of Dutchmen, with red wavy hair and caps of various kinds. Their noses were long and pointed. Their eyes were the color of sharks. The trunks of their bodies, however, were normal just like those of ordinary people." Hirabayashi, 1957, p. 327.

197—About the clothing of the Russians, a Japanese reported: "A considerable number wore robes of furs sewn together, while others wore robes of thick cloth [of] something resembling cotton. They wore trousers, which covered their legs closely down to the socks." Hirabayashi, 1957, p. 327.

198—Apparently these are Matsumae, Sado, Saga, and Noto. Hirabayashi, 1957, p. 323.

199—Atlas Russicus . . .Atlas Russien, published in 1745. The maps referred to are the "Mappa generalis totius Imperii Russici" and the "Ostium fluvii Amur cum parte australiori terrae Camtschatkae."

200—Kunashiri. Hirabayashi, 1957, p. 323.

201—Eleven men died during the voyage. Barratt, 1981, p. 36.

202—Hokkaido? See the "Mappa generalis" in the Atlas Russicus, 1745.

203—Spanberg and Walton were often in conflict and their relationship had steadily worsened. Barratt, 1981, p. 35; Golder, 1914, p. 227. Undoubtedly Spanberg accused Walton of going off on his own.

204—Part of the east coast of Fukushima Prefecture, presumably. See Hirabayashi, 1957, p. 323, where this identification is made for 36°42' N. Lat.

205—According to Lensen, (1959, p. 53) this is near Awatsu Village in Nagasa County in the province of Awa (Chiba Prefecture) at about 35°10' N. Lat. Hirabayashi (1957, p. 323) states the town was in the neighborhood of Amatsuhana in Chiba Prefecture.

206—The account of Walton's voyage given by Müller is more detailed than the one supplied by Waxell. Here, for example, Müller includes the date and the name of the quartermaster. See Waxell, 1952, pp. 77-80. Both writers clearly had access to Walton's report on the voyage.

207—This was later used as an argument that Walton had not reached Japan, but might rather have been in Korea.

208—According to Lensen, (1959, p. 54) this was "A two-sworded samurai."

209—This detail is from Waxell (1952, p. 79) who states he had tasted it in Okhotsk. He reported: "It is dark-brown in colour and tastes by no means unpleasantly, though it is somewhat tart, which is perhaps due to the warm climate: however, its alcoholic content is very considerable."

210—Müller suggested that the problem originated in the weather at sea, rather than the climate where it was made.

211—Waxell (1952, p. 70) reported: "He [Walton] had noticed that in each Japanese craft was a number of stones, each of about two to three pounds weight. Perhaps the stones served as ballast, but being of that size, they could also have been used as projectiles, if things should have gone wrong."

212—At 33°30' N. Lat. according to Waxell's account, (1952, p. 79). This was near Katsuura, on the east coast of Wakayama Prefecture. Hirabayashi, 1957, p. 323.

213—The report was related quite differently by Waxell (1952, p. 80), who stated that the Japanese had given Walton the understanding that he could not anchor there, and that they wanted him to leave. The assistance in filling the water casks is not mentioned.

214—About scurvy, Krasheninnikov (1972, p. 111) wrote, "Everyone on the Kamchatka expedition proved this fact; to counteract this disease they used almost no other remedy except the tips of the tiny cedars, which they used to make a beverage by allowing them to ferment and then making a drink similar to kvas, which they drank like tea."

215—These maps are referred to above. A Walton map showing the expedition's route from the Lena River to Okhotsk was published in Scherer, 1777.

216—Spanberg was not only rewarded but was promised the command over the whole expedition, in place of Bering. Barratt, 1981, p. 37.

217—Part of the reason for this was the quarreling between Spanberg and Walton, as well as the confusion in the records kept on both of their voyages. Then, "Bering examined Spanberg's log book, finding there many errors, and Spanberg detected in Walton's enough faults to fill a sixteen page notebook." Golder, 1914, p. 227.

218—In defense of Spanberg, Waxell (1952, pp. 88-89) said, "Spanberg's map is based on actual experience and pays no attention to the statements or guesses of others." He went on to cite the damage done by the belief in Jeso and Da Gama Land and complained "It is after all an easy matter, and one that requires no great knowledge, to sit in a warm room setting down on paper the distorted accounts and guesswork of others."

219—This accusation was made by Grigorii Skorniakov-Pisarev, commander of the Okhotsk region, with whom Spanberg had fought violently during the building of the ships for the expedition. Lensen, 1959, pp. 45-46, 48, 57.

220—The two interpreters were Shenanykin and Fenev, who had studied with the Japanese castaways Gonzo and Sozo. Lensen, 1959, p. 59.

221—Bering and Chirikov needed the *Gabriel* to transport provisions to Kamchatka for their expedition to America. Golder, 1914, p. 228.

222—Apparently Müller was incorrect. Spanberg went back to Iakutsk during this time, in order to obtain supplies for another voyage to Japan, and did not return to Okhotsk until June of 1741. Lensen, 1959, pp. 57, 59; Golder, 1914, p. 228.

223—The vessel was the *St. John*, 70 feet by 18 feet, with a crew of 78. Golder, 1914, p. 228.

224—There were three other vessels besides the *St. John*— the *Archangel Michael* with a crew of 40, the *Hope* with a crew of 33, and the *Bolsheretsk*, with 13. Golder, 1914, pp. 228-29.

225—This statement suggests that Müller was writing from incomplete records, for on this voyage Spanberg, separated from the rest of his fleet, continued his voyage in the *St. John* to 41°15' N. Lat., very near Japan. At that latitude, on 22 June, Spanberg called a sea council to determine the future course of the voyage. Opinions were divided. Because of contrary winds, sickness on board the ships, as well as the danger of going to Japan alone, some supported discontinuing the voyage. Other officers wished to continue until 10 July: as a compromise it was decided to proceed until 6 July. However, on 30 June at 39°35' N. Lat. the ship sprang a leak, and the *St. John* returned to the first Kurile Island. The three other vessels of the fleet were found there. Golder, 1914, pp. 229-30.

226—On 24 July, Schelting, in the *Hope*, together with the geodesist M.P. Gvozdev, sailed on a mission to chart the Okhotsk coast from the Uda River to the Amur River. The ships reached Sakhalin Island on 1 August, but the observations of the island were incomplete because of fog, and headwinds prevented him from continuing on to the mainland. Golder, 1914, p. 230.

227—Here Müller gives his evaluation of the failure of Spanberg's voyage to Japan which is undoubtedly the truth: Spanberg and his men did not *want* to make another voyage to Japan.

228—In 1741 the Admiralty College set up a committee to examine the records of the voyages by Spanberg and Walton. The report was issued in 1746, stating "Without any doubt it is clear that Captain Walton, judging from all circumstances, was really on the eastern coast of Japan and not in Korea . . . ." The committee was more cautious in its findings about Spanberg's voyage, indicating it was "possible" that he had been in Japan, "But to attempt from his journal to put his voyage on a chart and to locate correctly the islands he saw on the way and some of the Japanese islands is quite impossible, not only for an outsider, but for Spanberg himself." Golder, 1914, p. 227.

229—Jean Baptiste Bourguignon d'Anville, Philippe Buache, and Jacques Nicolas Bellin.

230—Waxell (1952, p. 91) said " . . . we were scarcely able to keep 20 carpenters working on the construction of our ships, as we were forced to send most of them to the storehouses on the Urak and to Yudoma Cross to assist in transporting our supplies from those two places. Thus it came about that a whole year passed without positive results." The period from 1738 to 1740 was extremely difficult for the expedition, which consisted of about 1000 members. Simply feeding, housing and supplying provisions for the expedition was a continual struggle; complaints flowed back to the government in a regular stream from expedition members and from officials in Siberia.

231—The vessels were 80 by 22 by 9 1/2 feet, with a carrying capacity of 220,000 pounds. They had two masts and were armed with 14 small guns. Stejneger, 1936, p. 221. The *Gabriel*, from the First Kamchatka Expedition, was also built in the style of the packet-boats used in the Baltic.

232—The Bay of Avacha was known to Bering because of the First Kamchatka Expedition. The first mate Ivan Elagin (spelled Jelagin by Müller; Yelagin by Stejneger) was sent to Kamchatka in the *Gabriel* to select a site for wintering in Kamchatka. Waxell (1952, p.96) stated that, "He brought us back the most exact information, of which we were very glad. He had also built quarters and storehouses there, so that we and the whole command were housed and sheltered from the moment we arrived."

233—Steller was an adjunct (the rank below professor) of the Academy of Sciences. He had met Spanberg earlier, and had petitioned to go with Spanberg on the second voyage to Japan. The government had not responded to his request when Spanberg and Steller arrived at Okhotsk in August of 1740. Because Bering needed Spanberg's ship for his own expedition and had no idea that the voyage to Japan would be repeated, Spanberg's expedition had to be delayed. Thus Steller decided to go with Bering to Kamchatka. Stejneger, 1936, pp. 200-203.

234—Chikhachev, who died of scurvy on 7 October 1741 while on the expedition, sailed with Chirikov; Khitrov sailed with Bering, as third in command. Khitrov kept a log book, with maps, of the voyage. One page of it is reproduced in Golder, 1922, I, opposite page 148.

235—Bering was going to sail on 15 August; on 12 August Spanberg returned to Okhotsk with the orders to make another voyage to Japan. The *Hope*, commanded by Khitrov, was going to leave on 1 September but was grounded on a sandbar at the mouth of the Okhota River. All the ship's biscuits for the expedition were ruined by this accident. See Stejneger, 1936, pp. 222-23. Steller, who hated Khitrov, cites this as the first misfortune of the expedition—one that prevented Bering from his original intention of wintering in America. Golder, 1922, II, p.20.

236—The *Hope* and a galliot, the *Okhotsk*. These were only going to Kamchatka to unload provisions. Stejneger, 1936, pp. 221-22.

237—According to Waxell (1952, p.92) the whole flotilla sailed together from Okhotsk on 8 September. De la Croyère and Steller were on the *Okhotsk*, commanded by second mate Vasilii Rtishchev. Stejneger, 1936, p. 223.

238—De la Croyère was responsible for making the astronomical observations; on 13 January 1741 he observed the eclipse of the first satellite of Jupiter. Stejneger, 1936, p. 233. Steller was charged with observations in natural history; Stepan Krasheninnikov, who had spent four winters in Kamchatka, had certainly accomplished most of the observations possible in the winter. Steller set his hopes on going with Bering (which was not settled at the time) to America. Stejneger, 1936, pp. 232-33.

239—Waxell (1952, p. 93) asserted: "We ourselves would gladly have put in to Bolsheretsk with our two packet-boats, but the water on the sandbanks outside the river's mouth was too shallow for us to be able to attempt it."

240—The *St. Peter* was sailing between Cape Lopatka and Shumshu Island, through Kurile Strait. Waxell, 1952, p. 93. Krasheninnikov (1972, p. 59) warned " . . . one must wait for low tide, for during high tide, waves come into the strait over a distance of several versts with such power and force that even when the sea is calm the waves are covered with froth and are 20 to 30 sazhens high."

241—This description is from Waxell (1952, p. 94) who stated, "We did not know what the ebb- and flood-tides were like there and so could make no computation." Because it was the time of the new moon, they met a very strong tide coming toward them through the straits. Waxell asserted, " . . . never in my whole life have I ever been exposed to such great danger as then."

242—" . . . for almost an hour we were unable to see from our position in relation to the coast that we had made any progress forward." Waxell, 1952, p. 94.

243—"Indeed, the boat was all but hurled up on to the deck among us. Where we were, there were 10 to 12 fathoms of water, yet I imagine that the ship can hardly have been 3 fathoms from the bottom when in the trough of a wave." Waxell, 1952, p. 94.

244—"At the same time we were afraid that we were going to lose the main topmast, for the wind was beginning to increase violently . . . we had to exert ourselves to keep the ship's head downwind; had we come athwart it among those waves there would have been no saving us." Waxell, 1952, p. 94.

245—This description is from Krasheninnikov (1972, p. 21) where the spelling is given as Suaachu.

246—"Avatcha Bay is one of the most wonderful natural harbors—or rather aggregation of harbors—in the world, consisting of a basin about 11 miles in diameter with nearly uniform depth of 11 to 13 fathoms, no dangerous reefs or sunken rocks, and a narrow well-protected entrance." Stejneger, 1936, p. 238.

247—Krasheninnikov (1972, p. 21) called these three large ports Niakina, Rakovina, and Tareina. He also wrote (pp. 86-87) that "The situation of this port is favored by its extent, its depth, and the way nature formed it and sheltered it from all winds; indeed it would be difficult to find another like it in the entire world."

248—"The church is one of the best ornaments of the place; it is nicely built, and well situated." Krasheninnikov, 1972, p. 325.

249—Stejneger (1936, p. 240) notes that the church was dedicated to the Nativity of Christ, not to the Apostles.

250—Müller is citing Waxell. "In a nutshell, this is the best harbour I have seen in all my days." Waxell, 1952, p. 96.

251—From Krasheninnikov, 1972, p. 21.

252—"But if you want to put into the harbour, then you must know that about half a German mile distant from it on your right hand are some submerged rocks where there is only nine feet of water. You must beware of those rocks." Waxell, 1952, p. 96.

253—Steller laid a good part of the blame for the problems of the expedition onto this transport of materials overland. Golder, 1922, II, p. 20. Golder (1922, I, p. 35) gave as the reason the unseaworthiness of the freight boats. Stejneger (1936, p. 224) extended this as a criticism by Steller against Khitrov, for bad seamanship, on the assumption that Khitrov had tried to sail the *Hope* to Avacha Bay and had failed. Waxell, however, stated "Our two provision ships put into Bolsheretsk itself to unload the stores they had brought, for it was by then too late in the year for them to be able to get round the southern point of Kamchatka. Nor had we any desire to let our two provision ships run any risks, for if anything should have happened to them our whole undertaking might have been upset." Waxell, 1952, p. 93.

254—"For eight dogs, which altogether could haul a load of 400 pounds, they receive as much as is usually paid for a horse in Russia." Waxell, 1952, p. 97. Krasheninnikov (1972, p. 231) said, "Four dogs can pull a load of about five puds, not counting the provisions for the driver and the dogs."

255—"Nor had the most of them ever been farther than five miles from where they were born, and now here were they having to go off with us, as they understood it, to the end of the world, and that, into the bargain, with their dogs which they loved above all things. In the main they did not care about money, having no means of using it; in fact most of them had no idea what money was." Waxell, 1952, p. 98.

256—The Kamchadals revolted and killed some Russians, who in turn put down the rebellion (using hand grenades in some cases) and punished the leaders of it. Waxell, 1952, pp. 98-99.

257—Waxell, 1952, p. 97. They were issued half rations of bread.

258—Steller says Bering sent a letter to him in February, 1741, asking for a meeting; Steller left immediately by dog sled for Petropavlovsk. In response to Bering's invitation to join the American expedition Steller noted his concern that he did not have permission from the Senate. Bering replied that he would accept the reponsibility. Steller then agreed to go on the voyage, which is what he wanted. Golder, 1922, II, pp. 15-16.

259—See Map XII.

260—Although Bering had a copy of this map, he apparently had not shown it to his officers prior to this meeting.

261—The bracketed translation was added in the 1764 English edition.

262—"On the basis of the new information given by this map we agreed that we ought to touch at that Juan de Gama's land." Waxell, 1952, p. 100. The text of the decision is given in Golder, 1922, I, pp. 38-39.

263—" . . . we were to follow that land from north to east or from north to west, depending on the direction it took, as far as the latitude 65 degrees north. After that we were to sail due west until we had passed the Chukchi promontory, the most easterly point of Asia. What we were trying to do was to determine the true distance along the parallel between North America and Asia." Waxell, 1952, p. 102.

264—"If we reached the 65th parallel in good season we planned to sail due west to the Chukchi country and determine the distance between America and Asia . . . .In planning the voyage we had to keep in mind that we were to be back in this harbor towards the end of September." Chirikov's report in Golder, 1922, I, p. 313.

265—In 1630 João Teixeira, "Cosmographo de Sua Magestade," prepared two manuscript maps in Portugal. See Wagner, 1937, II, p. 306, number 310. This conception of lands in the Pacific, with the presentation of the Land of Jeso, was published by Melchisedech Thévenot in his *Relations de divers voyages curieux*, published between 1666 and 1672.

266—The bracketed translation has been added in the 1764 English edition. The source supposedly used by Teixeira was a voyage made by João da Gama, a merchant, from China to New Spain in the late sixteenth century. Land is shown east of Japan; about it Wagner (1937, I, p. 138) asserted: "Nothing can be more certain than that Gama never saw any land in this vicinity, for the very simple reason that there is none there to be seen."

267—Philippe Buache, *Considerations géographiques et physiques sur les nouvelles découvertes au nord de la Grand Mer, appellée vulgairement la Mer du Sud.* Paris, 1753.

268—Müller is referring to the Dutch expedition of 1643 led by Maerten Gerritszoon de Vries, in search of land north of Japan. De Vries discovered two of the Kurile Islands. Maps of these are included in Buache, 1753.

269—"I think it would be only reasonable were such unknown lands first to be explored before they are trumpeted abroad as being the coasts of Yezo or de Gama, for unless such investigations are first undertaken, many a good sailorman will be most unwarrantably deceived. Those who produce uncertain things of that kind would do better to hold their peace, or, if they must exercise imagination and speculation, let them keep the results to themselves and not put them into the hands of others. I know that I am writing all too much about this matter, but I can hardly tear myself away from it, for my blood still boils whenever I think of the scandalous deception of which we were the victims." Waxell, 1952, p. 103.

270—Müller, in the passage cited here about the land of Jeso, tries to explain how the land seen, supposedly, by the Dutch in 1643 is no longer found in the area. He suggested "Earthquakes are very usual in those parts; therefore the Land of Jeso may, after the voyage of the Dutch, have been torn into several smaller islands by an earthquake." (Müller, 1758, p. 95).

271—Jean Baptiste Bourguignon d'Anville, Jacques Nicolas Bellin, John Green, Philippe Buache, and Joseph Nicolas Delisle.

272—Steller blamed this late start on the rebellion of the Kamchadals, stating " . . . the delays caused by the investigation of the rebels and the constant drunken state of Kolessov, the commander of Kamchatka, brought it about that we could not leave the Harbor of St. Peter and St. Paul before the beginning of the month of June, while in other respects the month of May was suitable and [originally] determined on." Golder, 1922, II, p. 20. Golder, the translator, added the bracketed word.

273—Steller was convinced that land was near. He wanted to continue the course they were on, but, he said: "Just at the time, however, the erratic behavior of the naval officers began. They commenced to ridicule sneeringly and to leave unheeded every opinion offered by anybody not a seaman, as if, with the rules of navigation, they had also acquired all other science and logic." Golder, 1922, II, p. 23. Steller, however, was wrong (*Ibid.*, p. 24, footnote 42). His arguments for his belief that land was near are also given in Golder., pp. 27-32.

274—Waxell (1952, p. 104) stated " . . . storms and mist made us lose our sister-ship the *St. Paul.*" Steller said there was "a slight storm" and, "owing to foggy and dark weather," the other ship was separated from them. Golder, 1922, II, pp. 23-24. Chirikov said, "On June 20, because of the continuous fogs, which are common in this region, and the stormy winds (which obliged us to heave to under the mizzensail) the Captain Commander and I became separated." Golder, 1922, I, p. 313.

275—The Senate's instructions dated 28 December 1732 contain the following: "Bering desires to have two ships for the voyage so that in case of a misfortune to one of them the other would stand by . . . Bering is to be in command of one of these vessels and Chirikov of the other. On the voyage they are to keep together, work together, and do all that is in their power to advance naval science." Golder, 1922, I, p. 30.

276—"For three days, as our agreement was, we searched for the *St. Paul* within the same parallel, where we had lost each other. But it was all in vain." Waxell, 1952, p. 104. Bering had given detailed instructions for procedures in case the ships were separated. Golder, 1922, I, p. 43.

277—The log of the *St. Paul* for 23 June 1741 records "At the fifth hour in the morning we gave up looking for the *St. Peter* and with the assent of all the officers of the *St. Paul* we went on our way." Golder, 1922, I, p. 288.

278—Khitrov's journal indicates that Bering consulted with Waxell, Khitrov, and Eselberg and it was agreed to continue the course south for one more day, because of signs of land. Golder, 1922, I, p. 70, footnote 19. On 26 June the course was changed to the north and east. *Ibid.*, p. 71.

279—On 14 July a decision was made by Bering, Waxell, Khitrov, and Eselberg to change the course. The log book states it was ". . .decided to steer N by E to the land sighted." Golder, 1922, I, p. 89. The official account of this decision gives as the reasoning the fact that the water supply was half gone and they were sailing farther and farther from Kamchatka. Golder, *Ibid.*, p. 90.

280—These are Waxell's figures, which differ slightly from those in the log book. Waxell, 1952, p. 105.

281—Waxell's figures (1952, p. 159) differ from the official log book of the *St. Paul*, (Golder, 1922, I, p. 290) which gives the latitude as 55°21′ N. Lat. and longitude 61°55′.

282—See the commentary on the De Fonte account in Chapter II, pp. 50-51.

283—Chirikov first sighted land near Cape Addington early in the morning of 15 July. A longboat went to seek a suitable anchorage in a small bay but reported that there was none. Chirikov continued northward for three days, to Lisianski Strait, where the longboat was again sent to shore. Golder, 1922, I, p. 314.

284—The longboat carried one small cannon and two rockets. If they could not land they were supposed to fire two guns; if they could they were to fire a rocket immediately after arriving on shore. They were to keep a fire going while on shore, as a signal to the ship. Golder, 1922, I, pp. 315-16.

285—The metal is not specified. Both English translations indicate brass cannons; Golder's translation of the appropriate text in Chirikov's report indicates a copper cannon. Golder, 1922, I, p. 315.

286—Chirikov's report states: "We had no signal of any kind from him. We saw them approach the shore, and that is all." Golder, 1922, I, p. 316. Later, however, a fire on shore was sighted. *Ibid.* Müller has taken this information from Waxell, who reported (1952, p. 159) "The boat pulled away from the ship; they watched it disappear round a headland and some while later noticed various signal flashes corresponding exactly with the orders given . . . ."

287—After letting off the longboat Chirikov intended to follow it closer to shore and to anchor; however, the mountains came right down to the water and there was no place shallow enough for him to anchor. At first they waited at the bay for Dementiev; later they were driven further off and then they returned to the same place on 23 July. They saw a fire on shore and when they shot off their guns as signals the fire on the beach got bigger. Golder, 1922, I, pp. 294, 316. Müller has taken his account from Waxell, 1952, pp. 159-60.

288—Naziazhev Polkovnikov (carpenter), Gorin (caulker), and Sidor Fadiev (sailor) in addition to Savelev. Golder, 1922, I, p. 295.

289—The journal and Chirikov's report (Golder, 1922, I, pp. 295, 316) indicate four men; Waxell (1952, p. 160) says that six men were sent ashore.

290—The small boat was sent ashore on 24 July. Golder, 1922, I, p. 295. Müller perhaps uses this date because Waxell (1952, p. 160) says three days had passed when the second boat was sent.

291—It is probable that both boats were destroyed by the strong current, rather than by Americans on shore. Golder, 1922, I, p. 311.

292—This statement is from Waxell (1952, p. 160). What Chirikov actually did was to sail toward the boats. Chirikov (Golder, 1922, I, p. 316) says "We went to meet them; as we drew near we noticed that they were not our boats, because their bows were sharp and the men did not row as we do but paddled."

293—It has been postulated that the call was the Tlingit "agou" meaning "come here." Golder, 1922, I, p. 311.

294—These statements about what Chirikov should have done are by Waxell (1952, p. 161) who concluded "Had he done this, Chirikov could have got some of his men back, if they had not all been killed already, or at any rate he could have taken a native for every man who was missing . . . all they got out of it was wisdom after the event."

295—Chirikov had ordered white handkerchiefs to be waved as a signal for the Americans to come to the ship. However, they paddled back to the bay, where the ship could not follow. Thus, Chirikov reports, "We became convinced that some misfortune had happened to our men." Golder, 1922, I, p. 317.

296—The Americans had been seen in the early afternoon; Chirikov remained there all day and in the evening moved offshore a bit further for safety, but kept a lantern out as a signal. Golder, 1922, I, p. 317. Waxell (1952, p. 162) is the source for this description of the weather conditions.

297—Waxell, 1952, p. 162. Chirikov waited and searched for the boats until 26 July, and then left the area, not returning to it again. Golder, 1922, I, p. 317.

298—Because the ship's boats had been lost they had no way to either explore the coasts or take on fresh water. On 26 July the decision to return to Kamchatka was made by Chirikov, Chikhachev, Plautin, and Elagin. Golder, 1922, I, p. 324.

299—Amid the general rejoicing, Bering expressed concern to Steller: "We think now we have accomplished everything, and many go about greatly inflated, but they do not consider where we have reached land, how far we are from home, and what may yet happen; who knows but that perhaps trade winds may arise, which may prevent us from returning? We do not know this country;

nor are we provided with supplies for a wintering." Golder, 1922, II, p.34.

300—Kayak Island. This island (Khitrov's journal, Golder, 1922, I, p.96) was named St. Elias Island by the Russians.

301—Steller protested, "For the officers were determined to have a cape on their chart notwithstanding the fact that it was plainly represented to them that an island cannot be called a cape, but that only a noticeable projection of land into the sea in a certain direction can be so designated, the same meaning being conveyed by the Russian word *nos* (nose), while in the present case the island would represent nothing but a detached head or a detached nose." (Golder, 1922, II, p.36)

302—Iushin's log book (Golder, 1922, I, pp. 92, 93) gives the name as "St. Aphinogena," referring to bluffs west of the entrance to Yakutat Bay.

303—At 8 a.m. on 20 July, Khitrov went to shore in the longboat. Steller (Golder, 1922, I, p.37) noted, "I asked to be sent with Khitrov, since after all he himself did not know everything, but in spite of his making the same request permission was refused." Steller was so anxious to go to shore that he protested violently and threatened to report Bering's action to the Senate and the Admiralty. For this, says Stejneger (1936, p. 265) " . . . a less lenient commander would have put the fiery scientist in the brig . . . ."

304—At 10 a.m. the smaller boat, with Steller on board, left the ship. As a sendoff, Bering had the ship's trumpeters play. Golder, 1922, II, p. 40.

305—Khitrov found a good anchoring place. As Waxell (1952, p. 105) reported, "However, Captain-Commander Bering did not seem inclined to make a long stay here."

306—Waxell (1952, pp. 105-6) indicated " . . . these little houses were lined with smooth boards and decorated with small carvings." Steller reported that the walls of the dwellings were so smooth that "it seemed as if they had been planed . . . ." Golder, 1922, II, p. 52.

307—Steller (Golder, 1922, II, pp. 52-53) recorded Khitrov's findings as "a wooden vessel, such as is made in Russia of linden bark and used as a box; a stone which perhaps . . . served as a whetstone, on which were seen streaks of copper . . . a hollow ball of hard-burned clay . . . containing a pebble which I regarded as a toy for small children; and finally a paddle and the tail of a blackish gray fox."

308—This is Müller's amplification of Steller's comment that " . . . their instruments, like those of the Kalmucks and the Asiatic Tatars of Siberia in former times, must be of copper . . . ." Golder, 1922, II, p. 53.

309—This is not surprising, in view of Steller's comments (Golder, 1922, II, pp. 36-37) at this landing: "Orderly management as well as the importance of the matter would now have demanded a harmonious consideration of what ought to be done, how to utilize the time and opportunity to the best advantage, what to explore on shore and how to go about it; furthermore, whether, considering the season and the provisions as well as the distance, the following up of the coast should be continued at this late time of year, or whether we should winter here, or, finally, try the straight way for home. However, all this was not considered worthy the calling of a council, but everyone kept silent and did as he pleased."

310—Sweet grass "completely prepared in the Kamchadal fashion." Golder, 1922, II, pp.44-45.

311—Steller found a place where "a couple of hours before" a meal had been prepared, but there is no indication that the people ran away after seeing Steller. Golder, 1922, II, p. 44.

312—Steller (Golder, 1922, II, p.45) wrote "I discovered . . . a wooden apparatus for making fire, of the same nature as those used in Kamchatka."

313—"When I was once on the top of the mountain and turned my eyes towards the mainland to take a good look at least at the country on which I was not vouchsafed to employ my endeavors more fruitfully, I noticed smoke some versts away ascending from a charming hill covered with spruce forest, so that I could now entertain the hope of meeting with people and learning from them the data I needed to make a complete report." Steller, in Golder, 1922, II, p.50.

314—The *Flora sibirica* of Johann Georg Gmelin was published in four volumes between 1747 and

1769, in St. Petersburg.

315—"The time spent here in investigation bears an arithmetical ratio to the time used in fitting out: 10 years the preparations for this undertaking lasted, and 10 hours were devoted to the work itself." Steller, in Golder, 1922, II, pp. 53-54.

316—Steller had delayed going back to the ship. Then: "Here I was given once more the strict command that, unless I came on board this time, no more notice would be taken of me. I consequently betook myself with what I collected to the ship and there, to my great astonishment, was treated to chocolate." Golder, 1922, II, p. 51.

317—This is from the report of Khitrov, noted in footnote 278.

318—The concern with getting water was one which had led to the famous remark made by Steller (Golder, 1922, II, p. 37) that same day: "Only on one point were all unanimous, viz. that we should take fresh water on board, so that I could not help saying that we had come only for the purpose of bringing American water to Asia."

319—This list of gifts is from Waxell (1952, p. 106) and does not agree with the list given by Steller (Golder, 1922, II, p.51) who felt they should have given the Americans knives or hatchets. Khitrov (Golder, 1922, II, p. 99) said that Bering decided on the gifts; " . . . namely, 16 ½ arshins of green material, 2 iron knives, 20 Chinese strings of beads, 2 iron pipes for smoking Chinese tobacco, called 'shar.'" Golder, 1922, I, p. 99.

320—Steller (Golder, 1922, II, p.60) noted "On July 21 in the morning, two hours before daybreak, the Captain Commander, much against his usual practice, got up and came on deck and, without consulting anyone, gave orders to weigh anchor." Waxell protested that they should stay until the water casks were filled, to no avail.

321—Steller's advice (Golder, 1922, II, pp. 67-68) about a more southerly route was rejected; they planned to sail northward along the coast. Because of the winds, they had to do a good deal of tacking. There were many islands, and, Steller says: "Our officers were long since weary of meeting land; but it was nevertheless indefensible to leave it without an investigation to assure themselves of its existence and to plot it on the chart." *Ibid.*, p. 69.

322—"During the night-time we sailed past several islands which we were unable to see, but I presume they were islands, because sometimes we sailed for two or three hours at a stretch through very calm water and with a light wind, yet at the same time making good speed. Suddenly we would come into large ocean waves and were scarcely able to manage the ship." Waxell, 1952, p. 107.

323—"It was a dark night and we had not made a landfall for several days; about midnight we had a bad fright on finding ourselves in only 20 fathoms of water and not having any idea what sort of a bank or shallows it might be." Waxell, 1952, p. 107.

324—"I decided to sail due south. For a long time the depth remained the same, but fortunately we eventually came out into deep water." Waxell, 1952, p. 108.

325—"Several days afterwards we passed an island. The weather was foggy and a sounding showed only 7 or 8 fathoms of water, so we hastened to drop anchor. When the weather cleared we saw that we had already passed the island." Waxell, 1952, p. 108. Steller reports (Golder, 1922, II, p.62) that during the night " . . . it was discovered on sounding that the ship was in four fathoms of water, though it was reported differently to the Captain Commander." Waxell's figures agree with the log, *Ibid.*, I, p.111, for 2 August; the island is now called Chirikov Island.

326—Khitrov's journal for 22 August (Golder, 1922, I, p.132, footnote 168) states: "On sick list, two sailors, two grenadiers, two marines, one Siberian soldier."

327—" . . . the mainland must be considered a broken coast . . . ." Waxell, 1952, p. 108.

328—For the text of the "decision to land in order to take on water" made by Bering, Waxell, Khitrov, and Hesselberg (Eselberg) on 27 August see Golder, 1922, I, p. 138.

329—The sailor was Nikita Shumagin; the whole cluster of islands is named for him. The island on which he was buried is Nagai. Golder, 1922, I, p. 142.

330—Here Müller has used the account of Waxell (1952, pp. 108-9) who added: "We at once made arrangements to have as much water as possible brought on board with the help of the longboat and we worked on that all through the night."

331—Steller went to shore with the smaller boat and found some springs of good water, but to Steller's disgust (Golder, 1922, II, p. 77), "In the meantime the sailors had chosen the first and nearest stagnant puddle and already started operations. I found fault with this water because it was stagnant and alkaline . . . and also because I observed at the beach that it rose and fell with the sea and consequently must be brackish, as it also betrayed the taste when boiled."

332—A rendering of Steller's statement about the effects of evaporation (Golder, 1922, II, p.77) that " . . . this water, after a short while in the vessel, would even increase in salinity from day to day and finally through standing became salt water, while on the other hand none of this had to be feared from the spring water."

333—The first water Steller had found was at some distance away; though he found good water closer, the sailors preferred to draw their supply from "the beloved salty puddle." Golder, 1922, II, p. 78.

334—"Our ship was not lying at all safely. Where she was, almost any southerly wind could pounce down upon us without us being able to run for shelter anywhere. That is why we wished to replenish our supplies of water in all haste, so that we might sail out back into the open sea." Waxell, 1952, p. 109. They were anchored between Nagai Island and Near Island; the danger is evident from Khitrov's map (Golder, 1922, II, p. 76).

335—Khitrov saw a fire burning on Turner Island and went there, with the results noted below. Steller (Golder, 1922, II, p. 88) asserted "If he had not gone at all or if, on not meeting anybody, he had returned betimes and thereby had not delayed the watering by depriving us of the yawl, we could have gotten out with the fair gale and been more than a hundred miles farther on our course."

336—Waxell (1952, p. 109) said he had no objection to the proposal, but wanted to get the ship safely anchored first.

337—Waxell (1952, p. 110) "As I by now knew that the fire we had seen was already entered in the ship's journal, and preferring to avoid the possibility of being made answerable in the future for not investigating it, I felt obliged to report this proposal . . . to Captain Commander Bering."

338—Khitrov's journal (Golder, 1922, II, p. 142): "Captain Commander sent me to the island . . . ." Waxell (1952, p. 110): "His decision was that it was reasonable to send the officer concerned himself, seeing that it was he who had made the proposal."

339—According to Khitrov's journal (Golder, 1922, I, p. 142) he took with him "1 assistant constable, 1 sailor, 1 cannoneer, 1 soldier, 1 Chukchi, and 1 Koriak interpreter."

340—Nagai, called by them Shumagin Island.

341—"One must, however, commend the officer for his presence of mind in hoisting a sail and steering the yawl straight at the waves." Waxell, 1952, p. 111.

342—The St. Peter anchored on the east side of Near Island, so the ship was not visible to Khitrov and his men.

343—Khitrov feared, not without reason, that the ship had abandoned him. Steller (Golder, 1922, II, p. 87) wrote, "When after some anxiety we arrived on board there was the greatest lamentation because Master Khitrov and his men were not yet at hand and it might be necessary to leave them on shore."

344—Waxell sent the longboat to the island the next morning. "By seven o'clock in the morning of 3rd September they were all back on board the ship, but the yawl had to be left behind as a sort of offering on that American island." Waxell, 1952, p. 112.

345—This was not the anchorage near Nagai Island, but rather near Bird Island, southeast of it. Golder, 1922, I, p. 337.

346—From Waxell, 1952, p. 113. Steller (Golder, 1922, II, p. 90) reports "We had scarcely dropped the anchor when we heard a loud shout from the rock to the south of us, which at first, not expecting any human beings on this miserable island twenty miles from the mainland, we held to be the roar of a sea lion."

347—The word Müller uses here is a boat. It is translated as canoe, in the sense of "a light, slender boat with pointed ends, propelled by paddles" as defined in the *American Heritage Dictionary*, which cites a kayak as "a watertight Eskimo canoe made of skins."

348—These were not calumets. Steller (Golder, 1922, II, p. 92) says an American " . . . took from the sticks lying behind him on the skin boat one which was like a billiard cue, about three ells long, of spruce wood and painted red, placed two falcon wings on it and tied them fast with whalebone, showed it to us, and then with a laugh threw it towards our vessel into the water."

349—Steller (Golder, 1922, II, p. 91) records: "As they now came gradually nearer constantly shouting while paddling, they began to talk to us intermittently, but, as nobody could understand their language, we only beckoned with our hands, that they might come nearer without being afraid of anything."

350—"The waves were striking very strongly against the island where the natives were and the whole coast was full of large, sharp stones which made it far from easy to land. Instead, I had a grapnel dropped some 20 fathoms from shore and let the boat glide in between the rocks until it was scarcely 3 fathoms off." Waxell, 1952, p. 114. The idea of "stormy weather" came from Steller's statement that the tide was rising and it was windy. Golder, 1922, II, p. 93.

351—Reference to the various accounts used by the author in preparing his book.

352—Steller (Golder, 1922, II, p. 94) asserted "They manifested especially great inclination towards our Koryak interpreter, who quite resembled them in manner of speech and in facial appearance."

353—Described by Steller (Golder, 1922, II, pp. 95-96) and Waxell, 1952, p. 117.

354—The Americans had only knives.

355—"As soon as they [the three men from the boat] had reached the shore, one of the Americans seated himself in his kayak and came out to me." Waxell, 1952, p. 115.

356—"I handed him a beaker of gin which he put to his lips, but spat the gin out again at once and turning to his fellows screeched most horribly." Waxell, 1952, p. 115.

357—Although Steller (Golder, 1922, II, p. 94) warned against it, they next gave the American a lighted pipe, "which he accepted indeed, though paddling away quite disgusted. The smartest European would have done the same if he had been treated to fly mushroom or rotten fish soup and willow bark, which the Kamchadals, however, consider such delicacies."

358—This was done, Waxell reported (1952, p. 115) because it was starting to get dark and a storm was brewing.

359—"The savages let the two Russians go at once, but they did not want to release the interpreter in whom they may have noticed some resemblance to themselves." Waxell, 1952, p. 116. Steller, however, said the Americans tried to hold all three men on shore. Golder, 1922, II, p. 94.

360—Steller said the people tried " . . . perhaps not with evil design but from sheer thoughtlessness, not realizing our danger, to haul the boat with its occupants ashore, where it would have been wrecked on the rocks." Golder, 1922, II, p. 94.

361—"As we were lying under a fairly high cliff, the two reports and their echo made a considerable din." Waxell, 1952, p. 116.

362—Steller (Golder, 1922, II, p. 95) said "Laughable as was the consternation to behold, it was nevertheless even more funny how they at once rose up again, scolded us because we had rewarded their good intentions so badly, and waved their hands to us to be off quickly as they did not want us any longer." On the other hand, Waxell (1952, p. 117) reported: "As we pushed off, I made smiling faces at the Americans and invited them to come out to us and aboard the ship."

363—Waxell (1952, p. 117) described the knife: "It was about eight inches long and in front broad and thick." Steller saw two knives and had a good look at one of them, stating that it was made of iron. From this he wondered whether the people knew how to smelt iron ore or traded for knives. Golder, 1922, II, pp. 97-99.

364—Waxell (1952, p. 118) noted "Their faces were red, but certain of them had painted theirs blue. Their individual features were like those of the Europeans, in contrast to the Kalmucks who are all flat-nosed. They were long-limbed and well formed."

365—This description of the Americans is found in Waxell, 1952, pp. 117-18.

366—"More I was not able to find out about the Americans' way of life and manner of subsistence, being hindered in this by language difficulties, for I had no one with me who could talk to them." Waxell, 1952, p. 118.

367—This person was Waxell, who stated (1952, p. 115) he used "an English book, de la Hontan's description of North America, which I had with me," in communicating with the Americans. The author, Louis Armand de Lom d'Arce Lahontan, based his *New Voyages to North America* (2 vols., London, 1703), on both experience and imagination.

368—Waxell (1952, p. 115) was convinced that his efforts to communicate via the English edition of Lahontan were successful. "I talked to them . . . These and several other questions I put to them so as to learn whether or not they really were Americans, and as they answered all my queries to my satisfaction, I was completely convinced that we were in America."

369—Waxell (1952, p. 118) said "They made us a present of two of their caps and of a stick five feet long, to the thin end of which were fastened feathers of every conceivable kind. They also gave us a little human image carved out of bone, which we imagined must have been one of the idols they worshipped." Steller (Golder, 1922, II, p.102) used the similarity of the hats to those of the Kamchadals and Koriaks and the feather decorations to those of the Indians of Brazil as an argument for supporting the American peoples originating in Asia.

370—Reference not identified. Müller's addition.

371—"Whether this was to wish us a good voyage or an expression of their joy at seeing us departing, on that I shall not express an opinion." Waxell, 1952, p. 119.

372—"We went southwards as far as possible so as to come clear of land, the wind being westerly and WSW." Waxell, 1952, p. 119.

373—"If, as it did, the wind occasionally veered round into the east, it was only a matter of a few hours before it had veered back into the west, where it remained for weeks on end." Waxell, 1952, p. 120.

374—The return voyage was begun on 6 September. In Waxell's official report on the voyage (Golder, 1922, I, p. 275) on the voyage he wrote, "We intended to go straight to Avacha Bay, but contrary winds from the west as well as violent winds hindered us and caused us much suffering." Steller (*Ibid.*, II, p. 106) said "Under these conditions, the late autumnal season and the great distance from Avacha, the courage of our sailors and officers dropped all of a sudden."

375—This quotation is from Waxell, 1952, p. 120.

376—Steller: "It was most fortunate that we caught sight of the land while yet day and before the storm came up which it did shortly afterwards, for otherwise we should certainly have run onto it in the night, or else . . . should have been driven by the southeast wind and been wrecked on it." Golder, 1922, II, p. 113. They were near Adak and Atka islands. *Ibid.*, p. 24.

377—"We could see that at some considerable distance inland there was a large volcano, and to this on our map we gave the name of St. Johannes." Waxell, 1952, p. 120. Probably the 5,740-foot mountain on Great Sitkin Island.

378—Stated by Steller (Golder, 1922, II, p. 115), who also recorded: "Half of our crew lay sick and weak, the other half were of necessity able-bodied but quite crazed and maddened from the terrifying motion of the sea and ship. There was much praying, to be sure, but the curses piled up during

10 years in Siberia prevented any reponse. Beyond the ship we could not see a fathom out into the ocean because we continuously lay buried among the cruel waves." *Ibid.*, pp. 115-16.

379—Waxell, 1952, p. 121. They had been driven some 350 miles southeast of the land they sighted on 25 September. Golder, 1922, I, p. 338.

380—By 2 October, when there was a brief period when the weather moderated somewhat, Steller reported that there were already 24 men sick, and two dead. Golder, 1922, II, p. 116. For 18 October Khitrov's journal records "On sick list: Captain Commander and 32 men." *Ibid.*, p. 191.

381—Waxell believed that the storm and "the continuing dampness" promoted the attacks of scurvy; the appetites of the men increased and at the same time provisions were running low. And, to add to the general misery, there was not much liquor left: "As long as it had lasted, it had kept the men in fairly good fettle. Deaths now became numerous, so much so that a day seldom passed without our having to throw the corpse of one of our men overboard." Waxell, 1952, p. 121.

382—"By now so many of our people were ill that I had, so to speak, no one to steer the ship." Waxell, 1952, p. 122.

383—This question had been raised as early as 7 September, and was raised several times, according to Steller. Golder, 1922, II, pp. 106, 116, 118, 119, and 120.

384—Waxell's report indicates that, following the storm in mid-October, "Although, on account of the hard labor and the continuous inclement weather, we were at the end of our strength, yet with the help of God we made every effort to reach the Harbor of St. Peter and St. Paul." Golder, 1922, I, p. 275. On 9 October, according to Steller, Waxell had tried to get Bering to agree to a wintering on "the mainland of America" (see Map XXIII), but Bering did not agree. *Ibid.*, p. 118.

385—See Maps XVIII and XIX.

386—This is Steller's deduction, and it is not warranted by comparison of the routes. Golder, 1922, II, pp. 121-22.

387—Waxell noted the discovery of three islands only— St. Mark, St. Stephen, and St. Abraham. Waxell, 1952, p. 122. Khitrov's journal (Golder, 1922, I, p. 199, footnote 112) records the discovery of an island, and says the "southern point of it bore true N." Presumably this is Kiska Island. The identity of these islands is not certain; from Müller's map it seems that they may be as follows: St. Macarius—Amchitka; St. Stephan—southern Kiska; St. Theodore—northern Kiska; St. Abraham—Buldir.

388—Semichi Islands, although there are three islands rather than two. Golder, 1922, I, p. 125. Waxell (1952, pp. 122-23) does not mention sighting these islands. Steller (Golder, 1922, II, pp. 126-27) was convinced that they had been in the Kuriles, "though the officers, to this hour, will neither admit nor believe it."

389—If they did believe these were the Kurile Islands, they would have needed to go north to reach Kamchatka; Steller (Golder, 1922, II, pp. 125-29) was most upset about the decision to sail so far north, suggesting ulterior motives, "Namely, they preferred to go north in order to be able to use the dire necessity as a pretext they would have to enter the mouth of the Kamchatka River and not Avacha (Bay). This we understood well enough, partly from the bad terms they were on with the Captain Commander and partly from the jealousy between Lieutenant Waxell and Master Khitrov."

390—Müller's comments about their position, with his name for the Near Islands.

391—Compare Steller's comment (Golder, 1922, II, p. 121) on 24 October that " . . . misery and death suddenly got the upper hand on our ship . . . .The small allowance of water, the lack of biscuits and brandy, the cold, dampness, nakedness, vermin, fright, and terror were not the least important causes."

392—Waxell, 1952, p. 122.

393—Iushin's log book for 24 October to 3 November (Golder, 1922, I, pp. 197-207).

394—"Those few who were still on their feet were dreadfully weak and exhausted, and so reluctant to do any work . . . .Their only wish, indeed, was that a speedy death might free them from their miserable plight. They told me that they would rather die than let life drag on in that wretched fashion." Waxell, 1952, pp. 122-23.

395—Waxell's (1952, p. 123) statement: "'With God's help,' I answered them, 'we shall soon sight land again; that will save our lives, whatever the land is like; perhaps we shall find there means to help us continue our voyage.'" This statement, as well as Müller's statement, suggests that the land they searched for was *not* Kamchatka, but the land east of Kamchatka that had been sought during the First Kamchatka Expedition, i.e., the Commander Islands.

396—This paragraph is from Waxell, 1952, pp. 122-23. Steller (Golder, 1922, II, p. 129) had this comment: "At God's mercy, under two leaders, betrayed and sold, we proceeded northward, through the 51st, 52nd, 53rd, 54th, and as far as the 56th parallel." The leaders he is referring to are Waxell and Khitrov.

397—The statement that they began sailing westward on 4 November is found in Steller (Golder, 1922, II, p. 129).

398—"Now it must be remembered that for a long time we had been unable to take an observation to determine our latitude, and because of the length of time that storms and dirty weather had persisted neither could we rely on our estimate of our latitude." Waxell, 1952, p. 123. According to Iushin's log book, an observation was taken on 25 October and the result was 50°51′; the dead reckoning for that day was 50°40′; by observation their latitude on 4 November was 54°30′; the dead reckoning for that day was 53°54′. Golder, 1922, I, pp. 198, 208.

399—Waxell (1952, p. 123) writes " . . . we drifted about the seas until 4th November, when we sighted land at eight o'clock in the morning." Steller (Golder, 1922, II, p. 129), on the other hand, says that they shortened sail " . . . so as not to run on the land. Everybody stood on deck and looked about for the land, as the thing was announced with very great mathematical certainty. To our great astonishment it chanced that towards nine o'clock land was seen." Iushin's log book states "we think this land is Kamchatka; it lies, however, between N and W, and it seems as if the end of it is not far." Golder, 1922, I, p. 208.

400—Waxell (1952, p. 124) says "During the night the wind increased considerably, forcing us to carry a lot of canvas so as to avoid drifting on to land."

401—" . . . all our big mainstays on the starboard side had parted, nor did we have anyone able to repair the damage with a knot or splice." Waxell, 1952, p. 124. By 4 November, 12 of the crew had already died; of the 65 remaining, Waxell says "there were only eight who, with great pain, could help themselves, and only three of these were able to be on deck." Golder, 1922, I, p. 340.

402—"To Captain Commander Bering, who had been tied to a bed of sickness for many weeks, I gave an account of our helpless condition in which we were more like a wreck than a ship." Waxell, 1952, p. 124. Steller (Golder, 1922, II, pp. 132-33) records it this way: " . . . Master Khitrov, who had already won Lieutenant Waxell over to his side and also brought around the petty officers and the crew, therefore proposed that, in view of the late autumn season, the bad weather, the unserviceable mast, as well as the distance from Avacha, and the small number of sailors and soldiers, feeble and sick, the Captain Commander should call a council, in which it would be decided to land in the bay to the west of us, where, at an estimated distance of six miles, a harbor was suspected."

403—In his report on the voyage Waxell (Golder, 1922, I, p. 276) says "The members of the crew announced that because of their sickness and feebleness they were no longer able to do their work at sea. Taking this into account the Captain Commander and the higher and lower officers agreed to look for an anchoring place where we might winter in order to save ourselves and not be entirely destroyed by such a dreadful disease. All the men agreed to this . . . ."

404—This is not reported in the accounts of the council; Waxell (1952, p. 125) says "After this [the council] we noticed that our two fore-braces had also parted on the starboard side."

405—Steller (Golder, 1922, II, pp. 133-34) writes: "The Captain Commander, it is true, insisted that since we had already risked and endured worse and could still use the foremast and since we had yet six casks of water, an attempt should be made to reach the port [Avacha]. However, both officers opposed his proposition, insisted on a landing in the bay, and persuaded all the petty officers and crew, who likewise assented but nevertheless were only willing to sign on condition that, as non-experts, they could be assured that this land was Kamchatka; if it was not, they would be prepared still to risk the utmost and work to the last." Khitrov swore it was Kamchatka. Bering asked the sailor Dmitrii Ovtsin to express his opinion; Ovtsin agreed with Bering and was told by the others to shut up. Steller did not give an opinion, but agreed to "add a written certificate regarding the sickness and the miserable condition of the crew."

406—Steller: "When towards four o'clock in the evening we were so near land that it appeared to be scarcely a mile away from us, and for three hours no officer had shown himself on deck, as was usual on all dangerous occasions, and all were gently and sweetly sleeping, I went to the Captain Commander and begged that he might order that at least one of the officers should remain at his watch, since it looked as though they were intending to run ashore without further precaution." Both officers came on deck. Golder, 1922, II, p. 135.

407—This paragraph is from Waxell, 1952, p. 125.

408—Waxell: "Here I must relate how in the midst of all our misfortunes we had an unexpected and undeserved stroke of good fortune. We had not made our sheet-anchor ready . . . and had we done so, it would probably also have been lost, and consequently we should have had nothing left which could have held us after we had got across the reef." Waxell, 1952, pp. 125-26.

409—After the first anchor cable broke, Steller (Golder, 1922, II, pp. 135-36) reports "The confusion became still greater by the constant breaking of the waves, the shouting and the wailing, so that no one any longer knew who should give or who should take orders." At this point Ovtsin and the boatswain forbad the throwing out of any more anchors, to let the ship get over the reef. After that "these men, who alone had retained their reason, let the last anchor drop . . . ."

410—From Waxell, 1952, p. 126.

411—According to Steller (Golder, 1922, II, p. 137) "Because I could see plainly that our vessel could not hold together longer than the first violent storm, when it must either be driven out to sea or dashed to pieces against the beach, I, with Mr. Plenisner, my cossack, and several of the sick men went ashore first." Later, when he went back to the place where the sick men were, he found Waxell, who was ill, on shore. Waxell said they were in Kamchatka, and would send for horses. Steller's journal is a day off in this section; he dates this 7 November.

412—Khitrov's journal (Golder, 1922, I, p.211) indicates "On the sick list are the Captain Commander and 48 others."

413—Waxell, 1952, p. 127. It is not surprising that Müller assumed Steller returned to the ship, for Waxell's text suggests this. However, Steller remained on shore. Some ptarmigans and some herbs were sent to Bering. Golder, 1922, II, p. 138.

414—Khitrov's journal (Golder, 1922, I, p. 212) records that ten of the sick were taken from the ship.

415—Waxell, 1952, p. 127. Steller (Golder, 1922, II, p.146) writes "The dead, before they could be interred, were mutilated by the foxes, who even dared to attack the living and helpless sick, who lay about on the beach without cover, and sniffed at them like dogs."

416—Waxell (1952, p. 127): " . . . he was laid in a little hollow specially arranged for him." Steller (Golder, 1922, II, p. 145): "In the afternoon the Captain Commander was brought to us on a stretcher and had a tent, made of a sail, put upon the spot that we had originally chosen for our dwelling place. We entertained him, as well as the other officers who had come to our pit, with tea."

417—According to Waxell's report (Golder, 1922, I, p. 340), the removal of the sick from the ship was not completed until 15 November; by that time seven more men had died. In his own account, however, he states (Waxell, 1952, p. 127) "The work of bringing the sick ashore continued, yet as late as 19th November I found myself still with seventeen men aboard, most of them lying in their beds, but five were dead." He went to shore on 21 November.

418—This description of scurvy is found in Waxell, 1952, pp. 199-200. Within the description, the material in parentheses has been added by Müller. The statement about the air is from Waxell (*Ibid.*, p. 129) who writes "I had not become badly ill until I took up my quarters in the galley. It was possible to keep a small fire burning there and I had assumed that it would be more comfortable and better to be there than to be burrowing in the snow ashore, so to speak, in the open. This hope, however, was most grievously disappointed; for the bad air and filth found its way even there from the holds where so many had been lying ill for two or even three months, attending to the needs of nature where they lay."

419—Waxell (1952, p. 128): "Of course, I had been attacked by the sickness while we were still out at sea, but I had forced myself to remain on deck and to keep moving the whole time."

420—The nicest thing that Waxell said (1952, p. 196) about Steller was that it was unfortunate he died so young, because he was "a great botanist and anatomist, well versed in natural science, and could have given the world really thorough information about Bering Island." Müller seems to have taken this from Steller's assertion (Golder, 1922, II, pp. 149-50) that in spite of the conditions on the island, "Nevertheless, we encouraged one another not to lose heart but with the greatest possible cheerfulness and earnestness to work for our own benefit as well as for the welfare of the others . . . ."

421—Where Müller got this information is unclear. According to his account, in mid-November Steller "assumed a twofold minor function, namely, to visit the Captain Commander off and on and to assist him in various ways, as he could now expect but little service from his two attendants, who often were not present when he asked for a drink of water." Golder, 1922, II, p. 151 and footnote 346.

422—Steller (Golder, 1922, II, p. 155) writes that Bering had made two voyages to "the Indies" rather than voyages to the East and West Indies.

423—To this point, the information in this paragraph is from Steller. Golder, 1922, II, pp. 155-56.

424—According to Waxell, Bering said "The deeper in the ground I lie, the warmer I am; the part of my body that lies above ground suffers from the cold." Because the sand came down the sides of the hollow in which he lay, Bering was half covered with sand when he died. Waxell, 1952, p. 135.

425—In his account to the Admiralty College Chirikov (Golder, 1922, I, p. 317) reported: "On the way we had contrary winds from northwest and southwest almost continually." The sightings of land were few, in spite of many signs of it. See Map XXIII.

426—It appears that Müller may have converted this date to the Gregorian calendar, for Chirikov reached Adak Island on 9 September, while Bering sighted land in this same area on 24 September. See Map XXIII.

427—"Towards nine in the morning, when it cleared a bit, we saw land to the west [Adak Island], about 200 fathoms away. . . . Near the shore, on both sides, there were many rocks above and below the water, and we could see the surf breaking over them." Chirikov's report in Golder, 1922, I, p. 320.

428—The Aleuts came to the ship in two groups—nine of them in the morning and fourteen in the afternoon. The Russians offered various presents which were not well received, except for knives, which were taken eagerly. Chirikov (Golder, 1922, I, p. 305) reported, "Although they spent three or four hours alongside and we talked a great deal, yet we do not know anything they said, and we could not persuade one of them to come aboard."

429—The ship had drifted dangerously close to the land. Chirikov (Golder, 1922, I, p. 320) said, "I, therefore, ordered to cut the cable (34 fathoms of which was still out) at the hawse hole, to put on all sail, and to go SE. This was done with God's help, but it was a narrow escape, for a strong wind blew off the mountains and from all directions." He added, "After we cleared the land we proceeded to sail a little more westerly than our laid-out course, but the head winds greatly hindered us."

430—Waxell (1952, p. 163) stated, "to supplement what they had, they distilled fresh water out of sea water. It was somewhat bitter, but not salt. They mixed it half and half with water from Kamchatka, and for a long time each of them received but a small ration a day."

431—"When it rained the crew set buckets and other vessels to catch the water from the sails; and, although it was bitterish and tasted of tar, yet the men drank it gladly and said that it was good for the health and that the tar bitterness cured them of scurvy." Chirikov in Golder, 1922, I, pp. 318-19.

432—With the water supply so low, they were reduced to only enough water to quench their thirst;

they cooked salt meat in salt water, and otherwise they had cold food supplemented occasionally with mush made with their precious water. Chirikov's report in Golder, 1922, I, p. 319.

433—In the journal for 26 September (Golder, 1922, I, p. 308) the record indicates that by this date Chirikov, plus two lieutenants and six crew members, were "very ill with scurvy."

434—Both the journal and Chirikov's report simply record this death without comment; the *Lettre d'un officier de la marine russienne*, however, reports that de la Croyère's death was caused, in part, by excessive drinking. See the commentary in Chapter II and later in this text.

435—Chirikov says that from 21 September on he was unable to go on deck. He worked on the courses to be sailed, but left the rest to Elagin. Chirikov (Golder, 1922, I, p. 322) wrote, "Elagin has good judgment, and, if it had not been for him and the strength which God gave him, some great misfortune would have happened to the ship."

436—During this voyage Chirikov reached the islands of Attu and Atka. Golder, 1922, I, p. 329.

437—Chirikov remained in Siberia until 1745; he returned to St. Petersburg then and was promoted. He died in 1748. Golder, 1922, I, p. 329.

438—Waxell (1952, p. 130) wrote, "The few of our people who were still able to stand on their own legs regarded this mishap to the ship as a great stride forwards towards our complete destruction."

439—Waxell (1952, p. 130) wrote, "the ship had scarcely been aground two days before the strong ebb and flow of the tide had made it sink eight or nine feet into the loose sand, of which the bottom there consisted."

440—Steller (Golder, 1922, II, p. 152) noted "Because of the high waves we were often unable for several days to reach the vessel in the boat for the purpose of landing as many of the supplies as possible." Once the ship was driven onto the shore, they could get the provisions, even though they were damaged. Waxell (1952, p. 133) said, "These consisted of rye-flour and some groats which had been lying for several days in the ship soaked with salt water, and thus it had to remain for sometime afterwards until some of us recovered sufficiently to be able to fish them up out of the water."

441—Waxell (1952, p. 130) wrote, "We could scarcely have hoped that the ship would remain at anchor almost in the open sea for the whole of the winter without being damaged, and if it had been driven out to sea, instead of on shore, we should have had to remain on the island for always, as there were no trees there with which another vessel might have been built."

442—In November, shortly after the shipwreck, three men were sent to the north along the shore to see if help could be obtained. They returned in six days, completely exhausted, according to Iushin's journal (Golder, 1922, I, p. 229).

443—In December three men were sent to the south, led by the sailor Anchiugov. According to Iushin's journal (Golder, 1922, I, p. 230), "He was gone about four weeks but did not learn anything definite. He said he thought that we were on an island. He could not follow the shore for any considerable distance because of the cliffs. He reported seeing many herds of sea otters."

444—This information is from Waxell, who said of the two exploring parties, "They returned after two days and reported that they had seen no human beings whatever, nor even discovered a single sign of their presence, not so much as a path or a fireplace, nor any indication that any had ever been there." Waxell, 1952, p. 131.

445—This Latin name is from Steller (Golder, 1922, II, pp. 218-19), who wrote, "Probably this sea otter is the same animal which the Brazilians on the western side of America according to the testimony of Marggraf called *jiya* and *cariguebeju*; and consequently this animal occurs, if not in all, at least in most places on the western as well as the eastern side of America."

446—Steller (Golder, 1922, II, p. 146) wrote, "The blue foxes (*Lagopus*), which by now had gathered about us in countless numbers, became, contrary to habit and nature, at the sight of man more and more tame, mischievous, and to such a degree malicious that they pulled all the baggage about, chewed up the leather soles, scattered the provisions, stole and carried off from one his boots, from another his socks, trousers, gloves, coats, etc., all of which were lying under the open sky and could not be guarded because of the lack of well persons."

447—Two more exploring parties were sent out in March, 1742. The first, led by Iushin, was blocked by a steep cliff about 50 versts from camp; the second, under Ivanov, went westward until blocked by steep bluffs, and later saw the sea to the west. Golder, 1922, I, pp. 232-33.

448—About the driftwood, Steller (Golder, 1922, II, p. 162) wrote, "That which was found in the neighborhood had been gathered early for building the huts and for fuel; in December we were already obliged to drag it in from a distance of four versts, in January and February from about ten versts, and finally in March even from fifteen to sixteen versts."

449—The description in this paragraph is found in Waxell, 1952, pp. 132-33.

450—Golder (1922, II, p. 162) indicated that there were "at least" five species of willow growing on the island.

451—"These foxes are not so soft in the hair as the Siberian blue foxes, and in my opinion this must be put down to the difference in their diet and especially to the raw damp air that there always is on Bering Island whether it be summer or winter." Waxell, 1952, p. 197.

452—Waxell (1952, pp. 133-34) reported, "What we were able to lay hands on was so little that we could only allot to each man thirty pounds of rye-flour a month, later reduced to fifteen pounds and finally to nothing, and also five pounds of wet groats and half a pound of salt."

453—"When spring came, we were all to try and live off plants and wild roots, so that we might keep 800 pounds of rye-flour for our voyage away from the island, if God should help us to leave." Waxell, 1952, p. 134.

454—Waxell (1952, p. 134) said, ". . . it was decided that we all, the high as well as the low, should enjoy the same ration without consideration of person or rank."

455—In his account, Waxell (1952, p. 135) said, "That was no place for exerting one's power and authority. Severity would have been quite pointless." In his report to the Admiralty College Waxell cited (Golder, 1922, I, p. 279) problems in commanding the men because of ". . . the great distance from the source of authority, which made it unsafe to hold them strictly to their work, and nothing could be done without the consent of all concerned."

456—"It is almost like a piece of leather and has to be chewed, chewed and chewed again, before it becomes slightly softened and can be downed bit by bit." Waxell, 1952, p. 138.

457—Steller's *De Bestiis Marinis* appeared in the 1749 volume of the *Novi Commentarii Academiae Scientiarum Imperialis Petropolitanae* (II, 1751, pp. 289-398, with plates).

458—Waxell (1952, p. 142) notes that when the snow was gone, they collected and ate herbs and plants which Steller helped them to select. Waxell said, "From my own experience I can assert that none of us became well or recovered his strength completely before we began eating something green, whether plant or root."

459—Steller (Golder, 1922, II, p. 220) wrote, "The best pelts bring in Kamchatka 20 rubles, in Yakutsk 30, in Irkutsk 40 to 50, and at the Chinese frontier, in exchange for their wares, 80 to 100 rubles."

460—This contradicts the statement of Steller, made in a letter written in November, 1742 to Gmelin. Steller, who was still in Kamchatka, wrote, "We brought back nine hundred sea otter skins of which I alone received eighty as my share." Golder, 1922, II, p. 245.

461—Waxell (1952, p. 141) wrote, "By the beginning of March the sea-otters, which had been gradually diminishing in number, were so wild from being hunted so much, that it was impossible to get anywhere near them."

462—This paragraph is from Waxell (1952, p. 137) who noted "It was easy to get the pieces down as we were never able to get all the oil out of them."

463—The fur-seal. It was described by Steller (Golder, 1922, II, pp. 224-26), by Waxell (1952, pp. 190-92), and Krasheninnikov (1972, pp. 149-55). Steller and Waxell call it the sea-bear.

464—The reference is to the circumnavigation of 1703-1704 of William Dampier, the English adventurer and buccaneer. His plundering of Spanish and Portuguese ships could have led to his hanging, but he compiled so much useful information—particularly about South America—that the Admiralty hired him for further explorations. The reference to the sea bear was not identified.

465—Waxell (1952, p. 141) maintained that "Sea-bear flesh is revolting, because it has a very strong and very unpleasant smell, more or less like that of an old goat." Steller (Golder, 1922, II, p. 225) reported ". . . the meat of these animals smelled like fresh white hellebore, thereby became repulsive to the taste, and in the case of many of the men induced vomiting with diarrhea."

466—From Krasheninnikov, 1972, p. 150.

467—Krasheninnikov (1972, p. 153) writes: "Another reason for the springtime retreat of the fur seal to the east and to deserted islands is very probably that by sleeping and resting and fasting for three months, they hope to get rid of all the fat they have put on, as bears do, who spend the entire winter without eating."

468—"When the sea-bears left the island in the month of May, we turned our attention on the seals, of which there were likewise large numbers." Waxell, 1952, p. 141.

469—Krasheninnikov (1972, p. 142) writes of this seal as follows: "The largest, which the natives call *lakhtak*, inhabit the Sea of Okhotsk and the Bering Sea, and are found from 56° to 64° latitude; it is different from the other species only in its size, which equals that of the largest bull." This animal is the bearded seal, the largest and rarest of the northern seals.

470—This description of the sea-lion is from Waxell (1952, pp. 192-93). He says "We did come across sea-lions on land on several occasions, but they were so dreadfully large, looked so strong, and roared so horrifyingly that we were afraid to attack them with our cudgels, and so left them in peace" (p. 193).

471—William Dampier, *A New Voyage Round the World*, vol. I (1697), pp. 90-91, 547.

472—Krasheninnikov (1972, p. 147) stated, "They have a bare neck, with a small mane of rough and shaggy fur."

473—The Steller's sea-cow was not the same as the other sea-cows, and Steller was the only naturalist who saw it. Descriptions are found in Waxell (1952, pp. 194-96), Steller (Golder, 1922, II, pp. 228-37), and Krasheninnikov (1972, pp. 157-59). In view of the fact that it was eaten out of existence by sea otter hunters not long after its discovery Krasheninnikov's statement (p. 159) that "There are so many of these animals around Bering Island that they alone would provide sustenance for all the inhabitants of Kamchatka" is especially stinging. For a translation of Steller's scientific description, see Stejneger, 1936, pp. 354-57.

474—The similarity was in the manner of eating. Steller (Golder, 1922, II, p. 232) said that the animals live in herds, like cattle on land, and "They eat in the same manner as the land animals, with a slow forward movement."

475—The lamantin—manatee or sea-cow; cf. "lamenter," to lament or wail.

476—Waxell (1952, p. 195): "In shape the sea-cow reminds you of an inverted Dutch ship's boat."

477—The travelers and accounts referred to are John Atkins, *A Voyage to Guinea, Brasil and the West Indies* (1735); William Dampier (see footnote 471); Peter Kolb, *The Present State of the Cape of Good Hope* (2 vols., 1731); Jean Baptiste Labat, *Nouveau voyage aux isles de l'Amerique* (6 vols., 1722); and, presumably, Duarte Lopez or Lopes, *A report of the Kingdome of Congo* (1597), where the Hogge-fishe is described on pages 28-29.

478—Charles de l'Ecluse (1526-1609); Joannes Jonstonus (1603-1675); John Ray (1628-1705); Jacob Theodor Klein (1685-1759); Petrus Artedi (1705-1735); Carl Linnaeus (1707-1778).

479—Charles Marie de la Condamine, *Relation abrégée . . . de l'Amerique Méridionale* (1745), pp. 154-57.

480—The only work which appears to be a possible reference here is Jacob Theodor Klein, *Historiae piscium naturalis promovendae missus* (Gedani: Litteris Schreibrianis, 1740-49).

481—Krasheninnikov (1972, p. 157) says that the beluga is so common that it does not need to be described; he describes the sea-cow because many naturalists "still cannot agree whether this creature should be classed as a fish or a marine animal."

482—The Danube River.

483—Müller's sources no doubt included conversations with Krasheninnikov and/or Waxell.

484—The relation between Gmelin and Müller is described in Chapter II; Müller seems to be caught between his own friendship with Gmelin and a desire to discredit Gmelin's account of Siberia—ascribing errors to being "overloaded with work."

485—Gmelin's observations were made in western Siberia, on the Enisei River, Müller's in eastern Siberia.

486—The second edition of Nicolaas Witsen's *Noord en Oost Tartaryen* (the first edition had the spelling *Tartarye*) was published in 1705, in two volumes; the page number given refers to volume two of the work.

487—Johann Anderson, *Nachrichten von Island, Gronland und der Strasse Davis* (1746, pp. 224-25).

488—One sea cow was enough to feed fifty men for two weeks. Waxell, 1952, pp. 194-95.

489—"Once we killed a young sea-calf which the ebb-tide had left high and dry among some rocks and which had been unable to get out again. It weighed some 1200 pounds and had a most delicious taste. If we had only had some spices and other things used for such dishes, it would have been as good as any European veal broth." Waxell, 1952, p. 194.

490—The description of the sea cow is from Waxell, 1952, pp. 194-96.

491—Waxell's (1952, pp. 142-43) version: "Not only was each individual allowed to voice his opinion, but he was asked straight out to give it, so that we might unanimously choose the best of all the different views. I explained to them that our plight was the same for one and all, and that the lowliest seaman longed for deliverance just as much as the first officer; therefore, we should all stand by each other as one man."

492—Waxell's (1952, p. 144) comment: "The despatch of the boat was a thing that could always be done, if nothing else proved better or possible, but I considered it unreasonable and dangerous to pin our faith on that, because it was bound up with too much uncertainty."

493—During a storm in February, the ship had been carried onto shore, so that "at the ebb, she was dry, yet at the flood the water was as high inside her as outside." Waxell, 1952, p. 145. Steller said (Golder, 1922, II, p. 168) they hoped to get the ship back to sea, until they realized that the vessel was almost full of sand.

494—They needed beams as rollers, in order to move the ship. Waxell, 1952, p. 144.

495—Waxell stated (1952, pp. 144-45) that this proposal was unacceptable because they did not have enough people or logs to move the ship, because the bottom of the ship was apparently damaged, and because the sea bottom was made of quicksand.

496—Waxell wanted this document, he said (1952, p. 146), because "If we did not succeed, I did not want the entire blame heaped on myself, and so I felt that such a precaution was called for."

497—Two men submitted a document to Waxell, protesting breaking up the ship. They felt that the plan would fail, "since no one had ever heard of a new vessel being built from a wreck." Waxell, 1952, p. 146.

498—Waxell (1952, p. 147) said, "With this work the other officers and I were always the first on the spot, so as the better to be able to put heart into the men."

499—Waxell (1952, p. 147) wrote, ". . . I encountered the vital obstacle that I did not have a single ship's carpenter, or rather only one, who was accustomed to this kind of work. We had had three good carpenters on board when we had sailed from Avacha, but they had died either at sea or on the island."

500—Waxell had a party to celebrate the event. He served *Saturnan*, a Siberian drink which was supposed to be made of butter, flour, and tea. Waxell (1952, p.148) says "Not having any of these ingredients, I used train-oil instead of butter, musty rye-flour in place of wheat flour, and crakeberry plants instead of tea." Even Steller (Golder, 1922, II, p. 178) reported ". . . we enjoyed ourselves fairly well."

501—Once they were able to solve the food-supply problem by using the sea cow, Waxell (1952, p. 151) noted ". . . our work made such fine progress that by the end of May the vessel had taken definite shape and all the frame-timbers were fixed in place."

502—"There was no lack of hemp and old rope for caulking, but we were extremely short of pitch with which to paint it over." Waxell, 1952, p. 153.

503—The description of preparing tar is from Waxell, 1952, p. 153. He said the tallow was part of his personal belongings.

504—Waxell (1952, pp. 153-54) wrote: "While busy building the new ship, we nevertheless found time to think of the other things that would be needed for the voyage, so that by the time our craft was almost ready we had also got our rigging, mast, sails, water-containers and a store of provisions as good as it was possible to have in those miserable conditions."

505—"The new vessel was quite finished at the end of July and all that we still had to do was to make the sliding bilge-block from which the ship might be launched." Waxell, 1952, p. 155.

506—Hooker—"A general name for fishing vessels which use lines and hooks rather than nets. It does not indicate any particular rig, build, or type." Kerchove, 1961, p. 377.

507—This paragraph is from Waxell (1952, p. 156), who wrote, "It was a peculiar mercy of God that there had not been the least breath of wind throughout the three days our new vessel had lain at anchor. The slightest blow would have greatly hindered us in rigging her and in getting our things aboard."

508—They sailed on 13 August, according to Waxell, 1952, p. 156, and the log book of the voyage in Golder, 1922, I, p. 243.

509—Waxell (1952, pp. 156-57) added, "To put it shortly, the ship fulfilled all our expectations and I know too for certain that in 1752 she was still being used as a transport vessel between Okhotsk and Kamchatka."

510—Waxell (1952, p. 157) writes "On 15th August we encountered a strong headwind between south and west and we all agreed to cut the boat's painter and let it go, for it was so heavy that it could easily have damaged our weak vessel."

511—This happened on 17 August. See Steller (Golder, 1922, II, p. 185) and Waxell 1952, p. 157.

512—Steller (Golder, 1922, II, p.186) reported, "Great as was the joy of everybody over our deliverance and safe arrival, nevertheless the news which we received from a Kamchadal at the very entrance [to the harbor] caused a much greater excitement. We had been regarded by everybody as dead or lost; the property which we had left behind had fallen into the hands of strangers and had mostly been carried away. Therefore, in a few seconds joy turned to anxiety in the hearts of all of us."

513—Waxell (1952, p. 158) said, "From the uttermost misery and distress we plunged into veritable superabundance, for there was a whole storehouse full of provisions, comfortable warm quarters, and other amenities, none of which we had been able to have that last winter."

514—Waxell set sail from Avacha on 2 September, but after one day, when a strong wind arose, "The vessel began to roll and to take a lot of water" (1952, p. 165). They returned to Avacha for the winter.

515—They arrived at Okhotsk on 27 June 1743.

516—Waxell (1952, p. 167) said, "I spent a full sixteen years on the Kamchatkan Expedition." The official ukase ending the expedition was issued in 1743, though several members of it continued their work in Siberia well beyond that date.

517—Steller left the expedition when it arrived in Avacha. He went to southern Kamchatka and to the Kurile Islands. His biographer, Stejneger, wrote (1936, pp. 395-96) that, "Among the more important objects of the trip was the securing of a better picture of the sea otter than the one made by Pleniser on Bering Island." In view of the value of its skin, Steller may have had another object in mind as well.

518—In the winter of 1743-44 Steller quarreled with Vasilii A. Khmetevski, the highest naval officer in Kamchatka. The latter made accusations against Steller to the Senate, claiming, among other things, that Steller had aided rebellious Kamchadals. Stejneger, 1936, p. 425.

519—The vice-governor was Lorenz Lange, who had been a diplomat under Peter the Great, and who had undertaken a mission to China on Russia's behalf. Lange acquitted Steller of the charges made against him in Kamchatka. Later, Steller, while drunk, had a serious clash with Lange as well. Stejneger, 1936, pp. 445-48.

520—The account of Steller's problems is confused. Steller left Iakutsk hurriedly on Christmas Eve, 1745, after the confrontation with Lange. The latter's report on the matter did not reach St. Petersburg until August, 1746, and in the meanwhile an order for Steller's arrest had been issued. Steller had difficulty with the customs inspectors at Tobolsk. Stejneger, 1936, pp. 452-54.

521—Steller was arrested and was taken part way back to Iakutsk. He had reached Tara before the second order—cancelling his arrest—was received. Stejneger, 1936, pp. 472-74.

522—Johann Theodor Lau, the chief surgeon on Chirikov's ship. Stejneger, 1936, p. 210.

523—The small biography, *Leben Herrn Georg Wilhelm Stellers* (Frankfurt, 1748), was written in response to these rumors. As noted in Chapter II, it is likely that Müller was the author of it.

524—For a short biography, see Vladislav Kruta, "Johann Georg Gmelin," in *Dictionary of Scientific Biography*, V, pp. 427-29.

525—These islands were Copper Island and the Near Islands in the Aleutians. In the period from 1743 to 1755, 22 fur hunting expeditions were sent out. Makarovna, 1975, p. 49.

526—This had been the policy after the First Kamchatka Expedition. For example, "An ukaz of September 20, 1733, by the Empress Anna Ioannovna directed the Siberian governor Pleshcheev to promote the fur trade, 'because it is better, and will cost the treasury nothing if the merchants and promyshlenniks themselves seek ways to distant places just as they found the ways to Kamchatka and other places previously unknown.'" Makarova, 1975, p. 38.

527—They also used *shitiki*, or sewn vessels, on the voyages to Bering Island.

528—The French edition appeared in Berlin in 1753, at the same time and by the same publisher as the German edition. See the bibliography. Because its French edition is the one best known, the citation to it here is given as *Lettre*, regardless of which edition is used.

529—The map, published separately, is titled "Carte des nouvelles découvertes au nord de la Mer du Sud, tant à l'est de la Siberie et du Kamtchatka, qu'à l'ouest de la Nouvelle France. . . par Philippe Buache."

530—Müller used the account of Waxell in preparing the *Lettre*. Because Waxell's account was not known until 1940, when it was published in Russian by Iu. I. Bronshtein, the relationship between Waxell's account and the *Lettre* was not demonstrated until this century. The *Lettre* is written in an eye-witness form and begins, "Your excellency is pleased to require my thoughts both on Mr. de l'Isle's new map. . . and his memoir. . ." (1754, p. 1).

531—Both the map and the memoir gave distorted views of the Second Kamchatka Expedition. On the map, for example, Bering's route is shown as if he only went as far as Bering Island, not to America, and the route to America is shown as that of Chirikov and de la Croyère. See Map XVI. The concern in Russia about this led to the preparation of a rebuttal—Müller's *Lettre*. See Andreev, 1959, pp. 5-8.

532—Arthur Dobbs, a wealthy Irishman, was a dedicated believer in a northwest passage through America, who for 20 years promoted the search for it. See Williams, 1962, especially Chapter II, for a full account of his activities.

533—Philippe Buache, "Nouvelles observations concernant les dernieres Connaissances venues de Russie. . . ," in *Considerations géographiques et physiques* (1753), pp. 51-55.

534—Müller is citing the *Journal des Scavans, combiné avec les Mémoires de Trévoux*, May, 1754, published in Amsterdam. The article appears on pages 185-95.

535—The *Lettre* (1754, p. 21) had noted that de la Croyère did not seem to be as affected with scurvy as the other men on Chirikov's ship, reporting that "It was wondered, that the great quantity of brandy which he swallowed every day had such a good effect, but it was soon perceived, that all the advantage he reaped from this inflammatory liquor, was to forget for some time his pain, while liquor was working in his body."

536—Valerian Lada-Mocarski, the compiler of the *Bibliography of Books on Alaska Published before 1868* (1969, p. 50) stated, "The importance of Müller's *Lettre*, as the first authentic and detailed record of Bering's Expedition of 1741, cannot be overemphasized."

537—This 60-page work was written in one month by Müller. Andreev, 1959, p. 6.

538—Müller is reminding us that the account he is giving is based on records of participants in the expedition. His earlier account, written in haste, had as its purpose the rebuttal of errors in Delisle's report. The present work is his attempt to give an accurate account of the expeditions.

539—In the English translation of the *Lettre*, this appears as follows (1754, pp. 17-18): "Well might therefore the name of the Pacifick Ocean be spared; or if it deserves to be so called towards the tropick, as it possibly may, sure it does not deserve that name in this place."

540—Delisle and Buache had said that the north parts of Asia and America were close together or joined. Müller (1754, p. 23) asserted ". . . I am of the opinion that formerly the land of Tschukschi, and the part of America opposite to it, were joined, but separated by an inundation, a volcano, or an earthquake, as has happened in other places; and thus the peopling of the vast American continent is more easily accounted for, than by any other hypothesis."

541—Müller lists seven major objections to the authenticity of the de Fonte voyage—beginning with the dating of it, questioning "that a Spanish Admiral should have reckoned by the years of King Charles of England's reign . . ." (1754, p. 26).

542—Dobbs (1754, p. 40) wrote ". . . although I am far from affirming it to be genuine, yet, as I think it still remains doubtful, until further discoveries are made, to determine whether it be true or false . . . it has been very ill translated, and incorrectly printed, and therefore can't support any chart to be made from it."

543—Jean Baptiste Bourguignon d'Anville, Jacques Nicolas Bellin, and John Green.

544—In the *Lettre* (1754, p. 30) the statement is made ". . . for my part, I should rather have been inclined to have made use of the name of New Russia, in imitation of other nations, who have called countries: New-England, New-Spain, New-France, New-Holland, &c."

545—Buache, 1753, p. 55. Buache states that the author of the *Lettre* "wants to give the name New Russia to the vast regions to the east of Siberia. . ." and holds the relation by de Fonte to be a forgery as "a result of Russian policy."

546—Müller (1754, pp. 31-32) stated "A judicious connoisseur and judge of such naval experiments, will not hesitate to give the preference to the informations of this compleat and indefatigable seaman, namely, Capt. Spangenberg, who made his voyage on purpose to take a particular view of the said islands; such a judge, I say, will always prefer this man's observations to those of other ships, who made theirs only by the way, and as it were accidentally."

547—This is part of the "Nouvelles observations . . ." which Buache presented to the French Académie des Sciences on 24 November 1753; it is printed in the *Considerations géographiques et physiques*, 1753, pp. 51-55.

548—Buache said that, in reconciling the maps in the Russian *Atlas* with the Dutch maps he believed "Zelenoi, Konozir, &c." were part of the land of Jeso (1753, p. 123).

549—Buache does not indicate this possibility; Müller, however, does suggest this (1758, p. 94).

550—Müller (1758, p. 95) tried to find a reason for the discrepancy between the observations of the Dutch and the Russians that "will prejudice neither party." He suggested that the Dutch could have seen one great land of Jeso which was later broken up into smaller islands by an earthquake, since earthquakes were common in the area.

551—The mapmaker was I.F. Truskott, an adjunct of the Geography Department of the Academy of Sciences. Andreev, 1959, p. 7.

552—The map reproduced here (Map XVIII) is one of the copies of this first impression.

553—There are very few changes in the plate used for both impressions. In the 1758 printing the word "Russes" has been changed to "Russiens" and the date has been changed; a "Route pour aller par la Mer a Kamtschatka" has been added and "I. Toumannoi" has been named. Streeter, 1969, VI, p. 2411.

554—After his return from the Second Kamchatka Expedition, Müller saw maps being prepared for inclusion in the Russian *Atlas* published in 1745. He began working on two maps of his own—a general map of Russia and a map of Siberia. These were finished in 1746, but Müller was refused permission to publish them because it had been agreed to keep the findings of the expedition secret. In April of 1746, the academy received an order to turn in all maps of the expedition. Müller's maps were not returned to him until the end of 1752. Andreev, 1959, pp. 3-4.

555—These are the reports of the explorations made of the northern coasts of Siberia.

556—For example, a cossack from Iakutsk, Mikhail Stadukhin, had searched (in 1644 and 1647) for a big island without success. Others had followed after him in search of this and other islands. Müller said (1758, p. 20), "it is noted first, that in all the descriptions of the voyages made between the Lena and Kolyma rivers, of which there are a considerable number in the archives at Iakutsk, there is not one word mentioned about this great island . . . ."

557—On the Delisle/Buache map of 1750 there is a small island between the mouth of the Kolyma River and the southern coast of a "Grande Terre découverte en 1723." See Map XV. The name Kopai had been given to this island on Shestakov's map, for a prince of the Shelagis who supposedly was held as a prisoner of war there. Müller, 1761, xx-xxi. Müller does not accept the existence of either the island or the large land and they are not shown on his map.

558—There are some differences in the two issues of the general map in the Russian *Atlas* of 1745. An illustration of whaling is shown along the northern coast of Siberia on the Russian issue; the other issue, in Latin, does not have this illustration, as noted by Buache, 1753, p. 4. Buache includes a copy of the illustration in his map number IV in the same work.

559—In the numbering, p. 50 is an error for p. 60; p. 139 for 137. These pages contain descriptions of the Chukchi Peninsula from accounts of travelers who went there, and commentary on Afanasii Shestakov's map and account.

560—This is a reference to a map of Philip Johann Tabbert von Strahlenberg, a Swede who had been in Siberia as a prisoner of war, and had made several maps of Siberia.

561—Here Müller is referring to the many accounts of the area that he had collected in the Siberian archives. He was particularly critical of Shestakov's map.

562—Puchochotschi Island appears on the map published in Amsterdam (see Chapter I) and on the Strahlenberg map. An almost identical land, with its northern border unenclosed, is shown on the Homann map. It is the land Bering was sent to explore in his First Expedition and he concluded that it was, indeed, part of the Chukchi Peninsula.

563—The Russian *Atlas* and the Delisle/Buache maps place the mouth of the Anadyr at about 63°; the correct latitude is nearer 65°, as Müller showed it on his map.

564—The Russian *Atlas* and the Delisle/Buache maps place the northern extension of this sea as about 61°; as Müller said, the sea reaches two degrees further north.

565—The "Observationes astronomicae," in *Novi Commentarii Academiae Scientiarum.* . . . Vol. III, 1753, pp. 444-73.

566—The longitude is closer to 142° east by current measures; Müller was figuring from the Canary Islands rather than from Greenwich.

567—The Russian *Atlas* and the Delisle/Buache maps show this part of the coast running north and south, with the Shantar Islands to the east. Müller said he changed this on the basis of accounts of voyages made in the area and because the Shantar Islands—though mountainous—were not visible from the mouth of the Uda River. See Map XXII.

568—Müller has placed all of the Shantar Islands south of the Uda River's mouth. As he predicted, later investigations would reveal the position, number, and size of the islands to be different from what he had indicated on his map.

569—Müller is referring to the maps made for the Chinese Emperor K'ang Hsi, who ruled from 1662 to 1722. The island is Sakhalin Island; the mapping of it is described in Du Halde, 1735, IV, pp. 12—15. D'Anville's "Carte générale de la Tartarie Chinoise" shows this island and is also included in this volume of Du Halde.

570—"Relation de la découverte de la Terre d'Eso, au nord du Japon," in Melchisédech Thévenot, *Relations de divers voyages curieux.* . . . 1696, II, pp. 1-4.

571—"Relation de la découverte de la terre de Jesso," in Bernard, 1725-38, IV: 1-17.

572—Because of the many editions of this work it is difficult to know which one Müller was consulting. For example, the *Castricom* account, "taken from the *Voyages au Nord*, vol. III," appears in Charlevoix, 1754, VI, pp. 65-77.

573—Presumably Müller is referring to the several-sheet "Carte de Asie" published by d'Anville in Paris in 1753. See Falk, 1983, entry #1753-7, p. 38. There is a copy of this map in the James Ford Bell Library.

574—In the map referred to in the preceding footnote, the geography is given by d'Anville as Müller describes it, except that "Blydenberg" is not indicated on the map.

575—Witsen, 1785, I, pp. 138-39.

576—Hendrick Cornelisz Schaep, commander of the *Breskes*, sailed from Batavia with another ship, the *Castricom*, on a mission sponsored by the Dutch East India Company in search of the land of Jeso. The two ships were separated at islands south of Japan. The *Breskes* continued alone, and the results of this exploration, because of fog, led to further confusion about islands in the North Pacific. Golder, 1914, pp. 121-122.

577—The *Castricom*, under command of Maerten Gerritsen Vries, sailed with the *Breskes* in the 1643 search for Jeso. Vries sailed from Hokkaido to Sakhalin, but because of fog did not see the strait separating them. Golder, 1914, pp. 121-22; Lensen, 1959, p. 23.

578—The *Castricom* account states that "Matsmei" is the capital of the country. Charlevoix, 1754, VI, p. 76. The Delisle/Buache map of 1750 shows it as a city on the island of Jeso. The 1753 Buache maps show it as a small island between Jeso and Japan. Müller's own map shows "I. Matsumai" north of Japan, but the western coast is shown with a dotted line to indicate the uncertainty about it.

579—Nadeschda appears (unnamed) on the Delisle/Buache map; Müller commented on this island earlier.

580—Müller is referring to reports from Japanese who were shipwrecked in Kamchatka or known to people living in the Kurile Islands.

581—Müller's earthquake theory.

582—Witsen, 1785, II, p. 866. There is an error in the page number of this reference as there is no mention of Jeso or of a van Keulen on this page; the correct page number was not identified. Johannes van Keulen was a seventeenth-century Dutch chart publisher; he was the first in a family of mapmakers whose firm continued into the nineteenth century.

583—This is a reference to the accounts of voyages to the Kurile Islands which Müller had collected.

584—See note 573.

585—Antoine Francois Prévost, editor, *Histoire générale des voyages*, 1752, X, facing page 480 (to illustrate the book of Engelbert Kaempfer). This map also appears in *Allgemeine Historie der Reisen*, 1753, XI, plate 22.

586—Charlevoix, 1754, I, p. 6. The Bellin map of Japan also appears in this volume.

587—The 1734 map of the Russian Empire by Ivan Kirilov is reproduced in Efimov, 1964, map 71. Müller has the river flowing into the north end of the bay.

588—Longitude measured from the Canary Islands.

589—By doing this Müller created his own imaginary land, for which he was sharply criticized. See Chapter II.

590—Delisle, 1752, p. 8.

591—Buache, 1753. Some of the maps indicate the sort of "turtlehead" shape on the coast of America that Müller has on his map. The Delisle/Buache map of 1750 did not have this.

592—One English proponent of northern passages, John Campbell, had earlier stated his reasons for believing " . . . that the Space between America and Asia is chiefly Sea, as we actually know it to be, between America and Europe, on the other Side." He believed that such a large land mass extending westward from America would destroy the balance between the lands and the seas—it would also (not unimportant to his beliefs) make any northern passages more difficult to sail. Harris, 1748, II, p. 1039.

593—John Green, *Remarks, in Support of the New Chart of North and South America*, 1753. This work contains a map composed of six sheets, with accompanying explanation. Green left western North America blank, noting that Delisle and Buache filled it with "the pretended Discoveries" of de Fonte.

594—Dobbs, "Observations," 1754, p. 47. He noted that the reason for this is because the coast they are considering is "above 600 leagues from any known part of America, except the northern part of Baffin's-bay."

595—In this section of his work Müller gives arguments for believing the land that is near the Chukchi Peninsula is a part of America, not an island (the "Isle de Bernarda") as shown on the Delisle/Buache map.

596—Here Müller argued against the Western Sea, the great body of water almost enclosed by North America, shown on the Delisle/Buache map.

597—Buache, 1753, pp. 11-12, cited Joseph de Guignes in support of his maps incorporating the de Fonte voyage. De Guignes (1721-1800) was a French Orientalist, and wrote *Histoire générale des Huns, des Turcs, des Mongols* (Paris, 1756-58).

598—Antoine Gaubil (1689-1759) was a French Jesuit in China. He translated a history of Genghis Khan, in addition to several other works.

599—This may be a reference to the travels of a Buddhist monk, Huishen, as recorded in the Chinese book *Liang shu*. In the fifth century Huishen sailed to a land named Fusang. From the description, the idea has been suggested that this was southern Mexico. See Kuei-sheng Chang and Jiu-fong L. Chang, "Chinese Exploration," p. 124, in Delpar, 1980.

BIBLIOGRAPHY FOR THE TRANSLATION

Akademiia nauk. *Atlas Russicus; mappa una generali et undeviginti specialibus vastissimum Imperium Russicum cum adjacentibus regionibus.* Petropoli: Typis Academiae Imperialis Scientiarum, 1745.

Allgemeine Historie der Reisen zu Wasser und zu Lande. 21 vols. Leipzig: Arkstee und Merkus, 1747-74.

Anderson, Johann. *Nachrichten von Island, Gronland und der Strasse Davis.* Hamburg: Georg Christian Grund, 1746.

Anderson, Matthew Smith. *Britain's Discovery of Russia, 1553-1815.* London: St. Martin's Press, 1958.

Andreev, Aleksandr I. "Osnovanie Akademii nauk v Peterburge." In *Petr Velikii: Sbornik statei.* Edited by A. I. Andreev. Moscow: AN SSSR, 1947, I:283-333.

Andreev, Aleksandr I. "Trudy G. F. Millera o vtoroi kamchatskoi ekspeditsii." *Izvestiia, VGO,* XCI:1 (January-February, 1959), 3-16.

Anville, See d'Anville.

Armstrong, Terence. "Bering's Expeditions." In *Studies in Russian Historical Geography,* edited by J. H. Bater and R. A. French, pp. 175-95. London: Academic Press, 1983.

Armstrong, Terence. *Russian Settlement in the North.* Cambridge: At the University Press, 1965.

Atlas Russicus. See Akademiia nauk, Leningrad.

Baer, Karl E. von. *Peters des Grossen Verdienste um die Erweiterung der geographischen Kenntnisse.* In *Beitrage zur Kenntniss des russischen Reiches und der angrenzenden Lander Asiens,* XVI (1872).

Bagrow, Leo. "The First Russian Maps of Siberia and Their Influence on the West-European Cartography of N.E. Asia." *Imago Mundi,* IX (1952), 83-93.

Bagrow, Leo. *A History of Russian Cartography up to 1800.* Edited by Henry W. Castner. Wolfe Island, Ontario: The Walker Press, 1975.

Bagrow, Leo. "Ivan Kirilov, Compiler of the First Russian Atlas, 1689-1737." *Imago Mundi,* II (1938), 78-82.

Bancroft, Hubert Howe. *History of Alaska, 1730-1885.* New York: Antiquarian Press, 1959; reprinted from the original edition of 1886.

Barratt, Glynn. *Russia in Pacific Waters, 1715-1825: A Survey of the Origins of Russia's Naval Presence in the North and South Pacific.* Vancouver: University of British Columbia Press, 1981.

Belov, Mikhail I. *Arkticheskoe moreplavanie s drevneishikh vremen do serediny XIX veka.* In *Istoriia otkrytiia i osvoeniia severnogo morskogo puti.* Edited by Ia. Ia. Gakkel', A.P. Okladnikov, and M.B. Chernenko. Vol. I. Moscow: Morskoi transport, 1956.

"Bering, Vitus." In *Russkii biograficheskii slovar'.* Edited by A.A. Pelovtsov. II (1900), 740-42.

Bering, Vitus. "Short Account" of the First Kamchatka Expedition. See Dall; Du Halde; Golder, 1922, I: 9-20; Strahlenberg, 1757, II:264-93; and Urness, 1982, 259-336.

[Bernard, Jean Frédéric, editor.] Recueil de voyages au nord. 10 vols. Amsterdam: J.F. Bernard, 1725-38.

Black, J.L. Citizens for the Fatherland: Education, Educators, and Pedagogical Ideals in Eighteenth Century Russia. Boulder: East European Quarterly, 1979.

Black, J.L. G.F. Müller and the Imperial Russian Academy of Sciences: 1725-1783 : First Steps in the Development of the Historical Sciences in Russia. In press, McGill-Queen's University Press.

Black, J. L. "G.F. Müller and the Russian Academy of Sciences Contingent in the Second Kamchatka Expedition, 1733-43." Canadian Slavonic Papers, XXV, no. 2 (June, 1983), 235-52.

Black, Lydia T. "The Question of Maps: Exploration of the Bering Sea in the Eighteenth Century." History and Archaeology Publications, Series no. 25. Office of History and Archaeology, Alaska Division of Parks, November, 1979, 6-50.

Boss, Valentin. Newton and Russia: The Early Influence, 1698-1796. Cambridge: Harvard University Press, 1972.

Breitfuss, L. "Early Maps of North-Eastern Asia and of the Lands around the North Pacific: Controversy between G.F. Müller and N. Delisle." Imago Mundi, III (1939), 87-99.

Bruzen de la Martinière, Antoine Augustin. Le grand dictionnaire géographique et critique. 9 vols. in 10. The Hague: P. Gosse, 1726-39.

Buache, Philippe. "Carte des nouvelles découvertes au nord de la Mer du Sud, tant à l'est de la Siberie et du Kamtchatka, qu'à l'ouest de la Nouvelle France. Dressée sur les Mémoires de Mr. De l'Isle." Paris: 1750.

Buache, Philippe. Considerations géographiques et physiques sur les nouvelles découvertes au nord de la Grand Mer, appellée, vulgairement la Mer du Sud. Paris: 1753. [Colophon: De l'impr. de Ballard, 1754.]

Büsching, Anton Friedrich, ed. Anton Friedrich Büschings wochentliche Nachrichten von neuen Landcharten, geographischen, statistischen, und historischen Büschern. 15 vols. Berlin: Haude und Spener, 1773-87.

Büsching, Anton Friedrich. Beytrage zu der Lebensgeschicte denkwurdiger Personen insonderheit gelehrten Manner. Vol. III. Halle: J.J. Curts witwe, 1785, 1-160.

Burney, James. A Chronological History of North-Eastern Voyages of Discovery. London: Payne and Foss, 1819; Amsterdam: Da Capo Press, 1969.

Bushkovitch, Paul. The Merchants of Moscow, 1580-1650. Cambridge: Cambridge University Press, 1980.

Campbell, John. See Harris, John.

Chang, Kuei-sheng, and Jiu-fong L. Chang. "Chinese Exploration," in Helen Delpar, editor, The Discoverers: An Encyclopedia of Explorers and Explora-

tion. New York: McGraw-Hill, 1980, 122-27.

Chapin, Seymour L. "Joseph Nicolas Delisle." *The Dictionary of Scientific Biography,* IV (1971), 22-25.

Chaplin, Peter. See Dall, William H., "Notes."

Charlevoix, Pierre Francois Xavier de. *Histoire du Japon.* 6 vols. Paris: Didot, 1754.

Chirikov, Aleksei. "Journal of the *St. Paul.*" See Golder, 1922, I:283-327; Lebedev, 1951, 134-429.

Coxe, William. *An Account of the Russian Discoveries between Asia and America.* London: Cadell and Davies, 1780, and fourth ed. London: Cadell and Davies, 1803.

Cracraft, James. "Did Feofan Prokopovich Really Write *Pravda Voli Monarshei?*" *Slavic Review,* XL (1981), 173-93.

Cracraft, James. "Feofan Prokopovich." In *The Eighteenth Century in Russia,* edited by J.G. Garrard, pp. 75-105. Oxford: Clarendon Press, 1973.

Cracraft, James. "The Succession Crisis of 1730: A View from the Inside." *Canadian-American Slavic Studies,* XII (1978), 60-85.

Cross, Anthony G. "British Knowledge of Russian Culture (1698-1801)." *Canadian-American Slavic Studies,* XIII (1979), 412-14.

Cross, Anthony, ed. *Russia under Western Eyes, 1517-1825.* New York: St. Martin's Press, 1971.

Cross, Samuel H. "The Contribution of Gerhard Friedrich Müller to Russian Historiography, with some consideration of August Ludwig Schloezer." Ph.D. dissertation. Harvard University, 1916.

Dall, William H. "A Critical Review of Bering's First Expedition, 1725-30, Together with a Translation of his Original Report on It." *The National Geographic Magazine,* II (1890), 111-67.

Dall, William H. "Notes on an Original Manuscript Chart of Bering's Expedition of 1725-1730, and on an Original Manuscript Chart of his Second Expedition; Together with a Summary of a Journal of the First Expedition, Kept by Peter Chaplin, and Now First Rendered into English from Bergh's Russian Version." *Report of the Superintendent of the U.S. Coast and Geodetic Survey Showing the Progress of the Work during the Fiscal Year Ending with June, 1890.* Appendix no. 19. Washington: Government Printing Office, 1891.

Dampier, William. *A New Voyage Round the World.* London: James Knapton, 1697. The copy in the James Ford Bell Library is volume I of a four-volume set of Dampier's voyages.

d'Anville, Jean Baptiste Bourguignon. *Nouvel atlas de la Chine.* La Haye: H. Scheurleer, 1737.

Delisle, Guillaume. *Atlas nouveau, contenant toutes les parties du monde.* Amsterdam: J. Covens & C. Mortier [1741.]

Delisle, Joseph Nicolas. "Carte des nouvelles découvertes . . . ." 1750. See Buache.

Delisle, Joseph Nicolas. *Explication de la carte des nouvelles découvertes au nord de la Mer du Sud.* Paris: Desaint et Saillant, 1752.

Delisle, Joseph Nicolas. "Memoir Presented to the Senate with Map Which Bering Used in Going to America." Translated by Frank A. Golder in *Russian Expansion on the Pacific, 1641-1850.* Cleveland: Arthur H. Clark Company, 1914, 302-13.

Delisle, Joseph Nicolas. "Nouvelle carte des découvertes faites par des vaisseaux Russes aux côtes inconnues de l'Amerique septentrionale avec les pais adjacents." St. Petersburg: l'Academie Imperiale des Sciences, 1754.

Delisle, Joseph Nicolas. *Nouvelles cartes des decouvertes de l'Amiral de Fonte, et autres navigateurs . . . Dans les mers septentrionales.* Paris, 1753.

Delpar, Helen, ed. *The Discoverers: An Encyclopedia of Explorers and Exploration.* New York: McGraw-Hill, 1980.

Dobbs, Arthur. *An Account of the Countries adjoining to Hudson's Bay, in the North Part of America.* London: J. Robinson, 1744.

Dobbs, Arthur. *Observations upon the Russian Discoveries.* London: A. Linde, 1754. In Müller, *A Letter,* 1754, pp. 35- 51.

Dodge, Ernest S. *Northwest by Sea.* New York: Oxford University Press, 1961.

Du Halde, Jean Baptiste. *Ausfuhrliche Beschreibung des chinesischen Reichs und der grossen Tartarey.* 4 vols. Rostock: Johann Christian Koppe, 1747-49.

Du Halde, Jean Baptiste. *Description géographique, historique, chronologique, politique et physique de l'empire de la Chine et de la Tartarie chinoise.* 4 vols. Paris: P.G. Mercier, 1735.

Du Halde, Jean Baptiste. *A Description of the Empire of China and Chinese-Tartary.* 2 vols. London: T. Gardner, 1738-41.

Du Halde, Jean Baptiste. *The General History of China.* 4 vols. London: J. Watts, 1736.

Ebulgâzî Bahadir Han. *A General History of the Turks, Mongols, and Tatars, vulgarly called Tartars.* 2 vols. London: J. and J. Knapton, 1729-30.

Ebulgâzî Bahadir Han. *Histoire genéalogique des Tatars.* 2 vols. Leiden: A. Kalewier, 1726.

Efimov, Aleksei V., ed. *Atlas geograficheskikh otkrytii v Sibiri i v severo-zapadnoi Amerike.* Moscow: Nauka, 1964.

Efimov, Aleksei V. *Iz istorii russkikh ekspeditsii na tikhom okeane.* Moscow, 1948.

Eichhorn, Carl. *Die Geschichte der "St. Petersburger Zeitung" 1727-1902.* St. Petersburg: Buchdruckerei der St. Petersburger Zeitung, 1902.

Ekspeditsiia Beringa: Sbornik dokumentov. Edited by A.A. Pokrovskii. Moscow: Glavnoe arkhivnoe upravlenie NKVD SSSR, 1941.

Engel, Samuel. *Geographische und kritische Nachrichten und Anmerkungen über die Lage der nordlichen Gegenden von Asien und Amerika.* 2 vols. Basel: Carl

August Serini, 1777.

Engel, Samuel. *Memoires et observations géographiques et critiques sur la situation des pays septentrionaux de l'Asie et de l'Amerique.* Lausanne: Antoine Chapuis, 1765.

Euler, Leonhard. *Die Berliner und die Petersburger Akademie der Wissenschaften im Briefwechsel Leonhard Eulers.* 3 vols. Berlin: Akademie-Verlag, 1959-76.

Falk, Marvin W. *Alaskan Maps: A Cartobibliography of Alaska to 1900.* New York: Garland Pub., 1983.

Fischer, Johann Eberhard. *Sibirische Geschichte von der Entdeckung Sibiriens bis auf die Eroberung diese Lands durch die russische Waffen.* St. Petersburg: Akademie der Wissenschaften, 1768.

Fisher, Raymond H. *Bering's Voyages: Whither and Why.* Seattle and London: University of Washington Press, 1977.

Fisher, Raymond H. *The Russian Fur Trade, 1550-1700.* Berkeley and Los Angeles: University of California Press, 1943.

Fisher, Raymond H. *The Voyage of Semen Dezhnev in 1648: Bering's Precursor, with Selected Documents.* Hakluyt Society, *Works*, 2d series, no. 159. London: Hakluyt Society, 1981.

Froidevaux, Henri. "Les etudes géographiques de Joseph-Nicolas Delisle sur l'Empire russe." *La Geographie*, XXXIII (January-May, 1920), 219-28.

Garrard, John Gorden, ed. *The Eighteenth Century in Russia.* Oxford: Clarendon Press, 1973.

The Gentleman's Magazine: For October 1743. XIII, 552. "Extract of a Letter from Petersburg."

Gibson, James R. *Feeding the Russian Fur Trade: Provisionment of the Okhotsk Seaboard and the Kamchatka Peninsula, 1639-1856.* Madison: University of Wisconsin Press, 1969.

Gmelin, Johann Georg. *Reise durch Sibirien.* 4 vols. in 2. Gottingen: Abram Vandenhoecks seel. Wittwe, 1751-52.

Golder, Frank A. *Bering's Voyages: An Account of the Efforts of the Russians to Determine the Relation of Asia and America.* 2 vols. New York: American Geographical Society, 1922.

Golder, Frank A. *Russian Expansion on the Pacific, 1641-1850.* Cleveland: The Arthur H. Clark Company, 1914.

Greely, A.W. "The Cartography and Observations of Bering's First Voyage." *The National Geographic Magazine*, III (1892), 205-30.

Green, John. *Remarks, in support of the New Chart of North and South America.* London: T. Jefferys, 1753, accompanied by a map in 6 sheets.

Grekov, Vadim I. "Naibolee rannee pechatnoe izvestie o pervoe Kamchatskoi ekspeditsii (1725-30 gg.)" *Izvestiia AN SSSR, seriia geograficheskaia* (Moscow) no. 6 (1956), 108-12.

Grey, Ian. "Peter the Great in England." *History Today*, VI (1956), 225-34.

Guignes, Josephe de. *Histoire générale des Huns, des Turcs, des Mongols, et des autres Tartares occidentaux.* 4 vols. in 5. Paris: Desaint & Saillant, 1756-58.

Gvozdev, Michael Spiridonovich. See Golder, 1922, I:22-4.

Hanway, Jonas. *An Historical Account of the British Trade over the Caspian Sea.* 4 vols. London: Mr. Dodsley [etc.], 1753.

Harris, John. *Navigantium atque Itinerantium Bibliotheca. Or, A Complete Collection of Voyages and Travels.* Edited by John Campbell. 2 vols. London: T. Woodward [etc.], 1744-48.

Harrison, John A. *Japan's Northern Frontier: A Preliminary Study in Colonization and Expansion with Special Reference to the Relations of Japan and Russia.* Gainesville: University of Florida Press, 1953.

Haven, Peder von. *Reise in Russland.* Copenhagen: Gabriel Christian Rothe, 1744.

Haven, Peder von. *Reise udi Rusland.* Soroe: Jonas Lindgren, 1757.

Herberstein, Sigismund von. *Notes upon Russia.* Translated and edited by R.H. Major. 2 vols. Hakluyt Society, *Works,* 1st ser. X, XII. London: Hakluyt Society, 1851-52.

Hirabayashi, Hirondo. "The discovery of Japan from the north." *Japan Quarterly,* IV:3 (July-September, 1957), 318-28.

The Historical Register for the Year 1730. XV:60 (1730), 291.

Hoffmann, Peter. "Gerhard Friedrich Müller—Die Bedeutung seiner geographischen Arbeiten für das Russland bild des 18 Jahrhunderts." Ph.D. dissertation. Humboldt Univerity, 1959.

Homann, Johann Baptist. *Grosser Atlas über die gantze Welt.* Nuremberg: In Verlegung des Autoris, 1716.

Homann, Johann Baptist. *Grosser Atlas über die gantze Welt.* Nuremberg: J.E. Adelbulner, 1725.

Ianikov, G.V. *Velikaia severnaia ekspeditsiia.* Moscow: Gosudarstvennoe izdatel'stvo geograficheskoi literatury, 1949.

Ides, Evert Ysbrandszoon. *Three Years Travels from Moscow overland to China.* London: W. Freeman [etc.], 1706.

Isnard, Albert. "Joseph-Nicolas Delisle, sa biographie et sa collection de cartes géographiques à la Bibliothèque Nationale." Comité des travaux historiques et scientifiques. *Bulletin de la Section de Géographie,* XXX (1915), 34-164.

Iushin, Kharlam. "Log book of the *St. Peter.*" See Golder, 1922, I:36-269.

J.L.S. *Neue Nachrichten von denen neuentdekten Insuln in der See Zweschen Asien und Amerika.* Hamburg, Leipzig: Friedrich Ludwig Gleditsch, 1776.

Justi, Johann Heinrich Gottlob von. "Zuverlassige Nachricht von dem merkwurdigen Leben und Reisen Herrn Georg Wilhelm Stollers, der Russisch Kaiserl. Akademie der Wissenschaften Adjuncti und Mitglieds." *Ergetzungen der vernunftigen Seele aus der Sittenlehre und der Gelehrsamkeit überhaupt*, V:4 (October, 1747), 362-84.

Kaempfer, Engelbert. *Histoire naturelle, civile, et ecclésiastique de l'empire du Japon.* 2 vols. La Haye: P. Gosse & J. Neaulme, 1729.

Kaempfer, Engelbert. *Historia Imperii Japonici . . . The History of Japan.* 2 vols. London: For the Publisher, 1727-28.

Kerchove, René de. *International Maritime Dictionary: An Encyclopedic Dictionary of Useful Maritime Terms and Phrases, Together with Equivalents in French and German.* Princeton: D. Van Nostrand Company, 1961.

Keuning, Johannes. "Nicolaas Witsen as a Cartographer." *Imago Mundi*, XI (1954), 95-110.

Khitrov, Sofron. Log book of the *St. Peter.* See Golder, 1922, I:36-269.

Kish, George. "Gerardus Mercator." *Dictionary of Scientific Biography*, IX (1974), 309-10.

Kish, George. "Guillaume Delisle." *Dictionary of Scientific Biography*, IV (1971), 22-25.

Klein, Jacob Theodor. *Historiae piscium naturalis promovendae missus.* Gedani: Litteris Schreibrianis, 1740-49.

Kopelevich, Iudif Kh. *Osnovanie Peterburgoskoi Akademii nauk.* Leningrad: Nauka, 1977.

Kopelevich, Iudif Kh. "Pervaia zagranichnaia komandirovka peterburgskogo akademiia (iz zapisok G.F. Millera o evo puteshestvii 1730-1731 gg.)" *Voprosy istorii estestvoznaniia i tekniki*, no. 2 (1973), 47-52.

Kornerup, Bjorn. "Peder v. Haven." *Dansk Biografisk Leksikon*, IX (1936), 478.

Krasheninnikov, Stepan Petrovich. *Exploration of Kamchatka: North Pacific Scimitar.* Edited and Translated by E.A.P. Crownhart-Vaughan. Portland: Oregon Historical Society, 1972.

Krasheninnikov, Stepan Petrovich. *Opisanie zemli Kamchatki.* 2 vols. St. Petersburg: Imp. Akademii nauk, 1755.

Kruta, Vladislav. "Johann Georg Gmelin." *Dictionary of Scientific Biography*, V (1972), 427-29.

La Condamine, Charles Marie de. *Relation abrégée d'un voyage fait dans l'interieur de l'Amerique Méridionale.* Paris: Veuve Pissot, 1745.

Lada-Mocarski, Valerian. *Bibliography of Books on Alaska Published before 1868.* New Haven and London: Yale University Press, 1969.

Lahontan, Louis Armand de Lom d'Arce, Baron de. *New voyages to North-America.* 2 vols. London: H. Bonwicke [etc.], 1703.

La Mottraye, Aubry de. *Travels through Europe, Asia and into Parts of Africa.* 3 vols. London: For the Author, 1723-32.

Lantzeff, George V., and Richard A. Pierce. *Eastward to Empire: Explorations and Conquest on the Russian Open Frontier, to 1750.* Montreal: McGill-Queen's University Press, 1973.

Lauridsen, Peter. *Vitus Bering: The Discoverer of Bering Strait.* Translated by Julius

E. Olson. Chicago: S.C. Griggs and Company, 1889. A reprint of this was made in 1969, which, unfortunately, does not include the maps.

Lebedev, Dmitrii M. *Plavanie A. I. Chirikova na paketbote "Sv. Pavel" k poberezh'iam Ameriki.* Moscow: AN SSSR, 1951.

Leben Herrn Georg Wilhelm Stellers . . . See Müller, Gerhard Friedrich. *Leben.*

Lensen, George Alexander. *The Russian Push toward Japan: Russo-Japanese Relations, 1697-1875.* Princeton: Princeton University Press, 1959.

Lisle. See Delisle.

The London Magazine, IX (1740), 155.

Maier, Lothar A. "Die Krise der St. Petersburger Akademie der Wissenschaften nach der Thronbesteigung Elisabeth Petrovnas und die 'Affare Gmelin.'" *Jahrbucher für Geschichte Osteuropas,* neue Folge, XXVII:3 (1979), 353-73.

Majors, Harry M. "Early Russian Knowledge of Alaska, 1701-1730." *Northwest Quarterly,* 4, (1983), 84-152.

Makarova, Raisa. *Russians on the Pacific, 1743-1799.* Edited and translated by Richard A. Pierce and Alton S. Donnelly. Kingston: The Limestone Press, 1975.

Marshall, Peter J., and Glyndwr Williams. *Great Map of Mankind: Perceptions of New Worlds in the Age of Enlightenment.* Cambridge: Havard University Press, 1982.

Masterson, James R., and Helen Brower. *Bering's Successors, 1745-1780.* Seattle: University Press, 1948. (Reprint of *Pacific Northwest Quarterly,* 38, nos.1 and 2).

Materialy dlia istorii imperatorskoi Akademii nauk. Edited by M.I. Sukhomlinov. 10 vols. St. Petersburg, 1885-1900.

Medushevskaya, O.M. "Cartographic Sources for the History of Russian Geographical Discoveries in the Pacific Ocean in the Second Half of the 18th Century." Translated by James R. Gibson. *The Canadian Cartographer,* IX:2 (December, 1972), 99-121.

[Müller, Gerhard Friedrich.] *Leben Herrn Georg Wilhelm Stellers, gewesen Adjuncti der Kayserl. Academie der Wissenschaften zu St. Petersburg: worinnen die biszher bekannt gemachte Nachrichten Deselben Reisen, Entdeckungen, und Tode, Theils wiederleget, Theils erganzet und verbeszert werden.* Frankfurt, 1748.

[Müller, Gerhard Friedrich.] *Lettre d'un officier de la marine russienne a un seigneur de la cour concernant la carte des nouvelles découvertes au nord de la mer du sud.* Berlin: Haude und Spener, 1753.

[Müller, Gerhard Friedrich.] *A Letter from a Russian Sea-Officer, to a Person of Distinction at the Court of St. Petersburgh.* London: A. Linde [etc.], 1754.

Müller, Gerhard Friedrich. *Nachrichten von Seereisen, und zur See gemachten Entdeckungen, die von Russland aus langst den Kusten des Eismeeres und auf dem ostlichen Weltmeere gegen Japon und America geschehen sind.* St. Petersburg: Kaiserliche Akademie der Wissenschaften, 1758. (*Sammlung russischer Geschichte*, III).

Müller, Gerhard Friedrich. *Nouvelle carte des découvertes faites par les vaisseaux russes aux côtes inconnues de l'Amerique Septentrionale avec les pais adjacentes* . . . . St. Petersburg: l'Academie Imperiale des Sciences, 1754. Second impression, 1758.

Müller, Gerhard Friedrich. "Opisanie morskikh puteshestvii po ledovitomu i po vostochnomu moriu s rossiiskoi storony uchenennykh." *Sochineniia i perevody, k pol'ze i uveseleniiu sluzhashchiia*, VII (January, 1758), 3-27; (February), 99- 120; (March), 195-212; (April), 291-325; (May), 387-409; VIII (July), 9-32; (August), 99-129; (September), 195-232; (October), 309-36; (November), 394-424.

[Müller, Gerhard Friedrich.] *Schreiben eines Russischen Officiers von der Flotte an einen Herrn des Hofes, die Charte der neuen Entdeckungen gegen Norden des Suder-Meers, und die Abhandlung, die zur Erlauterung derselben dient, bettreffend, welcjhe beyde von dem Herrn von L'Isle im Jahre 1752 zu Paris heraus gegeben worden sind.* Berlin: Haude und Spener, [1753].

Müller, Gerhard Friedrich. *Voyages from Asia to America, for completing the Discoveries of the North West Coast of America.* London: T. Jefferys, 1761.

Müller, Gerhard Friedrich. *Voyages from Asia to America, for completing the Discoveries of the North West Coast of America. The Second Edition.* London: T. Jefferys, 1764.

Müller, Gerhard Friedrich. *Voyages et découvertes faites par les Russes le long des côtes de la mer Glaciale & sur l'ocean Oriental, tant vers le Japon que vers l'Amerique.* 2 vols. Amsterdam: M.M. Rey, 1766.

"A Narrative of some Observations made upon several Voyages, Undertaken to Find a Way for Sailing about the North to the East-Indies, and for Returning the same Way from thence Hither; Together with Instructions Given by the Dutch East-India Company for the Discovery of the Famous Land of Jesso near Japan." *Philosophical Transactions*, X:109 (1674), 197-207.

Neatby, Leslie H. *Discovery in Russian and Siberian Waters.* Athens: Ohio University Press, 1973.

Nerhood, Harry, comp. *To Russia and Return: An Annotated Bibliography of Travelers' English-Language Accounts of Russia from the Ninth Century to the Present.* Columbus: Ohio State University Press, 1968.

Newton, Arthur Percival, ed. *The Great Age of Discovery.* London: University of London Press, 1932.

Novlianskaia, Mariia G. *Ivan Kirilovich Kirilov: geograf XVIII veka.* Leningrad: Nauka, 1964.

Nye Tidender om laerbe og curieuse Sager (Copenhagen), no. 17, 17 April 1730.

Obolensky, D. "The Varangian-Russian Controversy: The First Round." In *History & Imagination*, edited by Hugh Lloyd Jones et al. New York:

Holmes & Meier, 1981.

"Observationes astronomicae," In *Novi Commentarii Academiae Scientiarum*, III (1753), 444-73.

Oehme, R. "A French World Atlas of the 18th Century: The Atlas General of G.L. Le Rouge." *Imago Mundi*, 25 (1971), 55-64.

Okenfuss, Max J. "Russian Students in Europe in the Age of Peter the Great." In *The Eighteenth Century in Russia*, edited by J.G. Garrard, pp. 131-45. Oxford: Clarendon Press, 1973.

Omont, M. H. "Lettres de J.-N. Delisle au Comte de Maurepas et à l'Abbé Bignon sur ses travaux géographiques en Russie (1726-1730)." Comité des travaux historiques et scientifiques. *Bulletin de la Section de Géographie*, III (1915), 130-164.

Pallas, Peter Simon. *A Naturalist in Russia: Letters from Peter Simon Pallas to Thomas Pennant*. Edited by Carol Urness. Minneapolis: University of Minnesota Press, 1967.

Pallas, Peter Simon, ed. *Neue nordische Beytrage zur physikalischen und geographischen Erd- und Volkerbeschreibung, Naturgeschichte und Oekonomie*. 7 vols. St. Petersburg: J.Z. Logan, 1781-96.

Parker, John. *The Strait of Anian: An Exhibit of Three Maps in the James Ford Bell Library at the University of Minnesota, Portraying Sixteenth and Eighteenth Century Concepts of the Waterway between Asia and America, which is now known as the Bering Strait*. Minneapolis: The James Ford Bell Book Trust, 1956.

Pekarskii, Petr Petrovich. *Istoriia Imperatorskoi Akademii nauk v Peterburge*. 2 vols. St. Petersburg: Imperatorskaia Akademiia nauk, 1870-73.

Perevalov, V.A. *Lomonosov i arktika*. Moscow, Leningrad: Glavsevmorput, 1949.

Perry, John. *The State of Russia, under the Present Czar*. London: Benjamin Tooke, 1716.

Pesatskii, Vasilii Mikhailovich. *Vitus Bering*. Moscow: Nauka, 1982.

Pipes, Richard. Introduction to *Of the Russe Commonwealth, 1591*, by Giles Fletcher. Cambridge: Harvard University Press, 1966.

Polevoi, Boris P. "Petr Pervyi, Nikolai Vitsen i problema 'soshlasia li Amerika s Asiei.'" *Strany i narody vostoka*, part VII, *Strany i narody basseina tikhogo okeana*, book 3. Compiled and edited by Y. V. Maretin. Moscow: AN SSSR, 1975.

Prévost, Antoine Francois, ed. *Histoire générale des voyages*. 19 vols. Paris: Didot, 1746-70.

Reading, Douglas K. *The Anglo-Russian Commercial Treaty of 1734*. New Haven: Yale University Press, 1938.

Richter, Liselotte. *Leibniz und sein Russlandbild*. Berlin: Akademie-Verlag, 1946.

St. Petersburgische Zeitung, no. 22, 16 March 1730.

Sandler, Christian. *Johann Baptista Homann, Matthaus Seutter und ihre Landkar-*

ten: *Ein Beitrag zur Geschichte der Kartographie.* Amsterdam: Meridian Publishing Co. [196_]. Reprint of the original of 1886.

Scherer, Jean-Benoît. *Recherches historiques et géographiques sur le Nouveau-monde.* Paris: Brunet, 1777.

Schottenstien, Isaac Morris. "The Russian Conquest of Kamchatka, 1639-1856." Ph.D. dissertation. University of Wisconsin, 1969.

Siebold, Philipp Franz von. *Geographical and Ethnographical Elucidations to the Discoveries of Maerten Gerrits Vries commander of the flute Castricum A.D. 1643 in the East and North of Japan.* London: Trubner & Co., 1859.

Smith, Thomas R., and Bradford L. Thomas. *Maps of the 16th to 19th Centuries in the University of Kansas Libraries.* Lawrence: The University of Kansas Libraries, 1963.

Sopotsko, Arkadii Aleksandrovich. *Istoriia plavaniia V. Beringa na bote "Sv. Gavriil" v Severnii Ledovitii okean.* Moscow: Nauka, 1983.

Stejneger, Leonhard. "An Early Account of Bering's Voyages." *The Geographical Review*, XXIV:4 (October, 1934), 638-42.

Stejneger, Leonhard. *Georg Wilhelm Steller: The Pioneer of Alaskan Natural History.* Cambridge: Harvard University Press, 1936.

Stejneger, Leonhard. "Who was J.L.S.?" *The Library Quarterly*, IV:2 (1934), 334-40.

Steller, Georg Wilhelm. *Beschreibung von dem Lande Kamtschatka.* Frankfurt und Leipzig: J.G. Fleischer, 1774.

Steller, Georg Wilhelm. "De Bestiis Marinis." In *Novi Commentarii Academiae Scientiarum*, II (1751), 289-398, with plates.

Steller, Georg Wilhelm. *Journal of his Sea Voyage* . . . . In Golder, 1922, II:9-187.

Steller, Georg Wilhelm. *Reise von Kamtschatka nach Amerika mit dem Commandeur-Capitan Bering.* St. Petersburg: J.Z. Logan, 1793.

Strahlenberg, Philip Johann Tabbert von. *Description historique de l'empire russien.* Amsterdam, Paris: Desaint & Saillant, 1757.

Strahlenberg, Philip Johann Tabbert von. *An Historico-geographical Description of the North and Eastern Parts of Europe and Asia.* London: J. Brotherton [etc.], 1738.

Strahlenberg, Philip Johann Tabbert von. *Das nord- und ostliche Theil von Europa und Asia.* Stockholm: In Verlegung des Autoris, 1730.

Streeter, Thomas Winthrop. *The Celebrated Collection of Americana Formed by the Late Thomas Winthrop Streeter.* Vol. 6. New York: Parke-Bernet Galleries, Inc., 1969.

Sukhomlinov, M.I., ed. See *Materialy dlia istorii Imperatorskoi Akademii nauk.*

Sykes, Godfrey. "The Mythical Straits of Anian." *Bulletin of the American Geographical Society*, XLVII:3 (1915), 167-71.

Thévenot, Melchisedech. *Relations de divers voyages curieux.* 2 vols. Paris: T. Moette, 1666-72.

Tracy, James D., ed. *True Ocean Found: Paludanus's Letters on Dutch Voyages to the Kara Sea, 1595-1596*. Minneapolis: University of Minnesota Press, 1980.

Urness, Carol. "Bering's First Expedition: A Re-examination Based on Eighteenth-century Books, Maps, and Manuscripts." Ph.D. dissertation. University of Minnesota, 1982; New York: Garland, 1986.

Veer, Gerrit de. *The Three Voyages of William Barents to the Arctic Regions (1594, 1595, 1596)*. Hakluyt Society, *Works*, 1st ser., LIV. London: Hakluyt Society, 1876.

Vernadsky, George, senior ed. *A Source Book for Russian History from Early Times to 1917*. Vol. II. New Haven: Yale University Press, 1972.

Vucinich, Alexander. *Science in Russian Culture: A History to 1860*. Stanford: Stanford University Press, 1963.

Wagner, Henry R. *The Cartography of the Northwest Coast of America to the Year 1800*. 2 vols. Berkeley: University of California Press, 1937.

Warep, Endel. "Über einige Karten Russlands in J.B. Homanns Atlas vom Jahre 1725." *Petermanns geographische Mitteilungen*, CVII:4 (1963), 308-11.

Waxell, Sven. *The American Expedition*. Translated by M. A. Michael. London: Hodge and Company, 1952.

Waxell, Sven. Report to the Admiralty College, dated November 15, 1742. See Golder, 1922, I:270-82.

Waxell, Sven. *Den Stora Expeditionen*. Edited by Iuri Semenov, translated by Ulf Tengbom. Stockholm: Raben & Sjogren, 1953.

Waxell, Sven. *Vitus Berings eventyrlige opdagerfaerd 1733-43, skildret af hans rejse-faelle og forste officer*. Translated by Johann Skalberg. Copenhagen: Rosenkild og Bagger, 1948.

Waxell, Sven. *Vtoraia kamchatskaia ekspeditsiia Vitusa Beringa*. Translated by Iu. I. Bronshtein. Moscow, Leningrad: Glavsevmorput, 1940.

Weber, Friedrich Christian. *The Present State of Russia*. 2 vols. London: W. Taylor, 1723.

Weber, Friedrich Christian. *Das veranderte Russland*. 3 vols. in 1. Frankfurt, Leipzig: Nicolai Forsters und Sohnes, 1744.

Wiener, Philip P., ed. *Leibniz Selections*. New York: Charles Scribner's Sons, 1951.

Willan, Thomas Stuart. *The Early History of the Russia Company, 1553-1603*. Manchester: Manchester University Press, 1956.

Williams, Glyndwr. "An Eighteenth-Century Spanish Investigation into the Apocryphal Voyage of Admiral Fonte." *Pacific Historical Review*, 30:4 (November, 1961), 319-27.

Williams, Glyndwr. *The British Search for the Northwest Passage in the Eighteenth Century*. London: Longmans, 1962.

Williamson, James A. *The Cabot Voyages and Bristol Discovery under Henry VII*. Hakluyt Society, *Works*, 2d series, CXX. London: Hakluyt Society, 1962.

Witsen, Nicolaas Corneliszoon. "A Letter, not long since written to the Publisher by an Experienced Person residing at Amsterdam, containing a true Description of Nova Zembla, together with an Intimation of the Advantages of its Shape and Position." *Philosophical Transactions*, X:101 (1694), 3.

Witsen, Nicolaas Corneliszoon. *Noord en oost Tartarye*. 2 vols. Amsterdam: 1692.

Witsen, Nicolaas Corneliszoon. *Noord en oost Tartaryen*. 2 vols. Amsterdam: M. Schalekamp, 1785. This is a reprint of the edition of 1705.

Witsen, Nicolaas Corneliszoon. "A Summary Relation of what hath been hitherto discovered in the Matter of the North-East passage; Communicated by a good Hand." *Philosophical Transactions*, XI:118 (1675), 418-19.

Wright, John K. "The Open Polar Sea." *Geographical Review*, XLIII (1953), 338-65.

INDEX

Abulgazi. *See* Ebulgazi Bahadir Han

Academie des belles lettres (Paris), 138

Academie des Sciences, 11, 44, 45

Academy of Sciences, 31, 39, 131; *Atlas Russicus*, 40, 82, 91, 95, 131, 132, 136; Chancellery, 13; *Commentaries*, 52, 119, 128, 132; and Delisle, 44, 51; discord among members, 13, 30; establishment of, 11-12; Geographical Department, 65; gymnasium, 10, 30; Historical Assembly, 51; Historical Department, 51; and Japanese castaways, 74; support for, 30; library of, 3; and Müller, 40, 51, 65; and the "Normanist" controversy, 51; plan for,11-12; and SKE, 32, 79; and Steller, 81

Account of the Russian Discoveries between Asia and America (Coxe), 44, 65

Admiralty College, 18, 75, 85; and Bering, 16, 32; and Koshelev, 82; and Müller, 67; and newspaper article, 22; and SKE, 32, 79-80, 89; and Spanberg, 95

Aldan River, 69, 72, 88

Alexandrov, Yuri, 94

Amazon River, 121

America, 27, 28, 54, 55, 133; accounts of voyages to, 67; and Bering, 101; and Chirikov, 116; and Chukchi, 87, 138; and earthquakes or floods, 130; Russian expansion to, 3; and SKE, 79, 99, 100

Americans: canoes of, 108; come to the ships, 102, 107, 116-17; description of, 109; exchange of gifts, 104, 109- 10; give Russians whale meat, 107; huts of, 103; shouting of, 110; similarity to Siberian peoples, 130

Amur River, 96, 132-33

Anabara River, 83

Anadyr, 71, 77, 78, 99, 122, 132, 136

Anadyr River, 76, 77, 132

Anadyr Sea, 78, 132

Anadyrsk, 77, 78, 86

Anderson,(G.)Johann, *Nachrichten von groenland*, 123

Anian, Strait of, 5

Aniwa, Cape, 134

Anna Ivanovna, Empress, 20, 22, 34, 36

Anville, JeanBaptiste Bourguignon d', 73, 96, 100, 130, 134; "Carte d'Asie," 136

Apraksin, Fedor Matseevich, 16, 17, 69

Archangel Michael (ship), 89

Arctic coast explorations, 38, 44, 53, 54, 66, 67

Arctic explorations, SKE, 81-86

Argun River, 80

Arkhangelsk, 81, 86, 88, 123

Armstrong, Terence, 66

Artedi, Petrus, 121

Atkins, John, 121

Atlas Russicus (Academy of Sciences), 40, 82, 91, 95, 130, 131, 132, 136

Avacha, 99, 100, 101, 104, 110, 137

Avacha, Bay of, 74, 96, 97, 98, 117, 126

Avacha harbor, 97, 98, 111

Avacha River (Suaatscha), 98

Baidars, 71, 78

Baikal, Lake, 80

Ballast, 126

Baltic, 70

Barents, Willem, 5

Bears, white, 81

Belaia River, 72, 77

Bellin, Jacques Nicolas, 73, 96, 100, 130; *Histoire Generale des Voyages*, 136

Belskaia Crossing, 72

Beluga, 122-23

Beresov, 82

Berichten von gelehrten Sachen (Gmelin), 122

Bering, Vitus Jonassen, 3, 15, 30, 31, 69, 75, 77, 88, 95, 130; biography of, 15-16, 105- 6, 114-16; FKE, 17-18, 69- 74, 78; FKE, instructions for, 17, 25, 55-56, 69, 71; FKE, map for, 25; FKE, map of, 56, 70; FKE, and Chukchi people, 25, 71; FKE, decision about ending voyage, 25, 27, 55, 71; FKE, search for land to east, 28, 74; FKE, and Delisle, 20, 45; FKE, newspaper article about, 19-22, 29; FKE, "Short account" of, 20, 29, 42-43, 45, 67; SKE, proposals for, 32-36, 55, 78-79; SKE, and academic contingent of, 36-38, 79-81, 127-28; SKE, officers for, 80; SKE, prepa-rations for voyage to America, 89, 97, 103, 111-13; SKE, and Chirikov, 100-1; SKE, and Steller, 67, 99, 115; SKE, reports of, 38, 53

Bering Island, council meetings on, 124, 125; description of, 14, 119, 128; departure from, 126; exploration of, 118; food supply, 119; hunters sailing to, 128; death of men on, 114-16; place to land on, 113;

naming of, 116; ship-wreck at, 117-18; ship built at, 124, 125

Biron, Ernst-Johann, 36

Biscuit, 87

Black, J.L., 12, 40

Blanco, Cape, 101

Blumentrost, Laurentii, 11, 13, 30

Blydenberg, 134

Boats: leather, 71, 92; fishing, 90,91; trading, 82

Bolshaia River, 72, 97, 136, 137; Bering arrives at, 70; Shestakov at, 76, 77; Spanberg arrives at, 89; ship repairs at, 96; Spanberg at, 92; Walton at, 95

Bolshaia River (ship), 89

Bolsheretsk, 76, 97; astronomical observations at, 137; FKE arrival at, 70; provisions brought from, 98, 99; Spanberg winters at, 89, 96

Boston, 50

Bows and arrows, 108, 109

Brandy, 87, 88, 91, 94, 108

Brass, use of, 90

Bredal, Peter, 42

Breskes (ship), 134-35

Brunel, Olivier, 4

Bruzen de la Martinière, Antoine A., Dictionnaire Geographique, 73

Buache, Philippe, 131, 137, 138; Considerations Geographiques et Physiques, 100, 129, 130, 131; and Company Island, 100; and Japan, 96; and Jeso, 133, 135

Burough, Stephen, 4

Büsching, Anton Friedrich, 54

Bykovskii Mys, 83

Cabot, John, 4

Cajucks, 82

Calendars, 65

California, 43, 101

Calumets, 107, 110

Campbell, John, 42

Canada, 50

Canoes, 84, 125

Canoes, American, 108, 109, 116

Carp, 104

"Carte d'Asie" (Anville), 136

Castel, Father, "Dissertation sur . . . Kamtschatka," 73, 88

Castricom (ship), 79, 100, 130, 131, 133-136

Catherine I, 13, 19, 69; establishes the Academy of Sciences, 12; and Bering, 17; and Delisle, 45

Catherineburg, 75, 80

Caves, 114

Cedar trees, dwarf, 84

Chancellor, Richard, 4

Chaplin, Peter, 67

Charlevoix, Pierre F.X. de, Histoire du Japon, 73, 133, 136

Chendon River, 84

Chesterfield, Earl of, 42

Chichagov, Vasilii I., 54

Chikhachev, Ivan, 96-97, 117

China, 53, 133

Chinese, trade with, 120; voyage to America, 138

Chirikov, Aleksei, 20, 25, 39, 53, 88, 99, 124, 130; accounts of voyage to America, 53, 67; and FKE, 29, 69, 70; illness and death, 117; and latitude, 111; meets Waxell at Eniseisk, 127; and route of, 27, 45, 50; separated from Bering, 100; and SKE, 55, 78-79, 80; supply depot left by, 126; voyage to Kamchatka, 97; voyage to America, 101-2, 116-17

Chotycztach stream, 84

Chukchi, 86, 132; fighting of, 76, 77, 78; and FKE, 17, 25, 71, 72; and Müller, 55; translator for, 106, 107; and tribute, 75

Chukchi, Land of the, 87, 130, 138

Chukchi Peninsula, 27, 28; See also Chukotskii Nos

Chukchi Sea, 66

Chukotskii Nos, 52, 71, 75, 78, 80, 131-132; See also Chukchi Peninsula

Church at Avacha Bay, 98

Ciphering schools, 12

Clusius (l'Ecluse), Charles de, 121

Coins, 90, 94

Columbus, Christopher, 4, 8, 121

Commentaries (Academy of Sciences), 52, 119, 128, 132

Commentarii rerum Moscoviticarum, (Herberstein), 4

Company Land, 36, 38, 79, 100, 134

Considerations Geographiques et Physiques (Buache), 100, 129, 130, 131

Copenhagen, 19

Copper, use of, 103

Cossacks, 6

Coxe, William, Account of the Russian Discoveries, 44, 65

Cows, 122

Cruys, Cornelis, 16

Dampier, William, 120, 121

Davis Strait, 107

De la Croyère. See Delisle de la Croyère

Delisle, Guillaume, 15, 34, 36, 138; maps by, 8, 10; and Peter the Great, 10

Delisle, Joseph Nicolas, 28, 29, 30, 52, 68, 131, 135; and the Academy of Sciences, 15, 44; and de Fonte, 50, 128; and

Ebulgazi book, 15; *Explication de la carte . . .* , 128; and Kirilov, 15, 44; map for SKE, 36, 52-53, 68, 79, 99, 100; and maps of Russian discoveries, 44, 45, 137, 138; memoir of 1750, 36, 45, 50; and newspaper article concerning FKE, 20, 27; sketch map, 20, 27

Delisle de la Croyère, Louis, 80, 96, 97, 99, 128, 129; criticized by Müller, 52, 68; death of, 117; joins the SKE, 36-37, 79; and Delisle map of 1744, 45, 50, 53; travels on the Lena, 81

Dementiev, Abraham, 101, 102

Description . . . de la Chine (Du Halde), 67, 69, 73

Description of Kamchatka (Krasheninnikov), 67

Description of North America (Lahonton), 109

Description of Siberia (Müller), 51-52

Dezhnev, Semen, 37, 52, 55, 56

Diagilev, Ivan, 94

Dictionnaire Geographique (Bruzen de la Martinière), 73

"Dissertation sur . . . Kamtschatka" (Castel), 73, 88

Dnieper River, 122

Dobbs, Arthur, 43, 50, 53, 54, 129, 130; Müller's comments on, 137-38

Dogs and dog sleds, 70, 98

Don River, 122

Donau River, 122

Driftwood, 114, 118

Du Halde, Jean Baptiste, 45, 54; *Description . . . de la Chine*, 67, 69, 73; maps, 73, 133

Ducats, Dutch, 90

Dutch, and northeast passage, 4

Dutch East India Company, 6

Dvina River, 123

Earthquakes, 118, 121, 130

East India companies, 6

East Indies, 6, 53

East Siberian Sea, 66

Ebulgazi Bahadir Han, *Histoire . . . des Tatars*, 13, 15, 73 *Ecclesiastical Regulation*, 12

Edogawa River, 74-75

Efimov, Aleksei V., 22

Egach stream, 76, 78

Elagin, Ivan, 96, 98, 117

Elizabeth I, 139

Elton, John, 32

Endaurov, Egor, 80

Engel, Samuel, *Memoires et observations geographiques*, 54

Enisei River, 69, 80, 82, 83, 86, 103, 123

Eniseisk, 80, 117, 123, 127

Ensel, Richard, 31

Ermak, cossack, 51-52

Esso. *See* Jeso

Euler, Leonhard, 39, 43

Explication de la carte des nouvelles decouvertes (Delisle), 128

Fedorov, Ivan, 75

Ferro Island, 101

Figuroi Island, 135

Fir tree buds, 95

First Kamchatka Expedition, 22, 25, 139; instructions for, 16-17; Müller's account of, 66-67, 69-73; newspaper article about, quoted, 19; purpose of, 28-29, 54-56; recent studies of, 22; summary of, 3, 17-18. *See also* Bering; Chirikov; Spanberg

Fischer, Johann Eberhard, 38, 44, 51

Fish, 122; frozen, 84-85; smoked, 104

Fisher, Raymond H., 22

Flora Siberica (Gmelin), 104

Foggy Island, 105

Fogs, 89-90, 97, 110

Fonte, Bartholomew de, 53, 54, 101, 128, 130, 180; and Delisle, 45, 50

Food supply. *See* Provisions.

Forests, lack of, 114, 118

Fortune (ship), 70, 75

Foxes: American, 104; arctic, 114, 118, 119

Franconia, 127

Franklin, Benjamin, 50

Frederick the Great, 11

Fur seals (sea cats), 120

Fur trade, 6

Gabriel (ship), 17, 70, 75, 76, 77, 89

Gama, Juan de, 36, 79, 99, 100

Gama, Land of, 36, 38, 99, 100

Gaubil, Antoine, 138

Gazette de France, 38, 39

"Generalis totius Imperii Moscovitici" (Homann), 25

"Generalis totius Imperii Russorum" (Homann), 25

Gens, Jacob, 75, 77

Gentleman's Magazine, 39

Geodesists (land surveyors), 45

Gerdebol, (assayer), 75

Globes, 91

Gmelin, Johann Georg, 52, 54; on the beluga, 122-23; *Berichten von gelehrten Sachen*, 122; biography of, 127-28; and fire at Iakutsk, 37, 81; *Flora Siberica*, 104; joins SKE, 36-37, 79; and Russian administration in Siberia, 43-44; and Bering, 37; travels in Siberia, 80

Gold, pieces of, 93

Golovin, Nikolai, 34

Gorbei River, 70

Gordon, Thomas, 16
Green, John, 100, 130, 137
Greenland, 86, 107, 123
Grekov, Vadim, 19
Guignes, Joseph de, 138
Gvozdev, Mikhail, 75, 76
Harris, John, 42
Hasius (Hase), Johann M., 86
Haven, Peder von, *Nye og forbedrede efterraet-*
ningar om det Russiske rige, 42
Heemskerk, Jacob van, 87
Hemp, 125
Herberstein, Sigismund von, *Commentarii,* 4
Herbs, medicinal, 94-95
Hesselberg, Andreas, 105, 111
Histoire du Japon (Charlevoix), 73, 133, 136
Histoire Genealogique des Tatars (Ebulgazi
Bahadir Han), 13, 15, 73
Histoire General des Voyages (Bellin), 136
Historia quadrupedum (Klein), 122
History of Japan (Kaempfer), 31, 36, 73
Hokkaido, 6
Homann, Johann Baptist, "Generalis totius
Imperii Russorum," 25; "Generalis totius
Imperii Moscovitici," 25; "Kamtzedalie
oder Jedso," 22; map for FKE, 27, 29;
maps, 73
Homann firm, 40, 45
Hookers, 89, 126
Hope (ship), 89
Hudson Bay, 138
Hunting, importance of, 88
Hyndford, Lord, 42-43
Iaesma River, 123
Iaik River, 122
Iakutsk, 55, 75, 81, 83, 84, 85, 88, 89, 123,
132; Bering at, 69, 72; Chirikov at, 69,
70, 117; commanders at, 128; difficult
route to, 70; fire at, 80; Japanese brought
to, 74; Müller's discoveries at, 72;
Pavlutskii at, 77, 78; Shestakov's report
at, 76-77; Spanberg at, 69, 95; Waxell at,
127
Iakutsk (ship), 83
Iamal Peninsula, 5, 82
Iana River, 83, 84, 87
Ianikov, G.V., *Velikaia severnaia ekspeditsiia,*
66
Ice Cape, 8
Icebergs, 86
Icy Sea, 71, 72, 77, 79; alleged land in, 75,
87, 131; exploration of, 81-88; explorations east of the Lena, 83-86; impossibility
of navigation through, 86; reports of
voyages in, 85; usage of term explained,
65-66

Ides, Evert Izbrandszoon, 8, 25
Ilim River, 69, 80
Ilimsk, 69, 80
Inatzdare-Osim-Nokam, 74
"Incognita" land, 25, 27, 29
Indigirka River, 84, 85, 86, 87
Irkutsk, 37, 80, 89, 127
Irkutsk (ship), 83, 85
Iron, use of, 103
Irtysh River, 69, 80
Islands: between America and Kamchatka,
54, 56; danger for Bering's ship, 104; near
Kamchatka, 75
Iudoma Cross, 70, 72, 88, 89
Iudoma River, 69, 70, 72, 88
Iugor Shar, 81
Iukagirs, 77, 78
Ivan IV, 4
Jackman, Charles, 4
Japan, 53, 79, 134; and Jeso, 73, 133; journals
of voyages to, 66; reception in, described
in Walton's report, 93; SKE to make
voyages to, 79, 88; and Spanberg's voyage
to, 38, 90, 95, 96
Jedso. *See* Jeso
Jefferys, Thomas, 66
Jelmerland, 86
Jeso, 36, 79, 100, 130-31; confusion of geogra-
phers about, 133; description of, 6, 134-
35; and earthquake theory, 68; and
Kamchatka, 14, 73; and Spanberg, 38;
Witsen's report on, 13, 134-35
Jesso. *See* Jeso
Jesuits, 133, 136
Johnston (Jonstonus), Joannes, 121
Journal des Scavans, 138
Junks, 91, 92
Justi, Johann H.G. von, 41
Kachikov, Joseph, 117
Kaempfer, Engelbert, 74, 90; *History of Japan,*
31, 36, 73
Kalmucks, 109
Kamchadals, 17, 74, 77, 98, 99
Kamchatka, 54, 112; Academy of Sciences to
report about, 79; Bering anchored off of,
72; Chirikov to return to, 102; coasts of,
followed on FKE, 70; commanders at,
128; dangerous seas to the south of, 97;
Japanese junks driven ashore at, 91; and
Jeso, 14, 73; Krasheninnikov sent to
explore, 81; location of, 20, 137; maps,
22; on Müller's map, 136; Spanberg's first
destination, 89; trade to, 73; voyage from,
to Japan, 88
Kamchatka River, 70, 72, 74, 77, 119, 136
"Kamtzedalie oder Jedso" (Homann), 22

Kang-hsi, Khan, 133
Kantemir, Prince Antiokh, 32
Kara River, 81, 82
Kara Sea, 4-5, 66
Karskoe More, 81
Kasat stream, 74
Katovaia, 98
Kazan, 80
Kazimirov, Lev, 93
Ket River, 69, 80
Keulen, Johannes van, 136
Khatanga River, 83, 86
Khitrov, Sofron, 96, 103, 105-7; illness of,
    115-16; proposal to build ship, 124
Kholmogory, 81, 123
Khroma River, 84
Kiakhta, 120
Kiev Academy, 12
Kigil River, 136
Kio, 74
Kirensk, 95
Kirilov, Ivan Kirilovich, 15, 34, 38, 79; and
    Delisle, 44; general map of Russia, 73, 95,
    136; memorandum on SKE, 34, 36
Klein, Jacob T., 121; *Historia quadrupedum*,
    122
Knife, American, 109
Koch', 87
Kohl, Johann Peter, 10
Kola Peninsula, 4
Kolb, Peter, 121
Kolivano-Voskresenskii *zavod*, 80
Kolyma River, 25, 27, 55, 86, 87; on Müller's
    map, 131, 132
Kopai Island, 131
Korea, 985
Koriak interpreter, 71, 107
Koriaks, 75, 76, 77, 78
Koshelev, Ivan, 82
Krasheninnikov, Stepan, 37, 54, 81; *Descrip-
    tion of Kamchatka*, 67
Krasnoiarsk, 80, 125
Krupischev, Tryphon, 76
Kunashir Island, 130, 135
Kurakin, Prince Boris, 45
Kurile Islands, 75, 89, 96, 97, 111
Kurilians, 92
Kuznetsk, 80
Kyrlak River, 83, 84
Labat, Jean Baptiste, 121
Lachtaks, 120
La Condamine, Charles Marie de, 121
Lahontan, Louis Armand, Baron de, 67;
    Description of North America, 109
Lamentins, 121
Lamuts, 76

Land connection between Asia and America,
    8, 10, 28, 54, 55, 69, 130
Laptev, Dmitrii, 80, 84-86
Laptev, Khariton, 83-86
Laptev Sea, 66
Larionov, Vasilii, 89
Lassenius, Peter, 80, 83-84
Lau, Dr., 41, 127
Lauridsen, Peter, 16, 19
Leibniz, Gottfried, 11
Lena River, 27, 69, 72, 73, 75, 80, 81, 83, 84
Lettre d'un officier de la marine russienne
    (Müller), 52, 53, 54, 55, 68, 128-29
Linnaeus, Carolus, 121
Lomonosov,Mikhail Vasilevich,43,44, 51, 53-
    54
London Magazine, 38
Longboats, 102, 108, 116
Lopez, Duarte, 121
Maia River, 69, 72, 88
Malygin, Stepan G., 80, 82
Manati, Cape, 126
Manatis. See Sea cows
Mandarins, 133
Mangazeia, 82
Maps: Academy of Sciences, *Atlas Russicus*,
    40, 130, 131; anonymous, 1744, 45;
    Anville, 136; Bering, 28-29, 42, 56, 70,
    73; Buache, 138; Delisle, G., 8-9; Delisle,
    J.N., for SKE, 34-36, 79, 99, 100; 1750
    and 1752, 45, 50, 68, 128, 137-38; sketch
    map, 20, 27; Du Halde, 133; Green, 137;
    Hasius, 86; Homann, 22-25, 27, 45, 73;
    Ides, 8, 25; illegal, of SKE, 40; Kaempfer,
    31-32; Kirilov, 73, 95, 136; Mercator, 5;
    Müller's of Russia and Siberia, 40, 52, 53,
    65, 68, 131-38; Spanberg, 91, 92; Strahlen-
    berg, 14, 132; Teixeira, 100; Vries, 6;
    Witsen, 8
Martinière, Antoine A. de la. See Bruzen de
    la Martinière, Antoine A.
Matkol rock, 71
Matsmai Island, 91, 92, 135
Matsol, Cape, 82
Maurepas, Jean Frederic, Comte de, 15, 20,
    45, 51
Memoir (Müller), 131
Memoires de Trevoux, 73, 88, 129
Memoires et observations geographiques (Engel),
    54
Mendocino, Cape, 10
Mercator, Gerardus, 5
Mercury's staff, 110
Mezen, 81
Mezen River, 123
Minin, Fedor, 82-83

Monthly Miscellany, 50
Morison, George, 31
Moscow, 56
Moscow School of Mathematics and Navigation, 12
Moskvitin, Ivan, 6
Müller, Gerhard Friedrich: and Academy of Sciences, 3, 12, 13, 30, 39, 51, 52; accounts of Bering expeditions, 53, 55, 56, 65; accounts of explorations criticized, 54, 56, 67; and authorship of Steller biography, 42; becomes Russian citizen, 52; and Bering, 3, 36-37; biography of, 10; collections on Siberia, 40; commentaries: on America, 137-38; on Dobbs, 137-38; on his map, 131-33; on Japan, 136-37; on Jeso, 133-36; on the northeast passage, 53, 86-88; on publications about Russian voyages, 128-31; and de Fonté account, 53; and Delisle, 20, 34, 51, 52, 68; Description of Siberia, 51-52; and Dezhnev, 37, 52; earthquakes and the Land of Jeso, 68; editor of newspaper, 13; and Engel, 54; and FKE, 45, 55, 56; and Fischer, 51; and Gmelin, 43, 44, 80; as historian, 32; and the Historical Assembly, 51; illness and death, 38, 52, 56, 81; as interpreter between Delisle and Bering, 20, 34; journey to western Europe, 30- 31; Lettre d'un officier de la marine russienne . . . , 52, 54, 55, 68, 128-29; and Lomonosov, 51; maps and mapping, 40, 45, 52, 132, 136, 137; Memoir, 131; and newspaper article, 27, 29; and "Normanist" controversy, 51-52; and northeast passage, 56; "Nouvelle Carte" 1754 and 1758, 53, 65, 68, 131-38; publishes Witsen's account of Jeso, 13; records from Siberian archives, 55, 56, 85; and reports from the Chukchi, 55; Sammlung, 30, 53, 55, 65; and Schumacher, 12, 13, 31; and SKE, 34, 36, 37, 79, 81; and sources used for his accounts of expeditions, 66-68; translates Kirilov's memorandum on SKE, 36; uses Du Halde's map, 133
Muravev, Stepan, 80, 81-82
Muscovy Company, 4
Muskets, 108
Mutnaia River, 82
Nachrichten von groenland (Anderson), 123
Nadeschda Island, 130, 134, 135
Nartov, Andrei K., 39-40
Navy, Russian, 54, 67
Nerchinsk, 80
New Russia, 130
Newspaper article, on FKE, 20, 22

Niakina, 98
Niphon, 91
Nizhne-Kamchatsk, 17, 70, 72, 76, 77
Noord en Oost Tartarye (Witsen), 8, 13, 123, 134, 136
Nordliche und ostliche Theil von Europa und Asia (Strahlenberg), 73
"Normanist" controversy, 51
North Cape, 4, 6
North Pole, 86
Northeast passage, 54, 56, 81-83, 87-88, 138; and Ebulgazi, 15; European interest in, 4-6, 10; search for, as goal of FKE, 19-20, 22, 27, 29-30; and Engel, 54; and Müller, 53, 86; and SKE, 79-80; and Witsen, 6; and Wood, 6-7
Northern War, 11, 16
Notes (St. Petersburg), 1742, 85
Noto, Cape, 91
Nouvelle Bibliotheque Germanique, 129
"Nouvelle Carte des Decouvertes" (Müller), 131-38
Novaia Zemlia, 5, 81, 86, 87
Nye og forbedrede efterraetningar om det Russiske rige (Haven), 42
Ob-Postman (ship), 82
Ob River, 69, 80, 81, 82, 86
Obdorsk, 82
Okhotsk, 70, 75, 88, 89, 126, 127; Chirikov's arrival at, 117; destination of second FKE voyage, 72; error in position of, 132-33; lack of provisions at, 96; Shestakov returns to, 76-77; shipbuilding at, 80, 89, 95, 96; Spanberg meets Walton at, 92
Okhotsk Sea, 122
Okhotsk Tungus, 76
Olenek River, 81, 83
Olutora River, 136
Osaka, 74
Osama, King of Japan, 75
Oskoi, Cape, 72
Ostafev, Ivan, 75, 76
Ostermann, Andrei, 34
Ostrogs (forts), 6, 75
Ovtsyn, Dmitrii, 80, 82
Pacific Ocean, 130
Packet-boats, 70, 89, 96, 97, 98, 125
Paren River, 76
Patience, Cape, 134
Pavlutskii, Dmitrii, 75, 77, 78
Pechora River, 81
Peledun sloboda, 72
Penzhina River, 75, 76, 132, 136
Peru, 50
Pet, Arthur, 4
Peter II, 13, 22

Peter and Paul, Feast of, 78
Peter the Great, 15, 73, 132, 139; and the Academy of Sciences, 3, 12; and belief in northeast passage, 22; and Bering, 16, 19, 27, 69, 116; and Cruys, 16; and French Academie des Sciences, 11, 44; library of, 12; and purpose of FKE, 54; and western Europe, 8, 10, 11
Petropavlovsk, 98, 99, 110, 111; astronomical observations at, 137; Chirikov returns to, 117; distance from America, 101; wintering at, 126
Philosophical Transactions, 6
Piasida River, 83, 86
Piatidesiatnik, 74
Plautin, Michael, 80, 117
Polevoi, Boris P., 22
Polo, Marco, 5
Poltava, Battle of, 13
Popov, (cossack), 71
Prokopovich, Feofan, 12
Promontories, 55, 71, 78, 84
Promyshlenniki (fur traders), 6, 81, 128
Pronchishchev, Vasilii, 80, 83
Prosperous (ship), 6-7
Provisions and food supply, 88, 89, 118, 119, 120, 125
Puchotzkoi Island, 132
Pumps, 126
Pustozersk, 81
Rainwater, 117
Raius (Ray), John, 121
Reindeer, 88, 99
Royal Society of London, 6, 11, 30
Rtishchev, Vasilii, 84
Russian Imperial Academy of Sciences. See Academy of Sciences
Russians: trade with Japanese, 94; exchange of gifts with Americans, 109-10; fighting the Chukchi, 77, 78
Sado Island, 91
St. Abraham Island, 111
St. Elias Cape, 103
St. Hermogenes, 103
St. John the Baptist, day of, 110
St. John's Mountain, 110
St. Lawrence Island, 25, 71
St. Macarius Island, 111
St. Paul (ship), 89, 96, 97, 98
St. Peter (ship), 89, 96, 97, 98, 112, 113
St. Peter (II) (ship), 124-26, 128
St. Petersburg, 69, 75, 81, 85, 127; Bering arrives at, 73; Chirikov arrives at, 117; Chirikov ordered to travel to, 127; Japanese brought to, 74; newspaper article on FKE, 19; officers from, 97; Spanberg

travels to, 95
St. Petersburgische Zeitung, 13, 19, 54
St. Stephan Island, 111
St. Theodore Island, 111
Sakhalin, 6
Sakhalin Ula Island, 134
Salmon, smoked, 103
Salt-meat, 87
Sammlung russischer Geschichte (Müller), 30, 53, 55, 65
Samoyeds, 82, 88
Sanktpeterburgskiia Vedomosti, 13
Satzma, 74
Savelev, Sidor, 102
Scandinavians and Russian history, 51
Schelting, Alexander, 80, 89, 95, 96
Scheuchzer, Johannes G. 73
Schigani, 81
Schumacher, Johann D., 30, 36; and the Academy of Sciences, 11, 12, 13; accused of embezzling academy's funds, 39-40; and Gmelin, 43; and Müller, 11, 31
Scurvy, 88, 105, 111; and Bering's crew, 105; characteristics of, 115; on Chirikov's ship,117; and Laptev's explorations, 84; and Lassenius expedition, 84; remedies for, 84-5, 119
Sea animals, as food, 119
Sea bears, 109
Sea beavers. See Sea otters
Sea cats, 120
Sea-charts, 91
Sea Council, 25
Sea cows (lamentin, manati), 109, 121-22, 123, 126
Sea lions, 109, 120, 121
Sea otters, 109, 118, 119, 120, 128
Sea routes. See Northeast passage
Sea water, distilling of, 117
Seals, 81, 109, 120, 122
Sealskins, 108
Second Kamchatka Expedition, 37, 56, 66, 127, 139; account by Campbell, 42; account by Delisle, 50; account by Gmelin, 43; account by Haven, 42; Müller's sources on, 67; purposes of, 3, 32-36, 79; unauthorized accounts of, 42-43, 45. See also Arctic explorations; Bering; Chirikov; Gmelin; Müller; Spanberg; Steller; Walton
Secrecy, oath of: and Gmelin, 43; and SKE, 34; and Steller, 39
Seduction Islands, 112
Selanoi Island, 130
Selenaia River, 82
Selenginsk, 80

Senate: and Chirikov, 127; and Delisle map, 99; and Müller, 81; and report on Kamchatka, 79; and SKE: Bering's proposals, 32; instructions to Bering, 85; preparations for, 79; report to Empress Anna, 34; and Spanberg, 95; and Steller, 127
Serdtse Kamen, 71, 78
Shallops, decked, 89
Shallops, double, 82, 83
Shantar Islands, 75, 133
Shcherbinin, Mikhail, 84
Shestakov, Afanasii, 75, 77
Shestakov, Ivan, 75, 76-77, 78
Shipbuilding, 95, 96, 125, 126
Ships, Japanese, 74, 92, 93, 94
Shitikis, 87
"Short account" (Bering), 20, 29, 45, 67
Shtinnikov, Andrei, 74
Shumagin's Islands, 105
Siberia, 3, 20, 81, 86, 131
Sievers, Peter, 16
Siktak, 81
Skuratov, Aleksei, 80, 92
Sledge bottoms, 92
Sloane, Sir Hans, 31
Sloops, 89, 90
Solikamsk, 127
Songar, Cape, 91
Southern Ocean, 72
Southern Sea, 138
Spanberg, Martin, 20, 25, 88, 100; Delisle's account of, 53; discoveries and maps, 130-31, 136; first voyage to Japan, 38, 88-94; and FKE, 27, 29, 69, 70; and Müller, 67; and SKE, 38, 42, 55, 78-79, 80; second voyage to Japan, 95-96
Speedwell (ship), 6-7
Spitzbergen, 86
Starodubsov, Sava, 125
Stejneger, 41
States Island, 36, 79, 100, 134
Steller, Georg Wilhelm, 39, 96, 97, 99, 111, 114; biography of, 40-41; death of, 127; heroism of, 39; journal used by Müller, 67, 68; and oath of secrecy, 39; to replace Gmelin on SKE, 38, 81; and scurvy victims, 115; and sea animals, 119, 120, 121; as source of illegal reports, 39; and troubles in Irkutsk, 127; and voyage to America, 103-4, 105, 107
Stone-foxes (petsi), 81
Storms, 106-7, 111, 118
Strahlenberg, Philip Johann, 13-14, 54, 95, 132; Nordliche und ostliche Theil von Europa und Asia, 73
Straits between Asia and America, 56

Sturgeon, 122
Sviatoi Nos (Holy Cape), 27, 84, 85
Swartz, Mr., 38
Sweden, 11
Sweet leaves, 103
Syn boiarskii, 125
Tackle, 125
Taimura River, 83
Tallow, 125
Tamari Aniwa, 134
Tar, 125
Tara, 80, 127
Tareinaia guba, 98
Tatarinov, Petr, 25
Tatary, 133, 134, 136
Tauisk, 75, 76
Taz River, 82
Teixeira, (cosmographer), 100
Thevenot, Melchisedech, Voyages au Nord, 133
Three Sisters Island, 130
Tides, 118, 119, 125
Tigil River, 136
Tiumen, 41, 127
Tobol (ship), 82
Tobolsk, 69, 73, 74, 75, 80, 82, 127
Tolbuchin, Gabriel, 89
Tomsk, 80
Trade goods, 90
Train oil, 120
Truskott, Ivan, 65
Tscherna River, 77
Tübingen, 43, 122, 127
Tumannoi Ostrov, 105
Tungus River, 69
Tunguska River, 80
"Turtle head" of land, 53
Turukhansk, 123
Tver, 80
Tylowka River, 82
Uboina River, 77
Uda, 76, 122, 133
Uda River, 75, 76, 122, 133
Urak River, 88, 89
Urakstoe Plotbishche, 89
Urup Island, 135
Ust-Kamenogorsk Krepost', 80
Vaigach Island, 81
Vaigach Strait, 81,86
Velikaia severnaia ekspeditsiia (Ianikov), 66
Vereshchagin, quartermaster, 93
Verkhne-Kamchatsk, 74
Voevoda, 78
Volga River, 122
Voyages au Nord (Thevenot), 133
Vries, Maerten Gerritsen, 6

Wakaschimar (ship), 74

Walrus, 81

Walrus tusks, 78

Walton, William, 67, 80, 89, 90; report of voyage to Japan, 92-95

Water, fresh: and Bering, 105, 111, 112, 113; on Bering Island, 114; and Chirikov, 116, 117; from America, 104; and Spanberg, 92; and Steller, 103; and Walton, 93, 94

Waxell, Sven, 80, 88, 114, 127; accounts by, 42, 52, 67, 68; calls councils, 113, 124; illness of, 115-16; succeeds Bering, 106, 119; transports provisions, 88; and voyage to America, 107-10

Western Sea, 138

Whales, 107, 109, 120, 122, 131

White Sea, 4

Whitefish, 123

Willoughby, Sir Hugh, 4

Winds, contrary, 106-7, 110, 116, 117, 126

Wine, Japanese, 94

Winsheim, 127

Witsen, Nicolaas, 6, 8, 13, 22, 54; account of the *Breskes* and the *Castricom*, 134-35, 136; influence of his early map, 10; and Jeso, 14-15; *Noord en Oost Tartarye*, 8, 13, 123, 134, 136

Wolff, Christian, 11

Wood, John, 6-7, 86

Ximo Island, 74

Yacht, birchwood, 89, 91

Yedso. *See* Jeso

Zimovyes, 75

Zitronnoi Island, 130, 135